Explaining Global Poverty

Global poverty has attracted increasing concern from the public and politicians alike in recent years. However, much public debate is based on a simplistic and flawed understanding of the historical production of poverty. This book explores how social inquiry informed by critical realism can provide a better explanation of global poverty than existing dominant approaches. Poverty, understood in terms of the non-satisfaction of human needs, is produced by historically specific social relations. The author argues that global poverty is neither natural nor the outcome of purely local histories, as implied by popular and mainstream academic analysis. In order to explain global poverty it is necessary to examine the structures and historical development of capitalism and imperialism.

The first part of the book examines the contrasting positions and assumptions of mainstream and critical approaches in Development Studies and International Relations. It defends historical materialism as a substantive approach to the analysis of poverty, which is consistent with critical realist philosophy. The second part of the book provides a substantive analysis of the production of poverty in Africa, through the specific case of Mozambique.

Branwen Gruffydd Jones is a Lecturer in the Department of Politics and International Relations, University of Aberdeen, UK.

Routledge Studies in Critical Realism

Edited by Margaret Archer, Roy Bhaskar, Andrew Collier,
Nick Hostettler, Tony Lawson and Alan Norrie

Critical realism is one of the most influential new developments in the philosophy of science and in the social sciences, providing a powerful alternative to positivism and post-modernism. This series will explore the critical realist position in philosophy and across the social sciences.

Also published by Routledge:

Critical Realism: Interventions
Edited by Margaret Archer, Roy Bhaskar,
Andrew Collier, Nick Hostettler,
Tony Lawson and Alan Norrie

Critical Realism
Essential readings
Edited by Margaret Archer, Roy Bhaskar,
Andrew Collier, Tony Lawson and
Alan Norrie

The Possibility of Naturalism
3rd edition
A philosophical critique of the
contemporary human sciences
Roy Bhaskar

Being & Worth
Andrew Collier

Quantum Theory and the Flight
from Realism
Philosophical responses to
quantum mechanics
Christopher Norris

From East to West
Odyssey of a soul
Roy Bhaskar

Realism and Racism
Concepts of race in sociological research
Bob Carter

Rational Choice Theory
Resisting colonisation
Edited by Margaret Archer and
Jonathan Q. Tritter

Explaining Society
Critical realism in the social sciences
Berth Danermark, Mats Ekström,
Jan Ch. Karlsson and Liselotte Jakobsen

Critical Realism and Marxism
Edited by Andrew Brown, Steve Fleetwood
and John Michael Roberts

Critical Realism in Economics
Edited by Steve Fleetwood

Realist Perspectives on Management
and Organisations
Edited by Stephen Ackroyd and
Steve Fleetwood

After International Relations
Critical realism and the (re)construction
of world politics
Heikki Patomaki

Capitalism and Citizenship
The impossible partnership
Kathryn Dean

Philosophy of Language and
the Challenge to Scientific
Realism
Christopher Norris

Transcendence
Critical realism and God
Margaret S. Archer, Andrew Collier and
Douglas V. Porpora

Critical Realist Applications
in Organisation and
Management Studies
Edited by Steve Fleetwood and
Stephen Ackroyd

Making Realism Work
Realist social theory and
empirical research
Edited by Bob Carter and
Caroline New

Explaining Global Poverty

A critical realist approach

Branwen Gruffydd Jones

LONDON AND NEW YORK

First published 2006
by Routledge
2 Park Square, Milton Park, Abingdon, Oxon, OX14 4RN

Simultaneously published in the USA and Canada
by Routledge
270 Madison Ave, New York NY 10016

Routledge is an imprint of the Taylor & Francis Group, an informa business

Transferred to Digital Printing 2009

© 2006 Branwen Gruffydd Jones

Typeset in Times New Roman by
Newgen Imaging Systems (P) Ltd, Chennai, India

British Library Cataloguing in Publication Data
A catalogue record for this book is available from the British Library

Library of Congress Cataloging in Publication Data
A catalog record for this book has been requested

ISBN10: 0–415–39212–8 (hbk)
ISBN10: 0–415–56869–2 (pbk)

ISBN13: 978–0–415–39212–9 (hbk)
ISBN13: 978–0–415–56869–2 (pbk)

In memory of Carlos Cardoso

Contents

Tables

Acknowledgements

This book is a substantially revised version of a PhD thesis, submitted to the University of Sussex in 2001. The book draws on material which has been published elsewhere. Thanks to the following for permission to reproduce selected and revised sections of original publications in this work: Routledge and Shahid Qadir for material in Chapters 1 and 3 from 'Africa and the poverty of International Relations', *Third World Quarterly*, 26 (5), 2005; Routledge and Jan Burgess for material in Chapter 4 from 'The civilised horrors of over-work: Marxism, imperialism and development of Africa', *Review of African Political Economy*, 30 (95): 33–44, 2003; Martin Elbl and PSR for material in Chapter 5 from 'Globalisation and the freedom to be poor: from colonial political coercion to the economic compulsion of need', *Portuguese Studies Review*, 10 (1): 108–28, 2002; Mervyn Hartwig and JCR for material in Chapters 3 and 6 from ' "The massive presence of the past and the outside": presences, absences and possibilities for emancipation in the current global condition', *Journal of Critical Realism*, 1 (2): 1–26, 2003; Victor Mendes, Gina Reis and the University of Massachusetts, Dartmouth for material in Chapters 1 and 7 from 'Appearances and realities of post-war reconstruction in Mozambique', *Reevaluating Mozambique: Portuguese Literary and Cultural Studies*, 10: 49–67, 2003; Routledge for material in Chapter 7 from 'Globalisations, violences and resistances in Mozambique: the struggles continue' in Eschle, C. and Maiguashca, B. (eds) *Critical Theories, World Politics and 'the Anti-Globalisation Movement*, Routledge, London, pp. 53–73, 2005; and again for material in Chapter 1 from 'Explaining Global Poverty: A realist critique of the orthodox approach', in Cruickshank, J. (ed.) *Critical Realism: the difference that it makes*, London: Routledge, pp. 221–39, 2003.

The doctoral research and subsequent writing which forms the basis of this book were made possible by funding from the Economic and Social Research Council (grant nos. R00429734736 and T026271069), which is gratefully acknowledged. So too is additional financial support to fund travel and language training, provided by the Centre for Culture, Development and Environment and the Politics and International Relations Subject Group at the University of Sussex, and the Department of Politics and International Relations at the University of Aberdeen.

I very much thank my doctoral supervisors, Richard Black, Julian Saurin and Marc Williams. In different ways and at different stages they provided wonderful support, guidance, encouragement, criticism, inspiration and friendship. I especially thank Richard for his willingness to support me despite my research taking a direction he seriously disagreed with; Marc for his faith and support during a difficult period of intellectual confusion and change; and Julian for his profound intellectual inspiration and solidarity. I also thank my examiners Peter Wilkin and Ronen Palan for their comments and encouragement.

This book stems from and is informed by a period of fieldwork in Mozambique in 1999, although the final outcome is only loosely related to the specific substance of fieldwork. A great many people in Mozambique gave me assistance in various ways, for which I am extremely grateful and without whom the research would not have been possible. They are too numerous to mention by name but include peasants in the countryside in Nampula; government officials in Nampula and Maputo; staff in aid agencies, local and international non-governmental organisations, managers and staff of cashew processing factories in Nampula and Maputo; journalists, academics and trade union officials. In particular I would like to thank Professors Arlindo Chilundo and Carlos Serra at the Universidade Eduardo Mondlane, and António Sopa and the librarians at the Arquivo Histórico de Moçambique, for their support and assistance; Eliézer Camargo and Chris Asante of World Vision (Nampula), Rodrigo Rico of CLUSA (Nampula), and Nick Kottak, for invaluable assistance in arranging interviews in the countryside; Armando Bento, Joel Pinto, Maria de Fatima Vale and Raoul de Castro who were excellent interpreters; Irene de Souza and Carlos Costa for providing much information regarding the cashew sector; Joaquim Salvador and James dos Santos for excellent language teaching and initial introduction to Mozambique; Soila Hirvonen, Ritva Parviainen and Gabrielle Anthmer for their friendship and wonderful hospitality.

I thank Alan Norrie and the editorial board of the Critical Realism book series, and Alan Jarvis, Yeliz Ali and Amber Bulkley at Routledge for their interest in this project and patience during the months it has taken to bring it to completion, and the three anonymous readers for their constructive criticism and suggestions.

I have been blessed with supportive and enriching friendships, many of which stem from the early days of the PhD. Thanks to Libby Assassi, Sally Baden, Bridget Byrne and Khalid Nadvi, Grace Carswell and Geert de Neve, Liz Challinor and Julio dos Santos, Neil Curry, Helen Cornish and Andrew Nesbit, İpek Demir and Mark Williamson, Cate Eschle and Denis Donoghue, Lucy Ford, David Galbreath, Iman Hashim and Burak Ülman, Seung Young Kim, Gabriela Kütting, Mark Lacy, João Leonardo Medeiros, Henry Neale, Eric Othieno Nyanjom, Clare Richards, Pam Shaw, Katja Wessolowski. Special thanks to Alison Ayers, Pauline Rose, Andrea Oelsner and Anders Widfeldt.

Very many thanks to Catrin, Angharad and my parents for their constant support, encouragement, humorous interest and tolerance. Finally, ongoing thanks to Elly Omondi for his loving support and solidarity, extended over a long distance.

Branwen Gruffydd Jones

Abbreviations

ANC	African National Congress
DCR	Dialectical Critical Realism
DFID	Department for International Development
DNPP	Direcção Nacional de Propaganda e Publicidade
DOD	Debt Outstanding and Disbursed
DS	Development Studies
ECLA	Economic Commission for Latin America
Frelimo	Frente de Libertação de Moçambique
G7	Group of 7
G8	Group of 8
G10	Group of 10
G77	Group of 77
GDR	German Democratic Republic
IFAD	International Fund for Agricultural Development
IFIs	International Financial Institutions
IFPRI	International Food Policy Research Institute
IMF	International Monetary Fund
IPE	International Political Economy
IR	International Relations
MNR	Mozambique National Resistance
MPF	Ministério do Plano e Finanças
NATO	North Atlantic Treaty Organization
NGOs	Non-Governmental Organisations
NICs	Newly Industrialising Countries
OECD	Organisation for Economic Co-operation and Development
OPEC	Organisation of Petroleum Exporting Countries
PAIGC	Partido Africano da Independência da Guiné e Cabo Verde
PIDE	Polícia Internacional de Defesa do Estado
Renamo	Resistência Nacional Moçambicana
SADCC	Southern African Development Coordination Conference
SADF	South African Defence Force

SDR	Special Drawing Rights
TMSA	Transformational Model of Social Activity
TNCs	Transnational Corporations
UEM	Universidade Eduardo Mondlane
UNCTAD	United Nations Conference on Trade and Development
UNDP	United Nations Development Programme
UNITA	União Nacional Para a Independência Total de Angola
USAID	United States Agency for International Development
USSR	Union of Soviet Socialist Republics
ZANU	Zimbabwe African National Union

Introduction

Why is Africa poor?

a protest without perception of what causes that against which one protests can remain an empty cry; it can be valid in its outrage and concern, but ultimately powerless in its ability either to identify the roots of the problem or to convince sufficient numbers of people of its validity.

(Halliday 1986: 2)

The world at the beginning of the twenty-first century is characterised by extreme differences in living conditions in different areas, by extremes of poverty and wealth, of scarcity and abundance. In Africa chronic malnutrition and hunger is widespread and people struggle to buy a decent pair of shoes. In Europe and North America the consumption of ready-chopped and washed salad vegetables is routine, child obesity is now recognised as a societal problem, video-recorders and walkmans are abandoned for DVD and I-Pods. There are significant differences in living conditions within countries and regions – poverty exists in the West and extremes of wealth exist in Africa. However some insight into the major extent of global inequality can be gained from briefly considering some social indicators from the UK and Mozambique.

Both the UK and Mozambique are unequal societies. In the UK the poorest 20 per cent of the population have 6.1 per cent of national income, while the richest 20 per cent have 44 per cent of national income. In Mozambique the poorest 20 per cent of the population have 6.5 per cent of national income, while the richest 20 per cent have 46.5 per cent of national income (UNDP 2004: 188, 191). The levels of wealth and poverty in different countries are described annually by the United Nations Development Programme (UNDP), measured according to their Human Development Index. This is a figure based on four social indicators: life expectancy at birth, adult literacy rate, joint gross enrolment ratio (the ratio between the number of children in school and the total school-age population), and real per capita GDP. Mozambique's Human Development Index (HDI) for 2002 was 0.354, while that of the United Kingdom was 0.936. The UNDP ranks all the countries of the world by HDI; the UK comes twelfth, Mozambique comes one hundred and seventy first, with only six countries having a lower HDI (all of them in Africa: Guinea-Bissau, Burundi, Mali, Burkina Faso, Niger, and Sierra

Leone) (UNDP 2004). Some comparative indicators of the UK and Mozambique are shown in Table 0.1.

In 2003, UK consumers spent £41.2 billion on clothing and footwear, £83.7 billion on recreation and culture, and £81.2 billion on restaurants and hotels (Summerfield and Gill 2005: 86). In 2003–04, UK households spent on average £76.4 per week on leisure services (Gibbins 2005 Table 4.1). In 2002, 87 per cent of UK households had a microwave oven, 89 per cent had a video-recorder,

Table 0.1 Comparison of social indicators, UK and Mozambique

	Mozambique		*United Kingdom*	
Adult literacy rate	46.5%		~99%	
Probability at birth of not surviving to age 40 years (2000–05)	56%			
Probability at birth of not surviving to age 60 years (2000–05)			8.9%	
Children under weight for age	26%		<1%	
Population below income poverty line:	$1 per day: 37.9%		50% of median income: 12.5%	
Population below income poverty line:	$2 per day: 78.4%		$11 a day: 15.7%	
Population below income poverty line:	national poverty line: 69.4%		$4 a day: <1%	
Births attended by skilled health personel (1995–2002)	44%		99%	
Physicians per 100,000 people	2		164	
Population with sustainable access to improved sanitation (2000)	43%		100%	
Population with sustainable access to improved water source (2000)	57%		100%	
Infants with low birthweight 1998–2002	14%		8%	
Life expectancy at birth: 1970–75	41.1 years		72 years	
Life expectancy at birth: 2000–05	38.1 years		78.2 years	
Infant mortality rate (per 1000 live birth): 1970	163		18	
Infant mortality rate: 2002	125		5	
Under-five mortality rate (per 1000 live births): 1970	278		23	
Under-five mortality rate: 2002	197		7	
Probability at birth of surviving to age 65 (2000–05)				
F M	26.3%	19.8%	89.4%	83.2%
Tuberculosis prevalence rate per 100,000 population (WHO) 2000 2002	472.93	547.40	11.92	11.99
Tuberculosis death rate per 100,000 (WHO) 2000 2002	52.153	60.634	1.167	1.173
Maternal mortality (per 100,000 live births) (1985–2002)	1,100		7	

Source: UNDP 2004, United Nations Common Database online data.

99 per cent had a colour television, 83 per cent had a CD player, 32 per cent had a DVD player, 95 per cent had a refrigerator, 93 per cent had a washing machine, 75 per cent had a mobile phone, 93 per cent had central heating (Rickards *et al.* 2004: 49). In England in 2000, 20 per cent of boys aged 2–19 and 27 per cent of girls were overweight; 5 per cent of boys and 7 per cent of girls were obese (Nessa and Gallagher 2004).

In Mozambique in 2002–03, 63 per cent of the population were classified as living in absolute poverty. 28 per cent of households owned a bicycle and 46 per cent of households owned a radio. 56 per cent of households had no house-hold sanitation facilities (Ministry of Planning and Finance (MPF) *et al.* 2004: 38, 42, 43, 56). In 2001, 53 per cent of the population were under-nourished, 26 per cent of children under five were under-weight for their age, and 44 per cent under-height for their age (UNDP 2004).

Why is this the case? Are these natural, accidental characteristics, just the way things happen to be in different places? Do such differences arise from local cultures, traditions, attitudes, or natural environments? Is there any necessary connection between conditions of life in different parts of the world? How do we understand this modern condition, what sense do we make of it, how do we explain it? There are of course various competing understandings of this global condition, which differ in the first instance according to one's position in society. One type of understanding arises from the lived experience of the poor – for example that of a peasant in Mozambique, producing with their own sweat and blood, growing corn, cassava and groundnuts and collecting the few cashew nuts the old trees produce; trying to sell a season's produce in the market for enough money to buy some clothes (probably second-hand from Europe or America) and to pay the hospital fee for a sick child. Such an understanding will necessarily differ, for example, from that of a World Bank economist in Washington or Maputo, or a New-Internationalist-reading, Oxfam-contributing environmentally conscious undergraduate student in Brighton or Aberdeen (wearing their 'Make Poverty History' wrist-band), or a work-hard-and-play-hard financial analyst in the City of London.

But what about ideas in society, beyond the particular views specific to any one individual? With the development of capitalism and the modern state in western Europe arose the aspirations for social science. Systematic, organised inquiry seeking to provide secure knowledge about the workings of society was conducted in universities and philanthropic or state institutions, with a view to understanding and resolving social problems. The production of knowledge in the service of policy, directed social change and social order extended beyond the confines of the European nation-state to the arena of foreign and international policy. More generally, over centuries of European expansion a changing discourse and public awareness about world society, world progress and a world social condition emerged, institutionalised and reproduced by public statesmen and women, philosophers, journalists, academics, and public institutions of various kinds. In the eighteenth and nineteenth centuries such ideas centred on an ideal of civilisation, and on distinctions between civilised and backward or savage peoples. In the post-war period of the twentieth century this discourse has taken the form of ideas about development, growth, progress, modernisation, catching up (or getting left behind), underdevelopment and poverty. This public discourse simultaneously describes and offers explanations of the global human condition. Explanations are offered so as to decide upon action, to rationalise, make judgements, and to provide legitimacy.

The fundamental concern at the centre of this book is to explain the modern condition of poverty in Africa. This general condition is explored in the particular context of Mozambique. The condition of poverty – in Africa, in Mozambique and in many societies of the so-called Third World – is a modern tragedy and a social crisis of enormous proportions. It is necessary to insist on and repeat the scale of tragedy and global disgrace manifest in Africa's condition of poverty, in the face of the normalisation and marginalisation of poverty. Yet the very same global era which produces simultaneously the world-historical tragedy of global poverty and its normalisation, thus giving rise to an urgent need for moral outrage, also produces a *hegemonic* discourse of moral outrage. Tony Blair famously referred to Africa's condition as a 'scar on the conscience of the world' in a speech at the Labour Party conference in 2001, and the former UK Minister for Overseas Development, Claire Short, brought to public debates over global poverty a renewed and sincere sense of outrage and determination to act. George Bush, leader of the sole imperial superpower, recently said 'the United States wants to help the people of Africa realize the brighter future they deserve' (Parker 2005). In October 2004, James Wolfensohn, former President of the World Bank Group, issued 'an urgent call to action to make the planet more equitable and safe, through the three pillars of poverty reduction, environmental stewardship, and education of the youth of the world'. Speaking at the Annual Meeting of the Governors of the World Bank and International Monetary Fund (IMF), he said

> It is absolutely right that, together, we fight terror. We must. The danger, however, is that in our preoccupation with immediate threats, we lose sight of the longer-term and equally urgent causes of our insecure world: poverty, frustration, and lack of hope. If we want stability on our planet, we must fight to end poverty. Eradication of poverty is central to stability and peace. It is still the challenge of our time.
>
> (Wolfensohn 2004)

Such pronouncements articulated by the powerful seem readily amenable to the tools of critical discourse analysis, while an explicit comparative analysis of the humanitarianisms of the dawn of the twenty-first century and the closing decade of the nineteenth century would be a fruitful line of inquiry. But it is equally important to provide a critique which counters the implicit *explanatory content* underlying this hegemonic expression of moral concern. The current global conjuncture, discursive and material, gives rise to a peculiar contradiction. As the stark reality of concrete conditions of oppression deepens, becoming ever more impossible to deny – evidenced in the moral outrage expressed by the leaders of transnational capital – the consensus among critical scholars rejects out-moded notions of reality and aspirations to explanation. The more urgent the need to understand and explain this world we inhabit, the more roundly such an ideal is abandoned by many who call themselves critical.

In the current context of what some call 'moral anxiety' and the ambivalence of postmodernity, this book takes an unfashionable position. Against the general critical climate in the social sciences which emphasises the normative as primary, this book foregrounds the importance of objectivity and explanation. In the face of the very crisis of modernity which produces and reproduces poverty alongside technocratic aspirations of social control and the disciplining effects of institutionalised knowledge practices, this book reconsiders the notion and possibility of *science* as a distinct form of knowledge about the social world. Is it possible to retain any commitment to the possibility of science in social inquiry? In other words, is there a possibility of producing forms of knowledge about social phenomena which have greater explanatory adequacy than lay knowledge? Can we really entertain the idea of making any claims to knowledge about '*social reality*'? Could it be that one of the most important ways for scholarship to contribute to the radical project of societal transformation and human emancipation is through objective inquiry and explanation of the causes of social conditions? Or is the very idea of such an enterprise irredeemably mired in the sins of Enlightenment and Modernity, forever tainted with the relics of a naïve positivism and desire for neutral certainty, for appropriating The Other? One aim of this book is to reclaim the terrain of objectivity and explanation as belonging to the project of critical social inquiry in the interests of emancipation.

The concern of this book centres not on the task of documenting, measuring and defining levels and extents of poverty, nor on the moral condemnation of poverty, but on the problem of explanation. Global poverty is a fundamental characteristic of the modern world, and most commentators share in condemnation of widespread poverty and suffering in areas such as Mozambique. However analysts adopt different approaches to understanding and explaining this problem, and these competing understandings inform social action. Marx was critical of 'the kind of criticism which knows how to judge and condemn the present, but not how to comprehend it' (Marx 1867: 638). What is it necessary to do to make the move from description to comprehension or explanation? The way in which different approaches to social inquiry move from empirical data to explanation is a crucial defining characteristic of their method. An initial clue to the connection between description and explanation made by different approaches can be found by considering the analysis of two social scientists who work on global poverty.

The problem of explanation was addressed squarely by Howard White in a lecture given at the University of Sussex in 1999 entitled 'Why is Africa Poor?'. White is a prominent development economist and his analysis constitutes an exemplar of the long tradition of orthodox Development Studies. He began by detailing various statistics similar to those given above, in order to illustrate the 'quite staggering' 'scale' of poverty in Africa. He then acknowledged the problematic nature of attempting to portray varying conditions of human life by citing a series of statistics. Instead he suggested an alternative way of thinking about, say, the figure of infant mortality (2 million for sub-Saharan Africa as a whole, in 1995): 'two million infants – that's a line of dead babies two hundred and fifty miles long, which stretch from here [Brighton] to the edge of Scotland' (White 1999). He emphasised what he called the 'globalisation of African poverty', by which he meant the extent that Africa is 'falling behind', or 'failing to catch up' in comparison to other regions of the world, in particular South Asia. He then moved to the task of explanation, citing a report on child health which starts with the words of a father: 'Can you tell me why this had to happen?'.

Julian Saurin, a scholar in International Relations (IR), is also concerned with questions of poverty, and he too addresses the problem from a global perspective:

> As US consumers spend $7.5 billion on 'lawn care' products and $9 billion on children's video games per year, US overseas aid stood at £10.1 billion per year (1989–1991). A quarter of the world's population does not have access to safe water; at least 12 million infants died before the age of five in 1992, with a further 175 million under-fives suffering malnutrition.
>
> (Saurin 1996: 664–5)

These two commentators share a common concern, and they appear at first sight to use statistics in the same way, as a rhetorical device for expressing global poverty and inequality. Underlying the apparently similar rhetorical uses of statistics, however, are radically different understandings of the nature and causes of the problems they have both identified. The first is that of development economics, itself characteristic of a broader dominant approach to social inquiry which is defined by its method and underlying assumptions about ontology (the nature of the world) and epistemology (how and what it is possible to know about the world). The second is that of historical materialism. These two approaches rest on different ontological and epistemological assumptions and consequently employ very different methods of inquiry. When Saurin uses numbers to express global poverty and inequality, he juxtaposes details of the conditions of life of the millions of poor in the world with an expression of the level and nature of consumption in the highly industrialised, mass-consumption society of America. On one hand he mentions aspects so fundamental to human existence as nutrition and safe water. On the other hand he mentions high consumption levels of lawn care products and children's video games – items which can hardly be considered fundamental. His mode of expression is suggestive of an understanding of a qualitative difference in the lives of different social groups in the world (a difference that is lost when one thinks quantitatively in terms of 'per capita income'); of a global connection between these differing conditions; an understanding that these two starkly contrasted conditions are not accidentally but necessarily related; and that this relation has something to do with global structures of accumulation. This is in contrast to White's view of the problem – that Africa is simply further behind on the path to economic development and prosperity already trodden by America and the rest of the 'developed world'.

This latter view, that Africa has been left behind, predominates. The approach producing such a view is dominant in academia and in society more broadly – in the various national and international, governmental and non-governmental institutions formally concerned with global poverty and development. Implicitly or explicitly the causes of poverty in Africa are located internally to Africa, and in the current era – in the *local present*. According to a poll conducted in the UK by the *Telegraph* newspaper, 79 per cent of British voters believe that corruption and incompetence are to blame for poverty in Africa (Sylvester and Sparrow 2005). There is a tendency even in normative discourse to look on at conditions of poverty elsewhere with the utmost concern but little awareness of the historical and current causal relations between the affluence of the West and the poverty of Africa. The tendency of expressions of moral and political concern in the West to remain silent about causal relations between wealth and poverty is captured by television journalist Charlie Brooker, in his review of the Brazilian programme *City of Men* for the *Guardian*'s weekly television and radio guide *The guide*:

> the sole problem with City of Men is that it's entertaining first and 'worthy' second – in other words, and to quote Johnny Rotten out of context, it provides a cheap holiday in other people's misery. Like a heart-rending feature on Rwandan orphans in the middle of a glossy Sunday magazine, it gives pampered western milquetoasts like you and me a chance to feel somehow engaged with the world, to feel concerned, well-informed, and sympathetic – but only from a safe distance. It might go well with a glass of pinot grigio, but no matter how much you like it, no matter how much you wring your hands and blub about how desperately sad the world is, unless you're moved to board a flight to Brazil with a 1,000-point plan of action in your pocket, all you've done is enjoy the spectacle.
>
> (Brooker 2004: 52)

This book does not provide a plan of action, but in addressing the task of explanation it emphasises above all the *global* relations of cause and conditions of possibility between the affluence of the West and the poverty of Africa. It argues that an adequate causal explanation of poverty in Africa today must apprehend the 'massive presence of the past and the outside' (Bhaskar 1994: 107) in the constitution of the local present.

In the current capitalist world order the global extension of cause and conditions of possibility are not readily apparent. This is primarily because of the ubiquity of commodified forms of social life, interaction and reproduction. Without an informed understanding of history and the nature and operation of capitalism and imperialism, it is not at all obvious how and why conditions of social life in spatially distant locales might be causally related. A shopper in a supermarket in the UK buying a packet of ready-cut green beans or salted cashew nuts will likely have no idea of the social conditions of the peasants and workers in Kenya or Mozambique who grew and packaged those beans and nuts, still less an understanding of the global structure of social relations and mode of accumulation which causally link these two very different practices, conditions and possibilities of living. If it is characteristic of capitalist society that the real nature of social relations are masked by the phenomenal forms of social life, as Marx and many since have argued, then in the era of global capitalism it is precisely the *global* nature of social relations which are obscured. Emphasis on the normative tragedy of global poverty is important but insufficient for explanation, which requires acknowledgement of the causal reality of the social relations which structure our daily activities, and which, generally unconsciously and unaware, we necessarily reproduce in a routine manner. W. E. B. Du Bois commented in 1946 on precisely this world-historical contradiction:

> Because of the stretch in time and space between the deed and the result, between the work and the product, it is not only usually impossible for the worker to know the consumer; or the investor, the source of his profit, but also it is often made impossible by law to inquire into the facts.
>
> (Du Bois 1946: 41)

In the 1960s and 70s theories of underdevelopment and dependency insisted that conditions of poverty are not a natural condition but a causal outcome, produced necessarily by the historical development of capitalism as a global system. This was one of their most important contributions which the recent critical approaches in Development Studies tend to lose sight of in their preoccupation with local diversity. Today it is important to reclaim these insights, given the ever worsening material conditions suffered by the popular masses (both rural and urban) in Africa, the enduring dominance of empiricism in Development Studies and institutional discourse, and the critical focus on questions of local agency, subjectivity, identity and difference at the expense of global structure. A theoretical and methodological approach which recognises capitalism as a necessarily global and imperial system with real necessary structural tendencies, and which is sensitive to the myriad, endlessly nuanced and uneven social forms and conditions produced by the operation of structural tendencies in very different combinations and contexts, is more important than ever.

This book defends critical realism as the most adequate basis for substantive inquiry into global poverty. Much of what is required for such inquiry is already there even if it has fallen out of fashion, while critical realism is not the only foundation upon which to attempt such reclamation. Critical realism is important in this context, however, because it highlights not only the pitfalls of empiricism but, through its emphasis on intransitive reality, cause, explanation and objectivity, it steers a path clear from the pitfalls of postmodernism. This argument necessitates a certain amount of discussion at the level of philosophy, setting out realist arguments about ontology and epistemology. In defending critical realism with respect to the specific question of global poverty, the book contributes more generally to the growing programme of substantive research informed by critical realism. However it must be stressed that the primary concern of the book is global poverty, rather than critical realism per se. Critical realism is discussed because of its importance for social inquiry in general, and in particular for explaining poverty; but ultimately the discussion of critical realism is subordinate to the overriding concern about poverty.

This study does not contribute in itself to a new interpretation of Mozambican history. Rather it seeks to emphasise the insights of existing work, within a general framework which is founded on the principles of critical realism and a theoretical and historical understanding of capitalism and imperialism. One of the problems of the contemporary institutionalised division of academic labour is the separation of African studies, and African history, from the study of development and international relations. Thus important studies of the historical development of capitalism in different regions, and the process and local effects of incorporation of distinct regions into the emerging global political economy over centuries, become ghettoised under the categories 'African Studies' and 'African History'. Meanwhile the study of development proceeds with scant reference to the framework of global capitalism, colonialism and imperialism. Mainstream Development Studies has become fully subordinated to questions of policy relevance, with its jargon of participation, empowerment and poverty alleviation, seeking to assist non-governmental organisations (NGOs) in their efforts to help the poor to help themselves. Much of Critical Development Studies has long since abandoned analysis of class relations, let alone imperialism. Meanwhile it is only in the aftermath of September the 11th, 2001, that IR scholars have suddenly re-discovered imperialism and empire. New insights on empire/imperialism now proliferate as the effects of twentieth-century neo-colonialism, long-suffered in Africa and elsewhere, suddenly become apparent to the West in the first few years of the twenty-first century. Meanwhile the poor of Africa remain in their daily struggles to make ends meet and live decent lives.

Part I

Poverty, need and objectivity in social inquiry

1 Poverty and development in Africa

Twentieth-century orthodoxies

Public awareness and concern about global inequality and conditions of widespread routine suffering in specific parts of the world emerged during the twentieth century. This social phenomenon and global condition came to be conceived in terms of *poverty* and *development*, and became an object of institutionalised social inquiry and policy. Specific bodies of theories, conceptual frameworks and terminology arose, influenced by existing philosophical and methodological commitments as well as by the prevailing geo-political context. In the twentieth century's intellectual division of labour poverty and development were the concerns primarily of Development Studies, and to a lesser extent International Relations (IR). Social inquiry about this global social condition was conducted not only in universities but also by government policy departments, international organisations, philanthropic or non-governmental organisations (NGOs), and think-tanks. The ideas in this area have varied in form, tone and content, subject to a variety of political, theoretical and philosophical as well as empirical influences and determinations. This chapter surveys the academic and institutional approaches to the problem of poverty and development in Africa which have risen to prominence during the twentieth century.

It is helpful to employ some concept which can capture the existence of certain common features underlying a variety of widely held ideas, by virtue of which such ideas are treated as components of a broader group. An appropriate descriptive term would be discourse, but the very word *discourse* has come to be associated automatically with the work of Foucault, suggestive of post-structuralist commitments. However paying serious analytical attention to the nature, form and causal efficacy of ideas is not the sole preserve of post-structuralist approaches; while conversely the notion that materialists are necessarily reductionist, ignoring the form and causal significance of ideas, is inaccurate. The term ideology is of course relevant, but this concept has specific meanings which are not reducible simply to the descriptive sense of a set of prevailing ideas sharing certain common underlying assumptions. A specific concept of ideology referring to knowledge which is misleading and non-scientific is important, and will be used at a later stage. This use of the term ideology is evaluative and cannot be employed at the outset.

The term orthodoxy will be employed here so as to avoid accidental suggestion of post-structuralist commitments secreted by the use of the very word discourse.

Pierre Bourdieu's development of the concept of orthodoxy is particularly helpful in this context. The aim here is to identify certain commonalities in form, explanatory logic and basic underlying assumptions which are shared by a variety of ideas about the condition of global poverty which rose to dominance during the twentieth century. Bourdieu developed the notions of orthodoxy and doxa to theorise the way in which a particular, contestable view of the world becomes established as a normal, natural and unquestioned truth, by means of a set of propositions which are assumed and so never examined and questioned (Bourdieu 1977, 1990). Bourdieu uses the term doxa to refer to a set of assumptions which are never identified and therefore never questioned, the 'universe of the undiscussed (undisputed)' (1977: 168). They exist outside the realm of that which is spoken about, thought about and discussed. The realm of doxa is delineated in negative terms, as that which lies beyond what does exist:

> The truth of doxa is only ever fully revealed when negatively constituted by the constitution of a *field of opinion*, the locus of the confrontation of competing discourses [. . .] It is by reference to the universe of opinion that the complementary class is defined, the class of that which is taken for granted, doxa, the sum total of the theses tacitly posited on the hither side of all inquiry, which appear as such only retrospectively.
>
> (Bourdieu 1977: 168)

Orthodoxy refers to what is dominant within the field of discussion. The orthodoxy does not yet have the full invisibility of the unquestioned, unseen and taken-as-given doxa, precisely because it is challenged and contested within the 'universe of discourse (or argument)' (Bourdieu 1977: 168). By defining orthodoxy in terms of the form, contents and *limits* of that which is discussed and disputed, Bourdieu draws attention precisely to that which is unspoken, not said yet which defines the content of discussion by constituting limits. This is important because it enables identification of a set of ideas as orthodox despite apparent difference and variety:

> the manifest censorship imposed by orthodox discourse, the official way of speaking and thinking the world, conceals another, more radical censorship: the overt opposition between 'right' opinion and 'left' or 'wrong' opinion, which delimits the universe of possible discourse [. . .] masks in its turn the fundamental opposition between the universe of things that can be stated, and hence thought, and the universe of that which is taken for granted. The universe of discourse [. . .] is practically defined in relation to the necessarily unnoticed complementary class that is constituted by the universe of that which is undiscussed, unnamed, admitted without argument or scrutiny.
>
> (Bourdieu 1977: 169–70)

The concepts of doxa, 'that which is taken for granted' and orthodoxy, 'straight, or rather straightened, opinion, which aims, without ever entirely succeeding, at restoring the primal state of innocence of doxa' (Bourdieu 1977: 160, 169) capture powerfully the way in which particular assumptions and views become established so as to appear normal and natural, thus defining the limits of what is thought about and how things are thought about, whilst themselves (the assumptions) going unseen and therefore unquestioned. An array of orthodox ideas about poverty and social conditions in Africa emerged during the first half of the twentieth century and have remained influential ever since, notwithstanding the elaboration of important critiques. These various ideas can usefully be conceived in terms of a 'field of opinion', the 'locus of the confrontation of competing discourses'. The point is not their formal agreement and uniformity, but the underlying doxa, 'that which is taken for granted', 'the sum total of the theses tacitly posited on the hither side of all inquiry'.

During the twentieth century the production of knowledge about poverty was conducted in a variety of institutional sites, in different locations and subject to different theoretical and practical influences. We can therefore identify distinct forms of knowledge which differ in form, style and content. A brief examination of some examples of the various ideas, which pays attention not only to content and form, but also to what is not said, reveals the existence of what Bourdieu might call a common underlying doxa. Four different instances of orthodox knowledge about the condition of poverty in Africa are considered here. In Development Studies, the central defining theme is the notion of Modernisation. In IR, attention to Africa has taken the form of analysis of the weaknesses of the 'new states' in the international system. The central source of policy discourse about poverty and development is the World Bank, whose basic approach to explaining poverty is influential throughout the institutional network, both governmental and non-governmental. Finally, this general influence is seen in the current policy approach to poverty alleviation in Mozambique.

Poverty, development and modernisation

The boundaries and form of the study of development cannot be delineated consistently in strictly disciplinary terms. Development Studies in itself, as the academic study of the problem of development and developing countries, encompasses Economics, Political Science, Sociology, IR, Geography and Anthropology. A particular approach to the question of development became dominant in all these disciplinary fields: Modernisation Theory. The core assumptions, method and attitude of Modernisation theory informed the work of economists, sociologists, political scientists and international relations theorists.

Modernisation theory emerged as a result of Western political scientists, sociologists and economists turning their attention to the manifold problems facing the countries of the Third World after decolonisation. In a sense the core of the problem was the inadequate living conditions of the majority of the population of former colonies, but this necessarily gave rise to concerns regarding economic policy, political management and public administration. It was apparent that existing theories and concepts available for comprehending societal problems in

Western industrialised societies were not necessarily readily applicable to these 'new', emerging societies. The response was to employ existing methodological procedures, especially those of comparison and correlation, to the analysis of the new states.

At the centre of Modernisation theory is the binary opposition traditional/ modern.[1] The problems of developing countries were seen to stem from their traditional nature. The dichotomy traditional/modern became a lens through which all aspects of society were portrayed (see Table 1.1).

Table 1.1 Modernisation theory's characterisation of traditional and modern societies

	Traditional	*Modern*
Economy	Predominantly agricultural, low technology, subsistence, small-scale, with a small, narrow and poorly integrated manufacturing base; low levels of saving; low or stagnant economic growth; inefficient	Industrialised, diversified, well integrated, with commercial large-scale agriculture; high levels of savings and investment, high rate of economic growth; efficient, dynamic
Politics/ political system	Based on relations of kinship, clan, ethnicity; political power takes the form of patron–client relations, patrimonialism, corruption, long-term personal rule; political change via military coups, or political repression, authoritarianism	Pluralist power-sharing democratic system, with institutionalized procedures for diverse interest groups in society to compete in an orderly, peaceful manner through representation and negotiation, allowing smooth peaceful transfer of power
Attitudes, value-systems	Religious beliefs and superstitions pervade many areas of life; fixed status, ascriptive values of moral economy and social identity; local and parochial	Secular, freedom of religious thought; individual achievement-oriented attitude; universal and cosmopolitan
Family relations	Extended family, relations of reciprocity and extended mutual dependence	Nuclear family, self-sufficient, independent
Social stratification	Highly stratified and unequal society, characterised by cleavages (ethnic, religious, regional, class, caste)	High degree of social mobility and opportunity
Material well-being	Widespread poverty, low life expectancy, high infant mortality, high prevalence of diseases, inadequate healthcare and sanitation, use of traditional medicine, low level of education and literacy	High level of consumption and material wealth, modern healthcare and sanitation, eradication or control of most serious infectious diseases, high levels of education
Workforce	Low-skilled workforce, unmotivated, prone to corruption	Highly skilled, disciplined and motivated workforce

The state of tradition was seen to be an original stage, a point of departure. A necessary component of this approach was a linear, evolutionary vision of social and historical change. The very notion of 'development' is imbued with directional teleology and a sense of progress. Modernisation theory rendered this explicit, with its formulation of the transition from an early stage of tradition (pre-modern, pre-capitalist, undeveloped, backward, agricultural, rural, irrational, tribal, poor) to the later, further advanced stage of modernity (capitalist, industrial, urban, rational, secular, wealthy and prosperous). This transition was achieved by economic growth and the formation of liberal, pluralist political institutions and culture.[2] The science of Development Studies was concerned with studying how traditional societies and economies could follow and achieve the same path of progress towards modernity already taken by the industrialised, developed countries. The very attributes of tradition were seen as obstacles, hampering the progression to modernity, which had to be overcome.

The linear teleology inherent in modernisation theory necessarily gave rise to a strongly comparative approach to social inquiry.[3] The description and specification of the stage of tradition and undevelopment was relational, defined in opposition and comparison to the later stage of modern development (Pletsch 1981). The logic of comparative analysis was applied not only between developing and developed countries (longitudinally), but among developing countries as well (laterally). The basic logic of longitudinal comparison entails positing an ideal or primary entity, and then comparing through empirical description the characteristics of other entities to specify their differences. The characteristics of the ideal state, society, economy, political system, form of government, police and military, bureaucracy and political culture were derived from an idealised analysis of Western societies. These particular forms were held to be the desirable, advanced and correct form, and the forms found in developing countries were held to be different, further behind or backward, and inadequate. In terms of comparison among and between the various new and developing states, the objective was to identify factors which influenced the process of change (social, political, economic), whether negatively or positively.

It was recognised by Modernisation theorists that the transition from tradition to modernity was not easy. It would not happen automatically, hence the need to build a 'science' of development, so as to better understand how the process could be achieved and managed, how a society's 'potential for modernization' could be realised (Zolberg 1968: 86). The science of development was necessary to inform policy because the process of modernisation required assistance from the more advanced states (Lasswell 1965). The question of assisting the transition from tradition to modernity within developing states was posed in terms of nation-building and institution-building (Rivkin 1968, Eisenstadt and Rokkan 1973).

The purported difficulties in transition were apparent in Africa in the decades after independence, as many countries developed features of authoritarian rule, militarism and conflict. From the perspective of modernisation approaches, this was an indication that the rapid changes involved in the process of transition could potentially unleash all sorts of social tensions generating instability and conflict. Institutional mechanisms for stable collective decision-making and peaceful political change were assumed to be features distinctive of modern, pluralist political systems. These features were absent from traditional, hierarchical societies in Africa, which were composed of a number of distinct ethnic groups with their own culture, language and communal interests. This meant that the changes of modernisation and the breakdown of traditional institutions gave rise to unregulated, conflictual forms of political competition involving ethnic rivalry, personal 'patron–client' relations, the militarisation of politics and banning of political parties and freedom of speech. The traditional social institutions and beliefs, when confronted by the rapid and multiple changes involved in the modernising process and in the context of economic scarcity, necessarily tended to give rise to further cleavage, division, conflict and instability.[4] A central concern of the study of development and modernisation was therefore the problem of political and social order and stability, and more generally the process of social and political change.[5] The key issue was how the transition from tradition to modernity could be managed in an orderly manner, so as to retain stability and avoid conflict and disorder.[6]

Africa's new, weak states in the international system

Questions of global poverty, and social conditions within African societies and elsewhere in the Third World, have until recently remained fairly marginal to the discipline of International Relations as a whole. Indeed Jackson has referred to poverty and race as 'some of the major taboo subjects of our time' (Jackson 1990: 10). This is in part due to the dominant state-centric approach which constituted a defining methodological given in IR for much of the twentieth century. IR – whether 'idealist' or 'realist' – was concerned with relations between states, and the external behaviour of states as they interacted in the context of the international system. An analytical separation between 'the domestic' and 'the international' was assumed, and the basic unit of analysis was the state. This automatically removed questions of the conditions of deprivation or affluence experienced by populations within states from the horizon of the discipline's concerns. Until recently, to the extent that Africa has constituted an area of inquiry in IR it has been in terms of the role of African states in the international system, the attributes of the 'statehood' of African states, and their internal 'weakness' *as states*, rather than the social conditions suffered (or enjoyed) by African peoples.

Standard accounts situate the institutionalisation of IR as a distinct area of inquiry in the first decade of the twentieth century.[7] Prior to the First World War the field of IR was mainly studied in Britain, and reflected Britain's interests as the world power; after the war IR scholarship reflected the interests of the 'satisfied powers' in wanting to avert future war (Smith 1987). IR scholarship was concerned with international law, international organisation and cooperation, the basic unit of analysis being the state understood in terms of a rational actor. The early approach has been termed idealism, or liberal internationalism. In the wake of the Second World War and the failure of the League of Nations to ensure the peaceful rational resolution of differences between states, the approach of political realism was formulated, informed by Carr's critique of utopian idealism (Carr 1939) and the systematic approach of Morgenthau (1948), which specified the timeless principles of international relations. Political realism also assumed states to be rational actors, but self-interested power maximisers rather than cooperative in nature.[8] State behaviour and the nature of international relations were understood to be rooted in Hobbesian laws of human nature. Critics such as Walker (1993) and Patomäki (2002) have pointed out that the apparently opposed theoretical approaches of idealism and realism actually mirror each other in several ways. They provide different resolutions to the same set of concerns about possibilities of international peace and cooperation or conflict and instability. One emphasises institutions, norms, rules, regimes of cooperation; the other multi-polar or bipolar structures, systems, balance of power and hegemony. A growing array of 'issues' have been analysed within this general problematic of cooperation or conflict, from security to the environment, North–South relations, and international trade.

From the late 1950s onwards a new concern entered the discipline of IR: the phenomenon of 'new states' in the wake of decolonisation. The process of decolonisation was treated by IR through the prism of existing conceptual frameworks, methods of analysis and underlying assumptions, and generally accommodated in terms of 'the expansion of international society', a fairly rapid numerical expansion in the number of states in the international system. '[T]he rest of the world was added on' (Gran 1996: 2), and analysis focused on the particular characteristics and problems of the new states, which tended to be weak, poor and developing.[9] IR scholars were concerned with the behaviour of the new states in the international system, how their behaviour as states differed from that of the older states and Great Powers, and the implications of these 'new states' for the stability and functioning of the international system itself. This entailed descriptive analysis of the new states, the patterns of relations among them, their foreign policies and alliances, the implications of their voting behaviour within the United Nations, the formation of new sub-systems within international relations. The implications of the new states for the international system was analysed for example in terms of their numbers, which shifted the traditional balance of power between the superpowers.[10]

Existing conceptual frameworks of liberalism and political realism regarding the nature of international relations were adapted in order to understand the peculiarity and specific features of the new states. The new states were susceptible to analysis of the features and behavioural patterns of all states: including power (absolute and relative, economic and military), foreign policy, diplomacy, ideology, national interest, institutional arrangements of international organisation. On the other hand these new states were clearly different, in terms of their attributes, behaviour and concerns. Therefore much analysis consisted of describing, enumerating and classifying the distinctness of the new states, through cross-national comparisons, and development of specific concepts of weak, small and quasi-states.[11]

Drawing on modernisation theory and comparative politics, the 'problems' of these new states were seen in terms of nation-building: how to achieve the transition from traditional culture to modern sovereign statehood, in a stable and orderly manner. This process was seen to be inherently difficult, obstructed by the specific cultural and socio-political characteristic of new states. Specifically, the primordial sentiments and groupings of kinship, clan and tribe gave rise to political 'cleavages' which tended to generate a political pathology characterised by corruption, opportunism, conflict and disorder.[12] These inherent tendencies within the new states were seen to have specific implications for international relations. The new states were seen as a potential threat to the stability of the international order:

> Conflict is, in fact, such an enduring feature of new states – both domestically and internationally – that their emergence inevitably poses new burdens upon the institutions of the international political system. [...] The general problem of regulating world political order in the era of new states is [...] a continuing one.
>
> (Kilson 1975c: xi)

The new states of the Third World, especially those in Africa, were understood as internally weak and deficient. Unlike the older European states, it was argued, their 'statehood' did not derive from the actual existence of various defining features of a sovereign state. Rather, it had been conferred upon them for normative reasons when they were incorporated into the international system. In modern 'international society' all states have the same rights to independence, sovereignty, self-determination and non-interference. All states are recognised as legally and politically equal in international society, regardless of their empirical characteristics (inadequacies). For IR scholars the basic definition of sovereignty, statehood and the international system are inherently linked. The process of decolonisation entailed the expansion of international society from the society of European states, to encompass all of the world.[13] This process was implicitly criticised for prematurely conferring statehood onto political entities which did not yet possess the appropriate attributes:

> The increase in the importance of the General Assembly has heightened the attraction of statehood, and the ease with which the United Nations has, after 1955, given its blessing and opened its doors to new nations has been largely responsible for the huge rise in the number of new states.
>
> (Hoffman 1975: 179)

> international society has become a global 'democracy' based on the principle of legal equality of members. Even the most profound socio-economic inadequacies of some countries are not considered to be a barrier to their membership: all former colonies and dependencies have the right to belong if they wish.
>
> (Jackson and Rosberg 1982: 16)

The result according to this line of analysis is that the statehood of Africa's states, which are empirically weak in terms of their internal characteristics, is guaranteed by the international system. Jackson's argument (1990) is that the nature of international relations and the international system itself has changed with the process of decolonisation, and it is necessary to understand this change in order to explain the condition of states in Africa and elsewhere in the Third World. The change in the 'game' was from the former regime of positive sovereignty, according to which recognition of sovereignty was based on the actual existence of empirical features, 'contingent on capable and to some extent "civilised" government' (Jackson 1990: 5), to a regime of negative sovereignty, in which the right to sovereign statehood derives from the normative structure of international society, regardless of the actual characteristics and capabilities of particular states.

One important exception to this general pattern was the focus on what became known as the 'North–South dialogue' and more generally the North–South divide, which attracted attention from International Political Economy (IPE) scholars in the 1970s and 1980s.[14] The very terms on which the South engaged in 'North–South dialogue' were informed by Third World critiques of the Western orthodox approaches to the problem of development. The elaboration of these critiques, mainly by scholars from the Third World, influenced the work of some IR scholars. Nevertheless the general tendency of IR was to incorporate the conditions and problems of Third World societies and states within the discipline's existing frameworks, theories and methods. The emergence of the Third World states onto the stage of international politics, which necessarily entailed emphasis on the problem of poverty and international inequality, did not provoke any significant re-thinking of the core body of IR theories. Indeed this process of intellectual absorption or incorporation (containment) mirrored the actual process of decolonisation, which stopped at the level of political independence of individual colonies. From the perspective of the European colonial powers and the United States, decolonisation would not and should not entail reform of the structuring of the international system itself: decolonisation was a question of 'domestic' or 'internal' political sovereignty and self-rule with no implications for international change. It was precisely this assumption that was challenged by the Third World Coalition in their collective effort to reform the international order, as a necessary corollary of independence and consistent with international norms of justice and equality (Bedjaoui 1979). These efforts were resisted and ultimately defeated, however. In perhaps a similar way the radical scholarship of Third World critics, which questioned and reformulated the very nature of the international system as a system of structured injustice and exploitation, has had little lasting impact on IR as a whole beyond the circles of those 'already' concerned with the 'issue-area' of poverty and North–South relations.

The World Bank and global poverty: 'from diagnosis to treatment'

The analysis of global poverty produced by the World Bank provides an exemplar of the institutional policy orthodoxy. The World Bank is particularly influential and its analyses are characteristic of an approach that is prevalent on a much wider scale. The World Bank is the world's hegemonic development institution, and the agenda and advice of the World Bank is central to any orthodox understanding of poverty and attempts at poverty alleviation. Although the Bank's particular position has varied over time (see Williams 1994 chapter 4), its general influence has steadily increased to its current hegemonic standing. The sheer volume of its output of publications is testimony to its efforts in this regard. Marc Williams observes

> The World Bank's resources are not only financial. Crucial to the Bank's role as a development agency is its function as a research institute. The Bank is in the forefront of thinking on development issues and its expert staff of economists, engineers and other professionals produce highly valued country studies, sectoral analyses and influential research publications on issues such as debt, capital flows and trade liberalisation. The Bank's output on development issues are frequently at the forefront of development thinking and set the trends in thought.
>
> (Williams 1994: 122)

Since the early 1990s the Bank has reintroduced poverty as a central concern, and the World Bank Group has adopted the slogan 'Our dream is a world free of poverty'. A defining feature of the World Bank's analysis is its mode of explanation. Poverty was the theme of the 1990 *World Development Report* (World Bank 1990). The report aimed to provide 'a better understanding of how many poor there are, where they live, and, above all, *why they are poor*' (World Bank 1990: 25, emphasis added). Examination of this key document reveals features which are definitive of the Bank's methodological approach.

The second chapter of the report is titled: *What do we know about the poor?* It starts:

> Reducing poverty is the fundamental objective of economic development. It is estimated that in 1985 more than one billion people in the developing world lived in absolute poverty. Clearly, economic development has a long way to go. Knowledge about the poor is essential if governments are to adopt sound development strategies and more effective policies for attacking poverty. How many poor are there? Where do they live? What are their precise economic circumstances? Answering these questions is the first step toward understanding the impact of economic policies on the poor.
>
> (World Bank 1990: 24)

The next section of the report presents an extended analysis under the heading *The characteristics of the poor*, which examines data from detailed household surveys from different countries, 'to estimate the number of poor people and to establish what is known about them' (World Bank 1990: 24). The characteristics examined include geographic location, type and quality of the physical environment; 'demographic characteristics' such as gender, and size and composition of household; ownership of 'assets' such as land and 'human capital' (education, health); occupational activities and main source of income; position in the surrounding society; and how the poor spend their incomes. This exercise in data analysis produces findings such as:

- Poverty as measured by low income tends to be at its worst in rural areas [...] The problems of malnutrition, lack of education, low life expectancy, and substandard housing are also, as a rule, more severe in rural areas;
- Households with the lowest income per person tend to be large, with many children or other economically dependent members;
- The poor usually lack assets as well as income;
- Poverty is highly correlated with landlessness [...] when the poor do own land, it is often unproductive and frequently lies outside irrigated areas;
- Agriculture is still the main source of income for the world's poor. [...] the greatest numbers of the poor, including the very poorest, are found overwhelmingly in rural areas. Their livelihoods are linked to farming, whether or not they earn their incomes directly from it;
- In many countries poverty is correlated with race and ethnic background.

(Word Bank 1990: 29–33, 37)

Thus a detailed *description* of poverty is built up from empirical data from many countries. The final paragraph of the chapter, headed 'From diagnosis to treatment', summarises:

This chapter's survey of what we know about the poor points to two overwhelmingly important determinants of poverty: access to income-earning opportunities and the capacity to respond. When households have secure opportunities to use their labor to good purpose and household members are skilled, educated, and healthy, minimal standards of living are ensured and poverty is eliminated. When such opportunities are lacking, living standards are unacceptably low.

(World Bank 1990: 38)

Thus according to the Bank's approach the common empirical aspects or characteristics of the condition of poverty constitute the 'determinants' of poverty, and explanation consists of identifying these characteristics by means of the examination of empirical data.

Rural poverty alleviation in Mozambique

In the early 1990s Mozambique was identified officially by the World Bank and UNDP as one of the poorest countries in the world. The goal of poverty reduction has been central to government policy since the early 1990s. This concern is formally articulated in government policy and embedded in the discourse and practice of a range of actors including the government,[15] non-governmental organisations,[16] bilateral and multi-lateral development banks and donor organisations,[17] international research institutions[18] and consultancies.[19] The recent *Action Plan for the Reduction of Absolute Poverty (2001–2005)* announces the Government of Mozambique's intention to 'develop a comprehensive and integrated poverty reduction strategy' (Government of Mozambique 2001: 4). This follows a decade of policy formulation and implementation with regard to poverty reduction which has focused specifically on rural poverty – a reflection of the fact that the majority of Mozambique's poor live in the countryside. The Poverty Alleviation Unit in the MPF was created in 1990, the Government's *Poverty Reduction Strategy For Mozambique* published in 1995, and in 1996, the document *Mozambique: Rural Poverty Profile*. While there are several debates and differences in approaches,[20] nevertheless it is possible to trace the contours of a distinct policy approach to rural poverty: a distinct way of conceptualizing the condition of poverty, who the poor are, and how poverty alleviation is to be effected. Here some of the most important characteristics of this approach will be identified, with some indicative examples.

Discussion of development in the countryside of Mozambique today is framed in terms of the 'rural poor', 'rural poverty alleviation', 'raising rural incomes', 'sustainable livelihoods', 'lifting the poor out of poverty'. The condition of poverty is considered and measured ultimately in terms of income, notwithstanding a range of other socio-economic factors which are taken into account, such as health and education. The poor can therefore be identified as a specific proportion or percentage of the total population of Mozambique: it was calculated that in 1996–97, 69.4 per cent of the Mozambican population lived in absolute poverty (MPF *et al.* 1998: 57–8). The majority of the population in Mozambique live in the countryside and are poor: 'with the vast majority of the population in rural areas, poverty in Mozambique is predominantly a rural phenomenon' and in rural areas the headcount of those living in absolute poverty rises to 71.2 per cent (MPF *et al.* 1998: 58). They are 'small-scale farmers', and they are poor because they produce mainly for subsistence, with very low incomes.[21] The small-scale farmer is conceived in terms of a rational economic agent who makes decisions about the allocation of resources in the context of prevailing conditions (price signals, access to markets) with a view to maximising their welfare through maximising income.[22] As such, small-scale farmers are often portrayed in terms of the private sector.[23] Small-scale farming is the largest sector of Mozambique's economy, which is primarily agricultural. Agriculture is therefore central to economic growth and poverty alleviation.

The approach to poverty reduction is centered upon 'raising rural incomes', increasing the monetary income of the small-scale farmer (Government of Mozambique 1995a, 2001). For some this is stated in very explicit terms,[24] for others it is simply taken as a given. This is to be achieved if they produce more 'cash crops', if they switch from subsistence to 'commercial' farming, producing higher-value crops for the market.[25] The rural population of small-scale or family farmers is seen as having tremendous potential for rapid economic growth and poverty alleviation (Government of Mozambique 2001: 4).[26] The basic logic of the current approach is as follows: Mozambique is an agricultural country and most of its population are poor small-scale farmers with low incomes; therefore the approach to reducing rural poverty and achieving economic growth and development for the country as a whole must include a central focus on the development of small-holder farming, producing for the market.[27] This will contribute to rural poverty alleviation by raising rural incomes, and to the growth of Mozambique's economy by increasing agricultural exports.

The way this is to be achieved is to ensure conditions of competition, to open up the markets in rural areas so as to enable small-scale farmers to better respond to price incentives and farm in a more efficient and productive manner. In an open market farmers are free to make their own decisions about how best to allocate their resources so as to maximise their income and welfare. The forces of competition will ensure that farmers receive the highest prices for their crops, and in turn farmers will respond to the higher price incentives by producing more cash-crops for the market, thus raising their incomes and reducing their poverty.

This view of rural poverty and approach to rural poverty alleviation is not specific to Mozambique, nor is it new. It is characteristic of the current orthodoxy throughout Africa and the Third World more broadly (Cleaver and Donovan 1995, International Fund for Agricultural Development 2001, African Development Bank 2002), witnessed in the considerable policy discourse on rural livelihoods which has emerged over the past decade (Carney 1998, Department for International Development 1999, Belshaw 2002, Ellis and Freeman 2004). Furthermore this form of analysis and policy recommendation with regard to rural poverty has been elaborated by the World Bank since the late 1960s (Williams 1994: 114–17).

The poverty of the orthodoxy: an empiricist doxa

These various strands of orthodox treatment of African states and societies by twentieth-century scholarship and institutional policy approaches vary in specific form and content. However underlying them all is the common ground of empiricism. Empiricism is a philosophical doctrine which assumes that the realm of reality – ontology, or what exists – consists only and entirely of empirical phenomena, things and events available to experience. The empiricist approach to knowledge assumes that the only things that exist and can be known about in the world are things which are available to experience; that is, empirical things – material objects, actions and behaviour, events. The empiricist or Humean notion of causation as constant conjunction of events or states of affairs follows directly from this assumption. If the only things that exist are empirical things, then it must be necessary to refer to one empirical thing in order to explain another. The empiricist looks for patterns of regularly recurring events or states of affairs, correlations, in order to identify universal 'laws' of the form 'whenever A, B'. For the empiricist, identification of such an empirical regularity constitutes explanation.

The empiricist commitments of orthodox approaches are not usually acknowledged explicitly. The unobvious underlying structure of the orthodoxy is the set of unacknowledged assumptions which define its method and which constitute, in Bourdieu's terms, the doxa of orthodox knowledge. Any approach to social inquiry entails a particular method – a set of principles defining how to go about finding out about the world (Bhaskar 1994: 48, Lawson 1997: xii). These principles themselves rest upon a particular model of what social phenomena consist of, and consequently the appropriate way to subject them to inquiry. Assumptions about the nature of the world and possibility of knowledge which necessarily underlie all scholarship are rarely explicitly spelt out or consciously acknowledged by practitioners. Underlying empiricist assumptions are manifest in the different forms of method – the way social phenomena are characterised and explained.

In both Development Studies and IR, as well as the policy literature, the treatment of the conditions of African societies employs the state as the basic unit of or framework for analysis. The precise range of concerns and methods applied vary both between and among economists and political scientists. The very separation in the intellectual division of labour between 'economic development' and 'political development' is characteristic of the externally related treatment of the 'spheres' or 'systems' of the political and economic,[28] mirrored again in the treatment of the analytically separable spheres or systems of the domestic and international. The logic of analysis consists of identifying empirical characteristics and patterns of behaviour of the state, its economy and society (such as an agricultural economy, lack of industry, poor infrastructure, lack of domestic capital, ethnic and regional divisions and cleavages, conflict, weak government institutions, corruption). These are then identified as the basic causes of other related attributes – political instability, rising poverty, lack of economic growth. The empiricism is manifest in referring to one set of empirical characteristics or events to explain or account for another set of conditions, either in the course of descriptive-explanatory analysis or more explicitly through statistical correlation. The process of development is understood as a 'dependent variable' which is caused and affected by a range of independent variables. Exercises in data-collection and comparison enable correlation among different internal variables to test hypotheses about the relationships between different variables, and how certain variables affect the processes of modernisation such as economic growth, poverty reduction and liberalisation.

Thus in the analysis of the World Bank examined above, after detailing the various characteristics of the poor it was concluded that the main *determinants* of poverty are access to income-earning opportunity, and the capacity to respond. This exercise in 'diagnosis' has not really identified causes. The procedure consists of identifying a pattern of the form 'a is associated with b', such as poverty is associated with rural areas, agricultural occupation, large families; and then arriving at a conclusion of the form 'a causes b', such as a lack of access to income-earning opportunities is a cause of poverty. At the level of description such statements are unproblematic. The problem is not the identification of a systematic relationship between the empirical variables observed, but the notion of causation embodied in this method. It might be the case that the observed relationship between a and b does indeed regularly or always occur. Nevertheless this does not *explain why* the relationship holds; it does not identify what causes a and b to co-occur. The statements of the World Bank, following analysis of vast data sets and numerous studies and cross-country comparisons, boil down to little more than a set of tautologies and observations about patterns of change. They observe the tendency for development to be characterised by unevenness; but they do not explain why such processes of agricultural, technological and infrastructural development have historically occurred in some contexts but not in others. Borrowing the words of André Gunder Frank, this mode of explanation actually tells us little more than that 'the poor are poor because they are poor – and the rich are rich because they are rich' (Frank 1978: 1).

The empiricist mode of descriptive 'explanation', which explains empirical phenomena with reference to other empirical phenomena, is necessarily ahistorical. The existence of many of the empirical conditions observed – such as poverty, conflict, authoritarianism, corruption, an atomised rural society of 'small-scale farmers' – cannot in themselves be disputed (though they could be differently characterised), but orthodox accounts fail to adequately historicise and explain these conditions. Rather than being seen as social conditions requiring theoretical and historical explanation, as the outcomes of distinct historical processes of social change rooted in relations extending beyond Africa, they are taken as given, as contingent features peculiar to this 'type' of society or state. Even the apparently innocent descriptive terms 'rich countries' and 'poor countries' silently suggest that it is almost contingent, accidental or natural that some countries happen to be rich and others happen to be poor. This innocent form of ahistorical description is similarly characteristic of the analysis of Africa's 'new states' in the international system: 'In proportion to their territories and populations, African governments typically have a smaller stock of finances, personnel, and materiel than Asian or Western governments, and their staffs are less experienced and reliable' (Jackson and Rosberg 1982: 8).

This naturalises particular social conditions, removing the need for sociohistorical explanation, instead suggesting there is something essentially African in the various phenomena described. Poverty in Africa is treated as a natural original position, while the obstacles to overcoming poverty are located internally in the various 'traditional' characteristics of African societies and economies. The phenomena of authoritarianism, corruption, instability and conflict which emerged in many African countries in the decades after independence are accounted for in terms of essential features of ethnicity and traditional African culture, which gives rise to patron–client relations and 'patrimonialism' characteristic of African politics. What these approaches fail to do is to explain the specificity of economic conditions, social relations, ideologies and identities, rivalries and tensions as rooted in the social relations and practices of colonial rule, and supported by the practices of neo-colonialism and more generally the global capitalist order.[29] In a similar fashion the 'ideals' of the developed, democratic, stable states of the West are treated ahistorically.

Underlying and enabling the comparative, correlative and analogous logic of the orthodoxy is an atomistic ontology. The orthodox logic of comparison assumes self-contained units of analysis, which are essentially alike in basic nature but have internal empirical features which vary, and can thus be compared and categorised. Systematic comparison of various units enables identification and definition of different types of the same unit, and the formulation of models. The unit is the state, national economy, or political system. The approach of Gabriel Almond, a key advocate of Comparative Politics and Modernisation Theory, has been praised for combining 'extreme simplicity with a sense of inclusiveness [... which] makes it possible to discuss political systems everywhere in the same terminology' (Gamer 1976: 248). By comparing a number of variables of a political system (such as extent of internal differentiation, religious or secular culture, sub-system autonomy, competitiveness) political scientists differentiate between specific types and sub-types which are situated on a linear scale: primitive systems, traditional systems (patrimonial, authoritarian, competitive, hierarchical, pyramidal), and modern systems (Almond and Coleman 1960, Apter 1965, Almond 1974). The same logic is manifest in the comparison of economies (developing and developed), and states (weak and strong).

The charge that the orthodoxy is ahistorical is perhaps misplaced. The problem is not a lack of history, but the particular understanding of history which is implied. The orthodox method of empirical description, correlation and comparison within and between like units embodies a linear and atomistic understanding of history, change, time and conditions of possibility. The processes of social change which give rise to specific conditions and social forms in a particular country are held to be discrete and isolatable from the histories of other countries. The process of historical change is assumed to be broadly uni-directional or teleological: there is one path of historical change (progress or evolution) along which all countries are travelling (developing). The difference is in the rate of change, the speed with which different societies manage to advance – if indeed they advance at all and do not simply fall further behind, as implied by the current ideology of 'failed states' (Rotberg 2003). It is the internal characteristics of different countries which determines their stage of advancement, and how quickly they can move ahead. The image is of a global game of catch up, a global marathon, in which as time goes on the gap between those in the lead and those at the rear continues to grow:

> The disparity between the more advanced and the less developed parts of the world, like those between the more advanced states themselves, became pronounced towards the end of the nineteenth century. Unlike those between the more advanced states, which had achieved a new equilibrium of power by 1945, it has become even more, not less, pronounced with the passage of time. The intensification of industrial and technological advance in the past fifty years has caught up together all those nations which had made some minimum progress before 1900 and has rebounded and cross-fertilised and levelled-up among them. It has not yet done more than scratch the surface of

less developed societies. It is this disparity that will dominate international relations before long, if it does not do so already.

(Hinsley 1963: 364)

The standard image of different countries proceeding at different paces along one historical path, with Europe in the lead, is explicit in this account:

By the standards of European development, in so far as they are relevant, westernised India still remains, despite all her efforts, a hundred years behind the Russia of 1917. Her social, political and intellectual outlooks, her caste and family organisations – all that complex of outlooks and aptitudes, of practices and beliefs, that is so closely attached to the stage that has been reached by the economic and technical structure of a society – are those, roughly speaking, of England under the Stuarts. China, Africa, vast rural sections of India, parts of Latin America and many other areas are even farther behind by these same standards.

(Hinsley 1963: 364)

The international order of things

This survey has shown that a defining feature of orthodox treatments of the modern African condition is what Bhaskar has called *presentism* – a focus on current conditions as if it were possible to adequately comprehend the present without serious reference to long historical structures and processes. This is closely related to other implicit features of orthodox approaches – the underlying ontological atomism which informs an atomistic approach to history and the international, which could analogously be called localism or internalism; the teleological evolutionism, assuming a linear march towards progress; and a latent and enduring racism embodied in the dichotomy traditional/modern, which is the successor of earlier ideologies about civilised/uncivilised peoples.[30] The result of presentist and localist analyses is that the twentieth-century condition of poverty is characterised and analysed in ways which divorce it from the history of the West, thus rendering modern poverty in Africa a natural and normal condition. Development Studies focuses on patterns and processes within the state, taking the international as given. IR examines the 'external' form and behaviour of states as they interact with each other, employing the ahistorical logic of comparison with European ideal forms. Both ignore the history of the structuring of the world order through imperialism and colonialism, the historicity, structure and development of capitalism, and the processes of dispossession which these have necessarily entailed and which continue relentlessly. 'The state' is treated both internally and externally as an institution in and of itself, amenable to comprehension without reference to historically specific processes of accumulation, property relations and class forces. Thus the current world order is naturalised, and poverty treated as a natural starting point rather than a historical and causally produced outcome.

The defining logic of these orthodox approaches is to portray a sense that social change in different societies takes place independently and endogenously. This is manifest positively in what *is* said, what is focused on and analysed: empirical phenomena within the spatial, social and temporal boundaries of the present state; and negatively in what is ignored or treated superficially: the past and the international, the contradictions of global capitalism and imperialism, globally structured processes of accumulation and dispossession.

It is at this stage then that we can properly identify the *ideological* character of orthodox ideas in their diverse manifestations. The term ideology is used here to indicate ideas which are flawed with regard to their characterisation and explanation of phenomena, and by virtue of these flaws, help to reproduce prevailing social relations related to the production of those phenomena (see Mepham and Ruben 1979). The ideological function of orthodoxy in the academic disciplines of IR and Development Studies, together with the post-war Development policy discourse, has been to present the social crises of former colonies as a natural or locally caused condition, rather than the product of Western expansion and impe-rialism. The orthodox conception portrays the existence of rich and poor countries in the international order as natural: paraphrasing Foucault, the orthodoxy is char-acterised through its portrayal of the global distribution of wealth and poverty as part of 'the international order of things'. The lack of serious theoretical attention to capitalism as a global system, imperialism, and the nature of causal social relations between the West and Africa over centuries is an ideological absence at the heart of all variants of orthodoxy. The result of this absence, in the words of W. E. B. Du Bois, is that 'The difference of development, North and South, is explained as a sort of working out of cosmic social and economic law' (Du Bois 1964 [1935]: 714).[31]

2 Critical perspectives

From global structure to local agency

By the 1960s and early 70s it was becoming apparent that policies informed by the orthodox understanding of development and modernisation had failed to bring about any significant improvement in social conditions in much of the Third World. Inequalities within the Third World and also on an international scale were growing rather than reducing. The post-war economic boom was reaching exhaustion by the end of the 1960s, to be followed by global economic recession, falling world prices and demand especially of primary commodities, the 1970s oil price rises and onset of the Third World debt crisis. In Latin America the post-war policies of national state-directed development had failed to bring about significant economic growth or improved living conditions for the majority. In Africa the euphoria of the 1960s wave of independence was replaced in the 1970s by signs of economic crisis. On independence many African economies were heavily dependent on export of a few agricultural commodities. Export agricultural sectors declined in the context of falling prices on the world market, while the little industrialisation that did occur was heavily reliant on expensive imported machinery, spare parts and raw materials. Political independence had not brought economic independence. The socio-economic crisis in many Third World societies provoked a crisis in orthodox ideas about poverty and development.

Meanwhile developments in the philosophy of science and social science had punctured confidence in positivism and empiricism. Important advances in the philosophical critique of positivism were made by philosophers such as Karl Popper, Imre Lakatos, Thomas Kuhn, Gaston Bachelard and Paul Feyerabend. In different ways they all stressed the fact that scientific knowledge is a social construct, the product of a social process taking place in society in a particular context in time and space. The discontinuous nature of the development of scientific knowledge was emphasised, against the positivist notion of scientific development as a process of simple accumulation of certain knowledge. Hermeneutic and interpretavist approaches to social inquiry rose to prominence, associated with and to some extent informed by the critiques of positivism.

In this global socio-economic and epistemological context the dominance and certainties of positivist social inquiry across the disciplines were dislodged. In the fields of Development Studies and International Relations two forms of critique emerged. The first was motivated primarily by the evident failure of the modernisation approach, and the deepening economic crisis in much of the Third World. New concepts and theoretical schemes were developed to explain the ongoing reproduction and increase in poverty and inequality, centring on relational and provocative concepts of dependency and underdevelopment, understood within the context of the world system. The second sought to elaborate a critique of both the positivist mainstream and the 'structuralist' alternatives. New approaches informed by the various 'posts' (post-positivism, post-structuralism, post-modernism, post-Marxism) proposed radically different conceptions of the very subject matters of Development Studies and IR, how they should be studied, and the purpose and role of social inquiry. This chapter examines these lines of critique which emerged during the last three decades of the twentieth century. The aim is not to provide a comprehensive survey of the various debates and positions, but to highlight the prominent contours and movement of debate.

Global structures: world systems, dependency and underdevelopment

Analyses of dependency and underdevelopment provided a radical alternative to the mainstream of Development Studies. These approaches originated in Latin America, and most of the ensuing contributions and debates related to conditions in Latin America, much debate taking place in the pages of the journal *Latin American Perspectives*. As with the classical Marxist theories of imperialism (Kiernan 1974), it is important to appreciate the political context as well as the analytical content of dependency theory. The analyses of dependency which sought to explain the predicament of Latin American societies were situated within broader debates among the Latin American left over questions of the possibility of socialism and revolution in Latin America, whether capitalist development would further the progress towards socialism, and whether a non-capitalist path towards socialism was possible (Palma 1978). Radical scholars later developed similar approaches to the analysis of social conditions in the Caribbean (Thomas 1974) and Africa (Amin 1972, 1976, Rodney 1972, Onimode 1982, Zack-Williams 1983), the latter emphasising Africa's structurally subordinate position in the global political economy, the ongoing legacy of centuries of European expansion and colonialism, the role played by the West in producing poverty in Africa, and the structural and historical relationship between contemporary conditions in Europe and Africa. The 'weakness' of African states, and phenomena of post-independence conflict, corruption and stagnation, was to be explained not in terms of internal characteristics of tradition and culture but the legacy of colonialism on internal economic and political relations, exacerbated by the structurally subordinate position of African states in the world system.

The dependency analyses sought to provide a critique of and alternative to both mainstream modernisation theories, and the 'structuralist' analyses informing the Economic Commission for Latin America (ECLA), a regional body of the UN established in 1948. The ECLA developed an important analysis of the particular constraints faced by Latin American economies founded on the work of Argentine economist Raúl Prebisch, which provided a moderate critique of modernisation theory. It criticised orthodox free trade theory premised on the notion of comparative advantage, by emphasising the declining terms of trade faced by exporters of primary commodities, the unevenly distributed benefits of technological development and problems of 'technology transfer', and the immobility of labour compared to capital, among other constraints facing the countries of Latin America. Nevertheless the ECLA outlook accepted broadly the possibility of national development within the context of global capitalism and advocated policies of state-directed national development, with the assistance of foreign investment, to counter the particular constraints experienced by developing countries. This took the form of import-substitution industrialisation, an attempt to overcome the weaknesses of dependence on primary-commodity exports through diversification of the economy based on industrialisation oriented towards the internal rather than the world market, with the support of state protection. The aim was to promote national and regional capitalist industrial development by focusing on the internal market, with the assistance of state policy and qualified foreign investment (for a concise summary see Larrain 1989: 102–7, Chilcote 1974: 10–11).

Dependency theory challenged the essentially reformist nature of the ECLA analysis with a more profound critique of capitalism, both in terms of its international structure and national class relations and contradictions.[1] The theories of world systems, underdevelopment and dependency emphasised the historical nature of the condition of underdevelopment as a product of world capitalist development. The widespread poverty and lack of industrialisation which characterised so many Third World countries were not a natural starting point but a specific outcome, the result of global relations and processes. They emphasised the inherently global or world-systemic nature of capitalism, in contrast to the framework of the national state or economy assumed by modernisation theory. They countered the myopia and ahistorical nature of mainstream Development Studies by emphasising a much longer perspective on world history and the histories of relations between core and periphery, stretching back in a significant and causal way five hundred years or more. Analysis of conditions within countries of the Third World had to be situated within the history and structures of global capitalism, colonialism and European expansion. This included analysis of both the social relations and economic structures of Third World societies. Social relations, culture and politics, and the economy were not conceived as separate 'spheres' which develop autonomously and are amenable to separate analysis, as in Modernisation theory, but as necessarily, internally or dialectically related elements of a system or structure, which itself is related to the global structures of the world system.

The specificity of the structure of social relations in the Third World was a legacy of European expansion, the development of global capitalism, and the specific experiences of slavery and colonisation. The structures of Third World social formations were thus historically and causally connected to the class relations of capitalism and imperialism on a world scale. This required analysis of the way in which current structures of social relations are the product of the history of colonialism and the structured incorporation of Third World societies into the developing capitalist world system; and of the ways in which the current relations are reproduced in part through their insertion in the international system. Analysis of the relationship between ruling classes of Third World societies and the international or metropolitan capitalist classes gave rise to concepts such as com-prador classes, decadent national bourgeoisie or lumpenbourgeoisie (Frank 1972). These concepts and class analyses highlighted the alliances and coinciding interests of the national bourgeoisie and the metropolitan or transnational bour-geoisie, and the role of the national bourgeoisie in reproducing and entrenching the insertion of national economies in the global capitalist system in a structurally dependent position.

The production of underdevelopment in the Third World arose from the same set of relations and mechanisms which produced wealth and development in the West. The simultaneous impoverishment of the underdeveloped world and enrich-ment of the West was argued to be the result of a continuous draining of surplus from the periphery/satellite to the core/metropole, via relations of monopoly and unequal exchange embedded in the international division of labour (Frank 1967, Emmanuel 1972). The modern pattern of global inequality and uneven develop-ment between industrialised rich countries and non- or semi-industrialised poor countries was explained not in terms of endogenous processes and institutions, but through analysis of global structures of accumulation linking the wealth of the core to the poverty of the periphery. The simultaneous production of development and underdevelopment was caused by relations of unequal exchange between core and periphery which enabled dominant central areas at various scales (regional, national, global) to exploit surrounding subordinate areas and appro-priate their surplus. As a result the West developed at the expense of the Third World, producing underdevelopment as the other side of the coin of development. Examining the processes and mechanisms of exploitation included analysis of the role of transnational corporations (TNCs) in the Third World (Radice 1975, Biersteker 1978, Evans 1979, Villamil 1979). Rather than bringing the assumed benefits of injection of capital and technology to assist the development of the Third World, foreign capital in the form of TNCs was shown to exploit their advantages by gaining from the availability of cheap labour-power and raw mate-rials, while exporting the profits to the metropole and manipulating costs, tax and profits through transfer pricing. Foreign investment distorted the pattern of eco-nomic development and consumption by concentrating on luxury goods for elite consumption, and failed to contribute to balanced growth through fostering broader linkages with the domestic economy. This simultaneously entrenched existing structures of inequality and exploitation between classes within Third World societies and reinforced their subordinate position in the world system. As such, where 'development' did occur it was seen as distorted or dependent development (Frank 1978, Cardoso and Faletto 1979, Evans 1979).

These approaches articulated a major critique of the prevailing orthodoxy of Modernisation theory, as well as the nationalist-reformist perspective of the ECLA. A barrage of criticism soon emerged from all sides however, leading eventually to a broad consensus that the dependency and underdevelopment approaches were inadequate. By the mid-1980s David Booth had concluded that these approaches 'have today, quite rightly, lost their pull' (Booth 1985: 762). Criticism exposed important flaws constraining some strands of analysis in the literature on dependency and underdevelopment.

Dependency theory was seen to employ an over-determining structuralism, explaining all that happened within a country as the result of the operation of global forces and structures, or its place within the world system. The result was a teleological approach which was necessarily pessimistic regarding the possibility of development in the Third World. Internal contradictions and struggles in Third World social formations were downplayed due to the overwhelming focus on external determination (Johnson, D. L. 1981). Dependency theory was criticised by many for ignoring the role of class struggles in historical process (e.g. Chilcote 1974, Brenner 1977, Petras 1981), and by some for representing the interests of the national bourgeoisie in the face of transnational or monopoly capital, rather than the interests of the rural and urban masses (Warren 1980, Johnson, C. 1981). Others such as Tony Smith argued against dependency approaches that the differential and uneven forms of development in the world were primarily the result of internal social institutions and relations and state forms, rather than the global system – thus reaffirming the basic tenets of modernisation theory (Smith 1979: 279–82).

Analyses of dependency and underdevelopment were accused of tautology, circular argument and functionalism (Smith 1979, Booth 1985). The tendency of some approaches to construct formal mechanical models, and the quest for a generally applicable theory of dependency for the whole of the Third World, resulted in static and ahistorical analysis and historically unwarranted generalisations. They were said to pay insufficient attention to the concrete, complex and differentiated histories of particular countries: 'failing to reflect the diversity and complexity of the real world, they were incapable of explaining it' (Booth 1994a: 3). Concepts of core and periphery, dependency and underdevelopment were criticised for being too blunt, vague and general to reflect the actual heterogeneity and diversity of concrete social formations and struggles (Petras 1981).

From a Marxist perspective the dependency and world-systems approaches were said to misunderstand Marx's basic theory of capital. They theorised capitalism as a global structure of exchange relations rather than a mode of production. Despite the Marxist rhetoric of dependency theory, the emphasis on relations of trade, exchange and the international division of labour in explaining the exploitation of the underdeveloped countries in the world system was argued to be inconsistent with a Marxist theoretical understanding of capitalism (e.g. Laclau 1971, Cueva 1976, Brenner 1977, Bernstein 1979, Weeks 1981). The definition of capitalism in terms of commerce, and production for exchange and profit, rather than as a specific mode of *production*, overlooked the historically specific nature of capitalist social relations, instead portraying capitalism as almost timeless (Teschke 2003: 137). It also led to the mistaken location of exploitation in the sphere of exchange rather than production, and between countries or regions rather than classes. Analyses centred on the static concepts of core–periphery or metropole–satellite were unable to apprehend the contradictions and dynamic developments *within* both 'core' and 'periphery', including struggles between and within classes, and competition between capitals and factions of capital (Petras 1981). The theoretical explanation of uneven development in terms of dependency relations or mechanisms of surplus appropriation was seen as simplistic and empiricist. According to writers such as Frank (1967), Baran (1968) and Amin (1976), mechanisms of unequal exchange and the consequent draining of surplus from one region to another produced stagnation/ underdevelopment in the periphery and growth/development in the core. This model failed to explain accumulation through the production of surplus value, instead providing a static, empiricist 'see-saw' model:

> this may be seen as an international application of the 'image of limited good' [...], where the world is seen as a cake and where, if one group has a large slice of the good things of life, others have to settle for a correspondingly smaller share. Alternatively, it might be described as the see-saw theory of development.
>
> (Harrison 1988: 97)

The criticisms from within Marxism varied. Some Marxists argued that the notion of dependency distorted understanding and obscured the progressive role of capitalist expansion in the Third World (e.g. Weeks 1981). Further criticisms were levelled regarding the relationship between dependency approaches and theories of imperialism. Some criticised dependency analyses for paying insufficient attention to imperialism (Fernández and Ocampo 1974, Angotti 1981), others for providing a superfluous alternative analysis which was unnecessary given the ongoing relevance and greater adequacy of the classical Marxist analysis of imperialism (e.g. Weeks 1981). In defence it was argued that the dependency theorists contributed to and updated rather than replaced the classical Marxist literature, providing a consistent analysis which reflected the different contemporary conditions in the post-war era. They also provided an important corrective to the generally eurocentric focus of the classical theories of imperialism (Johnson, D. L. 1981). Smith, however, argued that 'dependency theory in general substantially overestimates the power of the international system – or imperialism – in southern affairs today' (Smith 1979: 249).

Finally, critics from across the ideological spectrum, both Marxist (Warren 1980) and mainstream (Ray 1973, Kaufman *et al.* 1975, McGowan 1976, McGowan and Smith 1978) gathered empirical evidence of development and industrialisation in the Third World to challenge the conclusions of dependency theory. The evidence of growth and industrialisation in various countries including the newly industrialising countries (NICs) of South Asia were held to disprove the pessimistic 'stagnationist' determinism of underdevelopment theories, while the lack of correlation between dependency and underdevelopment was argued to reveal the vacuousness of the concepts (Lall 1975). Some of these latter forms of criticism took place on the terrain of positivism, conducting statistical bi-variate and multi-variate analyses to 'test' the validity of 'the theory of dependency' in a manner inconsistent with the basic methodological principles of the radical approaches, thus constituting an attempt to appropriate and disarm the radical critique.

Much of the criticism was pertinent for *some* strands of analysis of dependency, underdevelopment and world systems, and must therefore be heeded. Nevertheless it is not enough simply to list a 'litany of sins' and then dismiss the entire project: the 'shotgun approach to critique is bound to hit its target at some time' (Munck 2000: 144). Many critics tended to overlook the richness and variety of this substantial body of literature, focusing narrowly on only a few key works, in particular the analyses of Sweezy, Wallerstein and Frank. The range and sophistication of concrete historical studies produced, as well as the wide-ranging debates, responses and internal critiques, were seldom acknowledged by critics. This sometimes amounted to a simplified caricature of a much broader and differentiated set of positions against which to mount dismissive critiques. Thus Zeleza has acknowledged 'It cannot be overemphasised [...] that Frank, Amin, and Rodney did not entirely ignore class analysis as is so often asserted. Certainly their later writings have few equals in their analysis of the class structures of dependent capitalist formations' (Zeleza 1983: 35), while Munck concluded 'If a theory is assessed in terms of its openness to debate, reformulation, and progress, dependency theory must be judged positively' (Munck 1981: 165).

At its worst, the dependency and world systems literature was guilty of formalism, empiricism, vague abstraction, functionalism and determinism, while both criticism and defence were polemical. At its best, debate was serious and constructive, and the literature provided theoretically and historically sophisticated analyses of the concrete condition of capitalism in colonial and neo-colonial societies, exploring rather than ignoring the specific configurations, contradictions, mutual determinations and influences of social classes, forms of capital and accumulation through the dialectical relationship between local developments and global relations of power.

Local agency and discourse: critical development theory

In the 1980s the intellectual ferment in philosophy and the social sciences reached Development Studies.[2] The cycle of orthodoxy, critique and counter-critique had according to many resulted in an impasse in development theory.[3] Booth blamed this state of affairs on 'the intellectual framework of Marxism as such' (Booth 1985: 762), a sentiment echoed in Corbridge's sarcastic conclusion that 'Marxist development studies appeared to run out of steam because of their internal contradictions, just as some societies constructed in the image of Marxism-Leninism themselves had foundered in the 1980s' (Corbridge 1994: 93). The widespread rejection of structuralist and/or Marxist approaches must also be seen in the context of the general shift away from the left across the social sciences in the 1980s and 1990s, abandoning such 'old-fashioned' notions as class and structure and Marxism more generally. Aijaz Ahmad, in a trenchant critique, has characterised this 'later capitalist hermeneutic' as 'the "post-" condition' (Ahmad 1997). In this context new critical and 'post-development' approaches arose, informed variously by elements of post-structuralism/post-modernism, post-Marxism, and indirectly by the philosophical critiques of positivism.

Criticism was levelled at the intellectual project of Development Studies, both orthodox Modernisation theory and Marxist or structuralist approaches; as well as at the institutional discourse and practice of development policy. Modernisation theory was criticised for being eurocentric, imposing Western models and values on non-Western peoples (Mehmet 1999, Tucker 1999). The dependency and underdevelopment approaches were also criticised for accepting the same basic model of Western industrial development as Modernisation theory. Furthermore, by examining only technical and economic spheres, they were said to ignore the cultural and ideological dimensions of dependency and Western domination. The emphasis on structural determination, it was argued, meant ignoring the agency and views of local people: 'people are treated as objects to be studied rather than as subjects of their own development' (Edwards 1989: 118). Western scholars should abandon their arrogant faith that they know best, and adopt 'a humbleness which resists the idea of a "truth," [and ...] a willingness to let others speak for themselves.' (Corbridge 1994: 96). Consistent with the new critical emphasis on knowledge, power and language, dependency and other 'Western' theories were even criticised for the symbolism of their terminology:

> the use of metaphor to add impact is significant. First, there is a pervasive spatial metaphor of 'up/down', 'metropolitan centre/satellite', in which capitalism is portrayed as superior and central, or [...] a 'transcendental agent'. This is capped by a sexual metaphor (capitalism 'penetrating'), in which the powerful, superior, male West imposes itself on weak, inferior, captivated (and female) others. Indeed there is a further carceral image (the 'tied' worker) of development as punitive, as against modernization theory's vision of development as reform.
>
> (Hobart 1993b: 7)

Much of the critical development literature, in its critique of both orthodox and radical structuralist or Marxist approaches and in what it proposes as an alternative, echoes themes central to post-structuralism and post-modernism. Influences from Lyotard, Said, Foucault, Derrida and Levinas resonate throughout the critical development literature. In general there is a rejection of 'totalizing' 'meta-narratives' of knowledge, history and progress, which are seen to replicate in the realm of knowledge the 'appropriation of the Other' effected materially through colonialism and imperialism. Structuralist approaches, with their unwitting endorsement of Western-style development, fail to confront 'the logics of empowerment/enslavement which are built into all narratives of "progress"' (Corbridge 1994: 95). Universal meta-narratives and attempts at generalisation are rejected in favour of the local, particular and multiple (cf. Lyotard 1984). Drawing variously on the work of Foucault, Said and Derrida, new critical perspectives foreground the realm of ideas and discourse as the site of Western domination of the non-West, the locus of power and domination over the 'subjects' or 'objects' of 'development': 'The real power of the West is not located in its economic muscle and technological might. Rather, it resides in the power to define' (Sardar 1999: 44). The power of the West is exercised through hegemonic control of knowledge production, which denies Third World societies the space to speak for themselves:

> one group has the power to articulate and project itself and its worldview on others. The others thus become Others – objects to be studied, described and developed. Overpowered by the hegemonic discourse of the West, Third World societies are stunted in their capacity to articulate their own identities and worldviews.
>
> (Tucker 1999: 13)

In a seminal contribution Columbian anthropologist Arturo Escobar (1984–85, 1995) drew on the work of Foucault to analyse the relationships between power and knowledge in the discursive construction of the 'Third World' through the 'discourse of development'. He examined the way in which, through the ensemble of relations between institutions, powerful ideas, modes of authority and techniques of information and surveillance, the description of problems and prescription of solutions through development discourse were determined not by 'the objects with which it dealt but by a set of relations and a discursive practice that systematically produced interrelated objects, concepts, theories, strategies' (Escobar 1995: 42). The very idea that there existed 'developing' and 'developed' countries, a 'Third World' which was 'underdeveloped', was the product of the Western regime of order and truth 'reflected in an objectivist and empiricist stand that dictates that the Third World and its peoples exist "out there," to be known through theories and intervened upon from the outside' (Escobar 1995: 8). The ways in which power is exercised through discourse has since become a central theme in critical development literature.[4]

Rejecting the homogenising and universalising effects of both orthodox modernisation theory and radical structuralism, critical development theory is characterised by a renewed emphasis on the agency and knowledge of local actors, and the diversity and complexity of local contexts. Critical scholarship foregrounds the local, the indigenous, the grass-roots, the culturally specific and different, and the polyvocal (Schuurman 1993, Booth 1994b, Esteva and Prakash 1998). The determinism and economism of structuralist approaches are criticised for assuming that local people have no capacity for independent action and resistance. Instead emphasis is placed on the way in which diverse local actors negotiate their terms of engagement with the state, development organisations, NGOs and other powerful actors;[5] appropriate and subvert in their own interests the prevailing hegemonic discourses or interventions; and protect their own interests through diverse strategies of resistance. The diversity of ideals and practices of social existence found in different contexts is emphasised, in opposition to the presumed universality of 'progress': 'the singular therefore makes way for the plural' (Nederveen Pieterse 2000: 204). Local forms of knowledge and values are privileged rather than dismissed.[6] There is emphasis on listening, reciprocal dialogue and mutual respect, as an antidote to the oppressive and patronising nature of Western discourses which seek to know the Other: 'monologues must be replaced by dialogues' (Tucker 1999: 14); 'the mission of the development critics is thus to unmask these assumptions and reinsert the autonomous perspectives of the indigenous and oppressed' (Munck 1999: 201). Central themes of critical development are empowerment and participation, advocating a 'grass-roots', 'bottom-up' conception of development in which the values, aspirations, culture and resources of local people are placed at the centre. Some refer to the approach of critical development as 'post-development' because of its radical departure from the inherently top-down, homogenising, universalist, Western characteristics of what is known as 'development':

> a cultural politics of postdevelopment would seek to forge links between specific or site-based discourses and a broader field of radically democratic discourse such as postdevelopment. [...] This discourse is post development in the sense that it would involve a theoretical move beyond a structuralist framework to the language of reconstruction, transformation and possibility.
> (Fagan 1999: 188, see also Rahnema 1997)

The critical emphasis on local diversity and specificity, agency, values and culture provides an important and necessary corrective to some forms of structuralist and reductionist analysis, but cannot in itself be sufficient to explaining the production of global poverty, global inequality, uneven and under-development. If local agency is analysed at the expense of global structure, the move simply replaces one set of weaknesses with another. A crude but not altogether unfounded response might take the form 'if poor people have so much agency, why are they poor?' Steven Topik has articulated a pertinent call to revisit the spirit of dependency theory, to 'save the baby from the bathwater':

> We understand that local cultures and identities are 'invented' and 'constructed' rather than being simply historical communal legacies. Local resistances slow the pace of global forces and perhaps divert them somewhat, but since there are some 400 billionaires in the world who control around 40 per cent of the world's wealth, the local has not much slowed down the process of accumulation or the concentration of political power of capital. Local culture is very important for understanding how local actors view their own actions. It may be less important for understanding their ability to resist the forces of history. The most important question is not just local variation but the relations of power that such variation connotes.
> (Topik 1998: 99)

Similarly, critical analyses of development discourse have provided important insights into the particular form and history of development ideology, but the actual relations of unequal power and exploitation structuring the global capitalist order are not solely discursive. It will be argued in Chapter 3 that a critical realist approach provides the grounds on which to analyse the way in which global relations of power structure the varied and highly uneven possibilities of local agency and change. The final section of this chapter considers the potential of an approach in IR which reclaims historical materialism and brings questions of world structure and possibilities of emancipation to the fore.

Hegemony and world order: from political realism to Neo-Gramscian IPE

While Marxism was being abandoned in the field of Development Studies, an important strand of International Political Economy (IPE) within the discipline of IR sought to defend a particular approach of transnational historical materialism. This approach, known as critical IPE or Neo-Gramscian IPE, foregrounds the unequal power relations which structure the global system or world order. The origins of critical IPE were influenced broadly by the concerns of underdevelopment and dependency theory of the 1960s and 1970s (Linklater 2001: 23, Murphy 2001: 70), but the approach was shaped more directly through its critique of the IR mainstream.

The field of IPE, which emerged during the 1970s, set out explicitly to broaden the substantive focus of inquiry beyond the narrow confines of the Cold War-defined discipline of IR. During the 1950s–60s, at the height of the Cold War, IR was dominated by concerns about inter-state security and the possibility of warfare between states, above all between the great powers: in short, the problems of 'how to manage an apparently enduring relationship between two superpowers' (Cox 1981: 130). The rise of broader of IPE approaches, concerned with the politics of international economic relations and with relations between a greater variety of actors in world politics, can be attributed in part to events and changes of the 1970s.[7] The apparently enduring quality of the international system of the 1950s and 1960s was disrupted in the 1970s by the collapse of the Bretton Woods monetary system of fixed exchange rates, demands from the Third World for a New International Economic Order, the two oil price shocks, and new uncertainties for the United States in the wake of the Vietnam War. These changes revealed the inadequacies of mainstream IR analysis and prompted the emergence of the field of IPE. Scholars of IPE criticised the state-centric approach of orthodox IR. They insisted on the importance of non-state actors and institutions in the international political economy, such as firms and international organisations, and the influence of internal, domestic political and economic conditions on the relations between states in the international system. The substantive focus was broadened beyond inter-state security to include other 'issue areas' such as trade, international finance and the environment, while foregrounding change rather than assuming order and stability. Although widening the empirical vision of the discipline, however, much IPE continued to reproduce underlying assumptions of the IR mainstream (Murphy and Tooze 1991b, O'Brien 1995, Williams 1996: 46–9). Consequently a number of critics sought to move beyond the mainstream in terms of method and epistemology as well substantive focus. A new, critical approach to IPE has taken shape over the past two decades which has come to be known as Neo-Gramscian IPE.[8]

Neo-Gramscian IPE is distinguished in part by its explicit contrast to defining features of mainstream IR/IPE, in particular political realism. These include differences in method, substantive concern, and underlying purpose of social inquiry. Political realism is criticised for being state-centric, ahistorical and ideologically biased. Political realism rests on a number of core assumptions about the eternal nature of the world: that it is composed of states which interact in an inherently anarchic international setting, that states are unitary actors which rationally pursue their own material and security interests. The outcomes of world order or disorder depend on the balance of power between the various units in the system. The presence of one or two strong powerful states enables the maintenance of stability or hegemony; in the absence of a strong hegemony, disorder, conflict and chaos can prevail. According to political realism's atomistic ontology, analysis of the behaviour and interaction of the various units can be modelled using the techniques of game theory. Political realism is criticised for reducing the problems of international relations to material power relations, conceiving and measuring power crudely in terms of military might and monetary wealth. Although claiming to be 'value-free', 'objective' and 'neutral', realist IR is shown in fact to endorse the norms and interests of the powerful, to the extent that it fails to question the basis of the status quo and seeks only to solve 'problems' which prevent the smooth functioning of the US-dominated capitalist world order.

Neo-Gramscian IPE differs from the mainstream in several respects.[9] It advocates a critical, reflexive and historical approach to social inquiry which explicitly recognises and foregrounds its own values and norms, historical origins and epistemological assumptions. Rather than being concerned with the smooth functioning of the prevailing order it aims to question the very nature and basis of the historically produced status quo, with a view to achieve socially progressive and emancipatory change. It avoids the dangers of utopian idealism, however, by seeking to identify possibilities for emancipation through concrete analysis of the present. Human beings and their concerns and values are placed at the centre of analysis. The global political economy is seen not as an eternal, essential structure, but as a historically produced outcome of collective human agency, whose form changes over time according to historically specific and developing configurations between social forces and relations of production, forms of state and ideology (Cox 1987). In contrast to the positivism of political realism this approach foregrounds the role of ideas and knowledge, including IPE knowledge, in the production and reproduction of social reality. Attention to the historical configuration of social forces which form the basis of state power (Cox 1981, 1987) provides a more historical treatment of the relations within and power of different states and their position within the world order, in contrast to political realism's ahistorical treatment of the state and reductionist treatment of power.

Many critical IPE scholars explicitly advocate a turn to historical materialism, but qualify this in several respects so as to avoid the perceived ahistorical, mechanical structuralism of orthodox Marxist thought. Critical IPE draws on the work of Gramsci because his humanist approach addresses the ethico-political realm and pays particular attention to the role of ideas and culture in power relations, thus avoiding the economic reductionism seen to characterise so much Marxist thought. A number of Gramsci's concepts and theoretical developments are seen to provide important insights into the reproduction of power in the global political economy, centring on the notions of hegemony and historic bloc.

The notion of hegemonic power is a central concept of Neo-Gramscian IPE.[10] It refers to a system of structural reproduction whose stability rests on the alignment of different social groups (classes and class fractions) at national and international levels, whose real interests differ but who nevertheless subscribe to a common world-view or ideology. This approach is articulated via the Gramscian concepts of 'historic bloc' (the alignment of different social groups or forces across class and national/international divides) and 'hegemony' (the creation of a broad consensus which secures structural reproduction). These concepts are related: the alignment of potentially conflicting social groups and class fractions with different real interests is achieved in part through the spread of commonly accepted ideas articulated through social institutions:

> A successful bloc was politically organised around a set of hegemonic ideas which give some strategic direction and coherence to the constituent elements. For a new historic bloc to emerge, its leaders must engage in 'conscious, planned struggle'. This was not simply an issue of the power of ideology or indeed of 'capturing' the state. Any new historic bloc must have not only power within the civil society and economy, it also needs persuasive ideas and arguments (involving what Gramsci called the 'ethico-political' level) which build on and catalyse its political networks and organisation.
>
> (Gill and Law 1993: 94)

Gramsci's work is used to clarify this peculiar quality of capitalist power in the global political economy: the fact that it rests not just on superior material or coercive power, but also and indeed centrally upon *consent*. Neo-Gramscian IPE pays particular attention to the role of dominant ideas and the ways in which social consensus is constructed and spread, for example through networks and think-tanks, and through ideas which incorporate and reflect elements of popular 'common-sense' and are thus more readily accepted by the masses (Augelli and Murphy 1988, Rupert 2000). Moreover they see social self-understanding to be central to politics and the possibility of progressive social change, for such self-understanding in part defines the limits of possible social struggle and change:

> Progressive social change would not automatically follow in train behind economic developments [as suggested by Marx or at least 'the more mechanical and economistic interpretations of Marx'], but must instead be produced by historically situated social agents whose actions are enabled and constrained by their social self-understandings. [...] How, indeed whether, such change occurs depends upon struggles to delimit or expand the horizons of these social self-understandings.
>
> (Rupert 1997: 139)

The new IPE provides a critical approach which takes seriously questions of method, ontology and epistemology, which analyses global relations of power and domination, which is committed to human flourishing and the 'good life', and to a politics of change and emancipation. Stephen Gill explains:

> the normative goal of the Gramscian approach is to move toward the solution of the fundamental problem of political philosophy – the nature of the good society and thus, politically, the construction of an 'ethical' state and a unitary society in which personal development, rational reflection, open debate, democratic empowerment, and economic and social liberation can become more widely available.
>
> (Gill 1991b: 57)

Given such attributes this approach would seem to offer much to the analysis of global poverty, and it has been claimed that 'Gramscian IR sought to amplify the voices of the imperialised world, to rewrite international relations from the point of view of the interests and aspirations of the impoverished South' (Murphy 2001: 70). However so far it seems that the Neo-Gramscians have focused mainly on the ways in which ideas and ideology play a role in global power relations and the construction or maintenance of hegemony by the major powers (especially the United States) and the transnational capitalist class, rather than seeking to explain the condition of poverty as such. Neo-Gramscian analyses of the links and networks between transnational capital, Western governments, international institutions, think-tanks and formal and informal planning fora, and the processes by which the transnational capitalist class promotes specific ideologies and policy agendas (e.g. van der Pijl 1998 chapter 4, Gill 1991a) provide major insights into the mechanisms of reproduction and expansion of the capitalist global political economy. The spread of neo-liberal ideology and political and economic reform throughout the Third World over the past two decades is of profound significance, and the role played by the ideological representation of 'poverty alleviation' in legitimising the expansion of capital is central to this process. Enrico Augelli and Craig Murphy have studied the situation of the Third World in the global political economy in their book *America's Quest for Supremacy and the Third World: A Gramscian Analysis* (1988), in which they examine the role of ideology in the construction and maintenance of America's supremacy and power over the Third World during the post-war period. They draw on Gramsci's work to examine the reinforcing of current structures of international domination and the continuing marginalisation of the Third World through the global political economy (Augelli and Murphy 1988: 6). Their study builds on Gramsci's concepts of ideology and supremacy in analysing relations of American power and domination with respect to the Third World in the post-war period. They examine the nature, content, history and role of ideology, and the way in which contradictory common-sense and philosophies of American society inform and legitimate American foreign policy, thus becoming a 'material force' in legitimating and providing collective support for policies taken in the interests of America's ruling classes. Analyses of this kind are important in understanding some of the mechanisms of reproduction and expansion of the current global order, and the consequent reproduction of the social relations which cause poverty. However these ideologies 'are primarily buttresses to the underlying imperial structural relationships, the grease that keeps the obsolete machinery of international economy running' (Johnson, D. L. 1981: 112). They do not in themselves explain the production of poverty.

In addition to the focus on the transnational capitalist class and the maintenance of global hegemony the Neo-Gramscians also advocate analysing the global political economy from the 'bottom up' (Murphy and Tooze 1991b: 6, Gill 1993a: 25, 1993b: 8–13, Murphy 2001: 70). Roger Tooze and Craig Murphy (1996) have addressed specifically the question of global poverty. Their concern is to criticise the way in which the problem of global poverty has been consistently marginalised by the discipline of IR, including IPE. They attribute this 'blindness' mainly to the epistemology of the orthodoxy, in particular the mainstream assumptions regarding power as a resource, and the economic rationality of cost–benefit calculus assumed to inform the actions of people. These assumptions, they argue, lead the mainstream to ignore the power, self-understandings, knowledge and motivations of the poor. They advocate an alternative epistemological foundation upon which to conduct inquiry into poverty, built on five principles (1996: 696–8). Social inquiry has to be consistent; conditioned by external evidence; critical, reflecting on its own history as knowledge; democratic, privileging those ideas most widely accepted by the greatest number in unconstrained dialogue; and ameliorative, providing suggestions for action to improve the social world. With regard to the question of poverty they advocate a practice of inquiry which is consensual, listening to and incorporating the self-understanding of the poor themselves as knowledgeable and powerful actors in their own right. Here they echo central concerns of the critical development literature. Tooze and Murphy substantiate their recommendation with reference to the participatory praxis of NGO which serves to empower the poor: 'in situations in which the international NGOs have expected and sought-out complex, but relatively egalitarian alliances with local NGOs, poverty has been lessened' (1996: 698–9). They elaborate:

> the peculiarly consultative practices of many local–international NGO partnerships have seemed to reduce poverty much more effectively, and certainly at a much lower 'cost' than many of the big ticket projects of the large intergovernmental agencies. One explanation for this would be that the international NGOs are more effectively able to tap the creative knowledge, the 'innovative power', of the poor, with whom they work on a relatively equal basis. [...] The successful NGOs bring in the understandings of the poor.
>
> (Tooze and Murphy 1996: 700, 702)

Unfortunately their position has major problems. Their discussion of poverty is entirely abstract and unhistorical, which in itself gives the impression (doubtless unintended) that the fact of global poverty is a contingent, unfortunate state of affairs; the use of the term 'less advantaged' (Tooze and Murphy 1996: 697) to describe 'the poor' adds to this impression. Their discussion of NGOs is similarly ahistorical and abstracted from the current conjuncture of the global political economy, specifically the neo-liberal social order and global re-structuring which has given rise to the phenomenon of NGOs, and which the existence and practice of NGOs helps to reproduce (Pasha 1996, Petras and Veltmeyer 2001, Manji and O'Coill 2002, Kamat 2004). The failure to explain or historicise the production of poverty leads to naïve approval of the ameliorative capacities of those international NGOs which engage in a participatory manner with the poor. This fails to see that, however well-intentioned the members of individual NGOs might be and whatever immediate concrete results they might bring – perhaps a borehole for a village or the construction of a rural health centre – the discourse of 'empowerment' and 'participation' and the existence and practice of NGOs fit neatly within the logic of neo-liberal imperialism. Indeed Tooze and Murphy's use of the term 'ameliorative' is very accurate: such an approach can only ever provide amelioration of the existing state of affairs because it does not seek to remove the structural causes of poverty.[11]

Perhaps the most important weakness of Tooze and Murphy's position is the endorsement of a consensual notion of truth. Drawing on Habermas they define truth in 'democratic' terms: 'the preferable account of anything is the one that can be most accepted by the unconstrained discussion of the widest number of people' (1996: 697). Social inquiry into poverty then ought to include the knowledge of the poor; IPE scholars should learn from the poor (1996: 706). Academic knowledge about poverty and the 'power and logic of the poor' should be confirmed with 'those who are in the best position to understand those powers and that logic, namely, the poor themselves' (1996: 704), because the poor, as

> (complexly) rational beings, when unconstrained by force or fraud, are in a position to judge the validity of the statements of others, and the extent of such consensus is one central measure of truth, or, as some theorists would argue, the central measure of truth.
>
> (Tooze and Murphy 1996: 705)

This approach to the relationship between power and knowledge is shared by many Neo-Gramscians. The question of the truth of knowledge is situated not in the relation between knowledge and what it is about, but within the social constituencies and power relations of the producers and receivers of knowledge, the discussants or interlocutors. More generally many Neo-Gramscians have reacted against positivism and the perceived mechanical structuralism of orthodox Marxism by emphasising the role of agency and ideas in the reproduction of society and historical change. However their discussions of social ontology often imply a simple opposition or dichotomy between material structure and ideas.[12] This leads many Neo-Gramscians to prioritise the realm of ideas in their theorisation of social ontology, and their substantive explanation of situations of domination and unequal power.[13] Burnham has criticised the Neo-Gramscians in this regard, arguing that in their 'frantic attempt to escape the twin evils of "economism" and "idealism" they end up "unwittingly" in the "post Marxist" camp struggling to escape an economism which in reality owes more to the Second and Third International than to Marx' (Burnham 1991: 77, 79). This ignores the non-ideational contradictions in the social relations of capital, and the role of force, coercion and violence in the maintenance of hegemonic world orders.

Chapter 3 elaborates the richer and more adequate social ontology of critical realism, which distinguishes between the hermeneutic and inter-subjective aspects of the social realm and social practice, and the non-discursive, non-empirical but real and causally efficacious social relations which constitute society. It is the social relations which structure, condition and enable practice and agency, rather than the self-understandings of agents, which must be examined in order to explain the condition of global poverty. Also it is the relation between an explanation and what it is about – the structure of society and causes of social phenomena – which must be the basis for a relation of truth, rather than already-held beliefs in the society concerned, however widely held those beliefs. For as Andrew Collier rightly insists, '[t]here is a difference between something's being true and its being generally believed to be true' (Collier 2003b: 215).

3 Objectivity, need and the dialectics of emancipation

The philosophical critique of positivism has had a profound impact across the social sciences, including Development Studies and IR. The certainty and claims to neutrality of positivist social science have been disrupted, and exposed as serving the interests of the powerful and securing the reproduction of the status-quo. In the light of this many have abandoned hope of improving and accumulating scientific knowledge of the world through objective inquiry, either for deconstruction, negotiation and dialogue, celebrating a diverse multiplicity of shifting perspectives and local knowledges, or for explicitly normative approaches which foreground the goal of emancipation. Forms of post-positivist critical scholarship vary considerably. One characteristic which is shared by critical approaches in Development Studies and IR, however, is the tendency to throw out too much when they abandon positivism. It has been too easy to equate the problems of positivism with the aspirations and practice of science per se, and to reject, along with positivism, notions of 'truth', 'science', 'objectivity' and a knowable 'reality out there'. The routine use of quotation marks around these terms gestures the consensus of disapproval shared by all those who thereby affirm their critical credentials.

The philosophical intervention of critical realism and its emerging research programme has made a vital contribution in this context. By reclaiming reality (Bhaskar 1989) critical realism defends a non-positivist theory of ontology; the possibility, importance and emancipatory potential of critical naturalism in social inquiry; the objectivity and intransitivity of social reality, social relations, human needs and values; and the radical potential of social scientific inquiry. These insights have various implications for substantive inquiry about global poverty. Critical realism defends the objectivity of human need, while also foregrounding the historicity of actual need satisfaction or deprivation, and the historically specific social relations which determine need satisfaction. Acknowledgement of the structural constraints on need satisfaction entails rethinking the question of poverty and poverty alleviation in terms of oppression and emancipation, and shifts the terrain from policy reform to political struggle. But the intransitivity of the social relations which structure possibilities of need satisfaction for particular groups or individuals entails that agents' self-understandings of their situation are not necessarily sufficient to adequately comprehend the causes of frustrated needs. Critical social inquiry must endeavour to provide more adequate explanations of the production of social conditions of poverty, which includes the possible critique of lay understandings.

Reality, explanation and critique

The rejection of positivism which is shared across the spectrum of critical approaches in Development Studies and IR[1] has left an impoverished notion of reality and ontology. 'Reality' is either shunned altogether, assumed to exist but remaining unknowable, or conceived mainly in terms of inter-subjective under-standings. This leads to an understanding of what it means to be critical in social inquiry which necessarily involves an explicitly normative point of departure, and rejects the possibility of objectivity. Critical approaches have revealed that behind its façade of neutrality the orthodoxy has a 'hidden normative content' which tac-itly sides with the interests of the powerful, in technical control and domination, serving to 'de-politicise' social problems of poverty and oppression (Ferguson 1990, Neufeld 1995: 96–106). A critical approach which counters the exercise of power therefore entails explicitly siding with the oppressed and excluded, the grassroots, and an explicit commitment to change (George and Campbell 1990, Fals Borda and Rahman 1991, Escobar 1995: 215, Neufeld 2001):

> one of the hallmarks of critical interpretative theory is a very pronounced normative emphasis which, it is held, is inextricably entwined with the task of explanation and which is also precisely the point most obviously ignored or down-played by the mainstream. Thus central to critical interpretative theory is the emphasis on a knowledge-interests nexus which, it argues, needs to be radicalised in the pursuit of emancipatory rather than technical interests.
>
> (Rengger and Hoffman 1992: 133)

Critical IPE scholars have turned to the work of Gramsci because of the explicit ethical commitments of his approach:

> Gramsci does not believe that adherence to any 'scientific' method can assure 'objectivity'. As far as he is concerned, real science always involves the viewpoint of human beings in specific cultural contexts. [...] An inquirer's real desire to change something is the guarantee of her honest search for truth, the source of her 'objectivity'.
>
> (Augelli and Murphy 1997: 16, see also Gill 1991b: 56)

> The Gramscian analysis [...] challenges orthodoxy directly by the incorporation of values into the explanation and exegesis and with this the negation of the claim to 'objectivity'.
>
> (Tooze 1990: 277)

In contrast to this broad current of critical scholarship, critical realism retains a notion of a social and physical reality which is in principle knowable, and independent of what is known about it. This gives rise to a different basic understanding of what it means to be critical. One of the most important implications of critical realism for critical social inquiry is its theory of ontology and epistemology which show how a commitment to objectivity and to explaining social reality, is necessary and enables a potential empancipatory role for social science (Collier 2003b). This means that the orthodox concern to 'discipline power with truth' can be met in a way which is fundamentally critical, and yet does not reject the value of truth in social inquiry (cf. Krasner 1996: 108–9, Tooze and Murphy 1996: 682–3).

Bhaskar's early contribution in philosophy of science appreciated the crucial insights into the nature of science in the work of Kuhn, Fereyabend and others, but revealed an important weakness in their work which rendered their critique of positivism incomplete: none of them had challenged the empiricist ontology of positivism, its theory of reality. They did not distinguish between real objects of knowledge, which exist independently of what, if anything, is known about them; and scientific theories, which are 'objects in thought', social products. Therefore they collapsed the conditions of the production of knowledge onto knowledge itself. Bhaskar's theory of transcendental realism, set out in *A Realist Theory of Science* published in 1975, accommodated their insights while rejecting their false conclusions, because of its alternative realist ontology. He thus completed the critique of positivism and proposed a more adequate alternative (Bhaskar 1997). Today Bhaskar's critical realism has moved far beyond its early beginnings, through dialectics and transcendental dialectics to the theory of meta-reality (Bhaskar 2003), while critical realism as such has moved far beyond Bhaskar's own work through considerable developments by a large number of scholars. There is a tendency among some adherents of critical realism to portray the early work as only very basic, almost having been superseded by later developments. The 'first stages' of transcendental realism and critical naturalism are very important however, and their enduring significance for social inquiry ought not to be overlooked. The principal elements of transcendental realism and critical naturalism remain vital to critical realist social inquiry, whether or not it ventures into the realms of dialectics and meta-reality. These include the distinction between transitive and intransitive domains and the realms of real, actual and empirical; the notion of real tendencies which are transfactual; and the theory of ontology as structured, stratified and emergent.

The realist theory of science was developed through a transcendental method. Bhaskar began with the practice of experiments in some branches of natural science, and explored what must be true about the world and about the nature and possibility of knowledge (ontology and epistemology) for scientific experiment to be both possible and necessary (Bhaskar 1997). His analysis established the intransitivity of objects of knowledge (their existence independent of what if anything is known about them);[2] the structured and stratified nature of reality (the ontological difference between causal powers and actual events);[3] the transfactual nature of causal powers, and consequently the potentially radical disjuncture, in open systems, between the operation of real tendencies or causal powers, and the production of actual events.[4] The world consists of complex structured entities, with various properties of different kinds – powers to act or do or 'suffer' certain things – which they have by virtue of their structures. There are different types of mechanisms, which act in specific necessary ways; and knowledge of their ways-of-acting constitute natural laws. Some mechanisms are more basic than others; and complex entities are made up of, but not reducible to, more basic structures. The real world is characterised by stratification and emergence. So for example the laws of physics are more basic than the laws of biology or chemistry. The laws of biology are ontologically dependent upon the laws of physics – they cannot break the laws of physics; but they are not reducible to the laws of physics. Higher-level strata have emergent properties which are specific to that level. So science is stratified according to the ontological stratification of real things in the world (Collier 1994, Bhaskar 1997).

The realist theory of science elaborates a powerful critique of empiricism which remains as important today as when it was first developed in the 1970s. Empiricist understandings of science, which constitute a misunderstanding of the actual form and practice of natural sciences, continue to inform much understanding and practice of social science. This is particularly the case in social inquiry about the condition of global poverty, as argued in Chapter 1. Empiricism continues to hold considerable sway in policy-related institutional sites of knowledge production such as the World Bank and the International Food Policy Research Institute (cf. MPF *et al.* 1998, Simler *et al.* 2004). Thus 'ideologies, derived from defective conceptions of those [experimental] sciences' still 'weigh, like a dead hand, heavily on the shoulders of many of the other sciences, and particularly of course the proto-sciences of society' (Bhaskar 1997: 260–1). Central insights of the early critical realism, including the intransitivity of both natural and social phenomena, are important for a realist understanding of society and the possibility of naturalism (i.e., a form of knowledge about social phenomena which is distinguished from lay knowledge by its greater adequacy with respect to social phenomena).

To establish the possibility of naturalism Bhaskar provided a transcendental analysis of an individual's intentional action – a basic given of the social world, as well as the focus of hermeneutic and interpretavist anti-naturalists (Bhaskar 1986: 121–2) and a central concern of critical development studies with its focus on local agency. Through transcendental analysis of the possibility of agency Bhaskar established the ontological reality and irreducibility of society consisting of structured social relations, ontologically distinct from individuals and social action but only ever manifest in and reproduced by social practice (Bhaskar 1986, 1998). Through ordinary practice, people continually reproduce society (Bhaskar 1998: 34). Particular social forms or relations might be sustained or changed as a result of ongoing practice, but they are never produced from scratch, from nothing. Any social practice – whether scientific, political, economic, cultural or linguistic – always uses already-existing 'material' in order to produce new outcomes, reproducing, changing and occasionally transforming the already-existing social forms. The model of society implied by this social ontology is termed the transformational model of social activity (TMSA) (Bhaskar 1986: 118–29, 1998: 31–7). The continual reproduction of social forms is the outcome of the totality of individual acts. It is not the intentional outcome of any particular act, but the unintended consequence of such acts. There is thus an ontological difference between people's practices, and the outcome of such practices which is the reproduction of society (Collier 1979, Bhaskar 1986: 123–4). Many critical approaches which emphasise the importance of agency in the production of history do not adequately differentiate the ontological difference between agency and structure: agency is central to the production of history because, for the most part, social structures are reproduced as the unintended consequence of routine practice; occasionally, they are transformed as the intended consequence of collective action. In other words, most of the time what agency does is to unintentionally reproduce structures. The emphasis on agency is often at the expense of structure, as in much recent critical development literature as well as some Neo-Gramscian scholarship. Neo-Gramscian IPE is said to provide 'a specific form of non-structuralist historicism' which 'stands in contrast to abstract "structuralisms" insofar as it has a human(ist) aspect. Historical change is understood as, to a substantial degree, the consequence of collective human activity' (Gill 2003: 55). However Bhaskar emphasises the importance of

> distinguishing categorically between people and societies, and correspondingly between human actions and changes in social structure [. . .] For the properties possessed by social forms may be very different from those possessed by the individuals upon whose activity they depend. Thus [. . .] purposefulness, intentionality and sometimes self-consciousness characterize human actions but not transformations in the social structure.
>
> (Bhaskar 1998: 35)

The transformational model of social activity avoids both the idealist voluntarism and mechanistic determination of other models of society, which see social relations as produced intentionally by people; or conversely see people and their actions as the automatic outcome of society. It is also distinguished from Giddens' model of structuration (Giddens 1984), by emphasising the ontological irreducibility (although existential interdependence) of actions and structures, and hence the ontological difference between the processes by which structure conditions (enables and constrains) agency, and the processes by which agency reproduces structure: 'People and society are not [. . .] related "dialectically." They do not constitute two moments of the same process. Rather they refer to radically different kinds of thing' (Bhaskar 1998: 33).[5]

The term society does not refer simply to inter-personal relations, connecting a mass of undifferentiated individuals one to another. Nor does it refer to inter-subjective understandings. It refers to sets or structures of relations between roles and practices. Different sets of relations exist, structurally linking different sorts of roles and practices – relations between parent and child, husband and wife, teacher and student, employer and worker, land-lord and tenant, state and citizen. These sets of relations themselves are to greater or lesser extents overlapping and interconnected. Society consists of the whole network of different interconnected sets of social relations. Marx's expression remains perhaps the most clear: 'society does not consist of individuals, but expresses the sum of the interrelations, the relations within which these individuals stand' (Marx 1858: 265). The sets of social relations which constitute society are real and causally efficacious but not empirical; they condition and enable, but do not completely determine, the actions and practices of people, by means of which they are instantiated and reproduced. In this sense then they are *analogous* to real but non-empirical relations and structures in nature, which are only manifest in their effects, and which condition but do not wholly determine outcomes (e.g. gravity) (see Bhaskar 1998 and Bhaskar 1986 chapter 2).[6] Being nonempirical, social relations are not immediately obvious; but being causally efficacious, they are in principle knowable (Bhaskar 1998).

It is the non-empirical reality and causal efficacy of social relations that structure, condition and enable human agency, which makes it important to reclaim some of what is rejected by much post-positivist scholarship in Development Studies and IR/IPE. Critical naturalism acknowledges the unique features of the social world which distinguish it from the natural or non-social world: subjectivity, inter-subjectivity and intentionality, the inherently meaningful and pre-interpreted nature of social practices and social phenomena. The people whose actions reproduce social structures have ideas and beliefs underlying, informing and motivating their actions, and according to which their actions are meaningful. In order to account for any social phenomenon it is necessary to examine prevailing ideas about it, how it is understood by the people involved. This is the importance of hermeneutics. However such ideas are usually not, in themselves, enough to provide an adequate explanatory account of social phenomena. This is in principle because of the ontological difference between people's actions, on one hand, and social structures and the process of their reproduction, on the other. The reproduction of specific social structures is the outcome of a totality of particular actions; but this is not the intention or motivation of any particular person. Beliefs informing actions might be wrong or inadequate in various ways; people might be unaware, or mistaken, about the social (as opposed to personal) conditions and outcomes of their actions. In a more historically specific sense, this is especially the case because of the increasingly globally extended nature of the social relations which structure and enable everyday lives and practices. Beliefs do inform actions, and therefore necessarily constitute part of the object of social analysis – the social scientist cannot simply ignore the understandings of the people concerned. But this does not mean that ideas held in society are necessarily correct with regard to the causes of social phenomena; and ideas are themselves objects requiring explanation. It is thus because of the ontological distinction between agency and structure, the existential interdependence but irreducibility of society and individuals and the duality of structure and praxis[7] that social science has an inherently emancipatory potential:

> unintended consequences and unacknowledged conditions may limit the actor's understanding of their social world, while unacknowledged (unconscious) motivation and tacit skills may limit his or her understanding of him or herself. Corresponding to each of these cognitive limits, human scientific knowledge promises a distinct emancipatory benefit.
>
> (Bhaskar 1986: 126)

With regard to the phenomenon of poverty critical social inquiry ought to concentrate on identifying the causes of poverty, which may or may not be already understood by the poor, rather than dwelling solely on the self-understandings of the poor. Because of the intransitivity of non-empirical social relations, it is not possible to privilege as a source of incorrigible explanatory insight the self-understandings of actors (Bhaskar 1986: 160–8) as for example Tooze and Murphy (1996) as well as many critical development works advocate. The way in which the practices and beliefs of agents (including the poor) are related to the causal production of their concrete conditions of life is through the unintentional reproduction of social relations. Therefore it is the social relations which produce poverty, rather than the practices and beliefs of the poor, which should be the object of inquiry seeking to explain poverty. An adequate social-scientific account might then provide a critique of lay self-understandings regarding the causes of poverty. This is potentially important because a variety of beliefs might be held about the causes of poverty – in terms of God's will, or bad luck, for example – which are factually incorrect but function to help reproduce the social order which produces poverty (see Serra 2003 and Chefo 2003). Hence the importance and emancipatory potential of the social-scientific commitment to objectivity:

> It is just this capacity to contradict such appearances which makes social science emancipatory. And to contradict appearances, social science must assume that *what is true is not the same thing as what is held to be true* – that is, it must make realist assumptions about truth.
>
> (Collier 1998: 55, emphasis added)

Poverty, objectivity and human need

The condition of poverty is not simply a discursive construct, the socially constructed product of patronising or racist attitudes of arrogance and paternalism inherent in the West's normalising gaze and social construction of the identity of the Other (Johnson 1991, Rahnema 1991, Escobar 1995). It is possible and necessary to reject Modernisation theory and its spurious and ideological dichotomy of traditional–modern, without also denying the existence of poverty. It is almost perverse that the climate of post-modernism and post-structuralism makes it politically important to insist on the objective reality of poverty, a social condition independent of discursive inter-subjectivity. Thus Upendra Baxi argues that the 'non-discursive order of reality, the materiality of human violation, is just as important, if not more so, from the standpoint of the violated' (1998: 129). In the critical rejection of all meta-narratives and reduction of knowledge claims to power and interests there is a consistent confusion and conflation between the transitive and the intransitive domains:

> there is no clearer metanarrative than the theory/discourse/ideology of development. It also follows that the Enlightenment notions of truth and objectivity mask the underlying power relations. A claim to truth is also a claim to power. Nor does anyone have a legitimate right to speak for others.
>
> (Munck 2000: 151)

But of course the empirical exercise of defining and measuring the extent and nature of poverty in different contexts, so beloved of development organisations and their (lack of) development 'league tables', does not in itself help in *explaining* the production of poverty, as was argued in Chapter 1. Both the critical emphasis on discourse, subjectivity and agency, and the mainstream focus on empirical variables, ignore (or are insufficient without acknowledgement of) the intransitive, causally efficacious and historical *social relations* which produce conditions of poverty and processes of impoverishment.

If the problem of poverty is re-posed in terms of inadequate satisfaction of human needs this immediately raises the necessity of referring to historical social relations in the explanation of poverty. This potentially shifts the terrain from the ahistorical technocratic reformism of the orthodoxy to a historically rooted and more radical critique of the structures of the status quo. However the question of human needs is in itself subject to considerable debate. Many critics question the objectivity of need on a number of counts. The assertion of needs which are objective and should be met regardless of what people might want is seen to have elitist and, at worst, totalitarian implications.[8] It is seen to license the deferral of decisions about what is best for people to a higher authority of experts and planners. These views are often informed by the experiences in many of the former cases of 'actually existing socialism' as well as the post-independence authoritarian states in Africa, whose economies were claimed to be organised on the basis of developmentalist planning to meet needs. Agnes Heller expresses this concern in her book *Dictatorship Over Needs* (Heller 1983).

A related concern is that positing a set of universal human needs denies human individuality, creativity and difference, implying that everyone has the same needs and values. A theory of objective, universal human needs is seen by many to constitute a form of essentialism which reduces human beings to static, ahistorical biological nature, denying historical specificity, difference and agency. Distinguishing universal needs from the diversity of wants that people have is seen to presuppose some metaphysical commitment to abstract universal human nature. It is argued that since all we can empirically know for certain is what people want, any attempt to specify needs requires metaphysical speculation about what is in principle unknowable (Ramsay 1992: 49, 1997: 223). Furthermore, the specification of 'universal' needs might only be privileging the needs and values of some particular society or group or way of life. This problem of cultural relativism is seen to arise from the relation between needs and ends.[9] Choices between ends depend in part on local customs, beliefs and values, so to identify 'universal' human needs would simply promote one way of life at the expense of others. For this reason it is argued that the notion of human needs is inherently normative and evaluative, and objectivity is impossible.[10]

Much of the debate about human need tends to oscillate between two poles of reductionist essentialism on one hand, and relativism on the other; and many commentators see no way out of this impasse. Kate Soper argues that any theory of needs which deserves the name would be one whose 'theoretical statement is to the effect that all theorisation about needs must necessarily live in the field of forces created by the antithetical poles of relativism and essentialism' (1981: 123).

She sees an antithetical tension between two discourses about needs. The first claims to be scientific and objective, rooted in biological and physiological facts about human nature and thus free from values. The second 'humanist' discourse is normative, recognising the values inherent in social phenomena and sensitive to the differences between cultures and individuals. For Soper, the first approach is at best capable only of vacuous generalities; anything beyond this tends to become essentialist and ahistorical, denying the politics of human needs. The second approach, in eschewing any universal or absolute needs or standard, leads inevitably to relativism and therefore provides no basis for critique of existing needs and the way they are met in any particular context (Soper 1993: 113–14).

Critical realism offers an important contribution to this debate, which has been developed by Maureen Ramsay (1992) and Sean Creaven (2000 chapter 3). Need can be specified in terms of the objects necessary to realise the potential powers of human beings as natural beings. The realist social ontology of causal powers, stratification and emergence addresses the simultaneously biological, social and individual basis of human need. The distinction between the transitive and intransitive, and the realms of real, actual and empirical, enable distinction between real needs, felt wants and expressed demand (Ramsay 1992). The satisfaction or denial of needs are shown to be determined by social relations. This means first that the explanation of poverty requires examination of social relations, and second that overcoming poverty and the frustration of need requires changing social relations.

The realist theory of ontology posits the existence of natural laws, natural necessity and natural kinds. Things in the world have structures by virtue of which they have characteristic ways-of-operating, causal powers and potentials; and are stratified, hence governed and affected by numerous laws of different strata. Things are more or less complex, being structured in different ways and composed of elements (themselves complex and structured) of different strata. Things in a higher stratum (psychological, social) will be composed of structured parts of lower, more basic strata (physical, chemical) (Collier 1994: 108). A plant is biological, but its elements, the parts of which it is made up, are chemical and physical. The notions of stratification and the hierarchy of strata do not apply to actual concrete things in the world, but rather to mechanisms. It is not that some things are physical, others biological, and others economic. Complex things might be composed of interacting elements governed by mechanisms of different strata (physical, chemical, biological and social) (Collier 1994: 116). The causal powers of mechanisms of higher strata are existentially dependent upon, but emergent from and irreducible to, those of the lower strata. They are rooted in, and dependent upon, the lower strata and therefore still governed by the laws of the lower strata (Collier 1979, 1994, Bhaskar 1997). Thus the mind is existentially dependent upon the physical/chemical existence of the brain; but the properties of the mind are irreducible to just chemical and physical processes. Human beings are complex beings, at once social, biological, chemical and physical. Human powers and potentials are rooted in the biological strata, and some are shared to a greater or lesser extent by other animate beings – the capacity for movement, vision, hearing, the capacity to feel pleasure and suffer pain and to cooperate with others.

Things in the world are characterised as the things that they are by their causal powers, powers to do or suffer certain things. Powers are real, but it is contingent whether or not they will ever be realised or their effects manifest. Thus a seed has the power to grow into a bean stalk; its powers will be realised if the necessary conditions of appropriate temperature, water, nutrition, space and light are available. The powers or potentials of an entity require certain conditions for their realisation, which are external to the entity. The needs of a natural being are the conditions necessary for the realisation of its characteristic powers. This is all very well but what about the nature and needs of beings which are both natural and social?

The question of human needs and human nature is uniquely complicated by the fact of human consciousness and intentionality. Human beings have a range of needs which are determined by the structural nature of their material bodies – for food, clothing, shelter, warmth or shade and exercise. But human beings have other powers specific to higher social and psychological strata, which are rooted in but irreducible to their biological being, in particular the capacity for language and symbolic representation, and the capacity for reflexive consciousness and reason (Bhaskar 1989: 79). Marx identified reflexive consciousness, and the ability to form plans and consciously carry them through, as what is definitive of specifically *human* nature, what sets human beings apart from animals. In his early writings (in particular the *Economic and Philosophical Manuscripts* written in 1844) Marx discussed at some length the question of human nature and the features distinguishing human from animal nature, a problem he posed in terms of the distinguishing features of human beings' 'species being'. This discussion formed part of an early anthropologically based critique of capitalism, as a system in which human beings cannot realise their true nature. He tended to associate human nature specifically with the activity of production; for example 'the productive life is the life of the species' (Marx 1844: 68). In capitalism workers are separated from the conditions of production, and are only united with these conditions in a process of production which is directed, owned and controlled by the capitalist. Marx saw such alienated productive activity as antithetical to human beings' true essence or nature.

Collier argues that there is no justification for choosing the activity of production above any other activity as characteristic of a human essence; this is an evaluative choice with no rational justification (Collier 1981: 5).[11] He argues that *all* activities that human beings engage in, both those they share with animals and those which are only human, are carried out in a specifically human rather than animal manner:

> Certainly, it is clear enough that we produce in ways that other animals do not. Marx is of course right about the imaginative pre-construction that distinguishes 'the worst of architects from the best of bees'; but this difference

is not peculiar to production; it also distinguishes the worst gourmets from the best of foxes in chicken runs, the worst lovers from the best of goats in rut, the worst of scientists from the best of curious cats, and so on. In short, even if our sharing a faculty with another species were any slur on that faculty, it is difficult to see how an 'essential' faculty could be picked out. *All human activities are cultural complexifications of natural functions.*
(Collier 1981: 11, emphasis added, see also Marx 1844: 94)

So human needs are the conditions necessary for the realisation of human powers or potentials. Human beings are social beings, with specific social characteristics and powers irreducible to their biological nature, but this does not mean that they cease to be biological beings because they are social (Timpanaro 1980: 45–6, Collier 1981: 9–10). The specific ways in which human beings realise the causal powers rooted in their common biological nature are governed by the laws of the higher social and psychological strata. Recognition of a common set of biologically rooted needs neither entails a notion of ahistorical static needs, nor does it deny human individuality. Collier's distinction (1990: 136) between abstract, biologically given needs and the determinate, social objects of need clarifies the seeming contradiction between the universality and particularity of human needs and their satisfaction which is so prominent in the debate about needs. The finite set of biologically rooted needs of human beings are real and necessary (defined by the causal powers of the 'natural kind', the human being); but they are abstract and general. The specific form and content of the objects by which human beings satisfy their various needs are historically specific and varied, co-determined by a range of social as well as physical factors.

Critics who deny the universality and objectivity of human need in the name of individual diversity reduce real needs to felt wants and expressed desires, which is an empiricist conflation. Maureen Ramsay (1992) has set out a detailed realist critique of liberal arguments which identify needs with wants. The identification of what can be known empirically with what exists is the key weakness of liberal approaches (Ramsay 1992: 52). Ramsay uses the realist *causal* criteria (Bhaskar 1997: 179) to ascribe reality to objective human needs, in contrast to the empiricist criterion of perceptibility. Needs can be identified and investigated empirically, by exploring the causal effects on people of the inadequate satisfaction of various needs (Ramsay 1992: 51, 56). Along similar lines to Collier, Ramsay distinguishes between objective needs, which are factual, empirically verifiable, rooted in biology, and which all human beings have by virtue of their human nature; and the wants, tastes and desires that people feel. Felt needs and wants might overlap with, but do not necessarily encompass the whole range of real, objective needs; and they are in principle distinct from objective needs. All people, regardless of their beliefs, have a set of objectively true fundamental human needs which can be considered intransitive; whereas the felt needs or wants that people have and express are partially determined by their knowledge and beliefs about the necessity, desirability and availability of different objects or activities, and are thus transitive. Beliefs can be false, knowledge can be incomplete; people might be mistaken or unaware about their real needs or the objects that can satisfy them. A person's beliefs, and the values and tastes informed by these beliefs, are themselves partially conditioned or determined by society and the person's position in society, as are the demands people make (Ramsay 1992: 121). Ramsay's argument thus foregrounds both the objectivity of human need and the social determination of the actual satisfaction or frustration of needs for particular people in particular contexts.

Human beings are unique among animate beings in that they self-consciously produce the means of their subsistence. This is a practical material process of interacting with nature, using already existing raw materials and working with tools in order to create the objects necessary to satisfy needs; and it is a reflexive, purposeful activity unlike the instinctive activities of animals (Marx 1867: 283). This difference is at the root of human history, notions of development and progress and the historicity of human needs. The human process of production, through which human beings self-consciously create the objects which satisfy their needs, involves cooperation, reflection and learning, and so is a process which develops. Knowledge about nature and techniques of production, as well as tools and other created means of production, is acquired, accumulated, passed on and developed. The ways in which it is possible for human beings to meet their needs are therefore not static and unchanging, as they are for animals. In the process new possibilities of production arise which themselves create new needs (or to be more precise, new concrete manifestations of abstract needs). Thus we have 'the power (or liability) to acquire powers or needs' (Bhaskar 1993: 145).

Precisely because the way in which human beings meet their needs is through self-conscious, intentional purposive activity, it is a *social* process which presupposes the existence of distinct sets of social relations between people. All activities by which human needs are met are therefore irreducibly social activities, involving social relations, and as such are only possible in society. The way in which a person meets their needs is not, and cannot be, through their own individual isolated activity, nor is it through instinctive behaviour (as with animals). It is through particular activities which necessarily involve the activities of other people, and which make use of knowledge and material products created by other people and previous generations.

A realist understanding thus shows that it is social relations which are explanatorily prior in explaining the concrete satisfaction or frustration of human needs in different contexts. The objects by means of which any particular individual can satisfy their needs depends upon the objects available in society, their position in society and their beliefs. As Marx observed,

> the worker who buys potatoes, and the kept woman who buys lace, follow the one and the other their respective choice. But the diversity of their choice is explained by the difference in the positions which they occupy in the world, a difference which is the product of the social organisation.
>
> (Marx 1847: 45)

Need, absence and the historical dialectics of emancipation

Realism thus establishes the objectivity of human need and the irreducibly social and historical cause of concrete need satisfaction or frustration. Poverty, as the routine *non-satisfaction* of historically satisfiable needs, is an objective social condition produced by historically specific social relations. This means that 'poverty alleviation' cannot be conceived in a technocratic sense of reform within the existing social order, if the structured social relations of that order cause the systematic production of poverty. Poverty as the routine non-satisfaction of historically satisfiable needs is not a contingent unfortunate state of affairs but a form of oppression; as such, 'poverty alleviation' has to be reconceived in terms of political struggle and emancipation rather than technocratic reform or philanthropy. But the intransitivity of both human needs and the social relations which cause their deprivation means that resistance to oppression cannot be conceived only at the individual or discursive and subjective level (Collier 1989: 138–9), while admitting the possibility, and perhaps necessity and emancipatory potential of a social scientific critique of lay knowledge and self-understanding with respect to the causes of poverty.

The ontology underlying a realist understanding of human need already implies an understanding of emancipation. As materially and socially dependent beings, realising the inherent potential for augmenting our powers requires gaining control over the various relations, objects and conditions upon which we depend (Collier 1990). Emancipation cannot be conceived in terms of freedom *from* determination or dependence, but rather in terms of increased control over the sources of determination.[12] This informs Bhaskar's early articulation of emancipation as 'the special qualitative kind of becoming free or liberation [...] which consists in the *transformation*, in "self-emancipation," by the agent(s) concerned, *from an unwanted to a wanted source of determination*' (Bhaskar 1980: 16, see also Bhaskar 1986: 171); he argues elsewhere that

> Emancipation is not to be confused with the amelioration of states of affairs. Nor does it involve the absence of determination. It consists in the transformation or replacement of unneeded, unwanted and oppressive sources of determination, or structures, by needed, wanted and empowering ones.
>
> (Bhaskar 1991: 145)

This initial realist conceptualisation of emancipation is enhanced by the developments of dialectical critical realism. With the elaboration of the ontological reality of *absence*, Bhaskar's dialectical critical realism (1993, 1994) integrates the problems of need, poverty, lack and oppression into a general dynamic understanding of social change, agency and history. Dialectical critical realism shows that the problem of poverty and need has to be radicalised in terms of oppression and emancipation, and why the pursuit of emancipation or the 'pulse of freedom' will necessarily involve struggle. Criticising the traditional, ontologically monovalent conceptions of purely positive being, Bhaskar defends the notion of absence as central to being, with real ontological status and causal efficacy, and at the root of change. An absence or lack can have causal efficacy and is thus real in a significant sense. An absence can be defined in terms of its causal effects, not simply in terms of what it is not:

> Absence is not just a metaphysical shadow cast by negative judgements, which are always reversible; it belongs to ontology, and is not reversible. The medieval philosophers were right: some facts are inherently negative, privations of being, and all ills are such.
>
> (Collier 2002: 165)[13]

Central to Ramsay's realist theory of human need is the causal fact that an unsatisfied human need will prevent the possible realisation of a particular potential or development of a particular causal power. This therefore constitutes a negatively causally efficacious *absence* or *lack*.[14] To meet that need requires intentional action which overcomes the lack, thus enabling the realisation of potentials and powers; and such intentional action is motivated by the experience of absence. In the terminology of dialectical critical realism this constitutes absenting absences, and is fundamental to human being in the world – when we are hungry, we produce or acquire food to eat. Without eating, we will be unable to grow, or have energy to maintain a healthy body and engage in physical activity, which constitutes the non-realisation of powers and potentials. When we eat food we are absenting the absence signalled by the experience of hunger, and in doing so enabling the realisation of human powers.

If for some reason we are prevented from satisfying our need, then we will (rationally and, other things being equal, necessarily) try to overcome whatever is preventing us from absenting the absence. Our material, social and rational being means that causally significant lacks are experienced as such, giving rise to conscious efforts to overcome the lack, and to overcome constraints which prevent the absenting of absences or the satisfaction of needs. It is the existence and experience of ontologically real, significant absence which motivates efforts to bring about change in the world. But it is the existence of real, causally efficacious social obstacles which prevent need satisfaction, which require the further process of transformative practice. Emancipation necessarily requires removing the basic causes which systematically produce specific forms of lack and absence suffered by specific groups. In ontological terms, what distinguishes emancipatory change and praxis from general social action and change is the overcoming of *structural constraints* on the absenting of absences. Critical realist dialectics thus conceives emancipation in terms of the absenting of constraints on the absenting of absences (Bhaskar 1993: 41–2, 207), and argues that the experience of lack and the rationality of human being gives rise to an *emancipatory dialectic*, the 'pulse of freedom'.

What are structural constraints, and how are they overcome? This is ultimately a substantive and historical question which cannot be resolved at the level of philosophy. Nevertheless Bhaskar's distinction between different forms of power relation provides some useful clarification. Power$_1$ relations constitute a capacity to do something or act in a certain way: 'the transformative capacity intrinsic to the concept of agency as such'; power$_2$ relations refer to relations of domination and control by one person or group over another: 'the transfactually efficacious capacity to get one's way against either (i) the overt wishes and/or (ii) the real interests of others' (Bhaskar 1993: 60, 153).[15] If power$_2$ relations systematically constrain the satisfaction of needs, then absenting the constraint (which Bhaskar terms constraint$_2$) will entail removing or transforming the power$_2$ relations which constrain the absenting of absences: this is transformative praxis. Dialectical critical realism also develops the general realist notion of stratification to elaborate a more complex model of social being: the four-planar model of social being. This distinguishes four types of relation: between a person and the material/ natural environment – material transactions with nature; among people through the objective structured relations between positions and practice – social relations; between one person and another person – inter-personal interaction; and intra-personal, intra-subjective relations (Bhaskar 1993: 258). This implies four different types of ontological relation of cause or dependency, with corresponding forms of potential freedom or oppression.

These distinctions mean that it is necessary to identify, in a particular context of oppression or exploitation, the basis of exploitation (power$_2$) and the causes of uneven distribution of power$_1$ among different groups. Bhaskar tends to skirt this necessity for theoretical and substantive analysis and differentiation between the nature and causes of different historical forms of social oppression. His use of the generic all-encompassing term 'generalized master–slave-type relations' to refer to *all* forms of oppression or exploitation serves as a convenient shorthand in developing his notion of dialectic, in particular with respect to absences and emancipation.[16] However it is not a helpful generalisation to make when it comes to substantive analysis, and therefore when it comes to understanding actual historical struggles for and possibilities of emancipation.

The umbrella term 'generalized master–slave-type power$_2$ relations' is misleading and glosses over the specificity of different types of social relations structuring unequal power in society, and the consequent need to analyse them, both theoretically and substantively, in their specificity as well as their totality and connection.[17] Bhaskar criticises Marx for prioritising inequalities arising from relations of production and the wage-labour–capital relation to the exclusion of other forms of social oppression, 'most obviously those of nationality, ethnicity, gender, religious affiliation, sexual orientation, age, health and bodily disabilities generally' (Bhaskar 1993: 332–3). This is a fairly standard criticism to make, often rehearsed by both Marxists and non-Marxists.[18] But critical realism shows that Marx's scientific practice respected the stratification of theoretical inquiry necessitated by the stratification of social reality. In his mature work Marx was not for the most part trying to theorise and explain each and every form of social oppression or the whole of social life; he concentrated on the relations specific to the capitalist mode of production as such. It seems entirely in accordance with critical realist methodological principles to distinguish, at the level of theory, between different forms of real mechanism. Distinguishing analytically between different forms and causes of social oppression does not entail *normative* privileging of one form of oppression over another. In reality many forms of social oppression – such as class-, race- and gender-based – are intrinsically related, as outcomes of social relations which historically co-exist with mutual and cumulative causal effect. But they nevertheless remain ontologically and analytically irreducible to each other. At a certain level of abstraction social inquiry can and must treat them in their own specificity before analysing concretely their mutual interaction. Moreover, it cannot be assumed at the outset that there is no significant explanatory priority between different forms and relations of social oppression. The four-planar model of social being *helps* in distinguishing different forms of oppression at different strata or levels of being: some, but not all, forms of oppression which are effective at the levels of subjectivity and inter-personal relations are parasitic upon, or necessarily related to, unequal relations at the level of transactions with nature (i.e. relations of class). Andrew Collier clarifies this as follows:

> There are of course numerous other forms of oppression in capitalist societies apart from class exploitation – along lines of race, sex, sexuality and so on. In some times and places, they are more severe than class exploitation. Why then should class exploitation take central place? My answer is that while other forms of oppression are causally linked to capitalism, they are not essentially linked to capitalism in the way that class exploitation is. Without a propertyless working class, no capitalism; racism and sexism on the other hand, while they are advantageous to capitalism which therefore tends to resist movements against them, are not essential to it; they could conceivably be abolished within capitalism, though it is unlikely. Conversely, insofar as they involve personal prejudice, there is no guarantee that they would automatically die out under socialism. But the structural pressure to retain them would be absent from socialism, making the fight against them a much easier task.
>
> (Collier 2001a: 16)

It was precisely the differentiation between a class-based and a race-based understanding of oppression that was central to the Mozambican liberation struggle, as argued later in Chapter 6.

Emancipation and the limits of philosophy

Critical realist philosophy demonstrates the objectivity of human need, and the necessity of social-scientific explanation of poverty as historically produced absence. To explain the social causes of absence or lack requires theoretical and historical examination of the social relations which structure the processes through which needs are met in different contexts. Such knowledge is necessary, though by no means in itself sufficient, for emancipatory struggles aiming to overcome the oppression of poverty. Here we meet the necessary limits on what philosophy as such can say about the condition of global poverty, and the process and possibilities of emancipation, in the current world order.[19] Philosophical discourse about emancipation is rooted, at a very general level, in the fact of humanity's mutual and dual dependence on nature and society, as sketched above. But beyond this general level, contemporary philosophical reflection on emancipation must be conditioned by the historical specificity of inequality, global poverty and oppression in the world today. Philosophy 'pursues a line of questioning with contingent historical origins and definite social conditions' and is practically conditioned (Bhaskar 1986: 12, 18). The philosophical concern with oppression and emancipation 'can no more be justified by philosophy, or philosophy alone, than boots can climb mountains; [it . . .] must instead be grounded in the wider horizon of historical experience' (Bhaskar 1986: 18). The concept of emancipation as such is an abstraction, but actual poverty and struggles for emancipation, along with 'revolutions, wars, plagues and people' are concrete phenomena (Bhaskar 1986: 112). Bhaskar has emphasised the importance of remembering that in the social domain, abstract inquiry must always 'have a concrete "mooring" – in history and geography, and in biography (individual and group) – which must be understood as a condition for the application of any theoretical constructs' (Bhaskar 1986: 112–13). With the development of capitalism, the satisfaction and deprivation of human need has taken a world-historical character, and the social causes of poverty and wealth are globally extended. To understand both the structural production of poverty and lack in any particular context in the world today, and the possibilities of and constraints on emancipatory struggles which attempt to overcome absences, it is necessary to analyse the specificity of capitalist social relations of production and the global processes of change involved in the development of capitalism.

4   Marxism, imperialism and Africa

The orthodox approaches in academic and institutional literature implicitly naturalise the condition of rural poverty. In response it is necessary to emphasise that the impoverishment of Africa's direct producers is a modern condition, a world-historical outcome of the global expansion and uneven development of capital effected through imperial relations. This requires an approach which acknowledges the specificity of particular contexts and conjunctures but nevertheless foregrounds the global structuring of the local, and the spatially and temporally extended conditions of possibility for social reproduction. In Development Studies the move away from the reductionism of dependency approaches to the critical focus on local agency, identity and difference has occurred often at the expense of attention to global structures. In critical IPE the rejection of positivism has also entailed a rejection of objectivity, an over-emphasis on ideology to the relative neglect of economic relations and coercive forms of domination, and an inadequate specification of social ontology in terms of inter-subjectivity and agency.

In the current climate of critical doubt regarding the possibility of explaining social reality it is all the more important to reclaim the core insights of historical materialism. Explaining the production and reproduction of local poverty in Africa requires a theoretical and historical understanding of the nature of capitalism and imperialism. Yet the point of departure here differs from the widespread consensus among critical scholars today. Historical materialism, as manifest in the mature works of Marx and Engels, aspires to provide an objective explanation of social reality, and this is one of the important ways in which it is consistent with the principles of critical realism. This is in contrast to the position of current critical scholarship which emphasises the centrality of normative commitments in the production of knowledge, and denies the possibility of objectivity. The potential importance of historical materialism and Marx's theoretical explanation of capitalism in relation to the question of emancipation rests on its nature as objective social science, not on the prior political commitments and solidarity of its adherents.

Critical realism, historical materialism and the analysis of African social reality

As Marxism was declining in popularity among scholars of Development, it was being introduced and developed in IR in the form of Neo-Gramscian IPE.

However while the problems of Marxist approaches in Development Studies (both real and perceived, to varying extents) can be attributed to lingering forms of positivism, manifest in overly functionalist or reductionist approaches, a weakness of the re-discovered historical materialism in some Neo-Gramscian scholarship is the over-emphasis on ideas and values at the expense of objectivity and non-discursive structures, mechanisms and contradictions.[1] Critical realism is therefore important in providing a defence of the realist underpinning of the historical materialism developed in the mature works of Marx, in particular his analysis of the workings of capital.

Critical realism and historical materialism

The move from critical realist philosophy to historical materialist substantive analysis is seen by some as problematic, even unwarranted. Critical realist philosophy does not 'legislate in advance' for the social sciences in terms of their substantive content (see Bhaskar 1998: 7 and chapter 1 generally), and critical realism does not necessarily entail Marxism. Many scholars are conducting critical realism-informed social inquiry into substantive issues without turning to historical materialism. On the other hand many Marxists see no need for critical realism. It is argued that historical materialism is defendable on its own terms, and reference to realist philosophy is superfluous or misleading; Marxists have a 'more obvious option than those heralded by Bhaskar: the Marxism of Marx' (Roberts 1999: 23).[2] The desire to reveal the 'authentic' version of Marx's method, or even to identify methodological features as the most important characterising feature of Marx's work, has been criticised (McLennan 1981, Roberts 1999). Nevertheless the case that historical materialism is consistent with the principles of scientific realism is worth making for several reasons.[3] Given the variety of interpretations of historical materialism it does matter how the underlying methodological principles are understood. Critical realist philosophy provides an independent set of arguments about method in social inquiry, which give specific reasons why the realist methodological principles underlying historical materialism are superior to those underlying forms of empiricist or idealist social theory. Much of this ground has been already covered persuasively elsewhere, so here only two points will be highlighted.

First, critical realism helps to reclaim what is lost in the turn to a 'humanist' approach to social inquiry which, against so-called 'mechanical marxism' (Gill 1993b: 3), emphasises the centrality of ethics, values, agency and praxis in relation to the construction of knowledge, and rejects the possibility of objective social science. Some of the central methodological claims made by critical IPE scholars are not in fact consistent with the historical materialism of Marx, with the result that some of what made Marx's approach superior to that of classical and vulgar political economy has been abandoned. Neo-Gramscians explain their turn to Gramsci on the basis that his work avoids the structuralism, economism and tendency to abstraction of much orthodox Marxism, and instead foregrounds human values and agency.[4] A central point of departure in Neo-Gramscian scholarship is Cox's often-quoted observation that 'Theory is always *for* someone and *for* some purpose. All theories have a perspective. Perspectives derive from a position in time and space, specifically social and political time and space' (Cox 1981: 128). The possibility of objectivity in producing social knowledge is denied; instead the claim to legitimacy in terms of knowledge is seen to rest on political commitments to the oppressed and to emancipatory social change.

However, Marx and Engels distinguished their approach from others precisely on the basis that theirs was a scientific method: 'our party [...] had the great advantage of having a new scientific outlook as its theoretical basis' (Engels 1859: 510). As Perry Anderson has pointed out, '[t]here were socialists before Marx: the scandal he introduced, which still affronts many socialists – not to speak of capitalists – today, was the aspiration towards a *scientific* socialism: that is, one governed by rationally controllable criteria of evidence and truth' (Anderson 1983: 14). Critical realism shows that evaluative judgements (and consequently imperatives for action) do follow from factual, explanatory accounts of social phenomena, which is the basis for the form of explanatory critique of which historical materialism provides a major exemplar (see Bhaskar 1998: 54–71). *As social scientists*, Marx and Engels did not claim to depart from political solidarity with the working classes or the oppressed, but on the contrary to provide an *objective* scientific analysis of the workings of the capitalist mode of production: 'it was the proud boast of Marx and Engels to have put socialist politics on a scientific footing, to have outgrown the stage of moralistic utopias' (Collier 1981: 3).[5] This is not, of course, to say that their analysis was *neutral*. Their work had major political implications and they were politically on the side of the oppressed. But the negative evaluative judgement of capitalist society, and the imperative to struggle to transform it, arise from the accurate, factual and explanatory account of its nature as an oppressive and exploitative social order (see Collier 1981, especially 13–22). Objective analysis *arrives at* evaluative conclusions, with normative and practical implications, rather than pre-existing normative commitments informing the content of explanatory analysis:

> Intellectual disciplines should seek the truth – and if the truth has political consequences, they should be followed. The legitimate project of 'politicizing' an intellectual discipline is simply spelling out the political conclusions that its well-evidenced results have, in the teeth of the positivist attempt to impose an alien neutrality upon the human sciences.
>
> (Collier 1998: 53)

Moral criticism of the existing order, solidarity with the oppressed, and a commitment to progressive social change are of course important but these do not in themselves guarantee the production of more adequate knowledge about the social world. The notion of explanatory critique in critical realism (see Bhaskar 1986: 179, Collier 1994: 169–90, Archer *et al.* 1998 part III) helps to clarify the specificity of the notion of critique in Marx's historical materialism. Some insist on the normative and practical dimensions of Marx's work over the objective and explanatory, citing the second half of the famous thesis on Feuerbach, 'the point, however, is to *change* it' (this has become a slogan of the anti-globalisation movement). But Marx was not an advocate of immediate 'direct action', nor indeed was Gramsci (Buttigieg 1992: 17). On the contrary both scholars firmly believed that successful political action requires a correct understanding of society, to which they devoted much of their lives to providing.

Second, the critical realist theory of depth ontology, differentiating between the realms of the real, actual and empirical, is important for defending Marx's analysis of capital. Much of his analysis requires the distinction between real, actual and empirical to be properly defended, in particular against empiricist refutations. The reign of empiricism holds such sway that empiricist criteria of 'scientificity' are often projected onto elements of Marx's theory of capital, which are then 'shown' to be proved wrong. It is often asserted that the labour theory of value has been shown to be wrong. Critical realism is important in first distinguishing between empiricist and realist understandings of theory and method, and then showing that the labour theory of value is based on realist principles, as Steve Fleetwood (2001) has argued. It does not rest on demonstrating quantitative relations between empirical values of wages and prices. More generally, the empiricist notion that social science can and ought to be able to make predictions is used to disqualify historical materialism. If prediction is held to be a defining criterion of the adequacy of a social scientific theory, and if Marxism is assumed to 'predict' the eventual transformation of capitalism into socialism and communism, then the collapse of the Communist Bloc in 1989 can easily be held up as 'proof' that Marxism was wrong all along. In countering such claims, it is helpful with the aid of critical realism to be able to shift the grounds of debate and the understanding of science.

The realist distinction between real structures and empirical events is important in understanding crucial features of Marx's work. The theoretical elaboration of the laws which describe the necessary way of operating of particular mechanisms and structures which are real but not empirical, and the explanation of actual events and empirical forms produced by different mechanisms operating under specific circumstances, are two related but different moments of social inquiry. Marx's appreciation of this difference is evident throughout his mature work. Most of *Capital* is dedicated to uncovering, theoretically, the laws of the real but non-empirical mechanisms of the structured social relations of capital. Much of this work does engage in detailed analysis of actual societies, but it does so in order to draw out the basic tendencies of capital as such. It is necessary to grasp this distinguishing realist feature of Marx's method, in order to see how aspects of his analysis of capital as such can shed light on historical developments outwith the time-and-space context of his analysis (or from which his theoretical analysis was abstracted) – in particular, colonialism, imperialism and the world-historical production of poverty in Africa.

In order to understand theoretically the basic tendencies of capital Marx often abstracted, in thought, from other relations or conditions which usually do actually exist in reality – and he knew this.[6] An important example is his abstraction from foreign trade, and his analysis of capital as if only one national economy existed. Marx always acknowledged the role of foreign trade in capitalism: 'Capitalist production never exists without foreign trade' (Marx 1885: 546). However his aim in *Capital* is to set out the laws and tendencies of the capitalist mode of production as such. In order to do so he abstracted from various complicating conditions and mechanisms which in reality of course are always present and have effects, but for the purpose of abstract theoretical analysis obscure the pure nature of specific mechanisms. The 'disturbing circumstances' Marx abstracted from often included, amongst others, those of foreign trade. For example in his section on Simple Reproduction he notes

> foreign trade, in so far as it does not just replace elements (and their value), only shifts the contradictions to a broader sphere, and gives them a wider orbit. [. . .] Bringing foreign trade into an analysis of the value of the product annually reproduced can therefore only confuse things, without supplying any new factor either to the problem or to its solution. We therefore completely abstract from it here, and treat gold as a direct element of the annual reproduction, not as a commodity imported from abroad by exchange.
>
> (Marx 1885: 544, 546; see also Marx 1867: 727, note 2)

It is well known that the analysis of 'capital as such' in the first volumes of *Capital* was the first part of a larger project which Marx never completed. His intention was to move on to analyse the more concrete phenomena of the state, foreign trade and international relations, the world market and crisis (the interconnection of these latter three being, said Marx, self-evident), presented in further volumes (Marx 1858: 108, 227, 1859: 19). Marx never did complete a systematic analysis of these other phenomena; hence André Gunder Frank's frustration that Marx 'relegate[d] our problems to a volume of *Capital* that he never came to write' (Frank 1978: 3). We are left with only scattered remarks, such as: 'The transformation of necessaries into luxuries by means of foreign trade [. . .] is important in itself [. . .] because it determines the whole social pattern of backward nations [. . .] which are associated with a world market based on capitalist production' (Marx 1894: 243). A realist interpretation of his method makes sense of this form of abstraction. Marx never thought that the *actual* world corresponded to the various simplified forms he analysed on the basis of abstraction, just as engineers never assume that in the actual world friction does not exist. Nevertheless in both cases the process of abstraction enables uncovering real laws and tendencies, in Marx's case some of the real laws and tendencies of capital.

Historical materialism and the analysis of African social reality

Is historical materialism, realist or otherwise, appropriate for the analysis of non-Western societies? Is Marxism a eurocentric theory? Can the concepts derived from analysis of capitalism in Western Europe be applied to the analysis of African or other non-European societies? Or does this automatically do violence to African social reality, by attempting to squeeze it into a pre-existing analytical framework derived from European history? The use of historical materialism as an approach to the analysis of social reality in Africa and other non-Western societies has been questioned on several grounds. Marxism is seen by some as a Western product, irredeemably eurocentric and therefore inapplicable to non-Western societies (e.g. Young 1990: 3). Chris Brown asserts that '[u]nquestionably, the two thinkers who have been most responsible for promoting a Eurocentric, developmentalist model of the world were Hegel and Karl Marx' (Brown, C. 2004: 328). For Foucault, Marxism's Western origins are indelible: 'Marxism exists in nineteenth century thought like a fish in water: that is, it is unable to breathe anywhere else' (Foucault 1970: 262 cited in Robinson 2001: 113). Marxism is criticised for subscribing to a 'metanarrative' of history, capitalist development and progress. Such criticisms are particularly pertinent for social inquiry concerned to explain the production of poverty in Africa, and must be taken seriously for both methodological and political reasons. The pernicious biases of eurocentrism, racism and white supremacy are alive and kicking today, both in some academic literature[7] as well as in popular consciousness (arguably rooted in ignorance of the world and history, and fed by the right-wing press).[8]

Many of the criticisms of Marxism as inherently eurocentric stem from the broader post-modern or post-structuralist rejection of *any* form of social theory which seeks to provide objective knowledge and explanation. The field of mainstream post-colonial theory is paradigmatic in this regard.[9] The very aspiration to articulate a general 'truth' whose validity extends beyond the context of the observer or subject, or to speak for or about others, is seen to be part of the universalising, civilising project of Western enlightenment, modernity and imperialism. It is true that the economic and political relations of European expansion and the violent conquest and dispossession of non-European societies over centuries were legitimised by various ideologies which rationalised brutal and dehumanising practices in the name of universal civilisation and progress. It is important to theorise and seek to counter the ideological and psychological (inter-subjective and subjective) conditions of possibility and effects of imperialism, within both metropolitan and colonial/neo-colonial societies. The phenomenon of racism was a necessary and irreducible component of European expansion, slavery and colonialism, and remains in some less overt form necessary to contemporary neo-colonialism. This is why, as Frantz Fanon observed, 'Marxist analysis should always be slightly stretched every time we have to do with the colonial problem' (1967c: 31). But it is politically disabling to conflate all commitment to truth, explanation, history, reason and universal humanity with the project of European imperialism.[10] It is illegitimate to reduce knowledge (or the aspiration to knowledge) per se, via imperialist ideologies, to relations of domination associated with imperialism. The best way to confront ideologies of any kind, including ideologies of racism and western supremacy, is to expose their factual falseness by providing a more adequate explanation of phenomena, and furthermore to expose their internal relations with (social necessity for and causation in) a particular social order (Bhaskar and Collier 1998), as Fanon did in his analysis of racism and colonialism (see especially Fanon 1967a).

Beyond the general dismissal of all types of meta-narrative, a more nuanced criticism questions the legitimacy of applying concepts derived from analysis of processes in one context to analysis of a different context (Zeleza 2003). This is a general hazard of social inquiry; historical materialism, however, is perhaps uniquely equipped to overcome it. One of the central charges of Marx's critique of bourgeois social science – the reason why he termed it 'bourgeois' – was that it was ahistorical: it failed to distinguish between the trans-historical and histori-cally specific features of social phenomena. As a result various specific features of a society – in particular, capitalist social relations of production – are portrayed as natural and eternal, rather than historically specific, demanding of explanation, and essentially transitory:

> The economists express the relation of bourgeois production, the division of labor, credit, money, &c., as categories fixed, immutable, eternal. [...] The economists explain to us how production is carried on in the relation given, but what they do not explain is how these relations are produced, that is to say the historical movement which has created them.
>
> (Marx 1847: 113–14)

Marx criticises the notion of the free isolated producing individual at the centre of the work of Ricardo and Smith (Marx 1857: 124). He argues that the classical polit-ical economists take as their starting point the individual of bourgeois society – a society of free competition – who appears to be 'free from the bonds of nature'. They do not see beyond the appearance to the real social relations through which these 'free' isolated individuals are dependent upon each other, in a state of unfreedom. This dependence is not manifest in personal relations of domination, as with tenant and land-lord, but in the impersonal relations manifest only through the exchange of things. They fail to see the historical specificity of this situation, and so assume the isolated individual to be common to all societies throughout history, rather than the particular product of a specific historically produced form of society. While the content of this critique is specific to Western industrialised capitalist societies, the methodological point is general, and crucial. Marx criticises the political economists for starting at the end point, assuming as given precisely the historically produced social and economic forms which require explanation: they 'obliterate all historical differences and [...] see in all social phenomena only bourgeois phenomena' (1857: 145).

In contrast, Marx begins his own analysis by identifying trans-historical features of humanity (Marx 1858: 85–8). These features – the necessity of pro-duction through social cooperation and interaction with nature, using tools and knowledge, involving some form of division of labour – are common to all soci-eties, indeed are part of what is definitive of being human. But Marx recognises that this in itself does not enable a sophisticated understanding of any particular society; in order to arrive at such an understanding it is necessary to distinguish the *particular* ways in which such common features appear in different forms in different societies. An understanding of the specificity of any particular society in any particular epoch demands attention to precisely what differentiates it from other particular societies; in other words focusing not on what human societies have in common, but what differentiates them (Marx 1857: 126). At the core of historical materialism is an insistence of the historical specificity of *all* societies. Such an approach cannot be judged inherently eurocentric. Thus in response to the criticism that historical materialism is eurocentric and therefore inapplicable to the study of African social formations, Kwesi Botchwey observed '[i]t is meaningless to accuse Marx of Eurocentricity because he spent the major part of his life studying the laws of motion of the capitalist system, instead of studying pre-capitalist socio-economic systems in Africa' (Botchwey 1977: 13).

It is true that Marx derived his theoretical understanding of capital mainly from analysis of capitalist society and development in England. But in the Preface to the first edition of *Capital* he explains the reasons for this, and this is one area where the argument for the realist underpinnings of Marx's approach is important. Natural scientists develop theoretical understanding of the operation of real mechanisms by isolating them in experiment to observe them operating 'in their pure state' (Marx 1867: 90; Bhaskar 1997). Social scientists however have no recourse to experiment; they cannot observe mechanisms in isolation, in their pure state. They can only observe the actual events and forms produced by various interacting mechanisms, and abstract from the prevailing, contingent and non-necessary factors to identify the properties and laws of the real mechanisms as such. In order to understand the laws of capital, Marx analysed the place where they were most fully developed at the time:

> What I have to examine in this work is the capitalist mode of production, and the relations of production and forms of intercourse that correspond to it. Until now, their *locus classicus* has been England. This is the reason why England is used as the main illustration of the theoretical developments I make.
>
> (Marx 1867: 90)

So to what extent can concepts such as class, state and mode of production be used in analysis of African societies without doing violence to their specificity? A central principle of historical materialism is that conceptual categories should arise from concrete historical research, rather than developing analytical models which are then imposed upon social reality (e.g. Marx and Engels 1845–46a: 36–7, 41). There are examples of conceptual development, for example in some of the literature on the peasantry and the 'articulation of modes of production', which lean too far towards abstraction or functionalism and begin to lose plausibility.[11] Analysis of classes and modes of production can become theoreticist, concerned more with terminology than with concrete analysis. Marx's own attempt to specify generic models of 'other' modes of production (in particular the generic Asiatic mode) was problematic and arguably one of the weakest aspects of his work. The tendency for conceptual frameworks to take on a life of their own at the expense of concrete analysis is a weakness found in many forms of social inquiry; it is neither the sole preserve of, nor inherent in, historical materialism. On the contrary, if the principles of historical materialism are respected then the common logic of 'history by analogy'[12] found in so much analysis of Africa (as observed in Chapter 1 with regard to Modernisation theory and the literature on 'new states') can be avoided.

Refusing the use of illegitimate analogies and conceptual transfers, however, does not imply endorsing the absolute and essential uniqueness and *difference* of societies; the 'peculiar features of state and civil society in the peripheral formations of Asia and the Middle East [and Africa ...] stem not from some sort of historical exceptionalism that might render them unintelligible to the Marxist method' (Ahmad 1985: 46). It *is* necessary to specify the differences between capitalist and non-capitalist social relations, the historical variety and diversity among non-capitalist societies and modes of production, and the specific effects arising from the historical combination of different production and exchange relations under different circumstances. This task is inherently difficult, hence the significant debates which have arisen, and it is always necessary that conceptual development is conditioned and informed by concrete substantive research. Likewise with the concept of class: while not trans-historical, at a certain level of abstraction the category might apply to a wide range of societies where productive activities are organised through social relations which give rise to antagonistic relations between different groups in society. But the empirical or substantive content of the nature of different classes – their bases of social power, their ideology or level of consciousness as a class, and the tensions, conflicting interests and struggles between or within them – can only be derived from substantive enquiry (Mamdani 1976, Shivji 1976). Whether or not, and what kind of, class relations exist in Africa or anywhere else, at any time, cannot be decided in advance of concrete historical enquiry. This was central to the thought and practice of Amílcar Cabral, as well as Samora Machel and Frelimo in the 1970s and early 1980s (Cabral 1969, Centro de Estudos Africanos 1982, Munslow 1985, Chilcote 1991: 47–64).

For some critics, the characterisation of Marxism as eurocentric is related to its narrative of progress: 'Marxism's universalising narrative of the unfolding of a rational system of world history is simply a negative form of the history of European imperialism' (Young 1990: 2). Many critical rejections or revisions of Marxism take as a point of departure the fact that 'the classical pretensions of Marxian critical theory, including the belief in irreversible and unilinear progress toward the fully autonomous society, have been cast aside' (Linklater 2001: 24). This association of Marxism with universalising conceptions of history parallels criticisms in the debates over human need discussed in the previous chapter: 'Critical theory in the Marxian mode has been opposed because its project of universal emancipation is host to totalising potentials [...] the normative focus of contemporary critical theory reveals a greater sensitivity to radical differences' (Linklater 2001: 30). There are two related parts to this kind of criticism: first the charge of a unilinear teleological understanding of history; second (and as a consequence), the belief that capitalism is necessarily progressive on a world scale.

It is often asserted that Marxism holds a teleological, evolutionist notion of history, which posits a number of distinct stages through which societies pass: primitive communalism, feudalism, capitalism, socialism, communism (e.g. Giddens 1981). According to the standard account, Marxism believes that at each stage contradictions between the forces and relations of production unfold until the relations become a fetter to the further development of productive forces, leading to crisis and transition or revolution to the next, higher stage. This view is then elaborated with the addition of other types of pre-capitalist society such as the slave society and the Asiatic mode of production. According to this perceived orthodoxy, all societies will eventually progress through roughly the same stages, with communism as the final end point. The idea that Marxism 'predicts' the coming of communism is part of this general stereotype. To the extent that this characterisation has any basis in the works of Marx and Engels it is in their earlier work, for example the observation in the *Communist Manifesto* that the bourgeoisie would create a world in its own image. However any adequate understanding of historical materialism must acknowledge the later works of Marx and Engels, which include corrections of various misinterpretations of their earlier statements.[13] Marx explicitly rejected the teleological transposition of the particular empirical characteristics of England's development onto the fate of all other societies, criticising such a view for

> transforming my historical sketch of the genesis of capitalism in Western Europe into a historico-philosophical theory of the general course fatally imposed on all peoples, whatever the historical circumstances in which they find themselves placed, in order to arrive ultimately at this economic formation which assures the greatest expansion of the productive forces of social labour, as well as the most complete development of man. [...] events of striking similarity, taking place in different historical contexts, led to totally disparate results. By studying each of these developments separately, and then comparing them, one may easily discover the key to this phenomenon. But success will never come with the master-key of a general historico-philosophical theory, whose supreme virtue consists in being supra-historical.
>
> (Marx 1878: 136)

It is widely held that Marx saw colonialism and capitalism as a progressive force in the continents of Asia, Africa and Latin America. Indeed, such a view has acquired the status of 'common-sense' (Ahmad 1992: 14).[14] Colonialism swept aside old stagnant social structures and traditions and brought with it railways, industry and the development of the productive forces, fostering the growth of the proletariat, and thus planting the conditions for capitalist development and an eventual transition to socialism. Marxism is thought to argue that capitalism will take root and develop in the Third World in more or less the same form as it did in Western Europe. Even the World Bank has cited a passage from the *Communist Manifesto* with approval (World Bank 1996: 1 cited in Renton 2001: 10), a move which echoes the earlier appropriation of Marx onto the side of Modernisation theory and neo-classical economics by the prominent development theorist Dudley Seers (1979).

These views are typically based on a few short pieces of journalism on India written by Marx and Engels in the 1840s and 1850s, along with selected passages from the *Communist Manifesto* and his often-quoted observation that 'the country that is more developed industrially only shows, to the less developed, the image of its own future' (Marx 1867: 91). This caricature is undermined, however, by considering the nature of these earlier pieces of journalism and the conditions in which they were written; by a wider survey of Marx and Engels' work, especially their more mature work of the late 1860s–1890s;[15] and crucially, as has been emphasised here, by a better appreciation of Marx's method of inquiry. Three aspects of Marx's analysis of capital which undermine these myths and which are important in the explanation of global poverty are the notion of primitive accumulation, the necessarily expansionary nature and tendencies of capital, and the destructive effects of the expansion of capital in non-capitalist societies.

Insights from Marx: primitive accumulation and the expansionary tendencies of capital

Marx's analysis of capital is necessary for an adequate explanation of the production of modern poverty in Africa, although it is by no means on its own sufficient. Marx never set out a fully elaborated theory of colonialism or imperialism, nor did he pay much attention to Africa. This must be partly explained by the historical context in which he wrote, before the onset of the 'new' imperialism in the last decades of the nineteenth century, when virtually the whole of the world's land surface was formally occupied by the competing European powers. Marx's analysis of capital nevertheless provides an important starting point, in particular the theoretical and historical notion of primitive accumulation, the demonstration of capital's necessarily global, expansionary nature, and the destructive effects of capitalist expansion.

Although Marx used the case of capitalism in England as the basis for developing a theory of the capitalist mode of production he never conceived such development as arising from and taking place solely within the confines of England. A key feature of his method of inquiry (see Marx 1858: 320, 460–1, 672, 1867: 273) was that his theoretical identification of the mechanisms and structures of capitalist accumulation pointed, logically and historically, to processes which must necessarily have taken place in order for specifically capitalist accumulation to take place. These processes and conditions of possibility were not confined to Europe.

The capitalist mode of production is characterised and distinguished from other modes of production by the continued ever-expanding accumulation of value. In his derivation of the laws of capitalist accumulation Marx assumes, from the outset, that the process of circulation constitutes the exchange of equivalents.[16] He shows that in simple circulation the only change that takes place is in the form rather than quantity of value. The practice of over- or under-selling does not lead to an increase in the total amount of value in circulation, merely in the redistribution of existing value: 'Circulation, or the exchange of commodities, creates no value' (Marx 1867: 266). The surplus must therefore come from production, and the only way that production can create surplus-value is if the value created through the process of production is more than the value consumed during the process. Marx thus identified the source of surplus-value in the sphere of production, arising from the consumption of labour-power as a commodity:

> In order to extract value out of the consumption of a commodity, our friend the money-owner must be lucky enough to find within the sphere of circulation, on the market, a commodity whose use-value possesses the peculiar property of being a source of value, whose actual consumption is therefore itself an objectification of labour, hence a creation of value. The possessor of money does find such a special commodity on the market: the capacity for labour, in other words labour-power.
>
> (Marx 1867: 270)

Labour-power as a commodity possesses this peculiar property because of the potential difference between its exchange-value as a commodity, and the amount of value produced when labour-power as use-value (capacity to labour) is consumed by the capitalist. Like all other commodities, labour-power has a value determined by the labour-time socially necessary for its production and reproduction: 'the value of labour-power is the value of the means of subsistence necessary for the maintenance of its owner' (Marx 1867: 274). Marx stresses that when labour-power is sold as a commodity it is sold as an effect, rather than as a cause; as something which has been produced, rather than as something which has the power to produce (Marx 1858: 307, 571, 575, 674). Workers sell their capacity to work. To the worker, their capacity to work is a commodity, an exchange-value; to the buyer, it is a use-value. The exchange-value of labour-power has been determined before it is sold, as with any other commodity. Its exchange-value is determined not by how much value it can produce, but by how much socially necessary labour-time went into its production: 'the past labour embodied in the labour-power and the living labour it can perform, and the daily cost of maintaining labour-power and its daily expenditure in work, are two totally different things' (Marx 1867: 300). If the general productivity of labour is such that the means of subsistence necessary for the maintenance of the worker can be produced, say, in half a day, then if the worker works for half a day, they have already produced the value equivalent to the value of their labour-power. If they then continue to work for the rest of the day, they are creating surplus-value for the owner of their labour-power: the capitalist.

Capital accumulation therefore presupposes two distinct conditions: first, the existence of labour-power as a commodity. This implies a class society composed of a property-less majority who own nothing but their own labour-power and who are free to own, and therefore to sell, their labour-power on the market as a commodity; and a class of property-owners. The second is a certain level of increased productivity, which presupposes a certain level of development of the forces of production:

> If the worker, in the whole of his working time, can produce not a farthing more than his wages, then with the best of wills he cannot squeeze out a farthing for the capitalist. Property is the offspring of the productivity of labour.
>
> (Marx 1858: 573)

The historical existence of capitalist accumulation means that 'the side which appears as capital has to possess raw materials, instruments of labour and necessaries of life so that the worker can live during production, before production is completed' (Marx 1858: 504), which implies that

> there must have taken place on the part of the capitalist an accumulation – an accumulation prior to labour and not sprung out of it – which enables him to put the worker to work and to maintain his effectiveness, to maintain him as living labour capacity. This act by capital which is independent of labour, not posited by labour, is then shifted from the prehistory of capital into the present, into a moment of its reality and of its present activity, of its self-formation.
>
> (Marx 1858: 504)

Marx elaborated these historical processes, or 'historic presuppositions' (1858: 459) at some length, bringing them together under the theoretical term *primitive accumulation* (see Marx 1867: 273, 873–5 and Marx 1858: 320, 459–61, 672). This refers theoretically to a mode of accumulation based not on the exchange of equivalents and the accumulation of surplus-value arising from the productivity of labour, as in the case of capitalist accumulation, but on buying cheap and selling dear, or on coercion, plunder and enslavement.[17] Concretely, it refers to the long and brutal history of, on one hand, the dispossession of agricultural societies of direct producers in Western Europe through the enclosures; and on the other hand, the conquest, pillage and enslavement of societies around the world in the Americas, Africa, China, Australia and Asia. Marx was quite explicit about the worldwide violence, bloodshed and destruction which constituted this moment of primitive accumulation on the part of European capital (see Marx 1867, part 8).

In this regard the charge of eurocentrism should be levelled not at Marx or historical materialism as such, but at some subsequent Marxist accounts of the history of capitalism which have ignored or underplayed the international dimensions of primitive accumulation in the rise of capitalism in Europe. Robert Brenner (1977) elaborated a lengthy critique of the analyses of André Gunder Frank, Immanuel Wallerstein and Paul Sweezy, key figures of the dependency and world-systems approaches. He criticised them for characterising capitalism in terms of trade relations and production for exchange. This led them to explain the rise of capitalism as a result of the spread of commercialisation and a trade-based international division of labour. Their account ignored the role of class relations and contradictions in productive forces, reducing class struggles to a formality.

These criticisms in themselves were important, but Brenner's alternative account, which centred on the class struggles in Europe, ignored the role of primitive accumulation through European mercantile trade, conquest, slavery and dispossession in the non-European world, instead placing emphasis on the importance of 'innovation' within Europe. Ellen Meiksins Wood has insistently defended Brenner's position (Wood 1999), and criticised 'anti-eurocentric critics' for disregarding the historical specificity of capitalist social property relations and conflating general forms of commerce, wealth and money with capitalism (Wood 2001).[18] She argues that the anti-eurocentric critics are themselves guilty of assuming that which has to be explained – that is, the historical novelty of capitalism. It is in Marx's identification of 'the transformation of social property relations as the real "primitive accumulation"' (Wood 2001) that the historical explanation of capitalism lies. In stating her case, however, Wood tends to emphasise changing property relations in Europe at the expense of foreign trade, as if this were enough in itself to account for the rise of capitalism.

A recent example is Benno Teschke's magisterial analysis of the rise of the international state-system in Europe from the eighth to the eighteenth century, which centres on the dynamics of social property relations underlying historically specific political forms and practices of state, sovereignty and geopolitics (Teschke 2003). Teschke echoes Brenner's critique of Wallerstein *et al.*, rejecting their equation of capitalism with production for the market in favour of a definition of capitalism in terms of its logic of production, based on a specific set of social property relations (2003: 139–42). He correctly insists that such a definition of capitalism 'requires a historical account of the origins of capitalist relations of production' (2003: 142). However his analysis emphasises the form of social property relations rather than the mode of production of value. Marx emphasises not only the social relations of capital, between the propertied capitalist and the 'free' property-less worker, but also (and *in part* made possible by these relations) the specific form of accumulation which is 'self-expanding'. This novel form of accumulation cannot arise out of thin air, but presupposes certain conditions. These include the relations between a dispossessed property-less class subject to 'purely economic' compulsion to sell their labour-power, which is the focus of Teschke's analysis, as well as those of Wood and Brenner. They also include already- accumulated property on the part of the capitalists, which makes possible the increased productivity of labour necessary for the production of surplus-value – 'capitalist production presupposes the availability of considerable masses of capital' (Marx 1867: 873). The processes and relations of accumulation through which the European ruling classes acquired the wealth which made possible the development of industrial capitalism extended far beyond the space of Europe, as summarised by Du Bois:

> 'Royal adventurers trading to Africa' in 1667 had among them members of the royal family, three dukes, eight earls, seven lords, and twenty-seven knights. With the end of the civil war in England, British merchants crowded upon the landholding aristocracy for an increased share in the profits of

industry. While the British were ostensibly fighting for dynastic disputes in Europe, they were really, in the War of Spanish Succession and in the Seven Years' War, fighting for profit through world trade and especially the slave trade. In 1713 they gained, by the coveted Treaty of Asiento, the right to monopolise the slave trade from Africa to the Spanish colonies. In that century they beat Holland to her knees and started her economic decline. They overthrew the Portuguese in India, and finally, by the middle of the century, overcame their last rival in India, the French. In the eighteenth century they raised the slave trade to the greatest single body of trade on earth.

> (Du Bois 1946: 54)

These globally extended conditions of possibility of the rise of capitalism in Europe hardly feature in Teschke's account which centres on changing social property relations. Indeed he emphasises that the rise of capitalism was *not* related to mercantile accumulation precisely because this was based on 'buying cheap and selling dear' (2003 chapter 6). As a result his account of the origins of capitalism centres on social changes within Europe, in 'an account of the regionally specific transformation of social property relations in the transition from feudalism/ absolutism to capitalism' (2003: 142). Following Brenner and Wood he insists that the rise of capitalism was unique to early modern England (2003: 145). He also highlights the importance of social property relations to explaining forms of international relations, in contrast to Weberians such as Michael Mann who fail to differentiate the different logics of foreign policy of capitalist Britain and her dynastic/absolutist counterparts on the European continent (2003 chapter 8). Teschke underlines that the difference between Britain and France's response to military competition during the eighteenth century was because of Britain's productive and expanding capitalist economy, which could sustain the financing of naval supremacy without risking internal social conflict arising from over-taxation (2003: 261–2). In his discussion both of the origins of capitalism and of the subsequent foreign policies and naval supremacy of Britain in the eighteenth century, Teschke pays insufficient attention to the international dimensions and conditions of possibility of Britain's capitalist economic power. He hardly mentions the importance of internationally structured processes of primitive accumulation which made possible Britain's naval supremacy and development of industry: the trans-Atlantic slave trade and slave production in the Americas, and later towards the end of the nineteenth century the importance of colonialism to European accumulation. The result is an impression that the rise of capitalism was an endogenous development which originated in Britain and then spread outwards, first to Europe and then, via the 'modernizing' effect of international relations (Teschke 2003: 250, 266), to the rest of the world.

The processes of accumulation over centuries which made possible the rise of capitalism in Western Europe were globally extended; capitalism cannot be explained solely on the basis of changes taking place within Europe. In contrast to the analyses of what Blaut (2000b) has termed the 'euroMarxists', Marx was always clear that, whilst capitalist production in its classical form might have first developed in one state, the *conditions of possibility* and social ramifications of such development were from the very start necessarily global in scope; '[i]t was Karl Marx who made the great unanswerable charge of the sources of capitalism in African slavery' (Du Bois 1946: 56). He was explicit about the necessary role of foreign trade both in the origin as well as the subsequent development of capital:

> whereas *the expansion of foreign trade was the basis of capitalist production in its infancy*, it becomes the specific product of the capitalist mode of production as this progresses, through the inner necessity of this mode of production and its need for an ever extended market.
>
> (Marx 1894: 344, emphasis added; see also
> Marx 1863: 253, 1894: 450)

Although he did not use such a term, it can thus be argued that Marx had a specific understanding of what we can call the global constitution of capital. Marx was always explicit about capital's dependence upon and reproduction of the world market and foreign trade (1858: 227–8; 528, 1894: 344, 920), and its necessary tendency to spread 'over the whole surface of the globe' (Marx and Engels 1848: 37); he also emphasised that the effects of such expansion were varied and uneven.

His analysis showed how and why the capitalist mode of production and accumulation is necessarily expansionary, requiring an ever-expanding orbit through which capital in its different forms can circulate. This is for a variety of reasons, in particular the competition between capitals (Marx 1858: 414, 552, 730, 751). Competition forces the continual search for improvements in labour productivity. The continual development and revolutionising of the forces of production is therefore a necessary tendency of the capitalist mode of production – 'the development of the productive powers of labour, which capital incessantly whips onward with its unlimited mania for wealth' (Marx 1858: 325). This means that more and more commodities can be produced from a given amount of labour-power, which requires expanding markets and expanding consumption capacity in order to realise the surplus-value contained in the commodities. The process of capital accumulation consists of the continuing expanding cycle of production (transformation of value and production of surplus-value), followed by realisation of value through sale of commodities, followed by re-investment of original value + surplus-value to start the process again. For this process to proceed, an expanding sphere of circulation and consumption is therefore necessary: 'a precondition of production based on capital is therefore *the production of a constantly widening sphere of circulation*' (Marx 1858: 407). The continual development of forces of production and expanding productivity of labour also entails expanding demand for raw materials.

Thus Marx explains how, for reasons inherent in the nature of accumulation of surplus-value and the mechanism of competition, the capitalist mode of production is necessarily expansionary, tending to spread throughout the world. The process of accumulation just described is a circuit, and so capital must be always in movement, always forming a circuit (Marx 1867: 709). If it is to remain alive capital must accumulate; if it is to accumulate it must ceaselessly perform this circuit. Therefore the necessary tendencies of expansion, both spatially and within society into ever more branches of production; of the revolutionising of forces of production, the rising productivity of labour and the cheapening of commodities; of the constant need for new labour-power alongside the simultaneous rejection of labour-power, and so on – all of these tendencies derive from this need of capital to continue to circulate, a circulation which is 'an expanding curve, not a simple circle' (Marx 1858: 266). The existence of a world market was both a necessary condition for the development of capitalist industry, and a continuously reproduced outcome of such development. For capital to flourish and accumulation to continue on an ever-expanded scale, production and exchange on a world scale, producing for and organised through a world market becomes increasingly necessary and characteristic.

Marx emphatically did not see the 'growth of the international character of the capitalist regime' (Marx 1867: 29) as a unifying or levelling process which would bring about a uniform pattern of development in all societies. Critical realism crucially clarifies his methodological distinction between the necessary properties and tendencies of real structures, and the empirical forms and outcomes produced by such structures operating in particular combinations and conditions. As discussed above, in developing his theoretical analysis of capital as such Marx often abstracted in thought from the various additional conditions and counter-veiling tendencies which existed in *actual* societies. Marx was however sensitive to the varieties of empirical social forms which emerge in the global history of capitalist development, and placed special emphasis on this point. From his analysis of capital as such, he argued that a necessary process in the development of the capitalist mode of production is the dispossession of rural populations, the destruction of modes of production based on use and their subordination to production for exchange and the logic of capital. But he insisted that in the actual world the ways in which such developments and changes take place, and the stages which are reached, constitute 'endless nuances', 'myriad forms', 'many intermediate stages' determined in each instance by the structural and contingent particularities of the specific conjuncture, both local and global (Marx 1858: 193). Thus he emphasises:

> the same economic basis – the same in its major conditions [...] display[s] [...] endless variations and gradations in its appearance, as the result of innumerable different empirical circumstances, natural conditions, racial relations, historical influences acting from outside, etc., and these can only be understood by analysing these empirically given conditions.
>
> (Marx 1894: 927–8)

One specific type of development to which Marx devoted attention was the effects of merchant capital on non-capitalist modes of production. Far from seeing the expansion of metropolitan capital into non-capitalist social formations as necessarily bringing about the development of productive forces, Marx analysed how this process can under certain conditions have considerable destructive effects without leading to any progressive development or transformation of productive forces (Marx 1894: 440–4). The dominance of merchant capital, which 'when it holds a dominant position, is thus in all cases a system of plunder' (1894: 448), does not tend to revolutionise the mode of production, but 'simply worsens the conditions of the direct producers, transforms them into mere wage-labourers and proletarians under worse conditions than those directly subsumed by capital, appropriating their surplus labour in the basis of the old mode of production' (1894: 453). He is quite clear about the non-progressive effects of such development:

> the most odious exploitation of labour still takes place [...] without the relation of capital and labour here carrying within itself any basis whatever for the development of new forces of production, and the germ of newer historic forms.
>
> (Marx 1858: 853)

> this form [...] impoverishes the mode of production, cripples the productive forces instead of developing them, and simultaneously perpetuates these lamentable conditions in which the social productivity of labour is not developed even at the cost of the worker himself, as it is in capitalist production. [...] It does not change the mode of production, but clings on to it like a parasite and impoverishes it. It sucks it dry, emasculates it and forces reproduction to proceed under ever more pitiable conditions.
>
> (Marx 1894: 730–1)

There is thus already much contained in Marx's analysis of capital which can help to explain the profoundly uneven forms of development across the world characteristic of capitalism. This unevenness, a necessary outcome of the various contradictory tendencies inherent to capital accumulation, is manifest in different forms, dimensions and scales, including qualitative, spatial and temporal, social and technological. Crucially, such unevenness is manifest globally at the level of the world market, between states: this is a routine, normal and necessary outcome of capitalist development on a global scale. As Anwar Shaikh has shown (1979, 1980, 1981), uneven development is a necessary outcome of international competition and world trade. However, in order to account for the historical specificity of poverty in Africa, a general account of capitalism is not sufficient. The history of colonialism and imperialism is central to explaining poverty in the Third World as well as the development of capital, and while capitalism is necessarily imperialist, imperialism is not reducible to capitalism. It requires analysis in its own right.

The imperial nature of capital

A general notion of imperialism can be posited which rests on the necessarily global character and conditions of possibility of capital accumulation.[19] Capitalist development has always presupposed external conditions of possibility: the development of capitalism in Western Europe was always, from the very start, premised upon external economic and political relations with other parts of the world. Marx's theory of capital also shows that the task of securing the conditions necessary for the circulation and expanded accumulation of capital is always political, requiring some form of state regulation and coercion, creation and maintenance of order; and that this in itself presupposes the existence of military force. The forms and manifestations of political power needed to protect and secure the social and material conditions for capital accumulation and expansion will depend in part on the forms and level of development of capital itself, as well as the particular structure of classes in any particular social formation. So too, the forms of resistance and struggle engendered by imperialist domination will vary historically.

The term imperialism can be used in this sense to refer to the social relations or the political order required to secure the external or global conditions for the accumulation of capital, regardless of whether the capital is itself nationally based. The necessity for imperialism arises from the inherently global conditions of possibility for the development and reproduction of capital. We can thus characterise imperialism as arising from the necessarily global, expansionary constitution of capitalism and manifest in the particular political order which develops to regulate and secure the accumulation of capital on a world scale. The specific form of imperialism is therefore not fixed – imperialism is not a trans-historical category. The particular character of imperialist forms and practices manifest in different eras must be carefully specified and explained on the basis of substantive research; they cannot be predicted in advance from theoretical definitions alone. Consequently it is also the case that the effects in societies subject to imperialism will also be varied and their particular forms must be specified in each case.

This concept of imperialism encompasses but is not restricted to the definitions or understanding developed by the classical Marxist theorists of imperialism. It foregrounds first the necessarily imperial nature of capitalism as a global system – a mode of production whose conditions of possibility are globally extended and which is inherently expansionary; and second, the historically specific forms that imperialism takes according to the historical conjuncture, co-determined by the development of capital and the conjunctural geo-political relations between states in the international system: 'Imperialism has been with us for a very long time, in great many forms, and constantly re-invents itself, so to speak, as the structure of global capitalism itself changes' (Ahmad 2004: 231). This notion of imperialism implies that while the classical Marxist theories remain important and insightful they are also to an extent historically circumscribed, and therefore not sufficient in themselves for understanding subsequent forms and developments of imperialism – hence the importance, in principle, of dependency theory, as well as theories of neo-colonialism. As Munck concluded, 'it is anachronistic for us to attempt to ground a theory of contemporary imperialism in *historically determinate* definitions relating to processes and ideologies of the early 1900s'

(1981: 167; see also Johnson, D. L. 1981: 108–9 and Ahmad 2004: 242). It is also important to remember that the classical Marxist analyses of imperialism were for the most part concerned more with the political implications of imperialism for the class struggle within Europe, in the specific context of inter-imperialist rivalry and impending war, than they were with the impoverishing effects of imperialism and the ensuing class and liberation struggles in non-European societies.

Three broad phases of imperialism in the history of capitalist development can be identified: mercantile imperialism, colonial imperialism and the latest stage which many term globalisation or empire but will be conceived here as neo-colonialism.

During the mercantile period of inter-continental trade and European expansion, the dominant classes in Europe accumulated wealth primarily by means of trade and dispossession. Merchants bought luxury goods from distant lands, purchased from the ruling or merchant classes of local societies. These were transported to growing markets elsewhere and sold at a profit. The development of mining and plantation crops in Latin America and the Caribbean, on the basis of slave labour, made the capture and selling of slaves a major branch of lucrative inter-continental 'commodity' trade. Because the source of wealth lay in the sphere of circulation, it was necessary to gain control over that process in order to secure advantage. Thus the specific mode of accumulation determined the form that imperialism necessarily took during the mercantile era. The competing interests of different European powers struggled for control and monopoly over trade routes, trade in specific goods or trade in specific regions, to secure their profits. These struggles were resolved by means of treaties, agreements, protective duties and monopolies; or through protracted wars and conflict, especially in the seas and coastal regions of the world. As Eric Williams and Du Bois emphasised, the bitter wars between the Dutch and the Portuguese, the British and the Dutch during the second half of the seventeenth century, and between Britain and France in the eighteenth century, were conflicts of rival mercantilisms, the struggle being 'fought out in the Caribbean, Africa, India, Canada and on the banks of the Mississippi, for the privilege of looting India and for the control of certain vital and strategic commodities – Negroes; sugar and tobacco; fish; furs and naval stores' (Williams, E. 1987: 40).

This mode of accumulation also determined, in a general way, the nature of effects on various societies around the world. The specifics would have to be identified in each case, but in general European merchant classes formed trading relations with the ruling classes of local societies. Particular and important patterns of social change resulted from such relations. In Africa the demand of European merchants for gold, ivory and slaves had major impacts within and between African societies. In general however the basis of local modes of production was not transformed.

Imperial relations took on a new form in the nineteenth century which was determined in part by the development of industry in Western Europe, made possible by the long period of primitive accumulation. With the development of capitalism in its classical form the technical and social organisation of production itself is reorganised according to the logic of capital, enabling accumulation of surplus-value within the sphere of production. Under these conditions advantage arises inherently from superior productivity rather than control of the process of exchange. Thus Marx observed in the nineteenth century: 'Today, industrial supremacy brings with it commercial supremacy. In the period of manufacture it is the reverse: commercial supremacy produces industrial predominance' (Marx 1867: 918). Britain, having attained naval supremacy and being the first to industrialise, enjoyed a position of inherent power during the first half of the nineteenth century, dominating the world market by virtue of its cheap manufactured goods. Britain initiated a series of international free trade treaties in the 1860s, which substantially reduced barriers of preferences and high tariffs between the leading European powers and their empires, thus allowing Britain 'freely to undersell everybody in all markets of the world' (Hobsbawm 1997: 52–3; see also Fieldhouse 1982: 177). By the second half the nineteenth century, however, other areas of Europe as well as North America were beginning to develop their industries and compete with Britain, weakening its supremacy.

The development of industry and the growing concentration and centralisation of capital generated new external needs for capital: for raw materials, for expanded markets and for new opportunities for investment. These could no longer be secured by means of the existing trading relations with foreign societies. The new expansionary requirements of industrial capital required a much more extensive reorganisation of local productive activities and capacities than hitherto. This, combined with the fact of competition between the various European powers, generated a need for control over whole territories and societies – the resources of nature and labour-power – rather than simply controlling trade at the edges and on the seas. The developing industries of nationally based capitals each needed to secure and increase their control of foreign territories in order to meet such needs. During the second half of the nineteenth century the industrialising powers of Europe rapidly sought to consolidate and expand their foreign 'possessions', laying claim between them to virtually the entire surface of the globe by the end of the century culminating in the 'scramble for Africa'. The necessity for foreign territorial occupation therefore arose both from the productive requirements of industrial capital per se, and from the requirement to keep others out. This phenomenon of inter-imperial rivalry was central to Lenin's and Bukharin's analyses of imperialism.

This new mode of capitalist accumulation based on industry thus generated new forms of imperial relations and new effects in the societies subject to imperialism. Meeting the needs of metropolitan capital, in terms of raw materials and productive investment, required a qualitatively new subordination and reorganisation of the productive activities of the conquered local societies. This in itself was necessarily resisted and the act of colonial occupation was violent, often involving long military campaigns of conquest (so-called 'pacification'). Subsequently, the task of reorganising local production in the interests of metropolitan capital required direct political control and coercion in the form of the colonial state. A social and international order of colonial imperialism emerged, with specific political, legal and ideological characteristics. The colonial social order was necessarily authoritarian and violent, and consequently was necessarily racialised (Fanon 1967b,c). The oppressive nature of the colonial social order necessitated a racialised ideology for its legitimation. The colonial ideology of European civilisation and non-European inferiority was manifest structurally not just within the colonies but in the institutions and norms of international law (Anghie 1999).

One of the most important processes of the twentieth century was the successful struggle for national liberation, whether by negotiation or armed struggle, by colonised peoples around the world. So what form does imperialism take today, in a world order no longer characterised by colonial empires but by a system of formally equal sovereign states? The current imperial order is that of the sovereignty of global capital, under the hegemony of the United States with the support of its subordinate allies, most prominent of which is the United Kingdom. A defining characteristic of the contemporary capitalist system is the separation of the political from the economic on a global scale. Ellen Meiksins Wood (1995) has shown how the development of capitalist social relations involves the shift of real social power to the 'purely economic' realm of production, and the consequent 'devaluing' of formal political equality. While the former colonies have attained formal political sovereignty and equality in the international state-system, there has been simultaneously an increasing shift of real social power to the economic realm on a global scale. After two world wars, the leading industrialised powers coordinate their interests through international institutions and regimes established to regulate the international capitalist order. These institutions are central in maintaining increasing control over the internal political and economic policies of formally sovereign states, in order to secure the global conditions for circulation and accumulation of capital. It was Kwame Nkrumah (1962, 1965) who drew attention to the multi-lateral nature of neo-colonialism. But there has been no fundamental break in the form of imperialism. The contemporary 'imperialism without colonies' (Magdoff 1978) still requires considerable political coercion and military power, in part because of the forces of resistance and reaction (whether progressive or reactionary) that any system of domination necessarily creates.

The long shift to the latest phase of imperialism was strongly resisted and contested by social forces around the world generated by the development of capitalism itself, including organised labour in the West and anti-imperialist movements for national liberation in the Third World. A second defining process of the twentieth century was the struggle against the rule of capital and attempts to create some form of socialist or communist path of development – in the USSR and the states of Eastern Europe; in China; Vietnam, Cuba, Mozambique, Angola, Nicaragua, Chile and many other countries. But, as Aijaz Ahmad (1992: 20–9) emphasises, the post-war period was also defined by the enormous growth in the productive power of capital – the remarkable development of forces of both production and destruction, and considerable concentration and centralisation of capital. The various attempts to create socialist/communist paths to development were eventually defeated by western capital's combination of superiority in routine production in the world market, and superior military might. In contrast to current notions of 'empire' as a form of decentred informal network (Hardt and Negri 2000), the concept of neo-colonialism is perhaps more appropriate. Contemporary imperialism, understood as the relations and social order through which the globally extended conditions for the circulation and accumulation of capital are secured, is no longer organised in the form of territorial colonialism but still requires significant military and political as well as economic coercion: 'through a vast network of military bases and permanently stationed naval fleets, flyovers, *in situ* "advisors," and US trained mercenaries, even this very literal imperialism of the past is wholly replicated today' (Brennan 2003: 201).

Part II

Explaining poverty

The massive presence of the past and the outside

5   The presence of the past

Slavery, colonialism and primitive accumulation

capital comes dripping from head to foot, from every pore, with blood and dirt.

(Marx 1867: 926)

In view of the present world catastrophe, I want to recall the history of Africa. I want to retell its story so far as distorted science has not concealed and lost it. I want to appeal to the past in order to explain the present. I know how unpopular this method is. What have we moderns, we wisest of the wise, to do with the dead past?

(Du Bois 1946: 80)

Whose interest does the use of a specified historical depth serve? Why is it that European scholars insist that Africans confine themselves to the post-1945 period – the so-called modern or contemporary period – while, in contrast, the British National Curriculum instructs history teachers to regard the post-1960s as current affairs?

(Amadiume 1997: 4)

Reclaiming the past

Orthodox accounts of poverty in Mozambique and Africa more generally are saturated with what Bhaskar calls 'presentism', as demonstrated in Chapter 1. The orthodox portrayal of Mozambique as an agricultural country with a population made up largely of small-scale farmers is at a fairly superficial level descriptively correct; but it is not simply descriptive. It describes in a way which silently obliterates the historicity of such a condition in the modern world. It is the very self-evidentness of this mode of characterisation which removes the need for explanation. The unspoken implication such an account articulates is that it is entirely a matter of chance, a contingent accidental fact, even normal and natural, that some countries happen to have developed a broad and deep structure of industrial production; that in some parts of the world agricultural production is carried out commercially, on a vast monocultural scale with intensive use of machinery, chemicals and hybrid seeds; whilst in other parts of the world such as Mozambique there is very little industrial development and most people are direct producers using hand tools.[1] The mis-treatment of the past is a defining feature of orthodox accounts of global poverty. History is typically either ignored or paid lip-service.

According to the linear and atomistic idea of history thus reproduced, the bottom line is that there are no causal relations between the poverty of Africa and the wealth of Europe. The incredible denial of history and global structure typical of current orthodoxies is epitomised in a recent remark made by Hilary Benn, UK Secretary of State for International Development, in the context of a discussion of 'failed states', an ideology which shares precisely these features: 'Imagine trying to pull the US or Canada out of absolute poverty without effective states to maintain law and order, promote growth and deliver services' (Benn 2004). His remark suggests that 'absolute poverty' is an original condition, and only those states with appropriate institutions and policies have been and will be able to 'pull' themselves 'out of' poverty. His remark is a condensation of the features of orthodoxy identified in the first chapter. It begs the most vital and deeply historical question: *how did certain societies get 'into' the condition of 'absolute poverty' in the first place?*

In the face of this silent obliteration of history, the 'silencing of the past' (Trouillot 1995), the long world-historical processes which have produced modern poverty in Africa must be foregrounded. This requires reconceiving the very notion of history, so as to escape from the common-sense notion of history as the chronological linear past of atomistic localised events. As Carlos Serra observes, 'things in life do not flow linearly, as phenomena following one after the other without memory of the past' (1986b: 58). Bhaskar's dialectical critical realism (1993, 1994) provides a more adequate ontological basis for conceiving of social change and possibility in time and space than the empiricism underlying orthodox accounts.[2] This is discussed here in a manner which is tentative and suggestive rather than fully worked out. A full understanding of dialectics arguably requires a wide knowledge of philosophy, and this book does not aim to engage in philosophical discussion as such, but rather to develop the implications of realist philosophy for substantive inquiry. Dialectical critical realism is difficult, the terminology complex and proliferous, and it is easy to get lost. Nevertheless it does contain significant implications for social inquiry which are well worth trying to highlight. The aim here is limited to trying to clarify some of these as they relate to the substantive concern of global poverty.

Realist ontology, including its elaboration in dialectical critical realism, provides a basis for conceiving of time, space, cause and history in a substantive way which is more adequate than the linear and atomistic assumptions underlying both orthodox academic knowledge as well as much popular discourse and common-sense. It seems to be necessary to be able to think about time, history and the past as instantiated in things and structures, rather than in terms of a one-dimensional chronological tunnel or line along which we pass steadily and against which events occur. Cause is central to realist ontology: the criterion for ascribing reality to something is causal rather than empirical, hence the ontological reality and significance of absence (Bhaskar 1993). Natural beings are characterised as the kind of things they are by their actual or potential causal powers (and one of the powers of human beings is to augment their capacities through conscious intentional action and production and self-conscious reflection). The notion of totality, understood in realist terms, refers to an entity or complex whose different parts are related internally or causally in some way. If social inquiry is to adequately grasp the ontological structure and extension of social phenomena it must apprehend their causal extension beyond empirical forms and actual events:

> To grasp totality is to break with our ordinary notions of identity, causality, space and time [...] It is to see things *existentially constituted*, and permeated, *by their relations with others*; and to see our ordinary notion of identity as an *abstraction* not only from their existentially constitutive processes of formation (geo-histories), but also from their existentially constitutive inter-activity (internal relatedness). It is to see the causality of a upon b affected by the causality of c upon d. Emergent totalities generate emergent spatio-temporalities.
>
> (Bhaskar 1993: 125)

Bertell Ollman's brilliant works on Marxist dialectics have developed the notion of internal relations as central to social and natural being and therefore to dialectical social inquiry (1993, 2003). However the realist recognition of the stratified, differentiated and open nature of the world means that we cannot assume from the outset that everything is part of a totality,[3] at least not in a sense that is useful in understanding and explaining social phenomena. These are by no means straightforward questions for social inquiry. It is not helpful simply saying 'everything is connected to everything else'; how far back in history is it necessary to look? To use Bhaskar's terminology, how can the beginning or end of a causally significant spatio-temporality or rhythmic be identified? 'When is a thing no longer a thing but something else? When has the nature, and so the explanation for the behaviour, of a (relative) continuant changed?' (Bhaskar 1993: 125). Dialectical social inquiry cannot simply *assume* totality; 'The drive to totality in science is given by the need to maximize explanatory power. But it is up to science to discover to what extent a subject-matter is internally related' (Bhaskar 1993: 123). Bhaskar therefore uses the term 'partial totality', arguing that '[i]n the social realm we are almost always concerned with partial totalities' (1993: 126).

The realist understanding of cause in terms of the real, trans-factual operation of structures in conjunctural combinations and circumstances to co-determine (co-structure or enable) outcomes is not empiricist and therefore not reducible to actual events and conjunctions or empirical action and behaviour. On this basis it is necessary to consider time and space as related and causal in a way which is not empiricist, not reducible to the realm of the actual and empirical (which is the realm of chronological time). Bhaskar captures this when he talks of time as being irreversible, and the causal extension of time, specifically of the causal presence of the past in the present. Because time, embedded or instantiated in social change and social structure, is irreversible and cumulative, it is necessary to acknowledge the present as being not wholly *pre*-determined, but in significant ways structured and circumscribed by the past. In this sense processes and events which occurred in the past might have ongoing causal efficacy in the present by making some things possible, and ruling out others.

The ontologically real understanding of time, space and possibility sheds a different light on the debates about eurocentrism discussed earlier. Brenner, Wood and Teschke are correct to insist on the historical specificity and distinctiveness of capitalist social relations; indeed this was central to Marx's account. But the rise and development of industrial capitalism in England and the rest of Europe was only possible because of relations and processes of change which took place elsewhere, in much of the rest of the world. It is in this causal sense that an account of the rise of capitalism within Europe which does not include its extended conditions of possibility is incomplete and eurocentric. Furthermore those processes were not only causally necessary for the development of capitalism in Europe, but had distinct, ongoing and cumulative causal effects far beyond Europe. An adequate explanatory account of the historical production of modern poverty in Africa must trace the emergence of the relations of European primitive accumulation, because of the profound and enduring causal effects of this historical process. In Bhaskar's terminology, primitive accumulation must surely be an 'existentially constitutive geo-historical process' (Bhaskar 1993: 139). This should not be taken as a kind of patronising argument of the form 'Africa's history has only been significant since the arrival of the Europeans'. African scholars have elaborated important criticism of approaches which examine Africa's history only in terms of European activity, even if from a critical perspective (Amadiume 1997: 4, Zeleza 2003). The common tendency to compartmentalise African history into pre-colonial, colonial and post-colonial 'subtly reinforces the view that dynamic movement in African history started with colonialism, that the multitude of generations that lived before the Berlin Conference were preparing for this great moment' (Zeleza 2003: 104). However the aim here is not to provide a historical account per se, but to provide an explanatory account of the making of contemporary poverty in Africa. In short, it is not possible to fully comprehend or account for the condition of modern poverty in Africa – or the condition of modern affluence in the West – without reference to the processes of European primitive accumulation, especially the trans-Atlantic slave economy and colonialism. The concern of this chapter is to trace some of the necessary causal relations between the internationally structured primitive accumulation over centuries which enabled the rise of capitalism and industry in Europe, and the structural impoverishment of African societies, with reference to the region of Southern Africa which constitutes contemporary Mozambique.

Slavery and primitive accumulation in Africa and Europe

> There can be little doubt but that in the fourteenth century the level of culture in black Africa south of the Sudan was equal to that of Europe and was so recognized. There is even less doubt but that Negroid influence in the valley of the Nile was a main influence in Egypt's development from 2100 to 1600 BC; while in East, South, and West Africa human culture had from 1600 BC to AD 1500 its monuments of a vigorous past and a growing future. What changed all this? What killed the Sudanese empires,

brought anarchy into the valley of the Nile, decimated the thick populations of East and Central Africa, and pressed the culture of West Africa beneath the ruthless heel of the rising European culture?

(Du Bois 1946: 44–5)

In the fifteenth century the regions of the Americas, Europe and Africa were not markedly different in terms of levels of socio-economic development (Abu-Lughod 1989, Wolf 1997 chapter 2). Within and between each region, more or less extensive networks of long-distance trade had emerged. North Africa was integrated in regional trade networks centred on the Mediterranean. Societies along the coast of East Africa were integrated into the substantial trade networks around the Indian Ocean (Wolf 1997: 41–4). Long-distance trade networks linked regional economies within Africa, in particular the trans-Sahara network (Niane 1984b). Within Africa, as in Europe, a variety of forms of socio-economic systems and political structures existed, ranging from large centralised states, kingdoms or empires to smaller decentralised societies. In Africa as in Europe and elsewhere, there was considerable variation in regional patterns of economic activity, settlement and population density. Across Africa, as in Europe and elsewhere, societies practised a variety of economic activities, including mining, iron work, pottery, cloth production, cultivation and livestock rearing, local, regional and long-distance trade.[4]

Prior to the impact of mercantile capital the social formations in the part of Africa which is now Mozambique consisted of various forms of clan-, lineage- or state-based societies, with different forms of hierarchical structure of social power. These societies practised various forms of agricultural production, cultivating cereals and keeping cattle (in areas not affected by tse-tse fly); in addition fishing and hunting were practised regularly and formed an important contribution to the diet.[5] Different forms and combinations of agricultural and pastoral production varied across ecological zones. Artisanal craft production such as pottery, carpentry, weaving, brick making, metal work and salt production were practised, to varying degrees of frequency and development according to environmental conditions. In some areas cotton cloth was produced, though this was not widespread. These activities were organised on the basis of family groupings and lineages. The division of labour was organised mainly according to sex and age. In general, family lineage groups were headed by chiefs or other forms of rulers (mainly men) with political, juridical and religious authority. They had authority over various social and economic matters including marriage relations and division of land (which was distributed according to need for use, not in the form of alienable property); and also relations with other groups, whether through trade or conflict. They did not usually engage directly in production, receiving tributes in the form of agricultural, craft and symbolic goods, as well as labour. Inherent to the reproduction of the structure of social power by such material means were ideas, beliefs, customs and rituals relating to the natural environment, spirits and ancestors.

Differences in the form of social and political organisation, language and culture existed and developed according to various influences including ecological conditions and productive activities, commercial exchange, migration and conflict. In certain areas forms of centralised state became established, though this was not generalised throughout the region; these included the State of Zimbabwe (~1250–1450) and the Muenemutapa State which dominated a large region extending between the Zambezi and Limpopo rivers from the mid-fifteenth to the end of the seventeenth centuries (Mar 1975: 16–23, Universidade Eduardo Mondlane 1988a: 61–73). Agricultural surpluses, and craft products including iron and copper items, skins, ivory and salt were exchanged with other social groups, both local and distant. Societies along the east coast of Africa entered into trade relationships with foreign traders from as early as the tenth century (Sutton 1972, Devisse and Labib 1984). These were mainly Arab, Indian and Chinese traders,[6] and later Portuguese at the end of the fifteenth century. The permanent settlement of people originating in the Persian Gulf increased progressively along the eastern coast of Africa between the ninth and thirteenth centuries, their presence extending from Mogadishu in Somalia to Sofala in Mozambique (Boxer 1969, Alpers 1975: 4, Serra 1986b: 11). Trading posts were established on islands and sheltered points of the coast, for example at Lamu, Mombassa, Zanzibar, the Mafia Islands, Kilwa, Kisiwani, the Kerimba Islands, Ilha de Moçambique, Angoche, Sofala, Quelimane. These facilitated the considerable system of maritime trade between Africa, the Persian Gulf and India, made possible by the patterns of wind characteristic of the air-masses of the West Indian Ocean: 'it was the mastery of the monsoons and their associated currents which enabled the Arab and Indian traders of the Western Indian Ocean to come to East Africa in order to exploit its natural resources' (Alpers 1975: 2; see also Devisse and Labib 1984: 655). The main items exchanged were gold and other metals, sandalwood and ivory from Africa, in exchange for cloth from India and porcelain and silk from China. In addition to the Arab-Swahili groups, communities of Indians became established along the African coast.

At the end of the fifteenth century the process of European expansion initiated a new era in which societies in different parts of the world came to be connected in qualitatively new and irreversible ways which causally linked processes of social change in disparate regions of the world. The period spanning the 1490s to the 1850s was the era of mercantile accumulation. European merchant capital became increasingly dominant throughout the world, with major effects on societies in Africa, the Americas and Europe. This was also an era which gave rise to the emergence and consolidation of exclusionary, divisive and racialised ideologies about different peoples, religions and cultures, arising from the encounters between Europeans and non-Europeans in the Americas and Africa, as well as the changing dynamics of relations between Europeans and Moslem Arabs with the rise of the Ottoman Empire which on both sides generated mutually reinforcing ideologies about the difference between Europeans and non-Europeans (Kasaba 1992).[7]

European expansion and the trans-Atlantic slave system

The main dimensions of early European expansion in the fifteenth century were the development of slave-based sugar production on the Atlantic islands of

Madeira, the Canary Islands, Cape Verde and São Tomé by the Portuguese, using slaves from West Africa; the expansion of Portuguese merchants along the West African coast and beyond developing trade in gold, ivory, spices and slaves; and finally the arrival of the Spanish and Portuguese in the Americas at the end of the century. This historical era is popularly known and celebrated as 'the age of discoveries'. It should be emphasised that for the most part the Portuguese did not 'discover' previously unchartered sea-routes nor previously unknown lands.[8] The very notion of European explorers discovering *peoples* was central to the racist ideology of European supremacy which legitimised the brutal treatment of non-European peoples over centuries. Thus Mozambican scholar Eli Mar relates 'according to the lessons we were given by the Portuguese colonists in primary school, we, the Mozambicans, were discovered by Vasco da Gama and his flottila at the end of the fifteenth century' (1975: 12). As he emphasises, the term 'discover' is appropriate when describing advances in the natural sciences, but when discussing peoples a more suitable term would be encounter. 'What for example would be the reaction of Germans, if we wrote that they had been discovered by Italians or by Turks, or that the Dutch were discovered by the Spanish?' (Mar 1975: 13). Roland Wright records the same reaction on the other side of the Atlantic: a traditional chief of the Onondaga Iroquois told him 'You cannot discover an inhabited land. Otherwise I could cross the Atlantic and "discover" England' (Wright 2000: 5). Trouillot's discussion (1995: 108–40) reveals powerfully that this is no mere semantic dispute: 'To call "discovery" the first invasions of inhabited lands by Europeans is an exercise in Eurocentric power that already frames future narratives of the event so described' (Trouillot 1995: 114).

The reasons for European expansion were numerous. Eric Wolf (1997: 108–9) attributes it to a crisis of feudalism in Europe, when the rate of growth of surplus-production slowed down, and increasing local resistance to further exploitation necessitated a turn towards external sources for the wealth necessary to maintain political and military power. The growing military and economic strength of the early Ottoman Empire, manifest in the capture of Constantinople in 1453, disrupted the eastern Mediterranean commerce, compelling expansion to the West and along the shores of the Atlantic (Sued-Badillo 1992: 76, Wolf 1997: 204). One of the main reasons for Portuguese exploration around the coast of West Africa was to gain control of trade in gold (Boxer 1961, Pinto and Carreira 1979, Devisse and Labib 1984, Oyebade 2000: 420). Until the Portuguese and Spanish 'stumbled on' the Americas (Trouillot 1995: 115), Africa was Europe's main source of gold. Referring specifically to Portuguese expansion in the mid- to late 1400s, the historian Charles Boxer notes the serious shortage of precious metals in Western Europe in general and Portugal in particular. This shortage resulted from falling production of gold and silver in central European mines, and the 'drain' of these metals to the East to pay for spices and other imports. Between 1387 and 1416 the price of gold in Portugal rose by 12 per cent (Devisse and Labib 1984: 661). Boxer suggests that this is one reason for the Portuguese quest across the Sahara, to seize Cueta in 1415 and secure a route to the gold-producing regions of the Upper Niger and Senegal rivers (Boxer 1961: 6–9). Blackburn notes that the Spanish and Portuguese monarchs were 'perennially short of cash' after the Reconquest of the Iberian peninsula from the Muslims that required agreements with the military aristocracy and the Church for payment and tax exemption in return for their support, which helps to explain 'the characteristic thirst for specie of the Iberian monarchs, and their willingness to consider money-making projects of exploration and colonization' (Blackburn 1997: 98; see also Pagden 1995: 66–7). Another important factor was the significant chronic shortage of grain in Portugal, prompting expansion to the fertile corn-growing hinterland of Cueta (Boxer 1961: 6–9, Birmingham 1993: 25) and the hope of large-scale production of wheat, vines and sugarcane in the Atlantic islands (Devisse and Labib 1984: 662).

The Portuguese first arrived in Mozambique in 1498 (Serra 1986b: 19, Birmingham 1993: 28), en-route to India. The Portuguese were able to continue round to India and China by benefiting from the navigational knowledge and techniques developed from the thirteenth to fifteenth centuries by Arab, Mediterranean and Chinese sailors (Devisse and Labib 1984: 655–6). Vasco da Gama, who had rounded the Cape of Good Hope and reached Malindi, was guided by the famous Arab pilot Ahmad-Ibn-Madjid to Calicut, 'the major emporium of the pepper trade on the Malabar Coast' (Boxer 1961: 13–14, Devisse and Labib 1984: 659). Having established the sea-route between Europe and Asia they sought to develop and protect the important trade in spices and other goods (Boxer 1969 chapters 1 and 2). The coastline of Mozambique was important to the Portuguese for two main reasons: first because of the strategic importance of the Ilha de Moçambique on the route to India. The Portuguese built fortified posts along the route at key points such as Ilha de Moçambique, Sofala and Mombassa. They established a colonial city at Goa in India and a trading post at Macau in China in order to organise and retain monopoly over the lucrative trans-continental spice trade, which they succeeded in doing for about 100 years owing to their superior gun-bearing ships (Boxer 1961: 14–16, Birmingham 1993: 28; Wolf 1997: 235–6). Second the Portuguese bought gold and ivory, brought to the coast from further inland, in order to trade in India for spices, which they would take back to sell in Europe in exchange for metals, textiles, cereals, navigation instruments and other items required to maintain the social power of both Lisbon and the empire more broadly (Serra 1986b: 26; see also Boxer 1969, Newitt 1973: 32, Wolf 1997: 44).

During this period Portuguese and other European, Indian and Arab peoples were present in Mozambique primarily as traders, situated mainly along the coastal strip, around the trading posts of Ilha de Moçambique, Quelimane, Inhambane, and the Maputo bay further south, and along the Zambezi valley. Relations of exchange with foreign traders were controlled by the dominant classes of the local societies – the various chiefs, heads of lineages and states. The impact of mercantile capital on societies in the region of Mozambique and throughout Africa was manifest in three general and related forms. First, production for exchange gradually acquired increased importance over production for local use, generating intensification of certain production practices. The basic organisation of local production remained essentially the same, but as trade increased the demands for surpluses and products such as gold grew, necessitating the intensification of these activities within overall social production. Second, this created increased levels of exploitation by the local ruling classes, in order to ensure increased production of the items required for external exchange. The local ruling classes organised and controlled the activities of gold mining, hunting elephants and rhinoceros and, later, slaves. The power of the local ruling classes came increasingly to depend upon control of external trade relations and extractive activities, and the consequent accumulation of weapons and symbols of prestige such as cloth and jewellery; this necessitated an intensification of relations of exploitation within local societies. Third, struggles between different social groups and factions increased, resulting in changing conflicts and alliances between different local and foreign groups contending for control over lucrative trade and exchange. The connections, alliances and conflicts between local ruling classes and foreign traders were all ultimately determined and driven by efforts to control and profit from trade in ivory, gold, slaves and other goods. Exchange took place 'at the edge' of the local societies, controlled by the dominant classes. The power of the dominant classes was increased through control of this trade: the power of the Chona ruling classes, which extended over a large area south of the Zambezi river, was enhanced by control of the export of gold; while further north the leaders of the Marave state controlled the trade in ivory (Universidade Eduardo Mondlane 1988a: 75).

This long period of mercantile accumulation constituted the first phase of insertion of the region of contemporary Mozambique into the emerging global economy. The processes of social change which took place during this period in Mozambique and the rest of Africa were conditioned by the general global process of expansion of European mercantile capital, which came to be centred on slave-based production and commerce in the Americas.

There has been a long debate over the actual numbers of Africans exported to the Americas during the slave trade.[9] Conservative estimates based on available records have concluded the figure is at least 13 million; Inikori judges that when allowance is made for missing and incomplete records, a realistic estimate is 15.4 million (2000: 391). This figure does not include the numbers killed in Africa in the process of hunting and capturing people, taking them to the coast for export into slavery:

> the processes leading to the export of those numbers – the wars, raids and other methods of slave gathering; the long march to the coast; the 'warehousing' of slaves on the coast awaiting shipment; the long keeping of slaves in ship holds before the vessels actually departed the African coast with their full cargoes – involved population losses that probably have been far in excess of the numbers actually exported.
>
> (Inikori 1979: 68)

The demographic impact was thus significant, in particular in Central Africa where it was devastating (Inikori 2000: 409). The demographic impact was far more than a simple numerical loss, because of the undermining of processes of social reproduction caused by slave-hunting. Although it is exceedingly difficult to provide some kind of counter-factual quantification of demographic impact, Inikori emphasises the significance of the fact that 'from 1500 to 1870, the growth of the African population lagged far behind that of any other continent during the same period' (1979: 70). The effects of the slave trade on socio-economic and political forms and processes in Africa included a decline in the range of productive activities such as iron production. This resulted on one hand from the fall in population and the generalised insecurity caused by slave-hunting; on the other hand from the time, resources and energy devoted to hunting slaves. The slave trade generated increased militarisation of socio-political structures and increased levels of conflict, using firearms supplied by European slave merchants. It led to the fragmentation and collapse of existing states, especially in Central and Southern Africa, such as the Kingdoms of Kongo, Muenemutapa and Ndongo (da Costa, A. N. 1982, Hilton 1985, Oyebade 2000: 423), and the rise of new military states and political classes based on slave trade and warfare, such as the *Ceddo* regimes in Senegambia, West Africa and the Yao in Southern Africa (Alpers 1969, 1975, Ishemo 1995, Barry 1998). Thus over several centuries the slave trade had major negative effects on socio-economic relations and conditions in Africa. It was above all a fundamentally parasitic process, detrimental to the progressive development of local productive forces and local economies. Boubacar Barry's conclusion with regard to the Kindgom of Waalo in West Africa has resonance throughout the continent:

> It is incontrovertible that Europe, by introducing the slave as a means of exchange, maintained the trade and thereby generalized slave raiding and the manhunt to the great detriment of the development of the forces of production. It matters little what was the exact toll in terms of human exports, when one realizes that for centuries the slave trade created an atmosphere of insecurity, incessant raids, and wars and caused misery and famine.
>
> (Barry 1979: 48)

The demand for slaves became significant in Mozambique only from the middle of the eighteenth century, later than on the west coast of Africa, although some trade in slaves had been carried out earlier. As José Capela has recorded in detail, the Portuguese first began exporting slaves from the west coast of Africa in the fifteenth century, destined mainly for Europe where there was a shortage of labour (Capela 1978, Pinto and Carreira 1979: 119–20, Sued-Badillo 1992: 77). Trade in slaves became a major activity with the development of sugar plantations first in Madeira (colonised in 1425), the Canaries, and Cape Verde, then São Tomé and finally Brazil in the sixteenth century: '[t]he Portuguese, disappointed at getting little gold, most of which remained in the hands of the Muslims in the north and east, rapidly reduced Africa to a single role – that of supplying manpower' (Devisse and Labib 1984: 664). Sugar had been introduced into Europe by the Arabs but was still rare; the development of sugar plantations using African slave-labour on the Atlantic islands paved the way for the subsequent production of sugar in the Americas and the trans-Atlantic slave trade (Pinto and Carreira 1979: 120). Between 1450 and 1500 the Portuguese captured around 150,000 Africans for export as slaves; during the first half of the seventeenth century around 200,000 slaves were sent to Brazil (Capela 1978: 113, 144). Slaves were exported mainly from the west coast of Africa – Guinea Bissau, the Congo and Angola. The greater distance around the coast defended Mozambique from 'this great human haemorrhage' (Capela 1978: 145) until 1645, when slaves were exported from Mozambique to Brazil following the Dutch capture of Angola in 1641. From then, between four and five thousand slaves were exported annually from Mozambique (Capela 1978, and Universidade Eduardo Mondlane 1988a: 99–100). The demand for slaves from Mozambique and the east coast of Africa increased in the middle of the eighteenth century with the development of French sugar plantations on the islands of the Indian Ocean. Between the 1770s and the 1790s the demand for and price of slaves rose considerably (Alpers 1975), and 'in each decade from the 1730s to the end of the slave trade they never exported fewer than 120,000 slaves from Central Africa and Mozambique, and the number from this area exceeded 180,000 in the last decade of the century' (Wolf 1997: 201).

In the early nineteenth century efforts were made by the British to put an end to the slave trade. The humanitarians' call to abolish slavery and the slave trade had gained the support of the industrialists in Britain (see Williams, E. 1987). With the development of manufacturing and industry in Britain, the old sugar monopolies were no longer in the interests of the dominant capitalist classes. Competition between the various sugar-producing economies was such that the old monopolies which sustained the slave-based plantation economies and hence the slave trade posed increasing constraints on England's rising industrial bourgeoisie, and the producers in the American colonies. The campaign for abolition, though dressed in a 'humanitarian cloak', was ultimately a campaign against the West Indian monopolies rather than slavery as such, as Eric Williams documented (Williams, E. 1987). The abolition campaign was therefore aimed primarily at specific regions of slavery and specific areas of slave import and export, focusing mainly on the slave centres of the West coast of Africa. In 1815 Portugal successfully negotiated the annulment of the previous agreement to abolish all trade in slaves; from then on prohibition only applied north of the Equator, exempting Brazil's trade with Angola, the Congo and Mozambique (Pinto and Carreira 1979: 132). In East Africa the slave trade continued to grow: 'All along the coast the demand for slaves steadily mounted, as Arabs, Brazilians, French, Spanish slavers from Cuba, and Americans discovered East Africa in the wake of the British anti-slave trade campaigns in West Africa' (Alpers 1975: 209; see also Inikori 2000: 391). The following observation was made by Captain W. F. Owen during his voyage along the East African coast in 1822–23:

> Quilimane is now the greatest mart for slaves on the east coast. They are purchased with blue dungaree, coloured cloths, arms, gunpowder, brass and pewter, red coloured beads in imitation of coral, cutlery, and various articles.

The free blacks of the country and banyans [Indians] carry on the trade inland for the merchants: and the arrival of one of these people among the tribes with his pedlar's stock is the signal for the general warfare when the weak become the victim of the strong. From eleven to fourteen slave-vessels come annually from Rio de Janeiro to this place, and return with from four to five hundred slaves each on an average. To contain the slaves collected for sale every Portuguese house has an extensive yard or enclosure, called a Barracon, generally surrounded by a lofty brick wall.

(Owen 1833: 292–3 cited in 1976a: 6, 1976b: 14)

Annual exports of slaves from Mozambique rose to around 20,000 in 1820 and reached a peak of over 30,000 in 1828 and 1829, in anticipation of a treaty with Brazil to abolish the trade in slaves (Newitt 1995: 250–1; see also Universidade Eduardo Mondlane 1988a: 102). Despite the eventual legal abolition in 1842, clandestine slave exports continued for many years, although on a reduced scale (Beachey 1976b: 15–25, Capela 1978, Pinto and Carreira 1979, Serra 1986b: 29).

The hunting and capture of slaves was concentrated in particular in the north of Mozambique (Alpers 1975 chapter 7, Universidade Eduardo Mondlane 1988a). In 1787 the Portuguese legalised the sale of guns, and thus

the hunting of men became generalised [. . .] Throughout the whole of the 19th century the political and economic panorama of the north of Mozambique was completely dominated by the capture, transport, marketing and export of slaves. The populations of origin Macua-Lomue were the main sacrifices. In this vast region, hundreds of thousands of defenceless victims were relentlessly pursued by the dominant classes of the Afro-Islamic coastal kingdoms, the Ajaua States on the Niassa plateau, the Macua kings and by Portuguese and Indian etc. traders. Dozens of thousands of Macua were exported to the Islands of Mascarenhas, Madagascar, Zanzibar, the Persian Gulf, Brazil and Cuba.

(Universidade Eduardo Mondlane 1988a: 102)

This final phase of the mercantile period had important effects on the local societies to a far greater extent than the trade in ivory and gold (see Serra 1986b chapter 3). New political structures and state forms emerged, arising from the organisation of hunting and selling slaves, controlled mainly by the local ruling classes, in particular the rulers of the Makua and Yao peoples in the north (see Ishemo 1995 chapter 1, Universidade Eduardo Mondlane 1988a chapter 6, Alpers 1975 chapter 7, Alpers 1969). Conflicts between local groups increased as they competed for the control over slave hunting, which was exacerbated and promoted by the Portuguese who profited from the slaves: 'the Portuguese slave trading in Central and East Africa resulted in the regions being ravaged by warfare arising from the demand for slaves to work in the Brazilian cane plantations' (Oyebade 2000: 423; see also Capela 1978, Universidade Eduardo Mondlane 1988a: 103). The long period of slave hunting led to more isolated and dispersed patterns of settlement, and considerable local migration, as people retreated into small groups and more remote areas for protection (Alpers 1975: 5, Serra 1986a: 98, Ishemo 1995: 23). Perhaps the major impact, however, was the significant depletion in the population caused by the slave trade, with some areas in the north of Mozambique experiencing total depopulation (Ishemo 1995: 23–4). The loss of the most active adults undermined the productive activities of those remaining, required for basic social reproduction, and the disruption of agricultural production caused by slave raids caused severe famine in the 1860s (Ishemo 1995: 23).

International trade, slavery and the development of capitalism in Europe

The processes of European primitive accumulation created a trans-Atlantic economic system which must be seen as a dynamic, structured totality, with differentiated relations and effects in the regions of Africa, the Americas and Europe. The parasitic political economies centred on slave-hunting and export in Africa, slave-based production in Latin America, the Caribbean and the southern states of North America, and the emergence of capitalism and industry in western Europe are each partial totalities causally connected by the processes of European mercantile accumulation through trans-Atlantic overseas trade. The history of slave-based production in the Americas is a major topic which lies beyond the scope of this study. The third side of the history of primitive accumulation is the rise of capitalism and industry in Western Europe, centred initially on the industrial revolution in England.

The necessity and significance of Africa for the development of Europe was first emphasised early in the twentieth century by W. E. B. Du Bois (1896, 1946), C. L. R. James (1938), Wilson Williams, a graduate student at Howard University (Williams, W. E. 1936, cited in Inikori 2002: 2), and above all by Eric Williams in his seminal *Capitalism and Slavery* (Williams, E. 1987, first published in 1944). The question has since been confirmed and further elaborated by others, above all the major work of Jospeh Inikori. On the basis of decades of meticulous and rigorous research, Inikori has firmly demonstrated the major significance of overseas trade with the slave-based economies of the Atlantic for the development of capitalism and industry in England and the rest of Europe. His work emphasises the emergence of the Atlantic world as a connected totality in which the histories of Western Europe, the Americas and Africa are necessarily connected by three and a half centuries of slave-based production and commerce (Inikori 2002: 156–8).

The colonisation of the Americas by Spain and Portugal in the sixteenth century, and later by France, Britain and the Netherlands in the seventeenth century, led to the emergence of a new Atlantic economic system in which export production in the Americas was central. The goods acquired or produced for export included gold and silver, sugar, cocoa, cotton, coffee, leather, tobacco, rubber, with sugar becoming the central product by the seventeenth century (for detailed analysis see Inikori 2002: 164–82). Inikori has conducted a detailed and extensive review of available research to estimate annual value of exports from the Americas to Europe from the sixteenth to nineteenth centuries (see Table 5.1).

Table 5.1 Annual value (f.o.b.) of export production in the Americas, 1501–1850

Years	£
1501–50	1,286,000
1551–1600	3,764,000
1601–50	6,268,000
1651–70	7,970,000
1711–60	14,142,000
1761–80	21,903,000
1781–1800	39,119,000
1848–50	89,204,000

Source: Adapted from Inikori 2002: 181.

The labour-power employed in the production of these export goods consisted mainly of African slaves transported from Africa (Inikori 2002: 183–96). The local populations of the Americas were initially coerced into labouring for the European colonisers but this soon proved unsustainable, mainly because of the drastic decimation of the local population as a result of European colonisation. The vast majority – around 95 per cent – of the native populations in the Americas had been exterminated within a few generations of European invasions as a result of the dynamic combination of military assault and disease (Ortiz 1992, Stannard 1992). Thereafter expanding production of commodities for export required expanding supplies of slaves from Africa. As the table indicates, slave-based production expanded explosively during the late eighteenth and early nineteenth centuries: '[i]n matters of export production for Atlantic commerce, the Americas were indeed an extension of Africa in 1650–1850' (Inikori 2002: 197).

The expanding trans-Atlantic commerce centred on slave-based production in the Americas was integrally related to the growth of intra-European trade, the commercialisation of social life and the development of industry in Western Europe from the sixteenth to nineteenth centuries (Inikori 2002: 203–14). European expansion and inter-continental trade was characterised by bitter rivalry among the European powers. These rivalries were initially mediated by the authority of the Catholic Church. The Papacy granted exclusive rights, privileges and duties to the Portuguese and Spanish monarchs to conquer and convert non-European (non-Christian) peoples and lands, derived from a series of Bulls and Briefs between 1456 and 1514 (Boxer 1969: 228–9). The division of the 'undiscovered' non-European world between the Crowns of Portugal (Brazil, Africa and Asia) and Spain (the rest of the Americas) was granted by Papal Bull *Inter Caetera* of Pope Alexander VI in 1493, and then renegotiated by the Iberian monarchs at the Treaty of Tordesillas in 1494. The authority of this decree was challenged by the Grotian doctrine of international law which proclaimed the freedom of the seas for all European powers (Pagden 1995: 48–9, Blackburn 1997: 187–93), and challenged in practice by the Dutch, British and French. The

Portuguese succeeded in retaining control of the trade in spices and slaves for most of the sixteenth century, despite the efforts of French and British. During the 60 years of Spanish rule in Portugal (1580–1640), efforts by other European powers to undermine Portuguese and Spanish supremacy in Atlantic commerce developed from sporadic attacks to international conflict (Pinto and Carreira 1979: 127–8), in particular between Portugal and the Netherlands: 'competition in international trade in Western Europe of the seventeenth and eighteenth centuries was, for all practical purposes, hardly distinguishable from war' (Inikori 2002: 253–4). During the eighteenth century the British and French gained influence, with Britain eventually coming to dominate the trans-Atlantic trade in slaves and the slave-based production in the Americas, as a result of war and diplomacy. Although the European powers practised mercantilist protection policies in Europe, commerce in the Atlantic basin functioned as a quasi-common market (Inikori 2002: 203–14). Britain gained most from this system, having gained naval supremacy and commercial advantage over Spain and Portugal. The Spanish and Portuguese, although the main intermediaries of the emergent trans-Atlantic economic system in the sixteenth and seventeenth centuries, 'reaped few of its benefits. The economies of these over-extended states were so weakened that they had to pass most of the American silver they acquired on to the Dutch and German bankers to whom they were heavily indebted' (Kasaba 1992: 10).

The participation of British merchants in buying, transporting and selling slaves from Africa to the Americas stimulated the production of export commodities required by the trade (Inikori 2002: 405–72), and the development of shipping services and the ship-building industry, both of which stimulated the development of coal and iron production, iron smelting and metal industries, in particular the production of iron nails, manufacture of guns, production of special copper and brass goods for the slave trade and slave vessels (Inikori 2002: 265–313). The slave trade stimulated the growth of financial institutions (banking, discount houses, the stock exchange, insurance and credit) to meet the particular credit and insurance needs of long-distance and long-duration, highly risky trade which eventually brought high profits; the development of financial institutions was further stimulated by the commercial wars for control of the Atlantic slave economy. The role of financial institutions in providing credit was significant in enabling the industrial revolution (Inikori 2002: 314–61). The expansion and industrialisation of textile manufacturing, which was at the centre of the industrial revolution, rested on overseas trade for the raw materials – raw cotton, wool, silk, flax, gums, indigo and other dyestuffs – the majority of which came from the Americas (Inikori 2002: 362–404). The expanding Atlantic markets were the major stimulus for the growth of the main sectors of Britain's manufacturing in the industrial revolution (Inikori 2002: 405–72). The industrial development of Western Europe and North America was thus integrally linked to and enabled by the enormous growth in international trade centred on African slavery in the Americas and the trans-Atlantic slave trade.

The analysis offered here does not constitute an empiricist 'see-saw' analysis of development and underdevelopment (cf. Harrison 1988: 97 cited in Chapter 2).

Rather it has traced in outline the differentiated but internally related processes of socio-economic change over centuries in Africa and Europe, centred causally on the emergence and growth of slave-based production in the Americas. This trans-Atlantic economic system enabled the accumulation which resulted in the industrial revolution in England, while producing a range of destructive and sometimes devastating effects on societies and productive activities across Africa. The emergence of industrial capitalism in Europe gave rise to new expansionary tendencies which eventually heralded a new and much more direct form of European involvement in and exploitation of Africa, in the form of direct colonial conquest.

The impetus behind European expansion in the nineteenth century, deriving from the development of industrial capitalism, was different from that during the mercantile period. In Africa in particular, the need was no longer for slaves, or commodities such as ivory and gold bought from local societies. The European bourgeoisie sought raw materials for their developing industries, opportunities to invest in production, and opportunities to sell their manufactured commodities. Rising competition between the developing industrial powers was manifest in all areas of the world market. During the nineteenth century the competing needs for expansion on the part of national capitals drove the different European powers to seek to consolidate their control over existing foreign territories and acquire new 'possessions' – the British in India and the settler colonies of Australia and New Zealand, the French in Indo-China, the Dutch in the East Indies (Indonesia). This expansion increased towards the end of the nineteenth century. Expeditions of 'explorers' and scientists set out, under the auspices of Geography and Philanthropic Associations, to discover the material potential of the interior of lands which so far had only been penetrated in coastal regions. During this period great commercial companies emerged, such as the British South Africa Company. Gold and diamonds were discovered in South Africa; Cecil Rhodes set out his grand project for supremacy at a continental scale, while Portugal pursued ideas about a 'rose-coloured map' of the Portuguese empire extending across Southern Africa from the Atlantic to the Indian Ocean (Nowell 1982). In addition to all-powerful Britain, other European powers started to expand: Belgium laid claim to Congo, and Germany seized possession of the strategic coastal regions of Namibia and Tanganyika. The ensuing tensions prompted the organisation of the Berlin Conference in 1884–85. Britain, France, Germany, Belgium, Portugal and other European countries, as well as America, met in Berlin to agree on the territorial division of the continent by means of peaceful negotiation, so as to avoid military conflict between the European powers. One of the principles agreed upon at the Berlin Conference was the need for 'effective occupation' of colonial territories, in both military and economic terms.

Colonial rule, metropolitan accumulation and the impoverishment of African societies

Colonial imperialism was a necessary and integral relation of a particular phase of capitalist development in Europe. Colonial occupation enabled new forms of primitive accumulation on the part of European capital. The historical and irreducible specificity of the phenomenon of colonialism must be recognised. The nature of the colonial social and international order are of major significance for understanding a range of conditions in contemporary Africa and contemporary international relations, but are overlooked in much Africanist, Development Studies, Political Science and International Relations literature. The racialised, violent and profoundly authoritarian nature of the colonial social order, and the specific policies of constructing rigid ethnic identities, have had lasting legacies and are important for understanding contemporary conflicts and tensions. The rise of authoritarian regimes across Africa after independence has to be understood in part in terms of the legacy of the authoritarian and violent nature of colonial rule. On the terrain of international relations, modern post-war development policy can only be adequately understood if situated in the context of the previous ideologies of colonial policy, including the emergence of colonial welfare and development policies from the 1920s. The post-independence crisis of African economies cannot be understood without analysis of their structural position in the international division of labour as a result of colonial rule.

Colonial conquest and rule constituted a rupture in the history of African societies, as Amílcar Cabral emphasised. The particular focus here is the way in which colonial accumulation rested on the exploitation of the African population, producing systematic and structural impoverishment of African societies. The following analysis elaborates some of the details, with regard to Mozambique, of a much more general process and condition.

As a colonial power, Portugal was subordinate to her other European rivals. Portugal was far less economically advanced than other European powers, but the loss of her empire in Latin America in the nineteenth century compelled her to turn to Africa and consolidate her old mercantile empire, protecting its claims from the encroachment of other European powers. Portuguese expansion into the interior of Mozambique began in the last decade of the nineteenth century, and was achieved only after long and difficult military campaigns to conquer local societies lasting into the 1930s. The particular conditions in Portugal meant that for the following three decades, until the rise of Salazar, most of the capital invested in Mozambique was of international origin – French, British, Swiss, South African and German. This took the form of investment in plantations and infrastructure; speculative purchase of the rights to vast tracts of land under concessions; and, in the neighbouring territories of South Africa and Rhodesia, considerable investment in mineral development. In addition to the local investment of productive capital, commercial capital continued to trade in the various commodities produced by the Mozambican peoples and required by European industries – oilseeds, rubber, copra and sisal. Such trade had existed for centuries, but was now subordinated to the requirements of industrial capital in Europe (Serra 1980).

The last decades of the nineteenth century and the early years of the twentieth century were characterised, in Portugal, by a series of conflicts and swings between the republican and monarchist ruling classes. Portuguese society was still made up of a mass of rural peasants and agricultural labourers, urban professional and merchant classes, the land-owning nobility and a small manufacturing industrial sector. In 1910 the monarchy was overthrown by the middle ranks of the army and Portugal was declared a republic (Birmingham 1993: 147). This process did not involve radical social change in Portuguese society. The middle-class leadership was soon replaced by an upper class republican government led by Afonso Costa, who reduced the role of the church, separating the church and state, and tried to reduce the public debt. Under such policies there were insufficient resources to meet the rising expectations for change among the proletariat. Close links were retained with Britain, whose support was seen as necessary to protect the colonies in Africa from German encroachment. This led to Portugal's entering the First World War in 1917, which bankrupted the economy. Portugal's economic crisis of the post-war years led to a military coup led by ultra-Catholic city of Braga in 1926 (Birmingham 1993: 152). António Salazar became Minister of Finance in 1928, and Prime Minister in 1932. The initial liberal reforms undertaken by the bourgeois monarchy of the previous century were replaced by a repressive autocratic oligarchy (Birmingham 1993).

Salazar's regime emerged in the context of the world depression of 1929–33. World trade fell by 60 per cent in four years, between 1929 and 1932 (Hobsbawm 1995: 94). The crisis of the US economy spread throughout the industrialising world, commodity prices collapsed, trade slumped and unemployment rose to dramatic proportions. This forced Portugal, in common with the rest of the world, to become economically more self-reliant. Previous policies of economic liberalism and free trade were abandoned, and the United States and Europe all sought to protect their economies. Salazar's policies of economic nationalism were thus similar to those adopted throughout the advanced capitalist powers of the world; however, the strategy of the *Estado Novo* was also a response to the particular conditions of Portugal. Since the fifteenth century the Portuguese social formation had been dominated by the land-owning and merchant classes. The fruits of mercantile trade and colonial pillage enabled a process of acquisition of land by the nobility, who retained a practical monopoly of overseas trade, with the king periodically redistributing wealth and privilege among the land-owning classes (Godinho 1971, da Costa, I. N. 1987: 8). As a result the economy was heavily dependent on imported manufactured goods and wheat, and dominated by foreign capital. The basic aim of Salazar's regime was to transform Portugal's society and economy away from its largely agrarian and trade-based character heavily dependent on foreign imports, by forcibly hastening the development of industry and an industrial bourgeoisie, and reducing the dominance of foreign capital in Portugal.

Salazar's strategy was to achieve rapid development of local industry on the basis of the internal market of the Portuguese empire, with direct state intervention in private productive activity through the *Câmera Corporative*, while restricting foreign investment in Portugal. This policy of *Condicionamento Industrial* (industrial regulation), initiated by law in 1931, was a central plank in Salazar's approach, the main instrument for the formation and concentration of capital in Portugal, and for structuring the division of labour between Portugal and the colonies (da Costa, I. N. 1987: 16, Pereira-Leite 1989: 86, 179). All industrial development was subject to prior state approval. This policy did not immediately produce results, but there was significant and rapid industrial growth in Portugal in the post-war period. Portugal remained neutral in the Second World War, and therefore was able to profit from the increased world price of commodities, while avoiding increased military expenditure. In a short period Portugal achieved a significant process of concentration and centralisation of capital and development of industry, although in relation to the more advanced capitalist states in Europe Portugal's level of industrial development was still very low.

The colonies in Africa played a central role in the overall economic strategy of Salazar's *Estado Novo*. Up until the late 1920s Brazil had remained important to Portugal's economy, as a market for exports, a destination for emigrants and a source of revenue in the form of emigrant remittances (Birmingham 1993: 164). The collapse of the world economy in 1930 brought a fall in trade with and emigration to Brazil, the United States and Europe. The Portuguese economy, heavily dependent on trade and the export of traditional agricultural goods, was affected badly by the fall in prices and contraction of markets (Pereira-Leite 1989: 174). With the loss of relations with Brazil, Portugal turned to Africa (Birmingham 1993: 164). Salazar's Colonial Act of 1933 aimed to integrate the African colonies directly into the strategy for rapid accumulation and development of industry in Portugal, primarily as suppliers of cheap industrial raw materials, and as protected markets for Portugal's manufactured goods. Raw materials central to Portugal's industrial development, in particular cotton, sugar, vegetable oils, as well as tobacco and sisal, were supplied by the colonies at a price below that of the international market. Between 1941 and 1964 the three export commodities – cotton, sugar and vegetable oils – constituted 90.5 per cent of the total exports sent from Mozambique to Portugal (da Costa, I. N. 1987: 29). By 1960, 82.8 per cent of Portuguese imports of raw cotton came from the colonies; in 1959 the percentages of imports originating from the colonies were respectively: oilseeds 100 per cent, sugar 92.2 per cent, sisal 98.5 per cent, palm oil 99 per cent, timber 56.2 per cent, maize 99.9 per cent, cocoa 100 per cent and coffee 99 per cent (da Costa, I. N. 1987: 33–4). The products of Portugal's industries, in particular textiles, wine, and a range of other manufactured goods such as shoes, olive oil, dairy products and soap were guaranteed secure protected markets in the colonies. This specific integration of the colonial economies within Portugal's economic development was secured by means of various legislation centred on the Colonial Act of 1933. This included the prohibition of the development of processing industry in the colonies which would compete with and divert material from Portugal's industry; a system of tariffs giving strong protection to Portuguese and colonial goods in the economic space of the Portuguese empire; restriction of foreign investment; and state control of external payments of the colonies (Universidade Eduardo Mondlane 1988b: 42–3, Pereira-Leite 1989: 198–208).

This process of rapid accumulation and development of industry in Portugal was only possible by means of brutal exploitation and repression of the peasant and working classes in both Portugal and the colonies: 'To speak of industrialisation in Portugal is to speak of colonial pillage, of brutal exploitation of Portuguese workers and of extensive privileges granted to the bourgeoisie' (da Costa, I. N. 1987: 16).

Accumulation and development in Portugal, in common with the rest of the European powers, rested in part on the structural impoverishment of the peoples of Portugal's African colonies.

Colonial rural labour policies: 'bloody legislation against the expropriated'[10]

> as soon as (in the colonies, for example) adverse circumstances prevent the creation of an industrial reserve army, and with it the absolute dependence of the working class upon the capitalist class, capital [...] rebels against the 'sacred' law of supply and demand, and tries to make up for its inadequacies by forcible means.
>
> (Marx 1867: 794)

As with most if not all of the European colonial regimes in Africa, the extraction of value from the rural populations of Mozambique, Angola and Guinea Bissau lay at the heart of the Portuguese empire's colonial regime of accumulation from the end of the nineteenth century to the early 1970s. What capital needed above all, whether trading or invested in mines, plantations, ports and railways, was the productive capacity of the local population, the Mozambican peoples. All capital accumulation rests ultimately on the extraction of value from productive labour. The worker is a fundamental necessity if accumulation on the basis of expanded reproduction of capital – accumulation originating in the sphere of production itself, rather than circulation – is to take place. But the existence of the free 'labouring poor' is, as Marx noted, an 'artificial product of modern history' (Marx 1867: 925). The capitalists and the state administrators went to Africa at the end of the nineteenth century with capital to invest; but they did not find there a society of free property-less individuals, ready for work. They had conquered and subordinated the local ruling classes, but still they faced societies of direct producers living on the land meeting their own needs, who therefore did not *need* to sell their labour-power or produce the goods required by capital. As José Capela observes, 'the indispensable element for production as much as for consumption was lacking: the free worker, producer and consumer in the system which was new to Portuguese Africa' (Capela 1977: 15). António Enes, Portuguese Royal Commissioner of Mozambique in 1895 and one of the most influential designers of Portugal's colonial policy at the end of the nineteenth century, saw the future of the colonies being dependent upon the introduction of industrialised agriculture, observing 'in East Africa agriculture requires capital, cannot be practiced without capital, and [...] the European colonization which will be able to flourish there is that which brings capital' and therefore the necessity of labour:

> The *obligation to work* is in no way the same thing as slavery: the negroes will be left free to choose the type, period and conditions by means of which they complete it; the rights of the workers to the fruits of their activity will be respected; no-one will be the owner of their persons or have usufruct of their abilities.
>
> (Enes 1946: 248, cited in Capela 1977: 55)

The theorists and practitioners of colonial rule in Mozambique – notably Oliveira Martins, António Enes (Portuguese Royal Commissioner in Mozambique 1894–95), Mouzinho de Albuquerque (Portuguese Royal Commissioner 1896–97), Freire de Andrade (Governor-General of the Province of Mozambique 1906–10), and José de Bettencourt – thus encountered the need to *produce*, by means of force, the labour-force and commodity-producers required by capital.

Under the ideology of liberalism and racist European supremacy, coercion was camouflaged by two principal mechanisms. The first was the monetary tax, the *imposto de palhota* (hut tax). The second was a series of labour laws resting on an ideology asserting the *moral* obligation for the local African population to work in order to improve their social and moral situation, in order to become more 'civilized'. The *indígenas* were defined as all those who were born in the overseas colonies of local father and mother, and who 'do not distinguish themselves by education and customs from the rest of their race' (da Silva Cunha 1960: 98, cited in Universidade Eduardo Mondlane 1983: 89). By means of the *imposto de palhota* the need for the local population to earn money was enshrined in legislation, thus providing legitimisation for the use of force, compulsory labour or forced emigration to the plantations of São Tomé as a means of punishment for failing to meet legal requirements (Capela 1977). Newitt records that '[p]enal labour was imposed for all sorts of infringements of the law ranging from failure to pay tax through to being improperly dressed or drunk' (Newitt 1995: 410). In this liberal ideological framework it was consistent therefore for the Governor-General in 1906–07, Freire de Andrade, to advocate increasing the hut-tax throughout the territory while simultaneously decrying the abhorrence of the illegal practice of *chibalo* (forced labour) (Freire de Andrade 1950: 348–50, cited in Capela 1977: 77–8).

The first steps towards initiating a new phase of colonial exploitation based not on slavery but on 'free' labour emerged in the 1850s, in the context of the period of modernising Regeneration in Portugal, and Britain's imposition of the abolition of slavery. The liberal Sá da Bandeira issued decrees prohibiting the institution of forced, unremunerated labour in Mozambique and Angola.[11] Instead he decreed that the existing tribute of 200 *réis* per household should be increased to 1,400 *réis*, payable in goods (at prices fixed by the colonial administration) or money, thus for the first time using the mechanism of tribute as a process of introducing the local population to the market economy, 'a first and tenuous step towards their insertion in the capitalist mode of production' (Capela 1977: 46). These measures provoked open resistance from the slave traders (Capela 1978: 273–5); nevertheless, despite their initial failure, Capela notes, this combination of legal measures implemented by Sá da Bandeira can be seen effectively as the birth of the infamous *imposto de palhota*, which came to have a crucial role in the final period of colonialism (Sá da Bandeira 1873 cited in Capela 1977: 47). The succession of such decrees which followed failed to have any effect in practice until the final decade of the nineteenth century, when the apparatus of some form of colonial state finally became established in the colonies.

Given Portugal's own underdevelopment in comparison with other European powers, capital initially expanded into Mozambique primarily in the form of concessionary charter companies financed largely by foreign capital, with exclusive rights over all aspects of social and economic organisation within their respective territories, responsible for military conquest, economic and infrastructural development, and administration within the territories of their concessions, in return for a percentage of their revenue paid to the Portuguese colonial state. The task of colonisation in Mozambique posed a number of problems to the companies and the colonial state: problems arising from the need for labour; the need for constructing the physical conditions for capital circulation – roads, railways, ports, bridges, and other 'public works';[12] and the need to maintain social order and control. The *imposto de palhota*, in combination with other administrative and legislative measures, was a mechanism implemented to overcome these problems. It was a means to compel the local population to earn money in order to pay the tax – thus compelling them either to produce goods for sale, or to sell their labour-power. It was a means of securing labour-power for plantations and building construction. And it was an important source of revenue needed to finance the administrative, policing and military forms of state apparatus. As Capela records, the importance of the *imposto de palhota* in these respects is illustrated by the large space it always occupied in official reports (Capela 1977: 68). During this period Mozambique was divided into areas under the control of the colonial state and areas under concession to private companies, and so there was no uniform policy. However, both state and concessionary companies introduced some form of *imposto de palhota*. Thus on July 9, 1892, the *Companhia de Moçambique* issued a decree stating that every owner of a hut located within the territory of the company was obliged to pay an annual tax of 900 *réis* per hut used for habitation. During the first two years the tax could be paid in money or goods; but from 1894 the tax would be payable only in money. Those who did not pay the tax would be obliged to work for a period – determined by the local salary rate – sufficient to pay the tax, increased by 50 per cent (Capela 1977: 60).

The collection of the *imposto de palhota* from the local population constituted a very significant component of the overall revenue for the state and concessionary companies (Capela 1977: 71–6, Neil-Tomlinson 1977, 1978, Serra 1980: 37–8, Newitt 1995: 407–8). By 1907–08 and 1908–09 the *imposto de palhota* was one of the two most important of all the sources of public revenue, the other being receipts from traffic on the Lourenço–Marques railway (Capela 1977: 75, citing Freire de Andrade 1950). The right to collect a wide variety of taxes was central to the monopoly granted to the concessionary companies. Neil-Tomlinson records that during the initial period of the Nyassa company's existence the tax revenues grew as the company consolidated its 'effective occupation' further inland. Annual *Imposto de palhota* revenue increased from £800 in 1898, to £1,275 in 1901, £3,105 in 1903, rising to £31,430 in 1912 and subsequently reaching £48,232 (Neil-Tomlinson 1977: 118). For a brief period after 1909 the company turned to labour recruitment for the South African mines, but during the 1920s, the last period of the company's existence, hut tax revenue again became central: '[f]or both the company and the people of Nyassa the collection of hut tax was the single most important activity of the administration. During the 1920s the company maintained a surplus of revenue over expenditure in Africa by repeatedly raising the level of hut tax' (Neil-Tomlinson 1977: 121). The rate of tax increased from 3 *escudos* in 1922, to 10 *escudos* in 1924, 20 *escudos* in 1925, 30 *escudos* in 1926, 50 *escudos* in 1927, and 85 *escudos* in 1928; the company's revenue from hut tax rose to £87,000 in 1927 and £95,000 in 1928 (Neil-Tomlinson 1977: 121–2). In real terms the hut tax was equivalent to one month's paid labour during the second decade, rising in 1927 to the equivalent of three months' paid labour (Neil-Tomlinson 1977: 123). Wage labour was scarce and so the tax had to be raised from more intensive cash cropping: 'virtually the entire product of African cash cropping and "wage" labour was consumed by the company' and in 1927 the hut tax accounted for 70 per cent of the company's total revenue (Neil-Tomlinson 1977: 123).

Throughout the territory, the collection of the *imposto de palhota* increased with increasing 'pacification' as more areas were brought under the control of the state or company administration. Carlos Serra records that in Zambezia, where the local equivalent of the *imposto de palhota* was a tax payable by each individual, called the *musokho*, the rate began at 0$80 ($ signifies *escudos*) in 1890, and rose to 1$20 in 1899, 1$60 in 1913, and 2$50 in 1921 (Serra 1980: 38). In 1923, it was raised to 10$00 for single men and 20$00 for married men (Serra 1980: 38, Ishemo 1995: 145). In the District of Moçambique (Nampula), under state administration, the hut tax was first collected in the coastal areas – Mossuril, Cabaceiras, Angoche, etc., – later extending further inland. In 1903, the colonial governor of the District of Moçambique ordered that the tax could be paid in goods in areas where there was not enough money, but in the coastal areas the tax was payable only in money. The governor established a list of products with which the tax could be paid: ripe groundnuts (shelled and cleaned), sesame, beeswax, rubber, corn, and rice – all export products (Universidade Eduardo Mondlane 1983: 116, citing Pimentel 1904).

The imposition of tax alone was not enough, however, to secure a supply of labour sufficient to meet the various needs of capital. Alongside the *imposto de palhota*, and intimately related, was the legal requirement to work, implemented with the backing of state coercion in the form of the *cypais*, African police – the lowest rung of the colonial state. This legislation rested on the ideological and racist definition of Africans as uncivilised, culturally and racially inferior, and lazy; people who therefore should be made to work so as to improve themselves. Thus a report presented to the Portuguese Government in 1901 asserted that in addition to being lucrative, the native tax is 'a just retribution for the tranquillity and progress which European Government guarantees to the occupied territories' (Costa 1901: 624–5, cited in Capela 1977: 67). The first legislation in Mozambique was introduced by António Enes in 1890. In 1898 Portugal's Colonial Minister Eduardo Villaca appointed a commission to review colonial labour legislation, which was headed by Enes (Vail and White 1980: 134, Universidade Eduardo Mondlane 1983: 89). Based on their recommendations, a new Labour Code for the Colonies was issued in Portugal 1899, which stated 'All the able natives in the Portuguese Colonies are subject, under this law, to the moral and legal obligation to provide, by means of work, for their sustenance and to improve successively their social condition' (Labour Code, November 1899, cited in Universidade Eduardo Mondlane 1983: 107). Vail and White report that under this code

> all male Africans between fourteen and sixty years of age were legally obliged to work, and this obligation could be fulfilled by (1) possessing an amount of capital adequate to supply one's needs or by practising a profession; (2) growing crops on land the extent of which would be determined by the government and which themselves would be exported under government supervision; or (3) working a certain number of months as fixed by local authorities. According to Article 34, such local authorities could compel labour for their own purposes, for the public service, or for private companies and individuals [. . .] The only people exempt from this imposition were women, men over sixty years, children under fourteen years, the sick and disabled, *cypais*, policemen, and recognized chiefs and headmen.
>
> (Vail and White 1980: 135, citing Silva Cunha 1955: 147–8)

The problem of labour remained a central concern of the colonial state administrators, plantation owners, and managers of the concessionary companies, throughout the period of Portuguese colonisation. In 1911, a Colonial Labour Code was introduced in Mozambique, officially enacting the Code issued earlier in 1899 in Portugal. In 1914, the *Regulamento Geral do Trabalho dos Indígenas nas Colónias Portuguesas* was introduced; and Álvaro de Castro, Governor-General from 1915 to 1917, argued that the *imposto de palhota* should be increased, that the *indígena* should be obliged to work throughout the year, either on his own land or for someone else, for a fixed minimum salary (Capela 1977: 90). Further legislation was introduced in 1926, the *Estatuto Político Civil et Criminal dos Indígenos*, and in 1928 the *Codigo do Trabalho dos Indígenas nos Colónias Portugueses de Africa*, which remained in force until 1962 (Vail and White 1980: 136, Centro de Estudos Africanos 1981, Pereira-Leite 1989: 167). This Code was supplemented by specific Regulations for Mozambique in 1930, *Regulamento do Trabalho dos Indígenas na Colónia de Moçambique*, which specified three types of compulsory labour: (1) for government agencies or municipalities; (2) for dealing with natural disasters; (3) for services related to the living conditions and agriculture of the *indígenas*, including road maintenance (Mondlane 1976: 94–6, Centro de Estudos Africanos 1981: 26).

The processes of forced extraction of value from rural societies increased significantly under the regime of Salazar's *Estado Novo*. The former autonomy of the colonies under the administration of Royal Commissioners was replaced with tight control from Lisbon. Administrative reform was enacted in 1933 through the *Reforma Adminstrativa Ultramarina*, which subjected colonial administration to mandate from Lisbon, with the role of Royal Commissioner being replaced by the Governor-General (Universidade Eduardo Mondlane 1988b: 42, Pereira-Leite 1989: 191). Administrative structures were set up to organise the coordination of economic activity in the colonies to conform with the overall plan of Portuguese development. The organisation of the production and marketing of raw materials for export to Portugal's industries was regulated by the state, which determined quantities and prices. Central to Salazar's strategy was the development of Portugal's textile industry, which was to be supplied with raw materials from the colonies. Mozambique became the main source of cotton: between 1931 and 1964 export of cotton from Mozambique to Portugal increased from 146 tonnes to 28,525 tonnes (da Costa, I. N. 1987: 54). This massive increase was achieved by means of various protective tariffs and price policies, state investment in irrigation, settlement of Portuguese families in Mozambique, and extension of the rail network (Pereira-Leite 1989: 370). Above all it centred upon compulsory cultivation of cotton by the African population which was introduced in 1938 – one of the first measures taken by Salazar's regime (Mondlane 1976: 85, Universidade Eduardo Mondlane 1988b: 29). Improved control of African labour therefore became central to the realisation of the Colonial Act at the heart of Salazar's policy. Indeed, Portugal's colonial policy was designed to be based on increased extraction of value from the African peasantry:

> In 1932, at the opening of the Imperial Conference in Lisbon, the Minister of the Colonies declared that government policy would be to avoid great works of promotion and expensive settlement of colonialists and to profit, in increased and more efficient ways, from the peasant, through constant work on the land.
>
> (Universidade Eduardo Mondlane 1988b: 41)

After failing to realise an increase in cotton production through persuasion, the state, under the administration of José Tristão de Bettencourt, developed more coercive measures; where necessary, district administrators who showed resistance to such measures were replaced (Universidade Eduardo Mondlane 1988b: 91–2). Each member of the population in the cotton concession areas was given seeds to grow, and had to plant specific areas of land; cotton had to be planted before other food crops; and those who failed to meet these regulations were punished through fines, physical abuse and imprisonment. These measures were enforced by the African police, *cypais*. Such measures to compel the peasants to produce in sufficient quantities the crops required by the companies and colonial state were not new, but they now became generalised throughout the country (Universidade Eduardo Mondlane 1988b: 92).

As a result, by 1943–44 the number of cotton producers rose to 791,000 – roughly 30 per cent of the Mozambican population of working age (Universidade Eduardo Mondlane 1988b: 92). Isaacman and Isaacman estimate that by 1945, taking into account 'the large numbers of minors and elders who also worked in their assigned family cotton fields', 'more than 1 million Mozambican peasants, primarily in the north, were producing enough cotton to meet the demands of the metropole' (Isaacman and Isaacman 1983: 45). Cotton production increased from 5.4 tonnes in 1938–39 to more than 40,000 tonnes in 1954, and during the period

1946–51 the colonies (mainly Mozambique) supplied more than 86 per cent of Portugal's cotton demand (Pereira-Leite 1989: 429). From 1942 cotton became the main export from Mozambique. The successful realisation of this articulation between Mozambique and Portugal was central to the colonial policy of the *Estado Novo* and the economic reproduction of the empire.

The structural impoverishment of the Mozambican camponês

What were the effects of the 'bloody legislations' of the *imposto de palhota*, the labour legislation and compulsory crop regime on the African peoples of Mozambique, their material conditions of life and possibilities for social reproduction? The specific nature and effects of colonial policy varied across Mozambique. In the South the role of labour migration to the mines in South Africa and Rhodesia was a major determinant of socio-economic change (see Covane 2001), while in the north plantations and petty-commodity production predominated. Nevertheless general observations can be made. The intensification of exploitation and extraction of surplus, either in the form of labour-power or the products of labour, undermined existing practices of production and social reproduction in a number of ways, without resulting in their total transformation. The effects of the *imposto de palhota* and the labour legislation constituted essentially a process of semi-proletarianisation in the countryside. Peasant communities remained on the land (though the best areas were appropriated for plantations and private farms), and still had to provide most of the means of social reproduction for the seasonal labour-force. A significant part of the cost of reproduction of labour-power was thus shifted from capital to the peasant society. The increased production for sale of crops such as cotton, groundnuts, rice and sesame, which were so important to the colonial state's export revenue and Europe's developing industries, left less time for people to produce the objects necessary to satisfy their own needs.

The fundamental effect of these various processes was a reduction in the capacity of local populations to meet their needs through their own production. Local artisanal practices declined, either because there was no time for them, or because of competition with imported manufactured goods. Serra records how in Morrumbala, in the area covered by the concession of the Companhia de Zambezia, 'the company started to sell hoes to the peasants at 1$00 each which led immediately to iron foundries being abandoned and to decline in the activity of the ironsmiths' (Serra 1980: 43). Similarly Arlindo Chilundo (2001) has documented the decline of local salt production in Nampula province. The imposition of the tax and forced labour regime structurally undermined the productive practices of African peoples, creating conditions of food insecurity, famine and disease (Ishemo 1989, 1995 chapter 5). A further result was the emigration of people away from the pressures and demands of the colonial state and companies, for labour, tax and produce. Many parts of the country, such as Niassa and Cabo Delgado, witnessed the exodus of whole communities to neighbouring provinces or colonies, in search of better conditions of life (Neil-Tomlinson 1977).

These processes of extraction of absolute surplus from the African societies, and reorganisation of their social and productive activities according to the various needs of capital, intensified during the phase of fascist-colonialism of Salazar's *Estado Novo*. Under Salazar's fascist-colonial regime Portuguese industrial accumulation rested on intensified extraction of value from the African population, which resulted necessarily and systematically in their impoverishment. Pereira-Leite records that in 1953 the total amount paid to the Mozambican producers for cotton amounted to 331 thousand *contos*; and the state tax receipts came to 180 thousand *contos*. In other words,

> On one side, the state received in the form of tax the amount which went to subsidise the price of exports given to the concessionaries of the cotton zones. On the other side, the African producers spent nearly 50% of the 'income' from their crops in paying tribute to the colonial administration. The great losers of the affair were without doubt these last whose sole benefit was balanced by the forced integration into the colonial market, and this with all the effects of disintegration of their traditional logic of production.
>
> (Pereira-Leite 1989: 429)

The compulsory cotton regime, with controlled marketing and pricing, enabled the Portuguese textile industry to acquire cotton from Mozambique at about half the world price. This was only possible because of increased exploitation of the direct producers:

> In 1939 the average price paid to African cultivators for first-class raw cotton was two cents per kilogram [...], which rarely provided sufficient remuneration for peasants to pay their taxes. By 1957, after a number of highly publicized reforms and price increases, the average yearly income derived by a family from cotton production in northern Mozambique was $11, barely covering its tax obligation to the state; and family income in the least prosperous regions was often less than $4.
>
> (Isaacman and Isaacman 1983: 46)

For the bulk of the Mozambican population in the cotton-growing areas the compulsory production of cotton in conditions determined by the existing mode and relations of production – direct producers, producing using human labour-power and hand tools, to meet their own needs as well as producing crops such as cotton – necessarily undermined their ability to meet their own needs through production. Cotton was grown throughout the country, irrespective of the suitability of soils, but most production was in the Districts of Moçambique, Cabo Delgado and Zambezia, which in 1941–44 produced 80 per cent of the total production; 48 per cent of the total came from the District of Moçambique (Universidade Eduardo Mondlane 1988b: 102–3, Chilundo 2001: 15). The increasing amount of time and physical effort which had to be devoted to growing cotton and rice, in order to meet the state requirements, meant that the time left for food production and other productive activities was marginalised. These other activities included building houses, making furniture, food preparation, caring for children (those too young to work), the elderly and the sick – in sum, the various activities necessary in order to ensure basic social reproduction. This was exacerbated by the absence of men on seasonal labour contracts or penal labour, in Mozambique or neighbouring territories. A survey in the district of Gaza in 1941 concluded that '50% of the women could not produce the forced cultures without seriously reducing food production' (Isaacman and Isaacman 1983: 54, citing the report of J. Anachoreta, Chefe da Sub-Delegação do Sul de Save, 1941). The state recognised that compulsory cotton production was causing a decline in food production, but:

> instead of removing the cause of the problem, which was the system of compulsory cultivation of cotton itself, from 1946/7, the colonial State gradually increased this system to include food crops as well. In this way, in the cotton zones, all the productive activities of the peasantry, not only that of cotton, came to be directed by the administration and by the agents of the concessionary companies.
>
> (Universidade Eduardo Mondlane 1988b: 131)

The increased production of cotton resulted in declining soil fertility (Universidade Eduardo Mondlane 1988b: 154–5) which contributed further to reduced food production. This was a particular problem in the densely populated district of Moçambique (now Nampula), but was common in many parts of the country. In the agricultural season 1950–51 poor weather conditions resulted in famine and a dysentery epidemic which resulted in the death of more than 3,000 people (Universidade Eduardo Mondlane 1988b: 153). The district of Moçambique is a fertile area where, traditionally, a surplus was produced and food exported to other less productive areas. In the first decades of the twentieth century the colonial governor of the district declared that it had the potential to become the granary of the colony (Chilundo 2001: 92). In the 1920s and 30s significant quantities of corn and other food crops were exported to other areas of the territory and even abroad (Universidade Eduardo Mondlane 1988b: 156). By the 1950s however there was a chronic risk of famine:

> If it was only the food crops which failed, the peasants had to resort to what was left of their income from selling the cotton and rice, after subtracting the various taxes, for buying food. It was even worse when, in addition, the cotton harvest also failed, leaving them with no possibility whatsoever of acquiring food from the rural *cantineiros*. Such situations arose again in 1959 in Murrupula and parts of Luluti, Mogovolas and Moma, provoking hundreds of deaths. It is evident that these situations were frequent.
>
> (Universidade Eduardo Mondlane 1988b: 155)

A widespread consequence of the increased pressure on the African population was a reduction in the variety of basic food products available in the countryside.

The consequent shift in diet resulted in rising malnutrition and disease, and periodic famines in the countryside. Serra records that in 1906 about thirty thousand people died of hunger in Zambezia, and in 1909 a colonial governor observed that 'the intensive development of the plantations has fatally turned the native away from his own crops' (Serra 1980: 44). The substitution of nutritious but more time-consuming cereals such as corn, sorghum and *mapira* with cassava, a tendency which had emerged in the early decades of the twentieth century, increased steadily as a result of the implementation of forced cultivation (Serra 1986b: 50). The crops of beans and groundnut were neglected, and often much of what was grown had to be sold in order to meet the monetary tax burdens (Universidade Eduardo Mondlane 1988b: 155). Cassava became increasingly important as a staple food. Cassava requires little maintenance as a crop, and grows all year round, in very poor soils. It is a basic carbohydrate, providing 'bulk' but with little nutritional value. Reports from the district of Moçambique in the 1950s indicated a serious problem of anaemia in the countryside, which caused lower birth rates and increased rates of infant mortality (Universidade Eduardo Mondlane 1988b: 156, referring to the district governor reports, de Almeida 1957 and dos Santos 1959). The food distributed to workers on plantations was also based principally and sometimes exclusively on cassava (Serra 1986b: 50).

Cassava is still today the basic staple for many people in Mozambique (Addison and Macdonald 1995: 3, MPF *et al.* 1998: 77). This is not a matter of 'choice', as celebrated by neo-liberals. It is not because of the preferences and culture of Mozambicans, nor because of the superior nutritious quality of cassava. On the contrary it is because cassava is a crop which requires the least time to produce, the least amount of labour for its production. Cassava is a food of poverty, characteristic of a society based on poverty. Marx explained this same logic operating in Britain in the nineteenth century:

> Cotton, potatoes and spirits are the objects of commonest use. Potatoes have engendered scrofula; cotton has largely driven linen and wool out of the market, although wool and linen are in many cases of much greater utility, if only from considerations of hygiene; spirits, again, have largely replaced beer and wine, although spirits, used as food, are generally recognised to be poison. [. . .] Why, then, are cotton, potatoes and spirits the pivots of bourgeois society? Because the least amount of labor is necessary for their production, and they are in consequence at the lowest price. Why does the minimum of price decide the maximum of consumption? Can it by any chance be because of the absolute utility of these objects, of their intrinsic utility, of their utility in so far as they correspond in the most useful manner to the needs of the worker, as man, and not of the man as worker? No, it is because, in a society based on *poverty*, the *poorest* products have the fatal prerogative of serving the use of the greatest number.
>
> (Marx 1847: 67)

The social and international order of colonial rule was a means of primitive accumulation for European capital (whether located in Europe or invested in the colonies), resting on the violent and coercive exploitation of the majority of African peoples, causing structural impoverishment. This form of extraction of surplus does not transform the local mode of production. Rather it 'clings on to it like a parasite and impoverishes it. It sucks it dry, emasculates it and forces reproduction to proceed under ever more pitiable conditions' (Marx 1894: 730–1). Essentially the same dynamic of mass structural impoverishment under colonial rule took place throughout Africa.[13] Thus in his analysis of French colonialism in Africa, Suret-Canale observes:

> The pre-colonial crop system, within its traditional social setting, provided a complete and permanent equilibrium between man and nature. Compelled thereafter, with means which were unchanged, to provide for his own subsistence and to furnish a surplus of export products as well, the peasant succeeded only in reducing this subsistence to a minimum, or even below: reserves kept back for traditional feasts or bad years disappeared. Every year there was famine. Malnutrition became a permanent feature.
>
> (Suret-Canale 1971: 297)

He records exactly the same process of dietary shift:

> In French Equatorial Africa [...] the average ration everywhere was below the 3,000 calories considered the minimum necessary for a man doing even light work. It was generally less than 2,000 and badly balanced, consisting almost entirely of cassava paste. Meat and fish, formerly eaten on a wide scale, became rare in the two generations following colonial penetration. [...] Forced labour had compelled the Ubangi to abandon millet, which was rich in fats, for cassava, which required less care in its cultivation; compulsory cotton cultivation worsened this situation by preventing crop rotation.
>
> (Suret-Canale 1971: 299)

The current structural condition of widespread rural poverty in Mozambique, as in the rest of Africa, is fundamentally a modern, world-historical social outcome, necessarily and causally related to processes of accumulation and development in Europe.

6 The presence of the outside

Revolution, counter-revolution and the production of absence

> The profound hypocrisy and inherent barbarism of bourgeois civilization lies unveiled before our eyes, turning from its home, where it assumes respectable forms, to the colonies, where it goes naked.
>
> (Marx 1853: 88)

> The field of social struggle within dependent nations does not uniquely proceed, at any given historical conjuncture, from the free unravelling of local histories.
>
> (Johnson, D. L. 1981: 113)

The rise of the discourse of development in the twentieth century constitutes a form of amnesia through which the past of colonialism, and its presence as neo-colonialism, are forgotten. Development policy, the international aid regime and the goal of poverty reduction are seen as the product of a benevolent world order. This world order is made up of sovereign states and rests on principles of political equality, self-determination, non-interference and mutual respect. It has grown from the original 'international society' which was born in Europe, and has since spread to encompass the whole world (Bull and Watson 1984). Some states are poor, others are rich, but the rich states help the poor states to develop, in a civilised and civilising, enlightened international system. Even some critical approaches in International Relations reproduce this narrative of Western civilisation:

> [m]odernity's qualities [the tendency to universalise rights, respect differences and reduce inequalities] are also evident in the recent development of the international society of states. Scope restrictions that prevented non-Europeans from gaining admission to European society have been lifted, at least for those groups with the power to constitute themselves as separate states. [...] The commitment to pacify the society of states without convert-ing it into empire is a [...] pronounced theme in the modern society of states.
>
> (Linklater 2001: 34)

The language and ideas about development have over time become consolidated into a powerful ideology which normalises global inequality and oppression, rendering global poverty a problem of moral concern, philanthropy and technical assistance, its roots and contemporary reproduction in relations of capitalist imperialism forgotten. This is consistent with the view of decolonisation as a process of 'transfer of power' by enlightened European powers, granting Independence to their former colonies and thus lifting the restrictions which had prevented non-Europeans from gaining admission to European/international society.

Given the role of development discourse in naturalising the international order of things, the Neo-Gramscian emphasis on the role of ideas in the maintenance of oppressive world orders is important:

> Hegemony is a structure of values and understandings about the nature of order that permeates a whole social system of states and non-state entities. In a hegemonic order these values and understandings are relatively stable and unquestioned. They appear to most actors as the natural order. Such a structure of meanings is underpinned by a structure of power, in which most probably one state is dominant but that state's dominance is not sufficient to create hegemony. Hegemony derives from the dominant social strata of the dominant states in so far as these ways of doing and thinking have acquired the acquiescence of the dominant social strata of other states.
>
> (Cox 1990 cited in Gill 1993a: 42)

However it was by no means just unquestioned values and understandings which maintained the structures of international power in the twentieth century. The role of force and coercion, orchestrated violence and brutality were central to securing the neo-colonial world order and ushering in neo-liberal globalisation. This was necessary because of the forces of resistance, struggle and revolution necessarily generated by the oppressive order of colonial imperialism.

In Bhaskarian terms, colonial rule in Mozambique as elsewhere was characterised by the systematic production of absence and lack for the majority of African peoples. The experience of lack and oppression gave rise to multiple forms of resistance which eventually consolidated in the revolutionary overthrow of colonial rule. The present of the twentieth century was, however, a structured present, and the possibilities for change in different contexts were heavily circumscribed by the globally unequal distribution of powers and capacities of production and destruction which was the product of the past. If dialectical critical realism is helpful in analysing this historical process in terms of transformatory praxis, emancipatory struggle motivated by absence and oppression – and thus emphasising the process of decolonisation as a struggle between oppressors and oppressed rather than a benign transfer of power – it must also be used to highlight the negative dialectic of counter-revolution. This chapter examines the determining presence of the outside or the international in the dialectic of revolution and counter-revolution manifest in the struggles of the Mozambican people for freedom and self-determination.

Decolonisation, neo-colonialism and the post-war international order

Decolonisation is portrayed by some as a process involving enlightened (or foolish) European powers granting Independence to their colonies, in the context of the new moral order (or disorder) of post-war international society (e.g. Kirk-Greene 1979, Gifford and Roger Louis 1987, Jackson 1990; for a critique see Grovogui 1996). Kedourie for example portrayed the process of decolonisation as an undesirable increase in international *dis*order, unleashed unwittingly by the decision of colonial powers to dismantle their empires. From the mid-1950s this process

> spread rapidly throughout Africa. 'Decolonization' suddenly became the settled policy of the British, the French, and the Belgians, a policy precipitately and thoroughly applied whatever the costs and consequences. The policy was, by and large, the outcome of a unilateral decision taken by the metropolitan authorities, rather than a response to some overwhelming or irresistible pressure exerted by the African populations.
>
> (Kedourie 1984: 351)

Such views are flawed on two counts. They tend to ignore, first, the extent to which decolonisation was the fruit of the struggles of the colonised to throw off the colonial yoke; and second, the determined efforts by European powers to retain their colonies, and to control the process of decolonisation in their interests. Western support for decolonisation was formally embedded in the post-war universal principles and international law regarding self-determination, sovereignty, equality and human rights, but was always also informed by and usually subordinate to neo-colonial economic and military geo-strategic interests. At the level of ideology, support for decolonisation was framed in terms consistent with the European civilising mission (Grovogui 1996, Anghie 2005). 'Self-rule' was the eventual goal to be reached when the colonised peoples were sufficiently mature. Concerns over whether Africans were sufficiently 'mature' for 'self-rule' were frequently voiced during discussions in Britain over the prospect of constitutional change and independence in her African colonies. In November 1947 a Conference of the Governors of Britain's African colonial territories was held in London. Papers prepared for the conference discussed the question of political change towards self rule, noting,

> The pace of change is still to some extent under control, but the direction can hardly be altered, and we must assume that perhaps within a generation many of the principal territories of the Colonial Empire will have attained or be within sight of the goal of full responsibility for local affairs.
>
> (Appendix II – General Political Development of Colonial Territories, African Governors' Conference November 1947, in Hyam 1992a: 199)

> In West Africa internal self-government cannot be achieved until territorial unity has become a reality, sufficient numbers of Africans have emerged qualified by their training and character to manage their own affairs on a territorial scale and the political leaders have become representative of and responsible to the people. In East Africa internal self-government can

only come when the Africans have developed to a stage at which they can play their full part with the immigrant communities in the government of the territories. [...] It is clear that in Africa the period before self-government can be granted will be longer than in most other parts of the Colonial Empire. Prophecy as to the length of this period is idle, but it may be said that in the Gold Coast, the territory where Africans are most advanced polit-ically, internal self-government is unlikely to be achieved in much less than a generation. In the other territories the process is likely to be considerably slower.

> (Appendix III – Constitutional Development in Africa,
> African Governors' Conference November 1947,
> in Hyam 1992a: 203)

Reactions to this paper at the African Governors' Conference, in November 1947, included the following. Sir Philip Mitchell, Governor of Kenya 'had been surprised by the capacity of the average East African to learn but he was per-turbed by his widespread lack of moral fibre'; Sir John Hall, Governor of Uganda, commented that 'The introduction of Africans into positions of execu-tive responsibility in the central government was impossible both now and in the immediate future [... in part] because of their general lack of character'; Sir Hubert Stevenson, Governor of Sierra Leone 'urged caution in giving any hope that self-government could come in a generation'; Mr Griffiths, Secretary of State for the Colonies, said he was concerned about 'the time factor. We knew how raw and ignorant were the peoples in an African territory but time was knocking at the door and the art of government had to be learnt' ('Constitutional Development in Africa': African Governors' Conference draft minute 5, Hyam 1992a: 303–6). Regarding East Africa, a draft statement to the House of Commons put forward in a Cabinet Memorandum in November 1950 by the Secretary of State for the Colonies stated

> When Africans have reached the stage of taking their full part and the other communities are sure of a future in East Africa we can hope for a state of har-mony and mutual confidence on which a Government in which all sections will participate can be soundly based. Until that stage is reached, and it will be some time before it is reached, it is essential that His Majesty's Government in the United Kingdom should continue to exercise its ultimate control in the East African territories, while allowing within that framework all reasonable freedom of action to the local Governments.
>
> ('East Africa': Cabinet Memorandum by Mr Griffiths:
> text of draft statement to be made to the House
> of Commons, in Hyam 1992b: 27)

This ideology informed not only the European colonial powers, but also the values and beliefs of America's ruling classes. America's post-war foreign policy towards the Third World from the moment of decolonisation throughout the

Cold War was tainted by a racism arising from America's own racial relations (Borstelmann 2001). Thus

> [t]he image of Third World leaders as volatile children was especially enduring for the administration. Sounding remarkably like his white South African counterparts, Foster Dulles lamented in June 1958 the 'tremendous surge in the direction of popular government by people who have practically no capacity for self-government and indeed are like children in facing this problem'. Whether these 'children' could mature remained uncertain to U.S. policymakers.
>
> (Borstelmann 2001: 111–12)

In practice, efforts by colonial powers to delay and control decolonisation were seen in colonial conflicts and wars in Algeria, Kenya, Madagascar, Malaya, Indonesia and Indo-China, as well as the Portuguese colonies; in routine restriction and disruption of African political organisation within the colonies prior to independence; in selective support for certain individuals or parties who did not threaten the European economic and strategic interests; in the assassination of radical independence leaders, such as Lumumba, Mondlane, Cabral and Machel;[1] and in diplomatic manoeuvres in the UN to block or undermine the process of decolonisation. Thus although Portugal's attempt to cling on to her colonies was one of the longest and most violent, it must not be seen as an exception to an otherwise enlightened process on the part of European powers.

The struggle for decolonisation has its origins in the routine and structural oppression of colonialism. As Mondlane wrote, 'As with all African nationalisms, Mozambican nationalism was born from the experience of European colonialism. The basis of national unity is the common suffering of the past fifty years spent under effective Portuguese domination' (Mondlane 1976: 107). The struggles for liberation from colonial rule across Africa grew from myriad smaller struggles for reform and resistance to oppression within the context of colonialism, as well as the growing international dimensions of struggle for reform including the Pan-African movement. These struggles usually entailed tensions and contradictions between rival African interests, rooted in the class structure of colonial society as well as the ethnic and regional divisions which had been deliberately created or entrenched by the colonisers (Nzongola-Ntalaja 1987, Mamdani 1996a).[2] It was such contradictions which the European powers sought to exploit and manage in the struggle over decolonisation.

The post-Second World War international order was formally built on values of sovereignty and self-determination, enshrined in the United Nations Charter of 1945, but this was only slowly extended to official international support for decolonisation. The war-time Atlantic Charter signed in 1941 by Franklin Roosevelt and Winston Churchill professed 'the right of all people to choose the form of government in which they will live' and the 'wish to see sovereign rights and self-government restored to those who have been forcibly deprived of them' (Atlantic Charter, in Brockway 1968: 103). Churchill construed this as applying only to Western peoples, although Roosevelt corrected him in affirming the universal validity of the charter ('Churchill and the Colonies, 1941' in Wallbank 1964: 68–9, Minter 1986b: 107). However it was not until 1960 that a formal call for decolonisation was articulated in the United Nations and thus made part of international law – and this only at the insistence of the independent Asian and African states, whose numerical superiority overcame the resistance of the colonial powers. The institution of the United Nations became a specific arena in which, on the formal terrain of international law, the struggle between the colonial powers and the formerly and still colonised was fought. This process in itself must be seen in dialectical terms, as a struggle over the potential of international law to serve, on one hand, as an ideological tool of legitimacy and regulation for the powerful, and on the other hand as a vital and emancipatory recognition and formal defence of the interests and rights of the weak against the strong (see Chimni 1993, 2003, Grovogui 1996, Koskenniemi 2000, Anghie 2005).

The struggle for and over decolonisation must therefore be understood in the context of the transition from one form of imperialism to another: from the territorially organised European colonial imperialism of the nineteenth century to a globally extended neo-colonial imperialism under the hegemony of the United States. The current phase of capitalist imperialism which has been developing since the Second World War is referred to here as neo-colonialism because of its multi-lateral nature, but it is dominated and underpinned by America's economic and military power. Neo-colonialism has various features or dimensions, which are discussed further in Chapter 7. It is characterised by the global dominance of the United States, in military and economic terms; by the further concentration and internationalisation of capital; but also by remaining rivalries within the industrialised world, between Europe, the United States and Japan. These features of neo-colonial imperialism have given rise to the liberal international economic order, regulated by multi-lateral economic institutions and regimes of international law to guarantee and extend global conditions for the accumulation of capital; and to the global extension of America's military power throughout the world. For much of the twentieth century these dynamics were influenced by Western rivalry with the Soviet Union, and Western imperial intervention in the Third World was routinely legitimised in terms of containing communist expansion.

The world economic depression of the thirties had led to an era of protectionism and isolated trading blocs, with the leading capitalist powers facing economic collapse and mass unemployment. It was argued that these conditions partly explained the rise of Nazism in Germany, resulting in the outbreak of the Second World War. By the end of the war the productive capacities of the European imperial powers had been largely destroyed and their foreign exchange reserves exhausted. The US economy had benefited from the impact of the war on the world economy, and more particularly from war-time financial arrangements with the European allies centred on the Lend–Lease system (Hudson 2003: 119–36). America was by the end of the war the largest and most technologically advanced economy, producing around one third of the world's total output, and by 1948 controlling three-quarters of the world's monetary gold (Williams 1991: 35).

American capital needed to expand: it needed expanded foreign markets to sell its goods, and new fields for foreign investment, including in Europe's raw-materials-producing colonies (Kolko 1988: 13, Hudson 2003: 131). America's plans for the post-war world order therefore did not envisage the maintenance of Europe's colonial empires, with their Imperial Preference systems. America's moral anti-colonial rhetoric rested firmly on the expansionary interests of American capital. The central components of America's post-war reordering were the reconstruction of the European economies through American aid and investment, so as to provide a market for American exports and bolster European capitalism against radical social change, and to establish an international economic order based on liberal principles of non-discriminatory free trade (Williams 1991: 19–20).

Given her overwhelming economic and military predominance in 1945, the United States 'almost single-handedly dictated' the emergence of the post-war inter-national economic order, with negotiations between America and Britain beginning during the war (Williams 1991: 18, Hudson 2003: 137–61). The International Monetary and Financial Conference of the United and Associated Nations, which took place at Bretton Woods, New Hampshire in 1944 involving 44 nations, was the culmination of these discussions and led to the establishment of a liberal interna-tional economic order, instituted in international organisations and agreements of the World Bank, the IMF and the General Agreement of Tariffs and Trade (Williams 1994). America's economic power and position as global creditor ensured these insti-tutions were designed in the interests of the United States. As America's economic supremacy has been attenuated by the rise of Japan and Europe as major economic rivals, these multi-lateral institutions have served to regulate the smooth functioning of the global capitalist system, reflecting the general interests of global capital rather than the particular conflicting interests of rival powers and capitals. They enable the major capitalist powers, led by the United States, to coordinate and unite collectively to impose reform on the rest of the world (Callinicos 2002).

One of the lessons drawn from the two world wars by the American and European architects of the post-1945 international order was that the integrated liberal international economic order they sought to establish, in order to enable the flourishing of an expansionary global capitalist system, would require 'more robust security arrangements than had existed under the League of Nations' (O'Brien and Williams 2004: 113). Securing a globally extended capitalist order required multi-lateral rather than simply national security arrangements. Central components of the West's post-war security arrangements were the North Atlantic Treaty Organisation, established in 1949, and America's global network of military bases and forces. NATO provided a formal structure to coordinate the enormous build-up of western military power in the post-war period. These components were complemented by diplomatic, economic and military support for friendly client states throughout the world, as well as the global counter-revolution against radical social change in the Third World carried out mainly through covert operations and interventions.

At the time of NATO's establishment Africa and much of the rest of the non-European world remained under colonial rule. Africa was seen by colonial military planners such as Admiral Richard Connolly 'in one sense as an aggregate of separate base areas and, in another, in its entirety, as a vast defence complex' (Coker 1985: 9). During the first decade of NATO's existence the colonial powers (mainly Britain and France, to a lesser extent Belgium and the Netherlands) sought to integrate Africa centrally within the alliance's security system and contingency planning (Coker 1985: 4–10). Their interests in incorporating Africa within NATO agreements were first to guarantee the protection of their control over colonial territories, and second to make use of the network of military bases and forces in Africa. These attempts were resisted by the United States and smaller NATO members, and so NATO was not formally committed to securing Europe's colonial territories in Africa. However according to Reid a secret understanding among the NATO powers did actually pledge 'consultation [...] in the event of a threat in any part of the world, including a threat to their overseas territories' (Reid 1977: 267 cited in Minter 1986b: 117).

As an alliance of the western capitalist world, the world of 'freedom', NATO was formally committed to democracy. The parties signing the Treaty in 1949 affirmed their determination 'to safeguard the freedom, common heritage and civilisation of their peoples, founded on the principles of democracy, individual liberty and the rule of law' (North Atlantic Treaty, in Brockway 1968: 139). This opening clause was subordinate to the security concerns of defending the capitalist west, however. Portugal was admitted as a NATO member from the beginning, signing the original agreement in 1949. Although a fascist dictatorship with no internal democracy, Portugal was considered a valuable military ally in the global war against communism. More specifically, Portugal's territory in the middle of the Atlantic, the islands of the Azores, were considered to be a crucial node in NATO's global defence strategy. America provided military aid to Portugal from the early 1950s (SIPRI 1975b: 248). While not considerable in comparison to US military aid elsewhere this was a significant contribution to Portugal's military capacity (as detailed below), such that by the early 1970s 'substantial portions of the Portuguese armed forces [were ...] American-equipped and American trained' (Minter 1972: 46).

Between 1945 and 1960 the western military alliance of NATO therefore served to bolster the European colonial powers and indirectly prolong their colonial presence in Africa. After 1960 and the wave of African decolonisation the West switched to a policy of supporting friendly client regimes such as Zaire and Kenya. The Western neo-colonial powers' ongoing support for their NATO ally Portugal, in the face of increased international pressure for decolonisation, was not inconsistent. It was guided by strategic interests regarding the Azores and protection of the Cape sea route and by economic interests in Portugal's African territories and the other white regimes in Southern Africa, and legitimised by the convenient spectre of communist expansionism.

Neo-colonialism and the struggle for Mozambican independence

In Mozambique and throughout Africa resistance against colonial rule and the violence, economic exploitation, political and cultural repression it involved had been constant throughout the twentieth century.[3] As Nkrumah wrote in 1942, 'Colonial existence under imperialist conditions necessitates a fierce and constant struggle for emancipation from the yoke of colonialism and exploitation' (Nkrumah 1962: p. xv). The various forms of resistance ranged from 'micro-resistance' or the 'weapons of the weak' (Scott 1990, Serra 1997b: 85), to the emergence of organisations representing and articulating the interests of Africans, such as the pan-African *Liga Africana* established in Lisbon in 1920 and the *Grémio Africano* established in Maputo in the early 1920s, which later became the *Associação Africana*. When this became more conservative as a result of intimidation and infiltration the *Instituto Negrófilo* was created, later compelled by the Portuguese state to change its name to *Centro Associativo dos Negros Moçambicanos* (Mondlane 1976: 112). Much resistance was unorganised and localised, consisting of numerous attempts by peasants and the small urban proletariat in Lourenço Marques and Beira to avoid, subvert or escape from the demands of the Portuguese colonial state and capitalist companies. These included emigration to other areas of the country or to neighbouring territories; deliberate sabotage of cotton production (Isaacman *et al.* 1979, Isaacman 1995, Isaacman and Chilundo 1995); fleeing from the workplace and organised strikes (Penvenne 1995). Criticism of the colonial regime was articulated by peasants, workers and the small group of urban educated Africans, through songs and poetry, and letters and articles in newspapers such as *O Africano* and *O Brado Africano*. In Mozambique and throughout the Portuguese empire, the colonial state deliberately took steps to prevent the formation of a national anti-colonial consciousness. These included restricting and repressing any expressions of subversive comment or criticism and on several occasions massacring striking workers,[4] while promoting Portuguese culture and values and simultaneously encouraging and reinforcing 'tribal' and ethnic identities and divisions (Serra 1997b: 84, 1997a: 140).

Explicit anti-colonial resistance aiming for national independence emerged in the activities of a number of different groups composed mainly of educated urban Mozambicans, within Mozambique but mainly outside in neighbouring territories, and in Portugal, France and America.[5] These groups formed contacts with other African independence movements, and had varied and sometimes conflicting interests and views on what type of struggle should be carried out, with what type of independence as an end. However in 1962 three distinct groups which had formed political parties in exile[6] came together, notwithstanding political differences, to form a single liberation movement, Frelimo – the *Frente para Liberação de Moçambique*, with Eduardo Mondlane elected as President of the movement.

Throughout the colonial period the Portuguese state was determined to prevent the development of anti-colonial organisation. During the 1960s Portugal's strategy for strengthening control over her colonies ranged from increased immigration of Portuguese settlers and an expansion in capital investment, to stationing thousands of Portuguese troops and strengthening the state mechanisms of repression and surveillance (Munslow 1983, Wield 1983). Barry Munslow records:

> A vast reorganisation and strengthening of the administration's military and intelligence systems took place. The secret police, PIDE, created new specialised sections based on the experience of the French in Algeria.

A Centre for the Co-ordination and Centralisation of Information was established, along with a Psycho-Social Action unit. Within a year of the start of the Angolan anti-colonial uprising in 1961, Portuguese military forces in Mozambique were increased from 3,000 to 12,000. The military budget for educational and psycho-social work rose by an incredible 2,000 per cent in 1961 over the previous year. This was to be doubled again in 1962. New riot police units and a special civil volunteer force were organised. Displays of napalm bombing, intended to intimidate the population, were staged in front of large crowds. A tough new governor was appointed with both civilian and military powers. Regulations were altered to permit the wholesale purchase of arms by Europeans.

(Munslow 1983: 83)

It was thus clear that the Portuguese state had no intention of negotiating a path towards independence for its colonies, and Salazar repeatedly refused to consider the option of a negotiated independence. Frelimo was therefore compelled to adopt the strategy of fighting for national independence of Mozambique through armed struggle, which began in September 1964.

By 1964 Portugal was already fighting colonial wars in Angola and Guinea Bissau. Between 1960 and 1968 the Portuguese army grew from 60,000 to 200,000, and national service was increased to four years (Munslow 1983: 102). In 1970 the deployment of Portuguese troops in Africa relative to population was five times greater than that of the United States in Vietnam in the same year (Minter 1972: 71). The proportion of the national budget spent on defence rose from 25 per cent in 1960 to 42.4 per cent in 1968 (Munslow 1983: 102). By 1971 Portugal was reported to have over 100,000 troops in Angola and Mozambique, and 30,000 in Guinea-Bissau. Over half the national budget was spent on defence, and Portugal's defence spending as a proportion of GNP was the highest in Western Europe (Bowman 1971: 24).

This major military effort, fighting a distant war on three fronts to preserve Portugal's African empire, would not have been possible without international assistance, both material and diplomatic. A fundamental condition of possibility for Portugal fighting the national liberation movements for ten years was support from her NATO allies. All of Portugal's military equipment was supplied by NATO allies, and Portugal received extensive and continuous military support from her NATO allies throughout the 1960s (Davidson 1970, Hall and Young 1997: 22). The use of externally supplied military resources in the African wars was either denied, or legitimised under the formality that the African territories were overseas provinces, thus part of Portuguese sovereign territory (Davidson 1970, Minter 1972: 100–13). But as Amílcar Cabral, the leader of PAIGC, the independence movement of Guinea Bissau and Cape Verde, observed:

Portugal is an underdeveloped country [...] Portugal would never be able to launch three colonial wars in Africa without the help of NATO, the weapons of NATO, the planes of NATO, the bombs of NATO – it would be impossible for them. This is not a matter for discussion. The Americans know it, the British know it, the French know it very well, the West Germans also know it, and the Portuguese also know it very well.

(Cabral 1973: 82)

In the early 1950s Portugal and America had signed a Mutual Defense Assistance Agreement, in the context of Portugal's membership of NATO. America provided considerable military assistance under this agreement, in 1960 signing a series of treaties with Portugal governing weapons production and exchange of patent rights and information (Coker 1985: 60). In 1961 Portugal received $238.5 million in arms and military training, and by 1963 a total of 2,288 Portuguese military personnel had received American training (Diamond and Fouquet 1970: 17, Minter 1972: 104). In 1963 the Kennedy administration agreed to supply Portugal with 30 fighter planes, and the American Export-Import Bank extended credit to Lisbon of $50 million and agreed to finance 50 per cent of the cost of building three warships for Portugal (El-Khawas 1975: 9).

During the 1960s the United States supplied Portugal with fifty Thunderjet fighters, thirty Cessna aircraft for training and security work, several Harvard trainers, and thirty Lockheed bombers, as well as five Boeing 707s, three 727s, and four 747s which regularly carried military passengers. France supplied substantial numbers of Alouette and Puma helicopters some armed with air-to-surface missiles, Panhard armoured cars, military transports (Nord 2502 Noratlas, Holste Broussard, Junker U-52), and frigates and submarines. West Germany supplied more than one hundred Dornier DO-27 light counter-insurgency aircraft carrying air-to-ground rockets, which were used extensively in Africa, at least twenty of which were sold in 1969; eight patrol boats; fifteen Nord 2051 D transport aircraft used as paratroop carriers in Angola and Mozambique; and 40 Fiat G-91 fighter-bombers, which were used in Guinea-Bissau and Mozambique to drop napalm, phosphorous and fragmentation bombs also supplied by Portugal's NATO allies. Britain supplied 150 Auster light aircraft to Portugal's air force, and 300 Austin Jeeps to her army. Portugal also received naval warships, patrol ships, minesweepers and submarines from Britain, Germany and France, which were used to patrol the Angolan and Mozambican coasts (Davidson 1970: 10–11, Diamond and Fouquet 1970: 16, Minter 1972: 133–8, 1986b: 234–5, SIPRI 1975b: 248–9, Mahoney 1983: 220).

When the UN General Assembly called for a ban on commercial sales of arms to Portugal in 1962 the United States opposed the resolution, and abstained in 1963 from a similar resolution passed by the Security Council (Diamond and Fouquet 1970: 16, El-Khawas 1975: 11). Western support to Portugal continued throughout the 1960s and early 70s. El-Khawas refers to a secret NATO document, published under the title 'Portugal Afrique: La Guerre de l'OTAN' in *Jeune Afrique*, 1974 July 13, which details American and European sales of arms, including defoliation chemicals, to Portugal in the early 70s (El-Khawas 1975: 17). Larry Bowman observed 'In Angola and Mozambique, America's commitment to non-violent solutions has little credibility for the liberation forces, when they are regularly bombed, napalmed, and shot at with American weapons and planes shipped to Portugal under NATO agreements' (Bowman 1971: 29).

Western support for Portugal rested on strategic and economic interests and dated back to the Second World War, although of course the Anglo-Portuguese alliance dated back centuries (Sherclif 1958). The Atlantic islands of the Azores were pivotal. During the final stages of the Second World War negotiations were held between the allied powers and Portugal, who had remained neutral, for use of the Azores as a military base. Britain first negotiated an agreement in 1943, invoking the ancient Anglo-Portuguese alliance (Minter 1972: 38, Crollen 1973: 26, 35). The agreement with the British included post-war guarantees to protect Portuguese sovereignty, including the colonies. After lengthy negotiations George Kennan then secured American military facilities on the Azores in 1944, also assuring US respect for Portuguese sovereignty in the Portuguese Overseas Territories (Minter 1972: 39, Crollen 1973: 37, El-Khawas 1975: 8). France later obtained a military base on the Azores, opened in 1965, in return for military supplies during the 1960s (Minter 1972: 138). The strategic alliance between the Western powers and Portugal continued and became entrenched during the Cold War through Portugal's membership of NATO.

In addition to the Azores, the geographic location of the southern African region was deemed by NATO and the US military to be important in global strategic terms (Coker 1985: 54–5). The region was important for protection of the sea route to the Indian Ocean region, for protecting access to strategic raw materials, and because of military bases in South Africa and the Portuguese colonies. The perceived importance of the Cape route increased after the closure of the Suez Canal after the 1967 Middle East war, forcing 80 per cent of Western oil supply to be transported via the Cape (El-Khawas and Cohen 1976: 39). Its perceived importance was further heightened by the increase in Soviet naval activities in the Indian Ocean in the late 1960s, and later the energy crisis in the 1970s (Coker 1985: 25, 46–7). In addition, US military aircraft flying to and from Indochina relied on over-flight and landing facilities in South Africa (El-Khawas and Cohen 1976: 24). More generally, fears of Soviet and Chinese 'expansionism' in Southern Africa were used to argue the need for 'containment' through alliance with South Africa, Portugal and Rhodesia (Mugomba 1976).

America's economic interest in Africa was as a source of raw materials, a site of foreign investment and a potential export market. With the expansion of America's economy in the post-war years America's need for raw materials increased, in particular the need for strategic minerals necessary for certain areas of high-technology industrial and military growth. Many of such materials are found mainly in Africa, especially central and southern Africa.[7] The substantial and highly profitable role of British and American investment in apartheid South Africa is well documented (First *et al.* 1973, Seidman and Seidman 1977, Minter 1986b). During the 1960s the economy of South Africa, along with that of Japan, was the fastest growing economy in the world and American investment increased significantly. The rate of return for British and American investment in South Africa and the Portuguese colonies was exceptionally high: a US government study noted 'US private investment is continuing at a high rate in South Africa because of unusually favourable returns' (US Government 1964 cited in Borstelmann 2001: 200; see also Bowman 1971: 27–8).

US economic involvement in Portuguese Africa also increased significantly during the 1960s and 1970s (Davis 1970, Minter 1972: 114–27, El-Khawas 1974). A year after the start of the war in Mozambique Salazar reversed his policy towards foreign capital and began to encourage foreign investment in the colonies, relaxing former restrictions on the operation of foreign capital and allowing a 100 per cent repatriation of profits. This, the 'single most important transformation in the political economy in this final period' (Munslow 1983: 87) was partly the result of the general shift in metropolitan and colonial policy in the late 50s and early 60s, but mainly because of the need for financial assistance in the struggle to retain the colonies. Mohamed El-Khawas records:

> largely as a result of African efforts, a United Nations resolution was passed in 1965 that recognized the relationship between foreign economic investment and Portugal's failure to grant self-determination and independence for the territories; the resolution requested that all specialized UN agencies refrain from granting assistance to Portugal and that all States refrain from any financial activity with Portugal that would impede the attainment of independence for Mozambique and Angola.
>
> (El-Khawas 1974: 300)

The UN's calls went largely unheeded, and the response to Salazar's reforms was an increase in foreign investment, mainly capital of South African, American and German origin. The appeal was made because investment in the Portuguese colonies yielded 'higher profits than anywhere else in the world' (El-Khawas 1974: 303; see also United Nations 1973). These investments were mainly in minerals and energy sectors including copper, natural gas, petroleum exploration (dominated by US capital) and iron-ore extraction; also in tourism, agricultural export processing and construction. It was at this time that the massive Cabora Bassa River Project was started in Mozambique, with significant South African capital. American investment in Mozambique and Angola increased consistently in the early 1970s (El-Khawas 1974).

These strategic and economic interests influenced the policy of the main Western neo-colonial powers – America, Britain, France, Germany – towards southern Africa over decades, leading to support for Portugal in maintaining her colonies, support for Rhodesia and apartheid South Africa as regional powers, and later, support for South Africa's strategy of regional destabilisation. The financial and military assistance that Portugal received from her neo-colonial allies was complemented by diplomatic support in the United Nations. While the majority of member-states backed resolutions criticising and attempting to restrain Portugal, the neo-colonial powers used their influence to block and undermine these efforts. The United Nations required colonial powers to report regularly on conditions in their non-self-governing territories. Portugal evaded this by implementing cosmetic reforms in 1951 which re-defined Portugal's colonies as Overseas Provinces of Portugal, and all the colonised peoples as Portuguese citizens (Wohlgemuth 1963, Udokang 1975). In 1959 the United States and Britain, along with Italy, France and the Netherlands abstained on UN Resolutions confirming Portugal's responsibilities as a colonial power. In 1960 the balance of voting power within the United Nations was transformed as a result of decolonisation in Africa and Asia, with African and Asian countries now forming the numerical majority. In December 1960 the African and Asian countries proposed the Declaration on Colonialism, which supported self-determination for all peoples still under colonial rule. Resolution 1514, proclaiming 'the necessity of bringing to a speedy and unconditional end colonialism in all its forms and manifestations', declaring the right of all peoples to self-determination regardless of 'political, economic, social or educational preparedness', and demanding the cessation of 'all armed action or repressive measures of all kinds directed against dependent peoples', was adopted by the General Assembly (United Nations 1960). The European powers and the United States abstained (Minter 1972: 51, Mahoney 1983: 189). Throughout the next decade a series of Resolutions against Portugal's colonial policies and wars were proposed to the United Nations (see United Nations 1970, Udokang 1975: 305–7 and El-Khawas 1972).

Under the Kennedy administration America initially switched to supporting decolonisation. Kennedy's apparent humanitarian motives and support for decolonisation were pragmatic, accompanied by concerns that delaying self-determination would lead to more radical and violent struggles in southern Africa, resulting in a loss of Western influence and growing Soviet influence (Samuels and Haykin 1979: 654, Guelke 1980: 651, Coker 1985: 34–5). In 1961 America supported UN resolutions calling upon Portugal to comply with UN policy against colonialism, after a series of revolts in Angola during which hundreds of Africans had been killed by the Portuguese.[8] The majority on the Security Council abstained, supporting Portugal's claim that events in Angola were of domestic concern (Mahoney 1983: 190). Salazar denounced the American stance as immature, weakening Europe's defences, serving communist expansion and violating NATO obligations (Emerson 1967: 73, Samuels and Haykin 1979: 656, Mahoney 1983: 198). His reaction was two-fold. First, he hired a public relations firm, Salvage and Lee, to promote Portugal's interests in the sphere of American public opinion (Minter 1972: 83–6, El-Khawas 1975: 6–7, Mahoney 1983: 214, Costa Pinto 2001: 17–19). Second, he threatened to withdraw permission to use the Azores. The agreement for US use of the military base in the Azores ran out in December 1962, and Salazar declined to renew it. The Azores was considered indispensable to US and NATO military strategy. In 1961 the Joint Chiefs of Staff had declared the military base in Azores essential to American security in case of trouble over Berlin (Schlesinger, cited in Diamond and Fouquet 1970: 16). In the early 1960s approximately 75 per cent of all military traffic between the US and Europe and the Middle East passed via the Azores base (Costa Pinto 2001: 19).

America continued to pursue what can be characterised as a form of 'constructive engagement', attempting to persuade Portugal to negotiate a path towards decolonisation through diplomacy and offers of substantial bilateral and multi-lateral economic aid (El-Khawas and Cohen 1976: 24–7, Samuels and Haykin 1979, Mahoney 1983: 203–20). This form of principled support for African decolonisation amounted to little more than 'leisurely planning and haphazard rationalization of contradictory interests and political postures' (Lockwood 1976: 11). While maintaining diplomatic efforts behind the scenes, the United States refrained from openly criticising Portugal or from endorsing any sanctions against Portugal which would have significantly restrained her colonial policy. From 1962 America consistently abstained or voted against all UN resolutions condemning Portugal's colonial policy, as did Britain (Diamond and Fouquet 1970, Minter 1972: 81, 133). America, along with Britain and France, abstained from UN Resolutions 1742 in 1962 and S/5380 in 1963, which requested all states to stop giving Portugal military and economic assistance; thus 'the powers most likely to furnish large-scale military assistance were not only free of any legal obligation to comply, but also had indicated their lack of approval of the measure' (Emerson 1967: 74; see also Mahoney 1983: 238–40).

The policy of the Nixon administration in the later 1960s, directed by Henry Kissinger, continued the option of affecting a public stance of moral opposition to colonial and racial policies in Southern Africa, while restricting actual practice to attempting quiet and friendly persuasion with Portugal and South Africa (El-Khawas and Cohen 1976: 28–30, 45–53). In the early 1970s American policy shifted decidedly in favour of Portugal, in diplomatic, military and economic terms (El-Khawas and Cohen 1976). The US voting position in the UN moved from abstention to support for Portugal and South Africa. In October 1970 the United Nations adopted a programme of action against colonialism, affirming the right of colonial peoples to struggle for their independence; 15 countries abstained, and the United States along with Britain, South Africa, Australia and New Zealand voted against (Minter 1986b: 248). In 1972 America voted against seven major UN resolutions on Southern Africa and colonial issues, and abstained from one other resolution (El-Khawas and Cohen 1976: 31, 46). The US advocated extending the NATO zone as far south as the Cape of Good Hope as a counter to the increased Soviet naval presence in the Indian Ocean, which was interpreted by Salazar's successor Marcelo Caetano as open support from NATO in Portugal's colonial wars (El-Khawas and Cohen 1976: 46–7). In December 1971 Nixon reached agreement with Caetano authorising a loan to Portugal of $436 million by the US Export-Import Bank, in return for use of the Azores base (El-Khawas and Cohen 1976: 47, Minter 1986b: 234). The guidelines regarding 'dual-purpose' equipment in the restrictions on US military exports to Portugal were relaxed, allowing export of helicopters, aircraft, large airliners, defoliants and other equipment (see Tables 6.1 and 6.2). In 1971 America sold Portugal two Boeing 707s and two Boeing 747s for use as military transport planes in Africa, and the Export-Import Bank supported the sale of twelve Bell helicopters for use in Mozambique, and a number of Rockwell photo-reconnaissance aircraft (El-Khawas and Cohen 1976: 47). Under Nixon America's annual military assistance to Portugal averaged one million dollars, in addition to support in

Table 6.1 Exports of American aircraft and helicopters to Mozambique and Portugal, 1965–72

	Mozambique		Portugal	
	No.	Value $	No.	Value $
1965	1	23,177	5	7,021,428
1966	—	—	1	14,667
1967	—	—	7	14,132,912
1968	1	105,122	14	25,370,505
1969	2	7,576,956	9	7,753,035
1970	21	808,030	10	16,458,548
1971	1	5,143,175	9	10,487,256
1972	13	881,678	10	57,936,468
Total	39	14,538,138	65	139,174,819

Source: Adapted from El-Khawas and Cohen 1976: 48; US Bureau of the Census, FT-410 Export Statistics.

Table 6.2 US exports of defoliation chemicals to Mozambique and Portugal, 1969–72 (in millions of dollars)

	Mozambique	Portugal
1969	—	57
1970	28	344
1971	88	115
1972	413	151
Total	529	667

Source: Adapted from El-Khawas and Cohen 1976: 50, citing 'Portugal Afrique La Guerre de L'OTAN', *Jeune Afrique*, 705, 13 July 1974, p. 64.

training Portuguese military personnel. American export of defoliation chemicals to Portugal, for use in the colonial wars, increased significantly (El-Khawas and Cohen 1976: 49), as detailed in Table 6.2.

Portugal was also supported by close cooperation with the neighbouring white regimes of Rhodesia and South Africa. Rhodesia's direct involvement in the war increased significantly after 1972 because of Frelimo's support for the ZANU force fighting for Zimbabwe's independence (Hall and Young 1997: 34). South Africa's apartheid regime ruled an increasingly advanced industrialised capitalist economy with various necessarily expansionary tendencies, including the need for access to external sources of labour, transport links and trade routes, markets and raw materials. Mozambique was particularly important to South Africa as a source of migrant labour for the mines, and as a major export route via Maputo port. South Africa therefore sought to defend its own regime against internal threats and their external sources of support, as well as to maintain control over economic relations with neighbouring territories. This included a policy of supporting the surrounding 'buffer' states under white rule (Davies and O'Meara 1984: 186).

The struggle for independence continued for ten years, during which time opposing interests within Frelimo struggled over the basic nature of their political, economic and military strategy, the resolution of which was crucial for the future of independent Mozambique. These conflicts centred on often sharply opposed views of the way in which production and distribution should be organised and the type of political structures created in the liberated zones, and on the definition of what the movement was fighting against, generating an internal crisis in Frelimo between 1967 to 1970 known as the 'two-line struggle' between 'proponents of a traditional African nationalist 'independence', and [...] those who believed that this would be meaningless unless accompanied by a social revolution' (Depelchin 1983: 80, 104; see also Munslow 1983: 102–13, Wield 1983: 82–3). The basic division was between a racial definition of the 'enemy' – the exploitation of Mozambicans being rooted in their domination by the white Portuguese; and a definition based on analysis of social relations of production – the exploitation of Mozambicans being rooted in their domination by capital, whose interests were protected by the colonial state. The anti-racist revolutionaries were led by Eduardo Mondlane, Samora Machel and Marcelino dos Santos; the cultural nationalists led by Uria Simano, Lazaro Nkavandame and Mateus Gwengere (Depelchin 1983: 80). These differences were debated at the second Congress in 1968, at which the group defending a more revolutionary approach, led by Machel, won support over the more conservative opponents, led by Nkavandame.[9] Thereafter Frelimo always insisted their war was 'a war of national liberation against Portuguese colonialism, against imperialism and against the exploitation of man by man', and not 'a war against the Portuguese people' (Machel 1982: 177).

The struggle for Mozambique's liberation from colonial rule and exploitation, the contradictions, experience and transformed understanding it generated, and Frelimo's solidarity with other liberation movements which was demonstrated consistently not just in rhetoric but in concrete practice at considerable cost to independent Mozambique, constitute a major historical instance of the kind of transformative praxis that Bhaskar discusses in his development of dialectical critical realism. It was certainly a struggle motivated by the experience of oppression. It was a struggle not for reform but to overcome the power$_2$ relations of colonial imperialism which constituted the primary obstacle to absenting the absences of impoverishment, oppression and underdevelopment. This is exemplified in Samora Machel's speech to the National Conference of Solidarity for Liberty and Independence of Mozambique, Angola and Guinea Bissau, at Reggio Emilia on 25 March 1973:

> The liberation struggle of the Mozambican people is a struggle against colonial fascist Portuguese domination, against imperialism, a struggle to install in our country a new social order that is popular and democratic.

Colonialism and Portuguese fascism are aberrations in our epoch. Colonial fascist domination is the worst form of negation and humiliation of the human person. Colonial war foments the most abject and horrible crimes which are repugnant to human conscience. [...] This struggle is that of the Mozambican people and of all peoples. As it is also a common struggle, our struggle to install in our land a new people's social order, which will liberate man from poverty and exploitation, will introduce justice in society and liberate the creative energy of the masses.

(Machel 1973: 153)

But substantive analysis of actual historical struggles reveals that the internal contradictions, and the external reactions of the powerful, pose far greater obstacles to the 'pulse of freedom' than is apparent when dialectics unfold at the level of philosophical reflection.

The struggle for social progress and transformation in Mozambique

When Independence was finally won in 1975 Frelimo was faced with the task of overcoming underdevelopment and 'the exploitation of man by man', or in Bhaskarian terms, of trying to absent the systematic absences of unsatisfied wants and needs. The source of poverty and lack of development was identified as being located not only in colonial domination but also in imperial capitalist relations of production. The broadly revolutionary vision of Frelimo had been consolidated during the years of the war, and in 1977 at the third Congress Frelimo officially declared itself a Marxist-Leninist party. As Barry Munslow records, this commitment to scientific socialism 'did not fall from the skies' (Munslow 1978: 94). In the words of Frelimo, it was the

affirmation of a process which was lived within the Mozambique Liberation Front, a rich, long and bitter process of class struggle [...] for us, Marxism-Leninism was not something we chose out of a book. It was in the process of the struggle that the people's interests asserted themselves and became more and more clearly demarcated from the interests of the colonialist exploiter and would-be national exploiter.

(Agência de Informação de Moçambique 1978 cited in Munslow 1978: 94)

Samora Machel later reaffirmed 'In our country Marxism is the product of the War of National Liberation. We did not proclaim Marxism after Independence. The war turned itself, in the process of its development, into a people's revolutionary war' (Machel, Press conference in Maputo, March 1980, cited in Centro de Estudos Africanos 1982: 39). Frelimo therefore attempted to direct a process of development, of absenting the lacks suffered by the majority of Mozambicans, through a popular and democratic process of reorganising the relations and forces of production in the interests of the needs and aspirations of the majority.

The attempts by Frelimo to construct a new path of social progress for independent Mozambique must be seen from their point of departure of already existing conditions, within Mozambique and in the broader regional and global political economy. Such a task was already inherently difficult, given the starting point of an economy and society structured by colonialism and inserted in a structurally subordinate and dependent position in the regional and global economic system. These major structural obstacles were compounded by the physical destruction of the ten-year war of liberation, the flight of Portuguese skills and capital on independence, and the desperately low levels of education and training of the Mozambican population. The productive capacities in Mozambique had been significantly weakened or destroyed, as a result of disruption and destruction during the liberation war and the rapid exodus of skills and capital on Independence. When it became clear that Frelimo would take power many of the 250,000 Portuguese settlers left, leaving around 100,000 on independence; the majority of those left within one year when land, property and services were nationalised after independence (Wield 1983: 85). The majority fled to Portugal, others to South Africa or Rhodesia; many took care to destroy the property they left behind. Mozambican society was largely illiterate, owing to the extreme racial discrimination practised by the Portuguese colonial state in terms of access to education and training (Universidade Eduardo Mondlane 1988b: 176–82). This rapid exodus of skilled and propertied Portuguese left Mozambique 'bereft of skills', as the colonial regime 'had not even trained clerks to staff the post offices, let alone engineers to service electrical generators or economists to evaluate development options' (Birmingham 1992: 59). Thus for example the railway system faced severe management problems because about 8,000 Portuguese workers left, of whom 400 worked in finances and accounting (Nhabinde 1999: 125); while there remained 'only thirty trained doctors for the entire population of 12 million' (Hall and Young 1997: 57). Any judgement of the strengths and weaknesses of Frelimo's policies and achievements must reflect appreciation of the various significant constraints posed by this already structured context of action.

The causal presence of the past was manifest more generally in the ways in which the structure of Mozambican society and economy, formed under colonial rule, generated specific constraints on possibilities of social and economic change (let alone transformation) in the post-independence years. The inequality in levels of education among Mozambicans on independence was one symptom of a profoundly unequal social structure rooted in the colonial reorganisation of society to meet the needs of metropolitan capital accumulation. The economic exploitation at the heart of colonialism was realised through political domination embedded in the extraction of surplus value from the rural population without transformation of conditions of production. On independence, Mozambican society consisted of a majority of 'semi-proletarianized' peasant producers in the countryside, and a small minority of educated semi-skilled urban 'middle classes', though with only a few years of education, some of whom had formed the lower administrative and policing strata of the colonial state. The senior members of Frelimo were drawn mainly from the educated urban classes – skilled and semi-skilled workers, nurses, secondary school students and teachers (Mondlane 1976, Munslow 1983, Wield 1983). In the countryside, rural society was characterised by considerable social stratification and variation within and between regions of the north, central and southern provinces.

Frelimo devised policies to reconstruct and develop the ability, within the territorial, social and economic space of Mozambique, to meet the needs of the population, and to attain greater self-reliance and autonomy in the international order. There was particular emphasis on developing and extending social services, especially healthcare and education, to the mass of the population, and developing agricultural production through state farms and collectivised peasant farming. Private property in land, housing and a range of services were nationalised, and enterprises abandoned by the Portuguese were brought under state control.

Such attempts and visions did not take place in a vacuum – no social action ever does, which is a central insight of the critical realist transformational model of social activity, as well as Marx's seminal observation that 'men make their own history, but they do not make it just as they please; they do not make it under circumstances chosen by themselves, but under circumstances directly encountered, given and transmitted from the past' (Marx 1852: 398). They did not start from scratch, but from the remnants of the already existing material and social conditions of colonial capitalist society prior to independence, including Mozambique's specific insertion into and relations with the regional and global political economy. This had various implications. First, attempts to reorganise production were constrained by the structure of the already existing economy and productive forces as they had been shaped by colonial capitalism, including the insertion of Mozambican economy into southern Africa's regional economy and the world market; as well as by the existing social capacities of the Mozambican population, in terms of the availability of skills. The attempts at economic reconstruction and transformation, in both agricultural and industrial sectors, proved imbalanced and poorly managed and coordinated, leading to inefficiencies and widespread shortages of basic goods (see Wield 1983, Egerö 1990: 83–107 and Abrahamsson and Nilsson 1995: 48–57).

Second, attempts to effect radical change in the existing organisation of production, for example through nationalisation of land, property and services, necessarily undermined the interests of certain social groups. One outcome was that in the effort to secure the pathway of revolutionary development, Frelimo's measures to resist 'subversive elements' became increasingly repressive. These ranged from sending opponents to political re-education camps; rounding up people judged 'unproductive' from the streets of Maputo and sending them to farm in the northern province of Niassa; to the onslaught against 'tradition' amongst the rural population. Another outcome was that certain groups within Mozambique were able to organise with other regional and global interests in seeking to destabilise independent Frelimo-led Mozambique.

Without ignoring the authoritarian tendencies of the socialist state and the (understandable) inefficiencies in economic production, the significant advances in the early post-Independence period must also be emphasised. The commitment to meet the needs of all Mozambicans was realised in remarkable improvements in primary healthcare and education. In 1982 the World Health Organisation held Mozambique up as an example of a 'very-low-income country' that had made 'extraordinary' strides in rural health and education. Within three years of independence 95 per cent of the country's children were vaccinated, and the number of primary and secondary school graduates had quadrupled (Ciment 1997: 65). Frelimo also achieved considerable success in striving to unite the peoples of Mozambique and overcome various existing social cleavages along lines of race, gender, ethnicity, regional variation, town and countryside. However, the very different living conditions and experiences of different Mozambicans, especially between town and countryside, posed significant constraints (both material and subjective) to realising a unified struggle for emancipatory change. Political structures and mechanisms were introduced, such as the *Grupos Dynamizadores*, in order to create an embedded popular democracy rather than simply trying to change society 'from above'. Some of these were modelled on the considerable mobilisation and cooperation between Frelimo and the rural societies achieved in the Liberated Zones of the north during the liberation war (see Centro de Estudos Africanos 1987). Nevertheless, attempts to bring about revolutionary social change were unpopular both among some members of the bourgeoisie who provided internal support for the external efforts at destabilization (Fauvet 1984) and, for different reasons, among the rural population.

The 'presence of the past' in the form of the given constraints of an impoverished society and structurally disadvantaged economy thus made the pursuit of socialist transformation in the interests of the masses inherently difficult. However, the 'presence of the outside' was far more significant. The major obstacle proved to be the deliberate efforts to destroy this project by externally orchestrated destabilisation of the most extremely violent form. The possibilities for the Mozambican peoples to act in their own interests by pursuing a socialist path of development were constrained not only by 'internal' presences and absences but, more significantly, by the globally uneven distribution of capacity to produce, and to destroy. The transformative praxis of the Mozambican revolution, in attempting not only to alleviate poverty (absent absences) but also to remove the causes of poverty and underdevelopment (absent the constraints$_2$ on absenting absences) by trying to create a socialist society, did not go unchallenged.

The neo-colonial world order, counter-revolution and the production of absence

Frelimo's programme of socialist transformation was deliberately and relentlessly undermined from the start, first by the white regime in Rhodesia and then by the white regime in apartheid South Africa, with the tacit support of the West. The war of destabilisation against Frelimo-led independent Mozambique began with the activities of the Mozambique National Resistance (MNR or Renamo) in the late 1970s. The MNR was originally formed in 1976 by the secret services of Ian Smith's regime in Rhodesia in response to Frelimo's support to the Zimbabwean independence struggle, and was organised in communication with the South African intelligence services (Fauvet 1984, Vines 1991). The MNR was supported from the start by various anti-Frelimo groups in Portugal and within Mozambique. Efforts to pursue progressive social change in Mozambique proceeded from an already structured society and there were plenty of interests against Frelimo and its revolutionary strategy remaining in Portugal, South Africa and Rhodesia. Paul Fauvet observes:

> neither the Rhodesians, nor South Africa Military Intelligence, worked in a vacuum. They availed themselves of Mozambican material that was already there, ready to be moulded into an anti-Frelimo force. [...] Here then were all the elements of a force to fight the newly independent state: white settler politicians in exile, former members of elite units in the colonial army, the embittered losers of political battles within FRELIMO, disgraced members of the FPLM.
>
> (Fauvet 1984: 108, 114)

In the late seventies the activities of the MNR consisted of numerous small raids focused in particular in central Mozambique; and spreading anti-Frelimo propaganda via a radio station based in Rhodesia called *Voz de África Livre*, set up by Rhodesia's Central Intelligence Organisation and run by the Directorate of Psychological Warfare (Fauvet 1984: 115, Martin and Johnson 1986: 9). The MNR's base was moved to Phalaborwa in the Transvaal in 1980 with the approval of British intelligence officers, in anticipation of Zimbabwe's likely independence (Fauvet 1984: 116, Martin and Johnson 1986: 13–16, Minter 1986b: 307). With Zimbabwe's independence in 1980, Frelimo hoped that Mozambique would now be free from the destabilisation activities of the MNR. Samora Machel declared that the 1980s would be the 'decade of victory over underdevelopment' (Nhabinde 1999: 33). However on the contrary the MNR's activities intensified, with renewed support and direction from South Africa.

South African direct support for the activities of the MNR in Mozambique increased after the fall of Prime Minister John Vorster in 1978. Vorster had followed a policy of 'détente' with South Africa's neighbours, trying to establish a 'constellation of states' in Southern Africa under South African leadership which would ensure the stability and regional dominance of apartheid South Africa from internal and external threats (Davies and O'Meara 1984: 67–8). This was undermined by Zimbabwe's independence and the establishment of the Southern African Development Coordination Conference (SADCC), through which the independent African states in the region organised to cooperate with each other and reduce their economic dependence on South Africa. Mozambique's port and rail facilities were key to this regional strategy (Leys and Tostensen 1982).

Vorster's successor P. W. Botha developed a more coherent and broad policy of 'Total Strategy' which integrated military, police and economic policy both internally and externally. This policy combined objectives to form pacts of non-aggression with neighbouring states, and consolidate and deepen economic ties and dependence of neighbouring economies through joint projects and foreign investment, with economic sanctions and military destabilisation which would undermine the viability of SADCC and prevent neighbouring countries from providing support to the ANC (Davies and O'Meara 1985: 189–91).[10] Botha reorganised the organisational and decision-making structure of the apartheid state, involving the centralisation of power in the hands of the Prime Minister and a major militarisation of the state (Davies and O'Meara 1985: 191–94). Investment in military equipment and activity increased significantly. By the mid-1980s military expenditure was more than twice that of 1978, and the South African Defence Force (SADF) claimed to have the most advanced weapons of their type in the world (Davies and O'Meara 1985: 194; Martin and Johnson 1986). Particular capabilities were developed for aggression against neighbouring states, including Reconnaissance Commandos (Recces) 'specialist units containing a high proportion of mercenaries for use in hit and run operations'. Of these, Recce no. 1 carried out the raid against ANC residences in Matola (near Maputo) in 1981; Recce no. 5 was responsible for training members of counter-insurgency groups including MNR and UNITA; and Recce no. 6 specialised in operations against Mozambique and Zimbabwe (Davies and O'Meara 1985: 195).

The transport network of the region, of which Mozambique's railways and ports were the pivot, was central to SADCC's attempt to reduce dependence on South Arica, and therefore became a central focus of South African external aggression (Nhabinde 1999: 15–16). As a central component of the broader aim to undermine the viability of SADCC South Africa's strategy was to systematically destroy the infrastructure upon which Mozambique's economy depended: railway lines and stations, tarred roads, bridges, oil pipelines and pumping installations, dams and factories.

The MNR also sought to deliberately undermine the social conditions of possibility of Frelimo's project and the stability of Mozambican society. This entailed physical attack on social infrastructure and deliberate terrorising society especially in rural areas. MNR attacks intensified notably from 1981. The MNR attacked and destroyed small towns and villages, and social infrastructure. By 1982 the MNR had destroyed 140 villages, 840 schools, 12 health clinics, 24 maternity clinics, 174 health posts, two centres for the handicapped and 900 rural shops; and had kidnapped 52 foreign technicians and killed 12 (Davies and O'Meara 1985: 202, Hall and Young 1997: 129). MNR documents captured from a headquarters in Gorongosa in 1985 contained details of a 'General Plan' agreed with South Africa, namely to destroy the Mozambican economy in the rural zones; to destroy the communications routes to prevent exports and imports to and from abroad, and the movement of domestic produce; and to prevent the activities of foreigners (cooperantes) because they are the most dangerous in the recovery of the economy (cited in Martin and Johnson 1986: 36, Hall Young 1997: 130). Commentators observed in 1986:

> No fibre of Mozambique society has remained untouched by South Africa's 'total strategy' and at least a quarter, if not half, of Mozambique's 13 million people are today 'displaced' in one way or another in their own country. The schools for their children, their access to medical care, their local store, their livestock, their access to markets, have been destroyed.
>
> (Martin and Johnson 1986: 31)

The complimentary strand of South Africa's Total Strategy was the application of economic 'techniques of coercion' (Davies and O'Meara 1985: 195). South Africa significantly reduced the volume of traffic sent via Mozambique's railway and port of Maputo, thus drastically reducing the tariffs paid to Mozambique, and also reduced the number of Mozambicans employed in the mines (Martin and Johnson 1986: 29). This had a major impact on Mozambique's economy which was heavily dependent on revenue from the railways and ports, and foreign exchange paid as wages to migrant mine labour. By 1984 Mozambique already estimated the costs of the destruction of the war to be US$ 3.4 billion (Nhabinde 1999: 43).

Thus after nearly a century of exploitation and impoverishment under Portuguese colonial rule, Mozambique's society and economy was then subject to systematic destruction, terrorisation and trauma. This brutal presence of the outside was most immediately the result of South Africa's apartheid regime, but again this policy was enabled and encouraged by the diplomatic and economic support received from South Africa's allies in the West.

America and the other Western powers' long-standing support for South Africa rested on alliances in the First and Second World Wars, the Korean War and the Cold War, as well as growing strategic and economic ties. America's global military network had important bases including a missile and satellite tracking station in South Africa, as well as the use of South African ports (El-Khawas and Cohen 1976: 40, Borstelmann 2001: 153). America's extension of the military base at Diego Garcia to include a naval base, in order to counter the Soviet build-up in the Indian Ocean, brought with it much closer cooperation with South Africa (El-Khawas and Cohen 1976: 40). South Africa had conducted a major military build-up during the 1960s. Major weapons imports reached $120 million in 1965, mainly from France, Britain and America, and the armed forces 'increased spectacularly'. America and Britain continued to sell military equipment to South Africa despite a series of UN embargoes (SIPRI 1975a: 92–5, SIPRI 1975b: 249–52). In economic terms America maintained a favourable trade balance with South Africa, American investment was significant and South African minerals were vital to key sectors of American industry, including the armaments industry (El-Khawas and Cohen 1976, Borstelmann 1993, 2001: 73, 153).

For a brief period during the late 1970s under the Carter administration America adopted a more pro-African foreign policy rhetoric but in substantive terms there was no major change in policy. Professed support for human rights and reform in southern Africa did not extend to supporting economic sanctions against South Africa; the assumption remained that reform would come through increased foreign investment (Guelke 1980: 658–9, Minter 1986b: 280–3, Borstelmann 2001: 248–59). The regional dynamics of Southern Africa worsened considerably with the arrival of Reagan in the White House. In the 1980s the Reagan administration's policy of 'constructive engagement' was initiated by Chester Crocker, US Assistant Secretary of State for African Affairs (Crocker 1980, 1992). Mamdani has argued that the aim of constructive engagement was 'to bring South Africa out of political isolation so as to better tap its military potential in the war against militant – and pro-Soviet – nationalism' (2004: 92). The professed aim was to attempt to persuade South Africa to reform its internal policies and to move towards stability in the region and independence for Namibia, on the underlying basis of good relations with South Africa, an ally against Soviet and Cuban expansion and communist revolution in Southern Africa. In 1981 Reagan said in a television interview 'Can we abandon a country that has stood by us in every war we've fought, a country that is strategically essential to the free world?', while Chester Crocker told South Africans in Pretoria that the 'top US priority is to stop Soviet encroachment in Africa' (cited in Minter 1986a: 294–5). Despite worldwide condemnation of the apartheid system and calls for economic sanctions the United States continued to trade with South Africa, including exporting security equipment to the South African military and police (Minter 1986a: 299–300). The United States also increased economic aid in the 1980s. South Africa's economy had suffered from the fall in the international price of gold at the start of the 80s, and the United States increased bank lending and used its voting majority to support South Africa's application to the IMF. The allocation South Africa received from the IMF was 'comparable to the increase in South Africa's military expenditures from 1980 to 1982' (Minter 1986b: 319).

The outcome of such support was to enable and encourage South Africa to continue its policy of external destabilisation. Reagan's 'constructive engagement' constituted a green light for South Africa's 'Total Strategy' of regional destabilisation which escalated throughout the 1980s on all fronts – in Namibia and Angola, and in terms of internal repression in South Africa, as well as the MNR's activities in Mozambique (Wright 1989: 160). Economic support enabled the intensification of brutal aggression. Between 1981 and 1983 South Africa spent ten billion dollars in its regional war (DNPP 1984: 7). Óscar Monteiro concluded that the policies of the Reagan administration effectively delayed the total liberation of Africa by at least ten years (Monteiro 2001: 61). The support of external neo-colonial allies was a major condition of possibility for South Africa's devastating campaign against Mozambique.

The US government did not give direct support to the MNR in the way it supported UNITA in Angola, but the organisation did receive backing from right-wing groups in America and other Western countries. This included support from right-wing and evangelical individuals and organisations in America, and links with Franz-Josef Strauss's Christian Social Union in Germany and Lonrho in Britain (Askin 1990, Austin 1994, Minter 1994, Ciment 1997: 117–8). Members of the US Congress argued for direct support to the MNR, but it was thought by the American Foreign Administration that official US support would deepen the conflict in Southern Africa, potentially provoking increased Soviet support and a more radical strategy from the ANC and its regional allies (Chan 1990, Abrahamsson and Nilsson 1995: 99, Ciment 1997: 152). Instead a compromise was reached: rather than providing direct support to the MNR America reduced the levels of financial development and emergency food aid to Mozambique over a number of years, which provoked in addition a reduction in multi-lateral aid from the UN agencies (Abrahamsson and Nilsson 1995: 99).

The major material and social destruction wrought by the MNR combined with a severe drought in the 1980s and rising oil prices and falling sugar prices. The result was the total collapse of Mozambique's economy, the threat of widespread famine, and increased dependence on external financial and food aid to provide the means for social survival. By the end of 1983 around 700,000 people in Southern Mozambique were starving, and Mozambique was one of the main recipients of American food aid (Ciment 1997: 153, Hall and Young 1997: 151–2). External assistance was conditioned not by the post-1945 international commitment to universal human rights, however, but by neo-colonial political and economic priorities towards Mozambique's role in the southern African region, influenced above all by the United States. Access to international financial aid and debt rescheduling was, in general, dependent upon neo-liberal economic reform. More specifically, the Reagan administration cut off food aid to Mozambique until Frelimo agreed to enter into negotiations with Pretoria, and cease to provide support to the ANC (Abrahamsson and Nilsson 1995: 100–5, Ciment 1997: 153). It was estimated that this suspension of food aid may have caused 100,000 deaths by starvation and disease in Mozambique (Ciment 1997: 153).

Negotiations with South Africa began in 1983 and led to the N'Komati Accord in 1984, under which both governments agreed to refrain from the use of force against the other state, and to prevent the use of their territories by any other 'state, government, foreign military forces, organisations or individuals which plan or prepare to commit acts of violence [...] directed against the other party' (DNPP 1984, Gomes 1984). In addition to negotiating with South Africa Mozambique was compelled to turn to the IMF and World Bank for credit and financial aid. Frelimo had always tried to increase its international autonomy as far as possible by following a policy of non-alignment, maintaining relations with both East (including both China and the USSR) and West, but by the early 1980s economic support from the Eastern bloc was no longer possible (Abrahamsson and Nilsson 1995: 98, Chan and Venâncio 1998: 13). Negotiations with the IMF and World Bank began in 1984.

The mid-1980s marked a turning point for Mozambique away from the quest for socialist transformation, as the very conditions for the basic reproduction of Mozambican society were no longer in Frelimo's control. In the context of its new dependency on the West, Frelimo moved away from the official rhetoric of

Marxism-Leninism and the commitment to socialist transformation. Access to credit from the international economic institutions was conditional upon specific economic and monetary policies, consisting of a reduction of state intervention in the economy and provision of services, liberalisation of the domestic market, and opening up to increased foreign trade and investment. Frelimo embarked on a programme of structural adjustment, the *Programa de Reabilitação Económica* (PRE), in 1987, and later reached agreement with the IMF and World Bank on debt rescheduling. Conditions imposed on IMF loans forced Mozambique to devalue its currency and cut back on food subsidies and health and education expenditure. This only led to further discontent among the Mozambican people, which 'in turn, led many to join forces with Renamo, thereby furthering South African aims and completing the circle' (Ciment 1997: 116).

After the N'Komati Accord South African capital started to explore opportunities to invest in Mozambique and increase economic collaboration (Nhabinde 1999: 44–5). South Africa also began to promote dialogue between Frelimo and Renamo (Martin and Johnson 1986: 32). However although Mozambique had begun actively to implement its side of the N'Komati agreement, restricting the ANC to a merely diplomatic presence in Mozambique, the MNR's attacks in Mozambique *intensified* after 1984. The MNR especially targeted economic and transport infrastructure in the South. In 1986 South African-directed destabilisation and destruction of infrastructure increased in the central and northern regions, in response to the international oil embargo (see Nhabinde 1999: 45–63). Nhabinde has provided a detailed examination of the long process of relentless disruption and sabotage of Mozambique's transport network by the MNR under direction of South Africa, elaborating the multiple ramifications for the Mozambican economy. He observes, 'The sanctions and the internal crisis had turned the "falcons" of Pretoria into wounded buffalos. The state of economic war was transformed into a state of real war throughout the region' (1999: 63).

The intensification of MNR activities in Mozambique was assisted in part by Malawi which allowed MNR forces to operate from Malawi. In September 1986 Samora Machel along with other Frontline leaders Kenneth Kuanda and Robert Mugabe confronted Kamazu Banda with evidence of Malawi's support to the MNR. In October Kuanda held a summit meeting of the leaders of the Frontline states, in order to find a diplomatic resolution to the hostile relations between Mozambique and Malawi over Malawi's breach of the Frontline against apartheid South Africa. Meanwhile South Africa was exhibiting mounting aggression towards Mozambique, after blaming Mozambique for a mine explosion in Transvaal (Mosse 2001: 139–41). Machel's trip to the regional summit in Zambia 'was a journey without return' (Mosse 2001: 141). The aeroplane carrying Samora Machel and thirty four others back to Maputo crashed into a hillside near Mbuzini in South Africa, killing all but nine passengers, in 'an accident that subsequent investigations indicated had been minutely prepared by the *apartheid* regime' (Mosse 2001: 141).

From the mid-1980s a number of forces in the regional and global conjuncture combined to result in negotiations between Frelimo and Renamo, leading to the peace accord in 1992, political reform and elections in 1994. The United States and Britain had persistently seen Mozambique through Cold War lenses, convinced its socialist policies were the result of Soviet influence. Frelimo's reforms in the mid-1980s contributed to the perception that Mozambique had finally moved away from Soviet influence, while public evidence of the barbarous destruction, torture and killings meted out by the MNR could no longer be ignored even by the United States after the publication of the Gersony report in 1988.[11] The United States and Britain, followed by other Western countries, began to provide military and financial support to Frelimo for defence and reconstruction of infrastructure. As resistance against apartheid within South Africa intensified, white support for the policy of 'Total Strategy' began to decline. With the collapse of the Soviet Union at the end of the 1980s it was no longer possible for the South African state to invoke the threat of 'Communist expansion' as legitimation of its internal and external aggression. In South Africa growing tensions between the military and capital created increased pressure for internal reform (Abrahamsson and Nilsson 1995: 109). International hostility to the apartheid regime also increased after Botha's declaration of a state of emergency in September 1985, and evidence of South Africa's continued support to the MNR which constituted a direct breach of the N'Komati Accord (Martin and Johnson 1986: 36, Nhabinde 1999: 52). This was expressed in international sanctions against South Africa. In Mozambique the costs of ongoing and intensified destruction by the MNR escalated. Access to international assistance continued to be conditioned by demands for economic and political reform and negotiation, and 'every reform demanded by the IMF that Frelimo agreed to encouraged harsher ones' (Ciment 1997: 154). Faced with continued threats to cut off international aid, Frelimo abandoned its policy of refusing to negotiate with 'South-African-financed bandits' (Ciment 1997: 154). The Peace Accord between Renamo and Frelimo was signed in Rome in 1992.

7 Neo-colonialism and the reproduction of poverty

Contemporary dialectics of accumulation and dispossession

> In place of colonialism as the main instrument of imperialism we have today neo-colonialism.
>
> (Nkrumah 1965: ix)

> The only part of the so-called national wealth that actually enters into the collective possession of a modern nation is – the national debt. [...] Along with the national debt there arose an international credit system, which often conceals one of the sources of primitive accumulation in this or that people. [...] A great deal of capital, which appears today in the United States without any birth-certificate, was yesterday, in England, the capitalized blood of children.
>
> (Marx 1867: 919)

> Newness largely appears as a fresh new set of rhetorical strategies offering its services in deodorizing the primitive accumulation that has operated without pause for six centuries.
>
> (Brennan 2003: 201)

The problem of global poverty and especially poverty in Africa has gained increasing public prominence in the West in recent years. Television reports, documentaries, speeches by politicians and rock stars (sometimes side by side), and pleas from NGOs such as Oxfam, World Vision and Save the Children bring the tragedy of global poverty into the popular conscience of the West with reasonable and intermittently increasing frequency. It is not easy at first sight to see beyond the seductive allure of the discourse through which the contemporary condition of global poverty is portrayed and discussed. Tony Blair speaks in tones of moral anguish and passionate conviction, while the language of the Department for International Development and the World Bank is replete with the need to help the poor to help themselves, through partnership, empowerment and participation. The UN Millennium Development Goals are admirable in their articulation of an insistence that the most basic needs be met throughout the world.[1] In 2005 Britain took the lead, in the context of its presidency of the G8, in urging the Western world to dig deeper and give more so as to make these goals attainable. In March 2005 the report of Blair's Commission for Africa reaffirmed the moral outrage and humanitarian passion for the 'parlous situation' of Africa. Tony Blair stated his determination to rally the West behind his plans to save Africa and Africans from slipping ever further into 'poverty and stagnation', proclaiming 'I believe that there is no more noble cause than galvanising the world to help transform the lives of millions of our fellow human beings in Africa' (Blair 2005).

In these apparently enlightened times does it really make sense to hark back to the old 1970s terminology of neo-colonialism? For those familiar with the history of capitalist imperialism, especially in its colonial form, these latest expressions of humanitarian concern articulated from the heart of global capitalism will suggest immediate parallels with earlier forms of humanitarian imperial ideology, not least at the moment of the conquest of Africa at the end of the nineteenth century. But these histories are not widely known, and so the poverty alleviation discourse holds popular appeal. This, together with a widespread abandonment of radical political economy and historical materialism in favour of analysis of identities, culture and subjectivity in isolation from political economy, make it all the more important to reclaim the concept of neo-colonialism and to situate both the condition of and the ideologies about global poverty in the structures of global capitalism and imperialism.

This requires delineating the contours and dynamics of the current conjuncture of global capitalism, and the place of poverty and ideology within it. The supremely technocratic appearance of contemporary imperialism reflects in part the changing relationship between money capital and productive capital. Lenin, Bukharin, Hilferding and others emphasised the monopolistic character of national capitals in Europe at the end of the nineteenth century, and the growing dominance of bank capital over industry. Global capitalism has continued to evolve and a centrally important development of the last quarter of a century, intimately linked with neo-colonialism, has been the enormous growth in speculative capital, international markets in securities and more generally the dominance of money capital over productive capital (Gowan 1999). While it remains true that both productive and financial capital share the interests of 'capital as such' (Clarke 1987: 394–5), nevertheless this changing relationship and the enormous growth of international financial capital and its liberation in the past quarter of a century is significant. New relations of global imperial domination exercised through international monetary and financial relations and regulation have emerged. These were rooted originally in the responses to the crisis of the post-war capitalist order in the 1970s, but subsequently developed into a distinctly strategic objective of reordering international and domestic relations of production in the interests of global and above all American capital. It is this global context of neo-colonialism in its neo-liberal form that has produced a *further* round of impoverishment in Africa, through new processes of primitive accumulation.

Neo-colonialism, the imperialism of our time

The notion of imperialism used here rests on the necessarily global and expansionary character and conditions of possibility of capital accumulation (see Chapter 4), and refers to the social relations and political order required to secure the external or global conditions for the accumulation of capital. The form of imperialism will therefore vary historically according to the conditions of global capitalism, the balance of social forces within societies and on a global scale, the relative strength of rival capitalist powers, and the form and fate of struggles within societies and internationally to resist or regulate capital. The defining features of imperialism identified by Hobson, Hilferding, Bukharin, Luxemburg and Lenin in the early twentieth century were the growing concentration of capitals in national economies, leading to monopoly situations; the significance of export of *capital* as opposed to commodities; the merging relationship between productive and banking capital to produce a 'financial oligarchy' of finance capital; the development of rivalries between the industrialised imperial powers and their monopoly capitals; and the consequent territorial division of the whole world among the biggest capitalist powers through colonial annexation. Lenin, following Hobson, emphasised in particular the parasitic characteristic of imperialism, arising from the dominance of money capital over productive capital, and the consequent influence of rentiers and speculators (Lenin 1917: 118–31):

> imperialism is an immense accumulation of money capital in a few countries [...] Hence the extraordinary growth of a class, or rather, of a social stratum of rentiers, i.e. people who live by 'clipping coupons', who take no part in any enterprise whatever, whose profession is idleness. The export of capital, one of the most essential economic bases of imperialism, still more completely isolates the rentiers from production and sets the seal of parasitism on the whole country that lives by exploiting the labour of several overseas countries and colonies.
>
> (Lenin 1917: 120)

The classical Marxist theories of imperialism did not pay a lot of attention to the form and effects of colonial imperialism in colonised societies, although this question was foregrounded by Rosa Luxemburg (1913 section three, especially 368–85, 411–16). Such questions were the central concerns of theorists from colonised societies such as Fanon, Cesaire, Nkrumah and Cabral. The theoretical notion of neo-colonialism was developed by Kwame Nkrumah (1965). Echoing Lenin's definition of imperialism as 'the highest stage of capitalism', he identified neo-colonialism as 'the last stage of imperialism'. Like Lenin, his analysis identified the forms and relations of capitalism as it continued to develop after the two world wars: the further concentration and centralisation of capitals on a world scale, the massive growth of financial monopolies, new forms of transnational capitalist cooperation alongside enduring inter-imperial rivalries, and especially the new world-dominating power and enormously dynamic and expansionary capitalism of America after the Second World War. Nkrumah was concerned with the way these features of capitalism produced particular relations of domination, exploitation and dependency in Africa and elsewhere, and analysed new and old forms of imperialism in their neo-colonial guise: the 'innumerable ways to accomplish objectives formerly achieved by naked colonialism [...] to achieve colonialism in fact while preaching independence' (1965: 239, 241). He emphasised the multi-lateral form of neo-colonialism, as the domination of former colonies was achieved through cooperation among the former colonial powers and the United States, and through multi-lateral institutions. He analysed the complex networks of extension of concentrated multi-national financial and productive capital. Through foreign investment the tentacles of foreign capital spread throughout every sector of Africa's economies, as financial consortia make

> the most sinister penetrations [...] From south to north, financial and industrial consortia have spread across Africa, busily staking out claims to mineral, metal and fuel resources, to forest and land produce, and erecting extractive and primary conversion industries in which they are entrenched as stanchions.
> (Nkrumah 1965: 65–6)

He emphasised the way in which international monopoly capital's control of the world market constrained possibilities for autonomous development in the former colonies, and already in the early 1960s drew attention to the role of debt and high interest rates imposed by Western creditors in extending neo-colonial control (1965 chapter 18). He also drew attention to the 'widespread and wily use of ideological and cultural weapons' (1965: 246) and the imperial monopoly control of news and film media; to the retention and expansion of Western military bases in former colonies; to the role of Western trade unions in promoting 'labour-management co-operation to expand American capital investment in the African nations' (1965: 245); to the role of American and other evangelical religious organisations and the American Peace Corps. He thus demonstrated that 'the methods of neo-colonialists are subtle and varied' (1965: 239).

Many of these features of neo-colonialism, analysed theoretically and empirically by Nkrumah in the 1960s, remain clearly visible today. Thus neo-colonialism is identified as 'the imperialism of our time', following Ahmad (2004: 231). The development of neo-colonialism in its current neo-liberal form was not immediate however, and it is necessary to acknowledge the important if contradictory struggles of the Third World for further reform and transformation of the post-colonial social and international orders after decolonisation. These struggles – some revolutionary, others elitist – took the form of a dialectic of Third World nationalism and internationalism. One of the central contradictions of post-colonial independence was the tension between the national and international processes and necessities of decolonisation. Colonial imperialism was fundamentally an international as well as national order, in economic, political and ideological dimensions. The fact of territorial colonial states presented a structural requirement for the anti-colonial struggle to begin with national political liberation. Yet equally the structures of international economic order and international division of labour established through European expansion and colonialism over centuries, and the post-war political and economic cooperation between the United States and Europe, presented a structural imperative for the anti-colonial struggle to move beyond the national to the international realm.

At the same time the initial process of *political* liberation potentially left intact the colonial legacy of economic structures and social relations within former colonies, thus requiring the continuation and radicalisation of the national anti-colonial struggle through internal social transformation. Yet at both national and international level, the unity engendered by the common struggle to throw off the colonial yoke overlay tensions and conflicting interests between rival groups or classes in the structured social formations of colonial and post-colonial societies. Social divisions and tensions were rooted in the deliberate colonial policies of divide and rule, along racialised, ethnicised, religious or regional lines, and exacerbated by necessarily uneven patterns of colonial capitalist development. In Africa these contradictions were further compounded by the nature of the 'balkanisation' of Africa's peoples, lands, resources and economies through the two rounds of partition effected in the 1880s and the 1960s (Nkrumah 1963, Mamdani 1990: 367). The major theorists of African colonialism and the anti-colonial struggle, including Fanon, Nkrumah and Cabral, grappled with these contradictions inherent in the quest for decolonisation, independence, liberation and unity.

The struggles and experiences of post-colonial societies have therefore necessarily been varied, according to the specificity of social relations and the balance of forces and interests in different societies as these had been shaped by the 'crucible of colonialism' (Ahmad 1992), re-shaped through struggles for independence, and subsequently by the different constraints, opportunities and imperatives arising from regional and geo-political location. It is helpful to employ Aijaz Ahmad's notion of the Third World nationalist project (Ahmad 1992: 17–34, 287–311, see also Amin 2003, 1994 chapter 5), and extend it to the corollary of the Third World internationalist project, in order to conceive of a discernible dynamic of struggle for social change in and among post-colonial societies in a way which allows for rather than ignores the diversity and contradictions of these struggles.

The projects of Third World nationalism and internationalism took varied forms, seeking greater political and economic autonomy and in some cases social transformation at the national level, and a more peaceful and just international economic, political and security order. The nature of the Third World nationalist project was in itself contradictory, often reflecting the interests of the national ruling elites rather than the majority of the peasant and urban working population, with tendencies towards authoritarianism and corruption (Fanon 1967d, Thomas 1984). Nevertheless the post-colonial national bourgeoisies generally sought to overcome their inherited structural dependence, and to increase their room for manoeuvre and autonomy in the international order, while simultaneously seeking to enforce internal reform or transformation to overcome some of the distortions of the colonial economy, enable greater national economic control and, in many cases, an increase in the standard of living of the majority. These strategies were accompanied by the Third World internationalist project: the sustained efforts of Third World states as a coalition to reform the international political, economic, legal and security order, through the Non-Aligned Movement, the G77 in UNCTAD and the campaign for a New International Economic Order (see Singham 1977, Singham and Hune 1986, Bedjaoui 1979, Chimni 1987 and Williams 1991).

Thus during the 1960s and 1970s there was an important dynamic of Third World nationalism and internationalism, which in several places including Mozambique developed in a revolutionary form. A faded slogan painted on a low wall surrounding a primary school in Lichinga, the provincial capital of Mozambique's northern province of Niassa, proclaims 'The Mozambican Revolution is an Integral Part of the Global Revolution'. This statement was not simply an instance of state propaganda of a Marxist-Leninist regime, but reflected an important dimension of world-historical reality of the twentieth century (Ahmad 1992: 17–34). Moreover, tragically, the defeat of Mozambique's revolution described in the previous chapter was an integral part of the *global counter-revolution* against all attempts at progressive reform and radical transformation in the Third World.

The various efforts to create a *post-colonial* social and international order, from the more limited and reformist of self-interested national elites to more radical and progressive attempts at structural change and transformation, were met at every turn by the Western neo-colonial powers, most specifically America, with an array of counter-revolutionary measures. An integral part of the West's Cold War strategy, especially on the part of the United States, was the 'containment' or destruction of radical and leftist regimes in the Third World through counter-revolutionary tactics ranging from direct military assault, assassinations, covert financial and military support of opposition groups and 'freedom fighters', to financial, military and police support to right-wing regimes. The case of Mozambique provides a major but far from isolated example of this global strategy. Meanwhile the campaign for the New International Economic Order (NIEO) was relentlessly undermined by the Western powers, above all the United States (Mortimer 1984). The global economic crisis of the 1970s and the subsequent development of the Third World debt crisis in the 1980s finally destroyed any hope of achieving progressive international economic reform. The effect of the crisis was to enable a radically different direction of reform: the *strengthening* of the international capitalist order combined with *internal* adjustment in the Third World on terms dictated by global capital.

The contradictions of the post-war capitalist order and the rise of neo-colonialism in its neo-liberal form

By the 1970s the post-war economic boom was reaching its limits. The current form of neo-colonialism has its immediate roots in the unravelling of the era of 'embedded liberalism', the unfolding of contradictions and crises and the manner of response to them, led above all by the new imperial power of the United States. In locating the specificity of the contemporary crisis of global poverty it is therefore necessary to trace the contradictory development of global capitalism in the second half of the twentieth century.

The post-war reconstruction of the centres of capitalist development – Europe and Japan – and the expansion of global economic activity had taken place within an international regime which was regulated to allow for national economic management, through international financial stability and restricted international flows of private capital. This regime, described by John Ruggie following Karl Polanyi as 'embedded liberalism' (Ruggie 1982), enabled domestic reform in the West through central planning and social democratic reforms (Halperin 2004 chapter 8). It arose from a historic class compromise reflecting the new balance of social forces in industrialised powers after the war: especially the strength of organised labour, and also of national productive capital over banking interests (Nkrumah 1965: xii, Davis 1987: 7–9, Helleiner 1994a: 164, Halperin 2004 chapter 8, O'Brien and Williams 2004: 117–18). The owners of capital accepted 'financial repression' (Gowan 1999: 14) at the international level in the interests of maintaining social order and security nationally. This required the pursuit of national economic development which enabled social welfare, with full or high employment, widespread improvement in living conditions and rising levels of consumption, in order to avoid the further radicalisation of the workers' movement in Europe (Davis 1987: 7–9, Halperin 2004). The masses of 'ordinary people' of Europe had been mobilised by Europe's ruling classes during the Second World War and 'Capitalists needed their cooperation not only in the war against fascism but also, after the defeat of fascism, in order to resume the war against socialism' (Halperin 2004: 249).

The post-war international order and the institutions established to regulate it were designed to provide international economic stability as a pre-condition for peaceful reconstruction and economic growth. International financial stability rested on the system of fixed but relatively adjustable exchange rates, centred on the dollar's fixed value in relation to gold. This was different from the pre-war Gold Standard, when all convertible currencies had been directly fixed in relation to gold. The Gold Standard system was inflexible and unable to survive the international financial crisis of the 1930s, as countries abandoned its discipline rather than face the domestic political consequences of the necessary adjustments it required. This move to floating exchange rates allowed the chaos of competitive devaluations as national economies attempted to mitigate the effects of global recession (see O'Brien and Williams 2004: 224–8, Helleiner 2005: 153–6 and Eichengreen 1985). Under the post-war Bretton Woods regime, convertible currencies were fixed or 'pegged' within certain controlled limits in relation to the dollar, allowing room for periodic adjustments in accordance with prevailing contingent economic circumstances and balance of payments deficits and under supervision of the IMF. The value of the dollar was held fixed at $35 per ounce of gold. The system of fixed exchange rates was based on the belief that exchange rate stability would be conducive to trade and foreign investment, and therefore be in the interests of all, and ensure peaceful development and stability.

The second, related feature of the post-war international order was the restriction of international flows of private capital, so as to avoid the disruptive effects of speculative flows of capital on national economies and exchange rates

(Helleiner 1994a: 163–75, 1994b chapter 2, O'Brien and Williams 2004: 117–18). The control of capital flows allowed for exchange rate stability and greater national autonomy in economic and monetary policy. The possibility of national economic autonomy was further upheld through the international financial institutions of the International Bank for Reconstruction and Development (World Bank) and IMF, created to provide long-term financing for the reconstruction of Europe, and short-term liquidity to countries facing temporary balance of payments deficits, respectively. Thus the needs for short- and long-term international lending were to be met mainly by public international bodies rather than private capital and banks. The restriction of international movement of private capital was not absolute, however, and during the post-war decades international financial markets developed free of regulation in the City of London, in off-shore centres and subsequently in New York (Helleiner 1994a: 169).

As outlined in Chapter 6 the post-war economic order was the result of war-time negotiations between the United States and the United Kingdom. Although generally in agreement, the United States wanted a more liberal regime while the United Kingdom favoured greater control of international monetary relations. The outcome was closer to America's desires, reflecting Britain's new post-war economic dependence on the United States (Williams 1994: 55, O'Brien and Williams 2004: 225). The provision of liquidity for post-war reconstruction did not come for the most part from the Bretton Woods institutions, which had insufficient resources or influence, but directly from the United States in the form of the Marshall Plan and direct investment of American capital. Thus the post-war international monetary and payments system came to be regulated not by the public multilateral institutions of the Bank and Fund, but by the US Treasury and Federal Reserve (Underhill 2000: 107–9).

This system contained an inherent contradiction which began to unfold as post-war economic reconstruction and expansion in the United States and Europe progressed, and was exacerbated by America's global military extension which necessarily accompanied her economic expansion. With the dollar as the international reserve currency global economic expansion would lead to a growth of dollars held abroad, eventually undermining America's capacity to sustain the fixed value of the dollar in relation to gold.[2]

America's ability to sustain the fixed value of the dollar began to decline for a number of reasons. First there was a major export of dollars during the post-war years, in the form of Marshall Plan aid to Europe and investment of US capital abroad, especially in Europe. The Marshall Plan, involving US government grants to Western Europe totalling around $13 billion, was intended both to aid Europe's economic reconstruction and, through doing so, to avoid revolutionary social change. Marshall Plan aid was given on condition of states committing to further liberalising the domestic economy and international trade (O'Brien and Williams 2004: 227). The second reason was the development of a growing deficit in the US balance of payments resulting from the high defence spending caused in particular by the Korean and Vietnam wars, as well as increasing US imports of manufactured goods (Hudson 2003 chapter 11). Over time the amount of dollars held outside the United States increased significantly. The direct dollar–gold convertibility meant that countries holding surplus dollars could exchange dollars for gold, leading to a continuous decline in US gold reserves. As already noted, after the Second World War US gold reserves amounted to three-quarters of the world's monetary gold. However by the late 1960s US gold holdings were significantly reduced to the extent that America's ability to sustain the fixed value of the dollar was threatened (Gowan 1999: 17, Hudson 2003: 16–17, 309, O'Brien and Williams 2004: 226–8). America's international monetary liabilities first exceeded internal gold reserves in 1960, and speculation against the dollar began in the developing financial markets during the 1960s (Underhill 2000: 110, O'Brien and Williams 2004: 227).

In the framework of the Bretton Woods exchange rate regime two solutions to this contradiction were possible. Countries holding dollars could adjust their own currencies, revaluing them in relation to the dollar thus restoring the competitiveness of US industry, stimulating US exports and reducing US imports, and hence redressing the US structural trade imbalance. The alternative would be internal adjustment in America, through reducing imports and military spending in order to reduce the deficit (Gowan 1999: 17).[3] Japan and Western Europe were unwilling to revalue their currencies because in doing so they would lose their international trade advantage over US industry (Williams 1994: 59–61, O'Brien and Williams 2004: 231).[4] Instead of contemplating domestic economic and social adjustment to sustain the Bretton Woods system the Nixon administration abandoned that system, officially breaking the link between the dollar and gold on 15 August 1971.

Gowan has argued persuasively that Nixon's decision to abandon the Bretton Woods system and allow the dollar to devalue was part of an aggressive strategy to maintain the hegemony of American capital in the face of growing rivalry from Europe and Japan and economic stagnation at home. While the declining sustainability of fixed dollar–gold convertibility was a contradiction inherent to the post-war Bretton Woods regime, this and the deep-rooted stagnation of the Western industrialised economies[5] 'formed the *background* to the changes initiated by the Nixon administration in international monetary and financial affairs: but the production crisis did not determine the *form of the response*' (Gowan 1999: 4).[6] Nixon's move sought to preserve and strengthen America's position of global dominance in the international financial economy which rested on the dollar's position as the global reserve currency.

For much of the post-war period America was the world's major creditor, but by the end of the 1960s had transformed into a major *debtor* (Hudson 2003: 20–4 and chapter 12). Yet uniquely among debtor economies America was able to turn this into an advantage (Hudson 2003). The importance of the dollar as a global currency enabled the United States to build up considerable budget and trade deficits, which were financed by other countries buying dollars and US government bonds (Davis 1985: 49, Helleiner 1994a: 167, Gowan 1999, Hudson 2003).[7] The United States was 'exporting inflation by flooding the world with dollars' (Hudson 2003: 312; Helleiner 2005: 159). This effectively meant forcing others to absorb the costs of adjustment required by America's large deficits (Parboni 1986, Helleiner 1994b: 112–13, Hudson 2003 chapter 11). Countries holding a surplus of dollars could no longer convert them into gold, and so had little choice but to buy US treasury bonds. This freed the United States from the usual constraints against allowing a growing balance of payments deficit. The US economy was not obliged to 'live within its means' as 'all constraints were removed on U.S. economic profligacy' (Hudson 2003: 20, 308). Breaking the dollar–gold link gave America far greater influence over other economies through its dollar policy (Parboni 1986, Gowan 1999 chapter 3, Duménil and Lévy 2004 chapter 12). The unavoidable revaluation of the currencies of Europe, Canada and Japan against the dollar after 1971 increased the competitiveness of US manufacturers, which meant 'foreign countries must accept increased unemployment at home resulting from loss of their export markets to US producers, in order that full employment could be fostered in the United States' (Hudson 2003: 342).

The fall in the value of the dollar and rise in other currencies, in addition to reducing the real value of America's foreign debt, forced a worldwide increase in prices of commodities and gold (Hudson 2003: 351). The 1974 oil price rise also operated to America's advantage and against her European and Japanese rivals.[8] The higher price of oil forced higher payments from the oil-dependent industrial powers of Europe and Japan; these 'petro-dollars' were then either used by Saudi Arabia and other OPEC states to finance imports, mainly from the United States, in particular Saudi Arabia's major arms imports; or were invested in US and European private banks. The United States had specifically vetoed proposals to recycle OPEC dollars through the IMF. The recycling of OPEC petro-dollars through private markets meant compelling Western Europe, Japan and OPEC to underwrite US deficits and policy autonomy (Helleiner 1994b: 111–14), because

> by purchasing an increasing amount of goods and services from the U.S. and by investing savings in U.S. financial markets, Saudi Arabia and the other members of the Gulf Co-operation Council (GCC) countries would technically transfer European and Japanese past surpluses to the U.S.
>
> (Kubursi and Mansur 1994: 318)

The effects of the first oil price rise were various. As the United States had anticipated, the OPEC countries could not absorb the volume of oil receipts and so invested them in Western banks, especially private banks, leading to an enormous expansion in international exchange of capital. The Western banks were eager to lend these so-called petro-dollars. Lending to Third World governments was considered a safe option, while there was relatively little investment opportunity in the OECD countries in the context of recession.[9] For their part many countries of the Third World, dependent on oil imports, began to suffer shortages of foreign exchange as a result of the hike in the oil price. They were able to borrow on favourable terms, at low interest, and invested the funds in long-term development projects, intending to pay back the loans from future profits and revenue arising from industrial development and economic growth.

The move to a floating exchange-rate system created more uncertainty and volatility in exchange rates, causing an increase in international speculative exchange. It was thus an important condition in enabling the subsequent shift, at both national and international levels, between the relative influence of money capital and productive capital (Davis 1985, Gowan 1999). This was further entrenched with the successive liberalisation of national capital controls, beginning with the United States in 1974, followed by the United Kingdom under Thatcher in 1979, and then by other European powers, Australia and New Zealand, and finally Japan, in the 1980s (Helleiner 1994a: 169–70, 1994b chapter 7, Gowan 1999: 40–1).

The interests and logics of money capital and productive capital are qualitatively different and potentially opposed (see Gowan 1999 chapter 2, Harvey 1999 chapter 10, Duménil and Lévy 2004: 96 and Clarke 1987). Marx observed that 'both interest and profit express relations of *capital*. As a particular form, interest-bearing capital stands opposite, not labour, but rather opposite profit-bearing capital' (Marx 1858: 853). Money capital performs a necessary function in any capitalist economy in providing liquidity and credit to enable investment and increase production and trade. However money capital does not always have to serve broader economic interests in this way. Holders of money capital favour a rapid circulation time in order to realise returns and minimise risks: 'for the money-capitalist absolutely any project which will offer a future royalty is what capitalism is all about' (Gowan 1999: 12); whereas the process of production requires long-term investment and stable economic conditions. The era of neo-liberalism is defined by the increasing subordination of the interests of production to those of money capital and speculation, through a shift in power to speculative and rentier capital and classes.

The liberalisation of capital controls enabled an enormous expansion in financial markets in the United Kingdom, the United States and off-shore centres, involving exchange of currencies, securities and derivatives. The profits made do not arise from the production of value either directly or indirectly (as in the supply of credit for productive investment), but from betting on future production and conditions, buying and selling claims to future streams of income (see Gowan 1999 chapter 2). This is a fundamentally parasitic form of accumulation: 'in reality the great bulk of what goes on in the so-called "global capital markets" should be viewed more as a charge upon the productive system than as a source of funds for new production' (Gowan 1999: 8; see also Duménil and Lévy 2005: 15, Davis 1985: 49–50, Hudson 2003: 32, Harvey 2004: 71–2). In addition the liberalisation of capital flows reduces the autonomy of states regarding social policy (O'Brien and Williams 2004: 228–30), and so the costs are shifted onto labour, as productive capital demands a more 'flexible' workforce in its effort to remain competitive. In the post-Bretton Woods era national and international economic regulation has been restructured in favour of global financial capital over local productive capital and local societies. In the Third World and former Soviet Union this restructuring has been hastened by new relations of unequal power and financial dependence which arose as a result of the complex combination of structural and contingent conditions and crises in the global economy in the 1970s and 1980s, and the way in which the leading industrial powers, above all the United States, responded to them.

The value of the dollar had continued to fall during the 1970s, after breaking the link with gold. By the late 1970s America's growing external deficit and rising inflation provoked a loss of confidence in the dollar, which began to lose more value. In order to restore confidence in the dollar America began a programme of stabilisation, led by neo-liberal Paul Volcker, raising interest rates and cutting government spending (Helleiner 1994b: 131–4).[10] In October 1979 the US Federal Reserve increased interest rates significantly. The interest rate rose sharply reaching close to 14 per cent by the end of the year, and rose further in 1980 reaching 17.6 per cent in April. Interest rates then fell during mid-1980, but rose sharply again in 1981, averaging over 19 per cent in June 1981 (Walsh 2004: 2–3). In the 1980s America continued to use the position of the dollar as a global currency to underwrite growing deficits. Reagan pursued a policy of economic expansion by cutting taxes and increasing military spending while maintaining high interest rates. The enormous deficits which resulted were financed by private foreign financial support – inflows of foreign capital from Japan, Latin America and elsewhere. Foreign capital was attracted by the high interest rates, the stability of the dollar and the depth of US financial markets (Helleiner 1994b: 147–8). Financial liberalisation thus enabled the United States to run enormous deficits while wielding considerable international power, and America strongly promoted financial liberalisation abroad as well as at home.

The strong dollar, the sharp rise in US interest rates and the recessionary impact this had on the US and European economies, combined with the second oil price rise in 1979 after the Iranian revolution, had devastating effects in the Third World. Many Third World economies, especially in Africa, are structurally dependent on the export of a relatively narrow range of primary commodities, especially minerals and agricultural goods: tin, copper, bauxite, diamonds, gold; coffee, tea, sugar, cocoa; bananas, pineapples; cotton, sisal, pyrethrum, vegetable oil; prawns, cashew nuts. This is a profoundly historical condition, a determining manifestation of 'the presence of the past', the enduring legacy of colonial rule and the international division of labour to which it gave rise. As Chris Okeke has emphasised, in contrast to the routine 'presentism' characteristic of discussions of Africa's debt crisis, the history of the slave trade and colonialism 'are important and not irrelevant to the problem' (Okeke 2001: 1491, 1491–4). After the Second World War the prices of primary commodities tended to suffer a secular decline in relative value, as a result of the inelasticity of demand for many of these commodities, changes in technology which reduced demand for specific raw materials, and enormous concentration in international markets allowing control over prices in the hands of buyers at the expense of exporters. It was precisely these structural problems, historically rooted and reproduced through the world market, which gave rise to the Third World's collective struggle to reform the *international* economic order.

This inherited structural condition was exacerbated by reduced global demand resulting from the global recession of the 1970s and 1980s, which caused commodity prices to collapse.[11] On the other hand with higher oil prices, the relative cost of manufactured imports grew considerably. The second oil price rise of 1979 threw many economies of the Third World into acute crisis. The steep rise in interest rates increased the value of their debts enormously, while their terms of trade steadily worsened and they were unable to meet the costs of the imports necessary to reproduce society and economic activity, let alone service their existing debts.[12] The changing global economic conditions had produced a crisis in the Third World where many economies were structurally unable to cover their trade balance nor repay the loans they had acquired under very different circumstances. It was the international response to this predicament which constituted a key moment in the emergence of the neo-liberal form of neo-colonialism.

The immediate response of the West, led by the United States, was informed by concern to preserve the stability of the international financial system and recover the funds of Western banks. The form of international response to financial crisis developed in the 1970s and 1980s, first in response to the collapse of the Franklin National Bank in 1974, and then to Mexico's debt crisis in 1982 (Helleiner 1994a: 171–2, 1994b chapter 8). Financial crises bring the danger of financial actors retreating to domestic markets and a return to exchange controls. It is thus in the interests of the liberal international financial order for leading states to respond to crises (produced routinely and necessarily by that very order, as Gowan emphasises, 1999: 34, 50[13]) in a way that protects the interests of international creditors. The cooperation of Western powers and their central banks was coordinated through the G10 and the Bank for International Settlements, led by the US Federal Reserve and the Bank of England. This enabled lender-of-last-resort action to avert financial collapse, and facilitation of re-scheduling arrangements between debtors and creditors, under new supervisory regimes (Helleiner 1994a: 170–2).

This early experience in crisis-response revealed a new role for the international financial institutions, in imposing stabilisation packages and structural reform on indebted economies. During the 1970s the World Bank and IMF had developed a number of specific mechanisms for additional financial support for developing countries, in response to their demands and in light of the particular economic difficulties they faced. Thus as Williams has demonstrated they were not wholly unresponsive to their Third World members. Nevertheless the *content* of the new mechanisms of financial support reflected the core liberal ideologies of these institutions (Williams 1994).

The debt crisis caused an acute need for additional finance on the part of indebted economies in Latin America and Africa, which enormously increased the potential for the West to dictate the terms on which further credit was given. This gave rise to a far more significant role for the IMF and World Bank than hitherto, as crisis managers (Pauly 1993, 1994: 207, O'Brien and Williams 2004: 271). This role was an opportunity to forcibly extend neo-liberal reform throughout the Third World and this was embraced by Western powers especially Britain and Germany and above all the United States, which had previously been unenthusiastic or openly hostile to the institutions (Williams 1994: 63, Gowan 1999: 31–2, 41, Duménil and Lévy 2004: 104). Simon Clarke's argument, which referred to the economic crises faced by the British economy in the 1970s, is all the more pertinent with regard to the debt crises of the Third World:

> it is through financial crises, that require the state to restore the confidence of domestic and international capital as the condition for their resolution, that capital ultimately imposes itself on the state and requires the government to subordinate popular needs and aspirations to the requirements of sustained accumulation.
>
> (Clarke 1987: 421)

The notorious Structural Adjustment Programmes of the 1980s, 1990s and onwards,[14] enforced through the mechanism of conditionality, were the embodiment of this new acute dependency and enhanced power of capital.

Revision of the IMF articles of agreement in 1977 enlarged the Fund's powers to enquire about and influence a broad range of member states' national economic policies which affected their exchange rates (Pauly 1994: 209–10). Since the 1980s the Fund has played a much more interventionist role, in imposing financial discipline on debtor states, than hitherto.[15] The declared purpose of the Fund as stated in its 1992 *Annual Report* is 'to help members identify the policy adjustments that may be needed to correct their balance-of-payments problems and thereby lay the foundations for sustained, non-inflationary economic growth' (cited in Pauly 1994: 210). The Fund operates with a standard set of assumptions regarding the 'proper' design of national economic policy, which are assumed to be generally applicable. They are neo-liberal principles, centred on balancing payments, maintaining low inflation, encouraging foreign investment, freeing domestic and international trade and promoting export-oriented growth, with all prices and allocation of resources determined by the free operation of market forces (see Williams 1994: 70–2, Helleiner 1994b: 115–21, Wade 2002 and Biersteker 1990). However the discipline of the Fund in imposing such policies is directed exclusively at economies of the South and, more recently, the former Soviet Union and Eastern Europe. This was not a role envisaged by the original architects of the Fund (Williams 1994: 56), and the Fund's major shareholders are not subject to the Fund's discipline (Williams 1994: 91, Gowan 1999: 43).[16] The imposition of structural adjustment on indebted economies of the Third World is one of the central mechanisms by which the Western capitalist powers, above all the United States, enforce local *internal* adjustment elsewhere to the contradictions and crisis of the global capitalist order generated principally and specifically by the actions and policies of the West. As Marc Williams observes,

> because of the structural power of capital, penalties have fallen mainly on the debtors, although the blame for the debt crisis lies as much with Western banks and Western governments as it does with Third World governments. Indeed, the often disenfranchised Third World populace, hardest hit by the draconian austerity measures imposed in order that the commercial banks and official agencies are repaid, bear no responsibility for the economic

disaster, and yet the workings of global capital determine that their sacrifices should form an important part of the solution.

(Williams 1994: 83–4; see also Gowan 1999: 35)

Through the mechanism of conditionality the institutions of the IMF and World Bank, acting in coordination with organisations of creditors such as the Paris Club, now wield an enormous influence on the specific detail of internal policy-making in indebted states, including monetary, fiscal, economic, trade, labour and social policies, institutional form and legislation. This is indeed a relation of neo-colonialism:

> The essence of neo-colonialism is that the State which is subject to it is, in theory, independent and has all the outward trappings of international sovereignty. In reality its economic system and thus its political policy is directed from outside. [...] Control over government policy in the neo-colonial State may be secured by payments towards the cost of running the State, by the provision of civil servants in positions where they can dictate policy, and by monetary control over foreign exchange through the imposition of a banking system controlled by the imperial power.

(Nkrumah 1965: ix–x)

Neo-colonial dialectics of accumulation and dispossession

Neo-liberal reform in Mozambique, which began in 1987 and increased significantly after the end of the war in 1992, entailed the standard recipe of currency devaluation, deregulation and liberalisation of trade, elimination of export and foreign exchange controls, privatisation, removal of internal price controls and subsidies, and reduction of social spending. These reforms were implemented during and after the devastating war between Frelimo and Renamo. With the end of the war around 80,000 soldiers were demobilised from both forces, and thousands of refugees and internally displaced people began to return. Regional and global processes of crisis, adjustment and reform resulted in thousands of Mozambicans returning from former employment in South Africa, and from the former GDR and the countries of the former Soviet Union. These overlapping conditions created a desperate societal need for order and security, through employment and provision of social services. Instead the social order was reorganised in the interests of the security of capital accumulation.

Since 1987 Mozambique has followed four successive IMF-directed reform programmes and has embarked on the fifth.[17] Measures implemented under these programmes have included (Government of Mozambique 2004, IMF 2004):

- Major adjustments of the official exchange rate, 1987–88.
- Progressive reduction in control of retail prices of commodities in internal market, from 1987.
- Provision allowing companies to lay off employees adopted, 1987.

- Secondary foreign exchange market established, 1990.
- Phasing out of the import licensing scheme.
- Export retention scheme abolished, 1992.
- Major tariff reform, 1991 – eliminated specific import duties and simplified the tariff schedule, establishing maximum tariff rate of 35 per cent.
- Privatisation or liquidation of large number of small- and medium-sized enterprises and utilities, 1987 onwards.
- Removing preferential interest rates for specific activities, 1987–92.
- Further removal of price controls, 1993.
- Implementation of market-determined exchange rate system, liberalisation of current-account transactions, gradual elimination of export surrender requirements, establishment of interbank foreign exchange market, from 1993.
- Privatisation of customs controls (UK-based Crown Agents), 1996–97.
- Reduction in state subsidies.
- Full liberalisation of interest rates, 1994.
- Development of interbank money market and bond market, 1996.
- Liberalisation of price of bread and wheat flour, 1996 – last staples on list of administered prices.
- Privatisation of banking system: In the early 1990s the commercial and central banking functions of the Bank of Mozambique were separated, and the commercial arm renamed Banco Commercial de Moçambique (BCM). BCM was partially privatised in 1996, as well as the Banco Popular de Desenvolvimento (BDM), renamed Banco Austral, in 1997. The Financial Institutions Law and Central Bank Law were passed in 1991. New foreign banks began operating in Mozambique in 1993. All commercial bank interest rates were liberalised in 1994.
- New, more liberal Investment Law, 1997.
- Introduction of Value Added Tax, 1999.
- Introduction of new income tax, and new codes covering fiscal incentives, and corporate taxes, 2002.
- Further liberalisation of tariff structure, reducing maximum tariff to 30 per cent in 1999 and 25 per cent in 2003, and average tariff reduced to about 13 per cent.
- Privatisation and regularisation of property rights and titles in rural and urban areas.
- A new Financial Institutions Law passed in 2004.

Measures to be undertaken under the current Poverty Reduction and Growth Facility include (Government of Mozambique 2004):

- Implementing steps to allow greater exchange rate flexibility.
- A new regulatory framework for microfinance activities.
- Preparation of a new foreign exchange law.
- Implementation of measures and revision of labour law to 'address labour rigidities', including simplifying the procedures for hiring expatriate staff, reducing retrenchment costs and facilitating temporary employment, 2004.

- Infrastructural development on the basis of World Bank loans: privatisation of electricity distribution and urban water systems; divestment of Government participation in telecommunications, national airline, ports and petroleum distribution.
- Long-term programme restructuring civil service and decentralising service delivery, through restructuring the ministries of Planning and Finance, State Administration, Education, Health and Agriculture.

Mozambique is widely regarded as one of Africa's success stories. According to recent figures from the UN Conference on Trade and Development (UNCTAD 2002: 4), Mozambique is among the 'high growth economies' of the Least Developed Countries, near the top of the table, behind only Equatorial Guinea and the Maldives. The World Bank notes approvingly 'Mozambique's growth rate has been well above the African average and among the highest in the world. [...] Economic growth was 8.3% in 2002 and is projected at between 7% and 12% annually until 2005' (World Bank 2003: 1, 3; see also African Development Bank 2002: 34–5, 79–81, 89). The IMF singled out Mozambique as a notable successful case of 'sustained adjustment' in Africa (IMF 2000). The European Parliament's Commission on Development and Cooperation observed:

> Since the end of the civil war and the first democratic elections in 1994, Mozambique has become one of the most successful nations of mainland Africa in terms of economic development and reconstruction, with an annual growth rate of 9 per cent between 1995 and 1999. With 60 per cent of its GDP financed by development cooperation, Mozambique has operated an efficient management and execution of the funds concerned, and has thus been able to benefit twice (in 1999, and again a few days after the end of the mission) from the IMF/World bank initiative for heavily indebted poor countries (HIPCs) for reduction of their external debt.
>
> (European Parliament 2001: 2)

Tony Blair joins in:

> Africa is changing – and for the better. There are plenty of bad news stories in Africa [...] but they can also overshadow the progress taking place. Mozambique and Ethiopia are just two countries that are enjoying sustained economic growth, and growth which is feeding through to their people.
>
> (Blair 2005)

Underneath the technocratic guise of policy advice and international approval lies the real, neo-colonial essence of neo-liberal reform through stabilisation and adjustment. The condition of financial dependency undermines the possibility of sovereign economic policy, while the kind of adjustments imposed entirely take as given the structures of the international economy, requiring internal adjustment to global crisis. First, the processes of stabilisation and adjustment effect a redistribution of wealth and power from the public to the private sector, within adjusting societies, and between them and the West. This constitutes a process of *accumulation through dispossession* (Harvey 2004). Second and relatedly, economic adjustment effects a process of social adjustment, realigning the balance of social forces within adjusting societies which strengthens those groups in favour of the neo-liberal agenda of transnational capital, and undermines those seeking greater protection and autonomy for a nationally oriented economic and social policy. Third, the effect is a further round of devastating structural impoverishment for the majority in society.

Accumulation through dispossession: debt, devaluation and privatisation

The condition of indebtedness and processes of stabilisation and adjustment have enabled a form of accumulation through dispossession, between classes structured nationally and internationally. High interest rates benefit creditors (Duménil and Lévy 2005). The rise of global interest rates from 1979 increased the cost of the debt owed by African governments beyond all proportion to the original sums borrowed (Onimode 1989). The stabilisation and adjustment packages enforced by the IMF and World Bank are designed in part to enable economies to service their debts, and as a result the debt crisis has constituted a massive transfer of wealth from debtors to creditors. Tables 7.1, 7.2 and 7.3 show the development of debt since the early 1980s, for Africa as a whole and for Mozambique, respectively. Between 1984 and 2000 Mozambique's external debt rose from $1,438.3 million to $7,037.6 million. Its ratio of debt service to exports rose from 7.8 per cent to 11.4 per cent, peaking at 34.5 per cent in 1995.

Thus through debt repayments a great deal of capital, which appears today in the countries of the G7 without any birth-certificate, was yesterday, in Africa, the capitalised blood and sweat of the poor. In addition to the transfer of wealth through debt repayments, two other mechanisms imposed as part of structural adjustment have enabled accumulation on the part of capital, usually foreign capital, at the expense of the Third World: currency devaluation and privatisation.

Central to IMF programmes is currency devaluation, which is said to contribute to both stabilisation and growth. The reasoning is that devaluation makes exports

Table 7.1 Africa's total external debt, 1970–2002

	Total external debt, current US$ (millions), average of period	
	Africa	*Sub-Saharan Africa*
1970–79	39,270	21,859
1980–89	180,456	104,676
1990–96	297,191	202,821
1997–99	317,325	221,539
2000–02	292,561	208,334

Source: UNCTAD 2004.

Table 7.2 Annual growth of total debt stocks,
sub-Saharan Africa, 1970–2004

Year	Total debt stocks, current US$ (millions)
1970	6,921
1971	8,730
1972	10,061
1973	13,114
1974	16,425
1975	19,635
1976	22,552
1977	31,680
1978	41,421
1979	49,039
1980	60,660
1981	69,211
1982	76,336
1983	86,880
1984	91,008
1985	107,041
1986	120,779
1987	147,764
1988	150,224
1989	157,072
1990	176,878
1991	183,450
1992	182,824
1993	194,865
1994	221,214
1995	235,435
1996	231,349
1997	220,816
1998	228,623
1999	214,960
2000	211,343
2001	203,187
2002	211,432
2003	231,360
2004	218,405

Source: World Bank 2005, Global Development
Finance on-line data.

cheaper thus increasing international demand, promoting economic growth
and bringing foreign exchange; makes imports more expensive, thus reducing
spending; and improves a debtor country's credit rating thus qualifying for loans
and attracting foreign capital. Throughout Africa and many other regions of the
Third World currencies have been devalued significantly over the past two

Table 7.3 Mozambique, total external debt and debt service, 1984–2002

Year	External debt, total (DOD, (current US$ millions))	Total debt service (current US$ millions)	Total debt service (% of exports of goods and services)
1984	1,438.3	16.7	7.8
1985	2,870.5	63.3	34.5
1986	3,491.7	104.8	54.6
1987	4,125.4	55.0	23.5
1988	4,163.2	70.3	27.1
1989	4,362.8	79.1	29.1
1990	4,649.7	78.5	26.2
1991	4,718.4	82.2	22.5
1992	5,130.3	82.7	22.9
1993	5,211.6	122.3	32.9
1994	7,271.7	123.3	31.2
1995	7,458.4	162.3	34.5
1996	7,565.9	140.7	26.0
1997	7,631.9	109.7	19.2
1998	8,289.3	103.6	18.0
1999	6,965.3	104.5	16.4
2000	7,037.6	87.7	11.4
2001	4,449.4	89.2	8.3
2002	4,609.3	75.6	6.1

Source: World Bank 2005, Global Development Finance on-line data.

decades, in some cases by many orders of magnitude more than the fluctuations in relative value between Western currencies and the dollar (see Ould-Mey 2003: 470–1). This indicates 'a real but invisible financial haemorrhage in the form of resource transfer from southern to northern economies [...] devaluation does not create wealth, [but] it does redistribute wealth across the boundaries of nation-states and/or currency-zone regions' (Ould-Mey 2003: 470). Mohameden Ould-Mey (2003: 470–2) has compiled data of change in exchange rate and currency value and change in export earnings between 1980 and 2000 for 37 developing countries and the Northern countries of the G7, and finds that

> for twenty years there has been a pattern [...] of massive currency devaluations and declining export earnings in the thirty-seven southern countries, and a similar pattern of rising export earnings and little or no currency depreciation in the seven northern ones.
>
> (Ould-Mey 2003: 470)

This structural pattern of enforced currency devaluation in the South has the effect of making 'southern labor and resources a lot less expensive for northern consumers, while increasing the dollar value of southern debt' (Ould-Mey 2003: 472).

In this way the structural re-impoverishment of Third World populations helps to under-write increasing levels of consumption in the northern industrialised powers.[18]

The Mozambican *metical* was devalued substantially in 1987 and has continued to depreciate in value in subsequent years, undergoing a second significant devaluation in 2001. Table 7.4 documents the changing exchange rate of the *metical*, in relation to the British pound and the American dollar (all three measured in SDRs[19]), over the past three decades.

Privatisation, another central plank of Fund/Bank adjustment programmes, enables foreign capital and local elites to acquire industrial enterprises, natural resources (agriculture, minerals, fuel) and public utilities at low prices, in order to release foreign currency to governments to service their debt, 'while the state must tax labor, not these enterprises' (Hudson 2003: 33). The investment-friendly environment compelled through conditionality ensures to foreign capital the benefits of tax breaks, profit repatriation, low tariffs, and a compliant and cheap labour force. Foreign investment through privatisations, often in minerals, export processing and utilities, is precisely the 'new wave of predatory invasion of former colonies' that 'operates behind the international character of the agencies employed: financial and industrial consortia, assistance organisations, financial aid bodies, and the like' (Nkrumah 1965: 50). Mozambique's programme of privatisation has been one of the most rapid and extensive in Africa (Cramer 2001): 'privatization has taken off in Mozambique at a more accelerated pace than in many other countries in Africa', with the result that now 'nearly all commerce is in private hands' (Basu and Srinivasan 2002: 34).

Economic adjustment, social adjustment

The imposed adjustment of accumulation effects a reordering of social relations by reconstituting public and private spheres and processes of production, accumulation and social distribution. As Gowan explains, it

> involves a shift in the internal social relationships within states in favour of creditor and rentier interests, with the subordination of productive sectors to financial sectors and with a drive to shift wealth and power and security away from the bulk of the working population.
>
> (Gowan 1999: vii–viii; see also
> Williams 1994: 84, Harvey 2004: 77–8)

The implementation of economic reform in Mozambique from the late 1980s has aligned the interests of members of the political elite with the international neo-colonial agenda instituted through the international financial institutions and creditor countries. This has entailed a social and ideological reordering of Mozambican society which systematically favours private accumulation. The creation of 'business-friendly environments' – the relentless endorsement of entrepreneurs and the private sector in pursuit of 'economic growth' – creates conditions in which practices of parasitic, primitive accumulation thrive. Mia Couto

Table 7.4 Exchange rates of Mozambique, UK and US, measured in SDR, 1966–2004

Year	Exchange rates (Units: National currency per SDR)		
	US	UK	Mozambique
1966	1	0.36	28.98
1967	1	0.42	28.86
1968	1	0.42	28.77
1969	1	0.42	28.65
1970	1	0.42	28.75
1971	1.09	0.43	29.92
1972	1.09	0.46	29.31
1973	1.21	0.52	31.18
1974	1.22	0.52	30.11
1975	1.17	0.58	32.16
1976	1.16	0.68	36.65
1977	1.21	0.64	39.54
1978	1.30	0.64	42.24
1979	1.32	0.59	42.50
1980	1.28	0.53	41.77
1981	1.16	0.61	41.61
1982	1.10	0.68	42.12
1983	1.05	0.72	43.09
1984	0.98	0.85	42.69
1985	1.20	0.76	45.22
1986	1.22	0.83	48.12
1987	1.42	0.76	573.14
1988	1.35	0.74	842.68
1989	1.31	0.82	1,077.23
1990	1.42	0.74	1,476.93
1991	1.43	0.76	2,639.72
1992	1.38	0.91	4,058.17
1993	1.37	0.93	7,339.15
1994	1.46	0.93	9,709.46
1995	1.49	0.96	16,187.9
1996	1.44	0.85	16,359.7
1997	1.35	0.82	15,574.4
1998	1.41	0.85	17,411.7
1999	1.37	0.85	18,254.4
2000	1.30	0.87	22,332.5
2001	1.26	0.87	29,307.5
2002	1.36	0.84	32,430.4
2003	1.49	0.83	35,450.3
2004	1.55	0.80	29,350.8

Source: IMF 2005a, International Financial Statistics online data.

has observed that such adjustment of accumulation has created some very rich people in Mozambique, but it has not created a wealthy Mozambique (Couto 2002).

The privatisation programme, which was 'bedevilled by lack of transparency' (Castel-Branco *et al.* 2001: 1), has been a causal process in the reordering of social relations. It is not only the fact of privatisation per se, but how it was achieved, which has created a structural condition conducive to parasitic, primitive accumulation. Privatisation was extensive and rapid, pushed through by the international institutions with no care as to regulation of the process, or implementation of appropriate regulatory or industrial policies by the state (Castel-Branco *et al.* 2001, Hanlon 2002). On the one hand this enabled a systematic process of personal enrichment of members of the political elite, within or connected to Frelimo, Renamo and the army. Castel-Branco *et al.* emphasise that in addition to pressure from the Bretton Woods institutions and bilateral donors, especially USAID, for privatisation and liberalisation,

> businessmen, high ranking army officers, and state officials pressed for privatization; it offered an investment opportunity for capital accumulated during the war through corruption and the extraction of a 'war tax' [...] Many senior officers, generals, and state officials were to benefit from privatization over the next decade.
>
> (Castel-Branco *et al.* 2001: 3)

Many companies were sold off cheaply and have not been rehabilitated, many loans have not been repaid and thousands of workers have been left without salaries for months or even years. On the other hand the largest enterprises, concessions and utilities – gas fields and other mineral resources, water services, port and railway transport corridors – have been sold to external capital.[20] These are the so-called 'private sector megaprojects' upon which Mozambique's current and projected economic growth are centred (IMF 2001), including the rehabilitation of the Cahora Bassa hydroelectric dam, and the MOZAL aluminium smelter.

Currency devaluation also effects an adjustment in social relations, through transferring wealth between groups within society (Mamdani 1994, Ould-Mey 2003: 478–80). Mahmood Mamdani has pointed out, with regard to structural adjustment in Africa, that the societal reconstitution from public to private and from social provision to private gain is exactly the core objective of IMF and World Bank policies. According to the logic of neo-liberal discourse, the initial 'shock' of 'demand management' promotes the longer-term aim to 'increase supply'.

> How can this be done? By a transfer of resources from those classes which tend to consume to those classes which have a tendency to invest, from the majority of workers and peasants and civil servants to the minority of entrepreneurs, from the working majority to the propertied minority, from the poor majority to the rich minority.
>
> (Mamdani 1994: 128)

In 1997, 78 per cent of Mozambique's population was living on less than two dollars per day. As noted in the introduction, the proportion of national income held by the poorest 20 per cent of the population was 6.5 per cent, while that held by the highest 20 per cent was 46.5 per cent (UNDP 2004: 188, 191).

Adjusted economies, adjusted lives

The technocratic policy of structural adjustment, defended as an obvious and innocent necessity arising from monetary imbalances between supply and demand and the 'misguided economic policies' of the past, is thus a fundamentally political and social process of change (Williams 1994: 92). The burden of capitalist crisis is shifted onto specific groups within society, which is manifest in very concrete conditions of insecurity and routine non-satisfaction of human need, collated conveniently under the umbrella category of 'poverty'. In the context of Mozambique this category of 'poverty' is not enough – further qualifications are required. It was calculated that in 1996–97, 69 per cent of the population was categorised as suffering *absolute* poverty, and 39 per cent categorised as suffering *ultra* poverty (MPF *et al*. 1998: 57–8).

In this manner statistics can indicate powerfully the contours of social crisis, but simultaneously do violence to the human condition through the process of abstraction. They are unable to convey the very concrete quality and experiential, lived nature of the condition to which they allude. A notion which better captures the dynamic, lived but also *caused* quality of poverty in Africa and elsewhere is that of *adjusted lives*, borrowed from the brilliant book by Nigerian writer F. Odun Balogun (Balogun 1995). This concept captures the fact that global restructuring, usually discussed in technocratic terms, enforces very direct changes in everyday conditions of living and survival for the majority in Mozambique and the rest of Africa, with multiple personal and social ramifications.

The process of currency devaluation has entailed a massive increase in the cost of living for the majority in society. Table 7.5 indicates the changes in the Consumer Price Index in Mozambique since 1985, which indicates a very substantial rise in the basic cost of living over the past two decades. The Consumer Price Indices of the United States and United Kingdom are shown for comparison, indicating the qualitatively less significant increase in cost of living suffered in the West over the same period.

With Mozambique's first devaluation prices rose 200 per cent while salaries rose only 50 per cent; with the second, prices rose 100 per cent and salaries only 50 per cent (Serra 2003: 28). In 2001 the minimum monthly wage was around $33.6 (665,706 *meticais*), enough for less than 40 per cent of the basic needs of an average-sized family of five, forcing families to send their children to work (*Mozambiquefile* June 2000, 299: 17–18). In 2003 the minimum wage increased to around $41 per month (982,717 *meticais*), and in 2004 to $46.7 per month (1,120,297 *meticais*). The General Secretary of the largest trade union, OTM, stated that with this increase the statutory minimum wage was still enough for only 35 per cent of the basic needs of an average family, not including electricity and water bills, education and health costs, and transport (*Mozambiquefile* June 2004, 335: 12 and *Mozambiquefile* May 2003, 322: 21). Added to and exacerbating the effects of this has been the imposition of charges for education and healthcare.

Privatisation and liberalisation have entailed the loss of livelihood for thousands of people. Since 1987 more than 1,470 companies have been privatised, a third of

Table 7.5 Consumer price indices, Mozambique, UK and US, 1985–2003

Year	Mozambique	UK	US
1985	0.681259	55.5507	62.4855
1986	—	57.4547	63.6469
1987	2.4866	59.8385	66.0279
1988	3.7333	62.7753	68.675
1989	5.23207	67.6701	71.9899
1990	7.69141	74.0822	75.8759
1991	10.2244	78.419	79.0892
1992	14.8751	81.3461	81.4847
1993	21.1523	82.6187	83.8899
1994	34.5171	84.6647	86.0772
1995	53.3062	87.5526	88.4921
1996	79.1551	89.6965	91.0859
1997	84.9882	92.5061	93.2153
1998	86.2463	95.6681	94.6622
1999	88.7126	97.1561	96.7334
2000	100.00	100.00	100.00
2001	109.05	101.821	102.826
2002	127.35	103.485	104.457
2003	144.448	106.50	106.828

Source: IMF 2005, International Financial Statistics online data.

which are now paralysed, their workers unemployed or with suspended contracts, and many other companies are in crisis with a risk of closure. Overall more than 116,000 workers had lost their jobs by 2001 (Sindicato Nacional dos Trabalhadores de Moçambique cited in Serra 2001: 10), and between May 2003 and June 2004 over 11,000 jobs were lost (*Mozambiquefile* June 2004, 335: 13). It is not just the 'worker' who loses their livelihood when they lose their job, but the five, six or more members of their family.

In the countryside, the economic adjustment of the past decade has been experienced directly through the increased cost of living, falling value of crops and increased uncertainty brought by the free market. During interviews conducted in rural areas of Nampula province and neighbouring Zambezia in 1999, a complaint heard routinely from all sides was 'our crops have no value':

> before, during the colonial period, you could go and take fifteen kilos of cashew to the shop, and receive two and a half *escudos*, and these two and a half *escudos* were enough to buy clothes – a *kapulana*[21] for the woman, a shirt for the man, trousers for the children and some other things, like cooking oil – with this two and a half *escudos*. But now, taking fifteen kilos of cashew to the shop, you could get more or less 150,000 *meticais*. But these 150,000 *meticais* are not enough to buy these things which you could buy with two and a half *escudos* of the colonial period. Yes. It is not enough.
>
> (group interview, Muatal, Muecate, Nampula, 30 June 1999)

The thing that is most difficult is the question of the market – the question of the market for our products – between us and the traders. The government doesn't set the prices beforehand. So now, we have to produce for the town, the city, and the buyers pay whatever they like. It is him who decides the price, the value of our product. So ... this is the biggest problem we have. Whereas there in town, the product of the trader is expensive. It doesn't correspond with the value of the product that we sell. This is the problem for us these days. We produce, and take it to sell – for example, groundnut, and the trader tells us how much he will pay for a kilo. We can't refuse because we will lose – so we take it to the market, and buy a *kapulana*, and the price doesn't correspond with the amount of groundnut we sold, in relation to a *kapulana*.

(group interview, Muatho, Murrupula, Nampula, 20 May 1999)

These days, we produce a lot. These days, we sell. But these days, what we buy with the money, isn't enough for anything. Why? Because the goods are very very expensive, they are expensive! You find – for example, forty *contos*,[22] fifty *contos*, is not enough to buy clothes for yourself and your family and children. [...] whatever people go to sell – two, three, four sacks of groundnut – they get, perhaps one hundred *contos*. Someone manages to get one hundred *contos*, but with this one hundred *contos*, he has to buy things to sustain the family, you need clothes for your self, for your children, salt, you also need money for the hospital fee or [...] say you want to eat fish – this money, it is not enough. It is good for nothing. Because the goods are very expensive. We manage to produce a lot [...] but the money is not enough to buy the things you need and save a bit for the house.

(group interview, Muchelelene, Murrupula, Nampula, 8 July 1999)

Here, these days [...] the produce we sell is undervalued. In terms of the prices of the traders, it is very low, in relation to the things we need to buy from the shops. So for someone to buy a bar of soap, for example, which costs 10,000 *meticais*, you have to take a lot of produce, because when you take one kilo it is not enough to buy a bar of soap. Because the price of a kilo of ground-nut is very low, so you have to take many kilos of ground-nut in order to be able to buy just one bar of soap. And then what about clothes for your wife, clothes for the children, you have to take so much produce. This is our difficulty, here in the countryside. [...] The money has very little value, whereas in the past the money was small but it had a lot of value – with one hundred *escudos* you could buy something. Now with 5,000 *meticais* you can't buy anything. There is no balance between the money and the goods.

(group interview, Minheuene, Muecate, Nampula, 2 July 1999)

the prices of things in the shops [...] they are always rising [...] so our situation remains, because we can't get enough to go and manage to buy things. ... however much we sell our produce the price is low, but we don't manage to buy things for a low price, because the prices are always high.

(group interview, Nabila, Gilé, Zambezia 18 May 1999)

Selling our produce is very difficult, because there are many products with a very low price, for example beans, corn, their prices are very very low; the only products which have a reasonable price is cashew and ground-nut. The rest have very low prices. We only sell them because we can't stay with rotting produce! The main problem for us is that when the harvest begins, we have groundnut, in our houses, prepared for selling, and we have no expectation that the price will rise, because we don't know if it will rise or not, it could happen that the price will fall. So instead of losing out, we take the ground-nut to sell. We take it to sell, but then, only at the end, after it has been sold, then comes the price rise. But also, we don't manage to store the produce, because of the condition of our lives. The level of life. We have many worries. If you only have produce in the house, when a child gets sick you can't take the produce to pay at the hospital! You have to go and sell so that you can take the child to hospital. So this is what forces us to sell our produce instead of saving it to sell later when the price is higher.

(group interview, Muculuone, Muecate, Nampula, 2 July 1999)

In the cities, towns and suburbs, thousands struggle to survive through petty 'business', buying, making or acquiring goods to sell to anyone with coins in their pocket: second-hand clothing and shoes imported from Europe and the United States, chocolate, chewing gum, boiled sweets, cigarettes, cooking oil, exercise books, pens, belts, hair clips, skin cream, bags, cotton thread, second-hand books, soft drinks, beer, fruit and vegetables, samosas, recycled metal and electrical parts. The sprawling, noisy *dumba-nengues* (informal urban markets), as well as the hard surface of city pavements, are the sites of the *vendadores da rua*, the celebrated 'micro-entrepreneurs' in Mozambique's 'market civilisation' (Gill 1995). This extreme context of 'market civilisation', in which individuals are pitted against each other in the routine and relentless struggle for survival, gives rise to precisely the behavioural patterns and conditions which, centuries earlier, Hume and Hobbes mistakenly assumed to be definitive of human nature per se – the 'propensity to truck, barter and exchange one thing for another' in a context in which life is 'nasty, brutish and short' (Serra 2003). In this world of adjusted lives, 'each day is a hard battle [...] [an] endless search for the bare necessities' (Serra 2003: 25). Without the stability of secure employment, the future is highly insecure and 'they know that they have to struggle hard to sell at all costs because "hunger does not take holidays"' (fieldwork diary of Coleti, cited in Serra 2003: 33). These celebrated 'micro-entrepreneurs' struggle in the intensely competitive markets to sell their goods in order to acquire food or exercise books for their eldest children (Serra 2003: 35). The propensity to sell anything for some coins which can be used to meet any need extends beyond the realm of the *dumba-nengues* to the *lixeiras* (city rubbish tips). The remarkable research of Carlos Serra's team has revealed in detail the lived world of *lixeiros* – those who survive by searching the city's rubbish dumps for items which can be sold or re-used: old cans and bottles, scraps of metal and plastic, discarded items of food, remnants of clothing, old tyres, and so on (Colaço 2001, Chefo 2003).

These new processes of further impoverishment result from a structural feature of the current global capitalist order. The costs of crisis and contradiction in the West, from over-production and the need for devaluation (Harvey 1999), are systematically passed on to others – from capital to workers in general, and far more seriously, from societies of the North to societies of the South. Again, this is precisely what Nkrumah identified: 'neo-colonialism, like colonialism, is an attempt to export the social conflicts of the capitalist countries. The temporary success of this policy can be seen in the ever widening gap between the richer and poorer nations of the world' (Nkrumah 1965: xii).

Conclusion

What critical development theory refers to as 'development discourse' has existed for a long time. Its current form can be traced back to the global conjuncture of the end of the Second World War (Sachs 1992) but its roots must be located much further back in colonial policy discourse. The ideology of development provides the dominant mode of apprehension of global poverty and inequality today. However this book has not focused on elaborating a critical analysis of the latest in development discourse. The current conjuncture requires more than that. The crisis of global poverty impinges intermittently onto the global public conscience but in the United Kingdom it has recently received very considerable popular and media attention, thanks to the 'Make Poverty History' campaign, Blair's Commission for Africa and the anticipation of the G8 Summit in July 2005.

There is something very problematic about the sudden wave of concern about poverty in Africa and the enthusiasm and determination to help. It is not the general humanitarian motivation as such which is problematic in itself, but the form of popular understanding of the problem of poverty which is articulated and disseminated by Tony Blair, Gordon Brown and Bob Geldof. There is a focus on the scale of tragedy of Africa's poverty, which naturally leads to a call to act, to do something. There is a sense of urgency – this crisis has gone on for too long – but also a sense of opportunity: 'Tony Blair and Gordon Brown have ensured that the issue of Africa will be there on the top table when the world's most powerful men meet' at the G8 summit in Scotland, July 2005 (Geldof 2005). There is a sense that what is required is 'political will', backed by popular will. If only the 'world's most powerful men' can be persuaded that poverty in Africa can't go on, and can agree on a plan and commit to it, then we in the west, in partnership with Africa, can really 'make poverty history'.

There is a profound *innocence* embodied in this campaign, at least in its media manifestation in the United Kingdom during 2005. The innocence arises in presenting the tragedy of poverty in Africa as purely tragedy, something for 'us' to feel concerned about, and want to help 'them'. The innocence works because 'we' in the West never have to question *the conditions of possibility of our own relative affluence*[1] and more specifically the causal connections between global poverty and wealth. The innocent humanitarian impulse of the campaign of Geldof, Blair *et al*. has wide appeal precisely because of the widespread and profound ignorance of world history which prevails. The humanitarian response to global poverty is parasitic upon ignorance of the structures of global capitalism and the history of colonialism and imperialism over five hundred years.

It is in part a concern about this relationship between ignorance of history and global structure, and the humanitarian impulse regarding global poverty, which underlies this book. Humanitarianism alone can never be an adequate response to global poverty and inequality because it ignores the structural production of social conditions and hovers in abstraction above the globally extended relations of cause and conditions of possibility which link wealth and poverty, accumulation and oppression. Humanitarianism is a safe response which does not threaten the status quo, the deeply historical, entrenched, instantiated structures of capitalism. The foreign aid regime and international NGOs provide an essentially ameliorative response which serves to channel popular concern away from the possibility of more radical organised political struggle. Perhaps the natural impulse to charity and philanthropy is itself only possible because of lack of knowledge of history; it is a response which rests on a 'presentist' and atomised, 'internalist' understanding of spatially distant social conditions.

This book does not conclude with an 'action plan' to reduce, let alone 'eliminate' the condition of poverty. It has been motivated by a prior concern to explain *why is Africa poor?* The approach followed here is in partial agreement with the many critical approaches which emphasise the causal significance and inherently political nature of ideas and their role in the production of the social world, but the politics of knowledge is approached here from a critical realist position which requires a concern with the explanatory adequacy of the content of knowledge, beyond the politics of knowledge production. One of the most radical implications of critical realism is its defence of objectivity and truth in critical social inquiry.

Ideas are significant because they inform our daily, routine actions and practices, by virtue of which, inadvertently, we reproduce society and the social relations which make our lives and living conditions possible. Some ideas present a mystified view of society and social conditions, and thereby help to secure the smooth functioning of society. Orthodox ideas about global poverty in their various forms identify poverty as a natural condition or the product of the (far away, spatially distant) local present. Poverty in Africa is because of the corruption of African rulers, because of the prevalence of civil war, because of inefficient economies which cannot compete in the global market, a lack of liberal political culture and functioning institutions. Such ideas prevent an adequate causal understanding of the historical production of poverty as a modern global condition, rooted in and reproduced by the global social relations of capital and the structures of imperialism.

Having a more adequate understanding of the social world and the causes of social conditions is not sufficient in itself to bring about significant change, to overcome social problems and change society. But it is an important starting point. This book has addressed the problem of explanation and sought to develop an explanatory account of the production of modern poverty in Africa.

While engaging in theoretical and methodological debates at a general level, the substantive moment of inquiry has examined the particular case of Mozambique. This is not just a book about Mozambique, however, and so it is important to draw out some general conclusions.

It has been argued that poverty in Africa is not a natural condition but a historically produced social outcome. It is the product of a very specific history, and sets of processes and social relations. Poverty is a condition of the frustration of historically satisfiable human need. The ways in which human beings meet their needs are through specific practices and activities connected by or organised through real social relations. The reproduction and satisfaction of the needs of an individual presupposes society because it presupposes the various practices and conditions necessary to provide the objects of human need. For very many centuries, the practices through which specific societies have met their needs and secured social reproduction have linked different societies through exchange and production as well as cultural and linguistic interaction. Thus the possibility and actuality of satisfaction or frustration of human need in different societies is rooted in historical social relations which have increasingly extended beyond the locale in time and space.

The modern condition of global poverty is a product of the development of capitalism on a global scale. The account here has not followed a mechanical analytical logic of development and underdevelopment between core and periphery, but has tried to trace specific mechanisms and processes of social change which have arisen in the long history of capitalist expansion, and which have caused systematic impoverishment, undermining the capacity of African societies to meet their needs. Capitalism as a mode of production centres on accumulation of surplus value in the realm of production through the exploitation of labour. The various contradictions of capital tend in most societies to produce poverty and unemployment alongside technological revolution and a mass of commodities. But the condition of global poverty is not simply the result of the normal operation of capital on a global scale. Capitalism is necessarily expansionary and requires an extended spatial realm and specific social and material conditions for continued accumulation to be possible. These general tendencies give rise to historically specific social orders of imperialism, and forms of domination, exploitation, accumulation and dispossession. So global poverty is not just the product of capitalism, but specifically the product of the necessarily imperial nature of capital.

The account here examined the long historical production of modern poverty through the concrete history of European expansion, slave trade, colonial rule, brutal counter-revolution and the logics of neo-colonialism in its neo-liberal form. The concrete details and contingencies of history will be different in different cases, but the most important and causally significant processes and relations which have been examined here are not unique to the case of Mozambique. The long era of mercantile and slave-based accumulation created the conditions of possibility for the rise of industrial capitalism in Europe while bringing new, parasitic, violent and sometimes devastating structures of accumulation in Africa.

The subsequent form of colonial imperialism constituted a major process of primitive accumulation on the part of European capital which rested on coercive extraction of value from African societies, producing the systematic impoverishment of African peoples. These processes were causally linked and remain instantiated in the structures of the global political economy despite the end of formal colonial rule. The ontology of critical realism foregrounds the causal and irreversible nature of time and the extension in time and space of social relations, structures and conditions of possibility. The past has ongoing causal efficacy in the structured present.

Poverty is a condition of frustrated objective need, a condition of lack and absence. Overcoming the absences which constitute poverty requires changing the social relations which routinely produce lack and this can only come about through social and political struggle. An adequate understanding of the causes of poverty and oppression is necessary but not sufficient, and actual struggles to change society will be confronted by the very structures they seek overcome. It seems surprising how easily critical scholars can talk of emancipation these days, but the history of the twentieth century shows us that changing society is not easy and will be resisted, often brutally. During the twentieth century the Western capitalist powers consistently undermined possibilities of radical social change in the Third World, both in specific societies and regions and in terms of the structure and regulation of the international economy. We therefore need to conceive of this period of capitalist world order in terms of neo-colonialism, in recognition that such policies are not unintended consequences of the well-intended, civilised actions of benign powers. The ruthless brutality with which the Western capitalist powers have sought to protect the interests of capital and prevent radical social change is seen in the long history of devastating war against Mozambican independence and self-determination. This history is not isolated or exceptional, but part of a much broader dynamic of twentieth-century imperialism.

The neo-liberal world order which has emerged from the wreckage of crisis and counter-revolution embodies new forms of primitive accumulation and impoverishment. Responding to structural economic crisis by imposing internal neo-liberal reforms effectively means passing the costs of globally produced crisis and risk onto the populations of the Third World, specifically, the workers, peasants and unemployed. It enables maintaining relatively high living standards and levels of consumption in the advanced industrialised countries, and reduces the need for politically dangerous economic adjustment in the West.

The restructuring of global capitalism since the 1970s and the renewed dominance of money capital over productive capital has produced the re-emergence of the essentially *parasitic* quality of imperialism, analysed by Lenin and Hobson at the beginning of the nineteenth century. The post-war regime of Keynsianism and the national bourgeois project in the Third World have been replaced, through counter-revolution and crisis-management, by a return to the pure qualities of capitalist imperialism on a global scale. The term neo-colonialism has been employed here because it is essential to recognise this historical conjuncture as a *further* round of globally imposed impoverishment on African societies, effected through new forms of domination with new mechanisms and ideologies. The new form and appearance of domination is epitomised in the supremely technocratic discourse and practice of international monetary relations. While Tony Blair's conscience is pricked by the plight of Africa's poor, the policies endorsed by the United Kingdom through the G7/G8 and the international financial institutions remain committed to neo-colonialism's neo-liberal project. Nevertheless the conditions of possibility of these new mechanisms of domination, anticipated with such foresight by Nkrumah, were produced to a large extent by formal colonialism. The colonial past is massively present in the fundamental economic structure underlying Africa's economic crisis and position of subordination in the global political economy today.

Notes

1 Poverty and development in Africa: twentieth-century orthodoxies

1 Key works include Apter 1965, 1968, Almond and Coleman 1960, Eisenstadt 1966, Kilson 1966, Rustow 1967, Lerner 1958 and Parsons 1960.
2 See Pye 1966, Pye and Verba 1965, Kuper and Smith 1969 and Post 1963.
3 See Almond and Powell 1966, Eckstein and Apter 1963, Apter 1958, Eisenstadt 1965, 1968, Gamer 1976, Kalleberb 1966, Black 1966 and Diamond *et al.* 1990.
4 See Zolberg 1968, O'Connell 1967, van den Berghe 1971, Lemarchand 1972, Huntington 1965, Eisenstadt 1966, 1973, Morrison and Stevenson 1972 and Mitchell 1960.
5 For example Zolberg 1968, Zolberg 1966, 1968, Apter 1973, Eisenstadt 1966, 1968, Kilson 1966, Southall 1961, Halpern 1963.
6 'Integration into a free society does not entail the total elimination of conflict from political life, but rather its containment within acceptable limits as indicated by a shift from force to power and authority. How that is achieved remains a central problem of the social sciences which far transcends the parochial concerns of particular disciplines or sub-disciplines within each' (Zolberg 1968: 87).
7 See for example Dyer and Mangasarian 1989, Dunne *et al.* 1999, Booth and Smith 1995, Smith *et al.* 1996 and Rengger 1999.
8 Within International Relations this tradition is generally referred to as realism, with the positions of classical and neo-realism distinguished. The term political realism is used here to distinguish IR realism from the philosophical position of critical realism.
9 See for example Kilson 1975b, Zolberg 1968 and Lyon 1973.
10 See for example Zartman 1966, 1967, McKay 1966 and Hoffman 1975.
11 For example Singer 1972, Rothstein 1977, Jackson and Rosberg 1982, Handel 1981.
12 Parsons 1960, Pye 1966, O'Connell 1967, Huntington 1968, Zolberg 1968, Kilson 1975a, c: pp. ix–x, Jackson and Rosberg 1982: 5.
13 Butterfield and Wight 1966, Jackson and Rosberg, 1982, Bull and Watson 1984.
14 See for example Williams, M. 1987, 1991, Mortimer 1984, Rothstein 1979 and Krasner 1985.
15 For example the *Unidade de Alívio da Pobreza*/Poverty Alleviation Unit within the Ministry of Planning and Finance, and the Policy Analysis Unit within the Ministry of Agriculture (formerly the Food Security Project, set up in 1992). See Governo de Moçambique 1995/Government of Mozambique 1995a; Government of Mozambique 1995b and Addison and Macdonald 1995.
16 For example World Vision Mozambique, CARE International, the Co-operative League of the USA (CLUSA), Actionaid, Oxfam and many others.
17 Including the World Bank and African Development Bank; the UNDP; the Mozambique Food Security Unit of the European Commission; governmental donor

agencies including the United States Agency for International Development (USAID), the Department for International Development of the UK (DFID), and similar agencies from numerous other donor countries in Europe and elsewhere.

18 For example the International Food Policy Research Institute (IFPRI).

19 For example consultancy firms such as Technoserve, Abt Associates, Deloitte and Touche.

20 For example the debate between Cramer and Pontara, and Pitcher (Cramer and Pontara 1998, 1999, Pitcher 1999).

21 This is the typical representation of rural poverty in the policy literature. The academic debate tends to be more nuanced, and many analysts highlight the numerous different activities people engage in to meet their needs – referred to in terms such as 'multiple coping strategies'. Indeed such approaches often celebrate the resourcefulness and ingenuity of rural peoples manifest in their diverse livelihood strategies. This positive evaluation perhaps derives from a desire to insist on the agency of rural people, rather than portraying them as victims of structural determinants. However there seems to be little analytical difference between celebrating the rural poor's ingenuity and resourcefulness manifest in their diverse livelihood coping strategies; and celebrating their *rationality* as rural decision-makers allocating their resources so as to best maximise their income and welfare. Both approaches see only empirical aspects of behaviour and fail to locate the condition of poverty as an outcome of distinct, historically specific social relations. A focus on social relations reveals the world-historical nature of modern rural poverty in Mozambique and the rest of Africa. Of course the 'rural poor' of Mozambique have *agency*; so too do the managers of transnational corporations, investment funds, credit-rating agencies. Their different social power arises from their different location within structures of social relations. Of course the rural poor of Mozambique make their own history, but they do so in conditions not of their own making or choice.

22 For example 'The strategies a household utilizes to maximize its income and food security are revealed by a number of factors, including the relationship it has established to the food market, the various means it has chosen to generate income, the manner in which it has chosen to spend its cash income, and finally the sources it utilizes to obtain calories' (Ministry of Agriculture and Fisheries 1992: 10).

23 'Going beyond subsistence production to production of marketable surpluses will require a strategy that also looks at smallholders (family sector) as part of the private sector, rather than as a distinctive and separate grouping. Whereas smallholder farmers tend to cultivate small plots of land, they are able to do much more. Policies and programs that aim to create the enabling environment for smallholders to take advantage of the availability of land in the country, and to increase areas under cultivation in ways which are environmentally sustainable, will be needed to expand private farming – including smallholders – in the country' (World Bank 1993: 30; see also World Bank 1996a: 21 and Abt Associates Inc. 1998: 12).

24 'Raising rural incomes' is a strategic objective of USAID's programme in Mozambique.

25 'Attainment of food self-sufficiency would maintain Mozambique at a low level equilibrium. In the post-war period economic growth will accelerate only if a successful transition from subsistence to production for market occurs, as well as diversification of production to include cash crops as well as food crops.' (World Bank 1993: 29; see also Government of Mozambique 1995a: 17, 18).

26 The Government of Mozambique's development policy does include an emphasis on the development of larger-scale commercial farming, within the framework of PROAGRI, the National Program for Agrarian Development. The aim here however is to characterise the particular approach to rural poverty alleviation and the way in which it is portrayed in relation to national development.

27 'The analysis has demonstrated that raising the farming output of smallholders is an effective way of reducing poverty. The argument is developed in three stages: small-holders constitute the vast majority of Mozambican society; smallholders are among the poorest people in the country; and raising smallholder production would reduce poverty directly, by raising incomes, and indirectly, by reducing the isolation of smallholder families.' (World Bank 1996a: 5; also in Government of Mozambique 2001: 4).

28 'The term *democracy* is used in this book to signify a political system, separate and apart from the economic and social system to which it is joined. Indeed, a distinctive aspect of our approach is to insist that issues of so-called 'economic and social democracy' be separated from the question of governmental structure . . . . Unless the economic and social dimensions are kept conceptually distinct from the political, there is no way to analyze how variation on the political dimension is related to variation on the others' (Diamond *et al*. 1990: 6).

29 Important critiques of the modernisation, pluralist and other Africanist approaches include Barongo 1978, Leggasick 1977, Ake 1973, Mamdani 1996b and Mamdani 1995. For analyses of the phenomenon of authoritarianism in post-colonial states, which situate it historically and within the global political economy, see Thomas 1984, Ahmad, E. 1983, 1980, Mamdani 1983, Johnson 1985 and Fanon 1967d.

30 See, among others, the brilliant work of Antony Anghie, e.g. Anghie 1999.

31 Du Bois is discussing the systematic absence in accounts of American history of serious discussions of slavery: 'Our histories tend to discuss American slavery so impartially, that in the end nobody seems to have done wrong and everybody was right. Slavery appears to have been thrust upon unwilling helpless America, while the South was blameless in becoming its centre' (Du Bois 1964 [1935]: 714), and the North and South refer to America, not the world. Nevertheless the essence of his critique applies to the contemporary orthodoxy of IR and DS.

2   Critical perspectives: from global structure to local agency

1 The literature on dependency, underdevelopment and world systems is enormous and it is neither necessary nor possible to provide a comprehensive review here. The aim is to present a summary view of the central contribution of the literature – its emphasis on global structure, capitalism and world history – whilst also indicating the variety of positions among both proponents and critics. Extensive reviews are available elsewhere, for example in Brewer 1990, Larrain 1989, Harrison 1988 and Chilcote 1974.

2 See Booth 1985, Corbridge 1990, Sklair 1988, Vandergeest and Buttel 1988 and Schuurman 1993.

3 This was discussed for example by Taylor 1979: p. ix, Booth 1985, Mouzelis 1988, Sklair 1988, Corbridge 1990, Booth 1994b and Gardner and Lewis 1996.

4 For example Escobar 1984–85, 1995, Ferguson 1990, Sachs 1992, Moore and Schmitz 1994, Apthorpe and Gasper 1996 and Grillo and Stirrat 1997. For a comprehensive overview, see Grillo 1997.

5 Long 1989, 1992, Drinkwater 1992, Berry 1993, Arce *et al*. 1994, Long and van der Ploeg 1994.

6 For example Chambers 1983, Chambers *et al*. 1989, Hobart 1993a, Scoones and Thompson 1994 and Misturelli and Heffernan 2001.

7 See Williams 1996: 46–7, Murphy and Tooze 1991b, Krasner 1996: 109, Cox 1981: 130, O'Brien 1995 and Biersteker 1993.

8 The range of developments which fall under the umbrella term 'critical' is of course very broad; one can be critical in different ways reflecting different core assumptions. A variety of perspectives emerged in the opening up of IR to alternative approaches influenced in

different ways by critiques of positivism, including feminism, post-modernism/ post-structuralism and social constructivism as well as critical theory and critical IPE. Richard Wyn Jones distinguishes between two approaches to critical IR/IPE. The first, exemplified by the work of Andrew Linklater, Mark Hoffman and Mark Neufeld, is influenced by the Frankfurt School (Habermas, Adorno, Horkheimer) and is concerned primarily with political and normative theory. The second, influenced by Gramsci, is concerned primarily with political economy (Wyn Jones 2001: 5). The focus here is on those who remain within the scope, broadly defined, of political economy. Prominent scholars who advocate and develop a critical approach to IPE include Robert Cox, Craig Murphy, Roger Tooze, John Maclean, Mark Rupert, Stephen Gill, Kees van der Pijl, Hazel Smith, Peter Burnham, Claire Cutler and Adam Morton. These and other critical IPE scholars by no means share the same approach in terms of substantive interests or methodological principles, indeed there is some debate among them. However they share an explicit aim to question and explain rather than take as given the status quo, and to explore questions of method; and many, though not all, draw on some form of Marxist thought, especially Gramsci's work.

9 For overviews see Murphy and Tooze 1991a, Murphy and Tooze 1991b, Tooze 1988, Cox 1981, Gill 1991b and Bieler and Morton 2004. Cox summarises critical IPE's opposition to the mainstream in terms of ontology: 'Neorealism has an explicit ontology . . . in which states, balance of power, Hobbesian power-seeking man, and the contractual basis of polity are presumed to be eternal interrelated components of world order. Critical theory has relativized neorealism so as to perceive it as an ideology of the Cold War. In a more positive sense, critical theory has envisaged a shift in ontology toward a more adequate depiction of the "real world" of the twenty-first century; so far this alternative ontology is only a work in progress' (Cox 2001: 46).

10 See Augelli and Murphy 1988, Gill 1991a, 1993c, Morton 2003 and Bieler and Morton 2004.

11 Tooze and Murphy's discussion of development practice is astoundingly naïve and suggests very little awareness either of the nature of the current development regime, or of the many critiques of the 'new orthodoxy' of development practice and NGOs (see for example Hearn 1998 and Henkel and Stirrat 2001). They refer approvingly to the micro-credit programmes of organisations such as the Grameen Bank, with little awareness of the role of micro-credit in the imposed neo-liberal financial restructuring of Third World economies, exposed by Heloise Weber (2002, 2004). Their approach seems little different in tone from that of the pseudo-radical Robert Chambers (Chambers 1983), whose work has been readily absorbed by the neo-liberal mainstream. The shallowness of the apparently radical impulse to listen to the voices of the poor as an end in itself is demonstrated by the fact that the World Bank has engaged in precisely such an exercise. See World Bank 1999, Narayan *et al.* 2000a,b and Narayan and Petesch 2002. Timothy Brennan's acerbic observation is pertinent in this regard: 'In this echo chamber, theory espouses a set of values that, at the level of ethics, is often painfully, and of course unintentionally, similar to neo-liberal orthodoxy' (Brennan 2003: 202).

12 For example, 'Gramsci's approach is consistent with the idea of historical structures, which are partly constituted by the consciousness and action of individuals and groups' (Gill 1993b: 22); 'beliefs and values are themselves just as real as the material structures and powers of the global political economy [. . .] all the global political economy is constituted by the reciprocal interaction of meaning and material capability' (Murphy and Tooze 1991a: 18–19).

13 Cox defines ontology as 'the attempt to identify the basic constitutive factors that help toward understanding and acting upon a particular historical conjuncture [. . .] the task is one of perceiving the historical structures that characterize and epoch. These structures, which are mental constructions, summarize the cumulative result of collective human action over time' (Cox 2001: 46). Gill emphasises the relationship between

ideas and hegemony as follows: 'The idea of an historical bloc – a concept which is one of the most fundamental innovations of Gramsci's political theory – is consistent in some ways with what Michel Foucault called a 'discursive formation': a set of ideas and practices with particular conditions of existence, which are more or less institutionalised, but which may be only partially understood by those that they encompass. Both concepts allow us to make sense of the way that practices and understandings come to pervade many areas of social and political life, in complex, perhaps unpredictable and contested, ways' (Gill 1995: 402). He places ideas and inter-subjective understanding as central to ontology in a similar manner to Cox: 'we may be in the throes of an ontological change or shift: a redefinition of the understandings and experiences that form basic components of lived reality. This includes mental frameworks – for example the way we think about social institutions and forms of political authority. Ontology more broadly involves shared understandings of the universe, the cosmic order and its origins; thus of time and space, and also of the interaction of social forces and nature [. . .] An ontology of the world includes our hopes, doubts, fears and expectations, our assessments of constraints and of human possibilities' (1997: 6).

3 Objectivity, need and the dialectics of emancipation

1 In IR there has been explicit engagement with debates in philosophy of science and the critique of positivism, for example George 1988, Hollis and Smith 1990, Neufeld 1995, Vasquez 1995 and Smith *et al.* 1996. In Development Studies the influence of philosophical debate is more indirect, via engagement with post-modernism and post-structuralism, as outlined in the previous chapter. See for example Escobar 1995, Gardner and Lewis 1996 and Parfitt's survey (2002) of the influences of post-modernism in Development Studies.

2 Things and events exist independently of experiences of them. This implies the existence of two distinct domains, which Bhaskar terms the transitive – consisting of knowledge, which is socially produced, developing and changing; and the intransitive – consisting of the objects of knowledge, which exist independently of knowledge. When scientific knowledge changes and develops, this does not mean that the objects of such knowledge themselves change.

3 The intelligibility of scientific experiment entails the ontological distinction between events, and the mechanisms which generate them. Causal laws, which are discovered in the process of development of science, consist of statements about the operation of different mechanisms – the characteristic 'way of acting' of different things. They refer to mechanisms; they are not statements about events or experiences.

4 The objects of scientific knowledge are not events, but structures and causal mechanisms; and scientific laws are statements about the ways-of-acting of things – generative mechanisms – not statements about empirical regularities of events. Scientific laws therefore make no claims about actual outcomes, just about the ways-of-acting, the causal powers, of things: 'The world consists of things, not events. Most things are complex objects, in virtue of which they possess an ensemble of tendencies, liabilities and powers. It is by reference to the exercise of their tendencies, liabilities and powers that the phenomena of the world are explained. Such continuing activity is in turn referred back for explanation to the essential nature of things. On this conception of science it is concerned essentially with what kinds of things they are and with what they tend to do; it is only derivatively concerned with predicting what is actually going to happen' (Bhaskar 1997: 51). This point is important because of the widespread mistaken assumption that to cite a law is to make a claim about what will happen; this confuses the universality of a law with the contingency of its actual realisation (contingent upon the conditions of closure): 'nothing is more fundamental to the physical sciences than the law of inertia, which states that bodies tend to remain at rest or in

uniform motion in a given direction. But nothing in the universe has ever remained at rest or in uniform motion in a given direction. This is no skin of the physicists' noses though, for although a cricket ball does not exemplify inertia, we need the law of inertia alongside the law of gravity and the laws governing air resistance in order to explain its flight' (Collier 1997: 22–3).

5 For critical discussion of Giddens' theory of structuration, and how critical realism differs, see Archer 1990, 1995 chapter 5, Porpora 1989, 1993 and Creaven 2000: 126–36.

6 Bhaskar is careful to differentiate critical naturalism both from unqualified positivistic naturalism which allows 'simple-minded transapplication of results derived from reflection on the conditions of the natural sciences to the social sphere' and from hermeneutical anti-naturalism, 'erected on a distinctive notion of social reality as pre-interpreted, conceptual or linguistic in character' (Bhaskar 1986: 118, 120). Critical naturalism defends that 'a *paramorphic* relationship between the natural and the human sciences can be set up capable of vindicating the idea that there are (or at least may be) knowable structures at work in the human domain partly analogous but irreducible to (although dependent upon) those discovered in nature' (1986: 118–19).

7 See Bhaskar 1998, 1986: 125–6, 1993: 115, 152–73. Bhaskar conceives 'the duality of social structure and human agency as transcendentally necessary conditions for each other. So it might be thought that they are on a par. But from the agent's point of view they are not. She is always treading on pre-trodden ground. [. . .] She is always, from birth to death, living in a pre-constituted world. She is always living in the past' (Bhaskar 1993: 142).

8 This argument is made by Fitzgerald 1977b, Flew 1977, McInnes 1977 and Heller 1980; see Ramsay 1997: 224, 1992: 50. See also Soper 1981: 5 and 1993: 128. Doyal and Gough 1991 argue that objective and universal human needs are identifiable, but Doyal notes elsewhere: 'The discourse of objective and universal human needs has been abused to reinforce a wide variety of relationships of dominance. The word "need" is one of the first to which self-proclaimed "authorities" have traditionally turned to justify their power and the morality of inflicting it on others. [. . .] When motivated by arbitrary self-interest, the pursuit of such dominance in the name of satisfying human need has led to moral outrages against both persons and the biosphere' (Doyal 1993: 113).

9 This is argued by Flew 1977, Barry 1965, White 1975, Frankfurt 1984 and Dearden 1972 (cf. Thomson 1987: 2 and Ramsay 1992: 3).

10 See in particular Barry 1965. Others who make similar arguments include Benn and Peters 1959, Taylor 1959, Fitzgerald 1977b and 1977a, Springborg 1981 and Soper 1981; see Ramsay 1992: 223 and Fraser 1998: 14.

11 However perhaps Marx's use of the concept 'production' could be interpreted more broadly, to characterise all human activities. Bhaskar's transformational model of social activity stresses the fact of self-conscious 'work on' already existing 'material' that is involved in any human practice: 'It applies to discursive as well as to non-discursive practices; to science and politics, as well as to technology and economics. Thus in science the raw materials used in the construction of new theories include established results and half-forgotten ideas, the stock of available paradigms and models, methods and techniques of inquiry, so that the scientific innovator comes to appear in retrospect as a kind of cognitive *bricoleur*. To use Aristotelian terms, then, in every process of productive activity a material as well as an efficient cause is necessary. And, following Marx, one can regard social activity as consisting, analytically, in *production*, that is in work on (and with), entailing the transformation of, those material causes' (Bhaskar 1998: 34; cf. Marx 1844: 92–3).

12 John Roberts has argued that a major difference separates the social ontology of Bhaskar and Marx: while both take seriously the need to identify universal or trans-historical attributes of human activity as such, Marx 'ensures that these universal characteristics have a historical dimension attached to their very core' (Roberts 2002: 240)

whereas this historical dimension is not integral to Bhaskar's emergent powers materialism. However the TMSA does emphasise precisely the historicity of social forms, both social relations and human consciousness (see Bhaskar 1986: 122–36, 211–23). Roberts stresses Bhaskar's emphasis on the openness of history, and the fact that people 'could always have acted otherwise' (239, 243) concluding that Bhaskar conceives of social life and human agency as undetermined. This is not the case. The TMSA and the theory of a structured and stratified, complex ontology composed of social relations and mechanisms, which are non-empirical, have real causal efficacy, and always only ever operate in combinations, configurations and conjunctures (thus foregrounding the necessarily historical nature of all social existence), means that there is a radical disjuncture between the realms of real, actual and empirical. Therefore there is no possibility of prediction of actual events or social forms from a theoretical knowledge of real tendencies and causal powers. But this does not mean an absence of determination or necessity. Bhaskar is explicit that 'freedom' does not mean absence of determination, but *increased control over* the various determinations that human beings are subject to, on the four planes of social being. Moreover the four-planar model of social being (discussed below) helps to distinguish further the different dimensions of determination (natural, social, inter-personal, subjective) and the interrelations between them, as Roberts acknowledges (2002: 244–5).

13 See Collier's discussions which qualify the notion of absence: Collier 2002: 164–5, 2001b and 1995.

14 An apparently similar notion was articulated earlier by Deleuze and Guattari: 'from the moment that we place desire on the side of acquisition, we make desire an idealistic (dialectical, nihilistic) conception, which causes us to look upon it as primarily a lack: a lack of an object, a lack of a real object . . . In point of fact, if desire is the lack of the real object, its very nature as a real entity depends upon an 'essence of lack' that produces the fantasised object' (Deleuze and Guattari 1984: 25, cited in Palan 2000: 222). However this is precisely an example of the importance of critical realism in specifying a *realist* theory of ontology and epistemology. Palan goes on to perform the following manoeuvre: 'as already hinted in the discussion of the distinction between needs and desire, it is possible to re-read the Marxist theory of capital as discourse. The Marxian theory of exchange value is a theory clearly based on Imaginary relationships' (Palan 2000: 225).

15 It should be noted that Anthony Giddens had already made a similar distinction, in his elaboration of structuration theory (Giddens 1984). However, as argued above, one of the important differences between Giddens' and Bhaskar's approaches is that Giddens' theory of structuration tends not to sufficiently distinguish the ontological irreducibility of individuals, practices and structured social relations, which is foregrounded in Bhaskar's TMSA.

16 The notion of generalised master–slave relations is defended because, he claims, all such relations of domination, exploitation, subjugation and control tend to produce particular attitudes on the part of the oppressed which serve to rationalise or compensate for their own oppression; and that characteristically the basic cause of oppression is hidden beneath fetishism and ideology, thus highlighting the necessity of critical social science for emancipatory struggles (Bhaskar 1993: 154).

17 A number of sympathetic critics have noted this weakness in the overly general use of the notion of master–slave relationships, and more generally Bhaskar's tendency to over-extend the limits of philosophy and venture onto the terrain of substantive inquiry without heeding the constraints of that terrain, for example Roberts 2002: 248, Sharpe 2003 chapter 10, Joseph 2001: 513–17.

18 Anthony Giddens (1981 chapter 10) made a similar point, and Andrew Linklater (1998) has argued that Marx concentrated too much on forms of exclusion arising from production relations to the neglect of other forms of exclusion based on representation and subjectivity. Norman Geras (1999: 163) has responded to Linklater with the

following: 'There is also, in this, a dialogical issue, if I may so put it. Who, today, of all the excluded, has least of a voice? Who, that is, in the major places and spaces of intellectual discourse? At the seminars, the national and international conferences, in the journals, the departments and faculties, and at the dinner parties and other social gatherings of the discursively busy communities of academics and intellectuals all over the world, it is not on the whole women or ethnic minorities or people as they are sometimes called of colour, and it is not gays or lesbians or those of an unconventional sexuality, who are the most absent. It is people in the "lower" economic categories, the economically marginalized, the impoverished, manual workers, the homeless, the chronically and the permanently unemployed, and all the wretched of the earth. Taken seriously, a truly dialogic perspective leads straight back into the social theory inaugurated by Marx.'

19 This is not to say that philosophical reflection on questions of need, freedom and emancipation is redundant, nor should it be judged on the same terms as substantive inquiry (as Roberts (2002) seems to do by comparing critical realism with Marxism). Philosophical inquiry *is* important but can only go so far. Philosophy should not be criticised for not doing what only substantive inquiry can do; however, philosophy can be criticised for over-stepping its limits. Some of Bhaskar's later work gives the impression of making an illegitimate move from philosophy to assertions about substantive processes and possibilities which are not sufficiently mediated by substantive inquiry.

4 Marxism, imperialism and Africa

1 This criticism is not valid for all those whose work falls under the label Neo-Gramscian. Mark Rupert (2003, 1995) emphasises that analysis of social power relations cannot be abstracted from the social organisation of production and interaction with the natural world, and explicitly situates his work upon a basis of critical realist philosophy (2000: 156 fn. 8).

2 Various arguments have been elaborated by Gunn 1989, Magill 1994 and Roberts 1999. John Roberts (2001) has defended the 'Marxist systematic dialectics' of Hegelian Marxists such as Tony Smith, Chris Arthur and Shamsavari against Bhaskar's dialectical critical realism, although others have drawn more sympathetically on the parallel concerns of critical realist and other variants of Marxist dialectics (e.g. Brown, A. 2002), seeking in some cases to develop fruitful syntheses (e.g. Arthur 2002). Ben Fine (2004), discussing mainly the work of Tony Lawson, has argued that critical realism is neither critical nor realist enough in terms of undermining mainstream economics and that alternatives rooted in Marxist political economy are more critical with regard to capitalism and have existed for far longer than critical realism.

3 There is a large body of work defending aspects of this case in different ways, which includes McLennan 1981, MacLean 1981, Sayer 1983, Manicas 1987, Collier 1989, Pratten 1993, Joseph 1998, 2002 and Marsden 1999. Furthermore, Morera (1990) has claimed a realist interpretation of the work of Gramsci. Joseph (2000) more modestly acknowledges the contradictions and tensions within Gramsci's work, arguing that some of Gramsci's work is compatible with realism and that it is worth developing these aspects more systematically. Mário Duayer and João Leonardo Medeiros (2005) have argued that the work of Georg Lukács has striking parallels with the earlier work of Bhaskar, although the reception of Lukács' work in the English-speaking world is hampered by the incompleteness and poor quality of the available translations.

4 The Neo-Gramscians have provided a major critique of political realism in IR, but they seldom actually refer to the 'mechanical marxism' they also claim to improve on. Perhaps their foe is 'that "mechanistic economic reductionism" which is something of

an urban legend among Marxists. Everyone knows of some Marxist, whose works they have not read, who is a mechanistic economic reductionist. But no one has ever read a work by such a Marxist' (Collier 1988: 545).

5 See Collier 1981, 1989, 1998: 53–4, Bhaskar 1986: 199–200.

6 '[I]n order to portray the laws of political economy in their purity we are ignoring these sources of friction, as is the practice in mechanics where the frictions that arise have to be dealt with in every particular application of its general laws' (Marx 1867: 1014); 'In theory, we assume that the laws of the capitalist mode of production develop in their pure form. In reality, this is only an approximation' (Marx 1894: 275).

7 Exemplars are the works of Samuel Huntington and with specific reference to the social crisis of poverty in Africa, Robert Kaplan (1996). In a more subtle form the English School of International Relations continues to reproduce an implicit narrative of the superiority of European values and institutions which are seen to have spread worldwide with the 'expansion of international society'. Remarkably, in a book written in 1992 Adam Watson speaks of 'primitive peoples of Africa' (1992: 277, 296).

8 The prevalence of racialised discourse with respect to Africa reproduced in popular consciousness in the West is manifest in the routine tendency to understand Africa's peoples in terms of tribes and tribalism. In my experience undergraduate students often persist in using the language of tribes when discussing Africa. To point this out is not to accuse any one individual of racism per se, but to identify the racialised character of popular understandings. It is worth quoting Mamdani's footnote: 'One might further ask what a tribe is. There was a time when the word possessed scientific content, when it characterized those social formations that did not possess a state structure – the communal, classless societies, as, for example, the Germanic tribes. Today, however, every single ethnic group in Africa is referred to as a tribe regardless of the nature of its social development. What is it that makes 2 million Norwegians a people and just as many Baganda a tribe? A few hundred thousand Icelanders a people and 14 million Hausa-Fulanis a tribe? There is only one explanation: racism' (Mamdani 1976: 3).

9 See Bhaba 1994, Young 1990, Williams, P. and Chrisman 1993. Critiques of post-colonial theory grounded broadly in historical materialism, some more sympathetic than others, have been articulated by Ahmad 1997, 1992, Larsen 2000, San Juan 1998, Dirlik 1994 and Brennan 1997. See Bartolovich and Lazarus 2002 for a collection of essays which engage seriously with the concerns of historical materialism and post-colonialism in a manner which avoids stereo-types or orthodoxies on both sides.

10 See Andrew Collier's essay 'Critical realism and the heritage of the Enlightenment' (2003a) for a rare critical defence of the enlightenment values of reason, universalism and progress. His arguments are important, all the more so for being deeply unfashionable among the left in the current conjuncture.

11 See for example Taylor 1979, Wolpe 1980 and Jewsiewicki and Létourneau 1985; for critical overviews see Zeleza 1983, 1997: 98–102 and Mafeje 1981.

12 See Mamdani 1996, Ayers 2003, 2006, Zeleza 1983, 2003, Depelchin 1992, 1981: 23 and Campbell 1988.

13 Sayer and Corrigan (1983) have refuted the common assumption that Marx's endorsement of Darwin is 'proof' of his evolutionism: 'what Marx celebrated in Darwin's book was precisely that "it deals the death-blow to teleology in the natural sciences." This forms part of a long-standing hostility on Marx's part to teleological explanations in history, which dates back at least to the text which first proclaimed the fundamentals of historical materialism, *The German Ideology* of 1845–46. There any idea that "later history is the goal of earlier history" is ridiculed as a "speculative distortion": "what is designated by the words 'destiny', 'goal', 'germ' or 'idea' of earlier history is nothing but an abstraction from later history' (Sayer and Corrigan 1983: 78, citing Marx 1861: 115 and Marx and Engels 1845–46b: 50; see also Marx 1858: 106). They also dispute the

argument that the views of the 'late' Marx differed in any significant way from the earlier work.

14 This standard portrayal of 'the Marxist position' is found for example in Roxborough 1979: 43, Linklater 1990: 97, Kiernan 1974, Warren 1980, Avineri 1969, Hobden and Wyn Jones 2001: 217.

15 Aijaz Ahmad has provided an extended critique of such views, in particular those of Edward Said and Bill Warren; see Ahmad, A. 1983, 1992 chapter 6 and 2001. See also Mohri 1979, Jani 2002 and Nimtz 2002.

16 The common view that Marxism explains capitalist profit as arising from the exploitation of workers through payment of 'unfair wages' is mistaken. Marx's explanation of the source of surplus-value is premised on the worker receiving the actual exchange-value of their labour-power, although he acknowledges that 'unfair' forms of exploitation of course do exist.

17 David Harvey (2004) emphasises that we need to understand primitive accumulation not as a historical *period* but as a form of accumulation which continues to be integral to the overall reproduction and expansion of capital accumulation. He therefore prefers to use the notion of accumulation by dispossession so as to avoid the suggestion that primitive accumulation refers to a fixed historical period. See also Depelchin 1981: 22 and Ahmad 2004: 248 for a similar discussion. This argument is followed in chapter 7.

18 Wood's main targets were André Gunder Frank and James Blaut. James Blaut (1993, 2000a) has set out important critiques of eurocentric accounts of world history.

19 This discussion refers to the historically varying forms of *capitalist* imperialism, underlining that capitalism as a system is necessarily imperialist. This does not however imply that the phenomenon of imperialism as such is confined to capitalism.

5 The presence of the past: slavery, colonialism and primitive accumulation

1 In 2002, 79 per cent of UK's and 86 per cent of Portugal's merchandise exports consisted of manufactured goods, compared to 8 per cent for Mozambique; 16 per cent of UK's and 13 per cent of Portugal's merchandise exports consisted of primary goods, compared to 91 per cent for Mozambique (UNDP 2004: 192, 195). The conditions represented in these figures are not historically accidental.

2 The attempt here to develop the insights of dialectical critical realism with respect to history, structure, the past and the outside, does not claim that this provides the *only* or even the best grounding for a non-empiricist understanding of history (see McLennan 1981). Indeed some of the most important critiques of orthodox narratives of world history have come from post-colonial critics who argue that the histories of the 'core' and 'periphery' be recognised as necessarily and causally related and mutually constituted, as 'intertwined and overlapping histories' (Said 1994) or 'connected histories' (Subrahmanyam 1997, 2005) rather than treated externally as parallel chronological trajectories.

3 This is one of the differences between Bhaskar's and Hegel's notion of dialectic and totality. See for example Bhaskar 1993: 129.

4 See Niane 1984a, Falola 2000, Barry 1998 chapter 1, Inikori 2002: 158–63, Abu-Lughod 1989, Wolf 1997 chapter 2.

5 For accounts of pre-colonial societies in the region of contemporary Mozambique, see Universidade Eduardo Mondlane 1988a chapters 1 to 4, Serra 1986a, Chilundo 2001 chapter 1, Adekunle 2000, Phiri *et al.* 1992, Bhila 1992, Alpers 1969 and 1975 chapter 1.

6 Devisse and Labib relate 'The Chinese indeed visited this coast of Africa in force during the fifteenth century. [. . .] as early as 1402 a Korean map gave an approximately correct, non Ptolemaic outline of southern Africa; in 1470 the Ming chronicles gave a precise description of a zebra; and a Chinese painting of 1444 depicts a giraffe' (Devisse and Labib 1984: 658).

7 This book aims to develop an explanatory account of the production of modern poverty in Africa, with specific reference to Mozambique. There is insufficient space to deal adequately with the realms of culture and ideology which have constituted a major integral and irreducible component of imperialism and colonialism. Thus the analysis here recognises the necessary and complex relationships between political economy, culture and ideology in the totality of social order but does not focus for the most part on ideological dimensions. Important analyses of the ideologies of European imperial expansion over centuries include Muldoon 1994, Pagden 1995 and Anghie 2005.

8 Referring to the eastern Atlantic bounded by the western coasts of the Iberian peninsular, Africa and the Atlantic islands of the Azores, Madeira and Canary Islands, Devisse and Labib note '[w]e have every reason to believe that Muslim ships were in many cases the first to link the coasts and islands, although there is no written record of their passage' (Devisse and Labib 1984: 660).

9 See Inikori 2000: 405–6, 1976a,b, Curtin 1969, 1976 and Anstey 1976.

10 Cf. Marx 1867 part VIII, chapter 28.

11 The institutions associated with the *Prazos* in Mozambique, and the *Serviço de Carregadores* (porters) in Angola (Capela 1977: 41–5). For analysis of the *Prazos* in Zambezia, see Ishemo 1995.

12 See Arlindo Chilundo's examination of construction of railways and roads in Nampula province (the District of Moçambique) during the colonial period on the basis of forced labour (Chilundo 2001).

13 See Shivji 1986 chapters 1 and 2, Turshen 1984 and Giblin 1986 for Tanzania; Mamdani 1976, 1982, 1986 for Uganda; Nzongola-Ntalaja 2002 chapter 1 for the Congo; Suret-Canale 1971 Part II chapter 1, especially pp. 294–305 for the French colonies; Onimode 1982 chapters 3–6 and Adesina 1994 for Nigeria; Mbuende 1986 chapters 3 and 4 for Namibia; Nzula *et al.* 1979 chapters 2 and 3 and Oculi 1987 more generally.

6 The presence of the outside: revolution, counter-revolution and the production of absence

1 Congolese Prime Minister Patrice Lumumba was assassinated in a conspiracy involving the CIA under Allan Dulles with encouragement or informal endorsement of Eisenhower, American diplomats, UN officials, and Congolese anti-Lumumba moderates, but ultimately planned and executed by the Belgians 'who carried out this odious act through a chain of command running from the ruling class in Brussels to Belgian non-commissioned officers in the Katanga gendarmerie' (Nzongola-Ntalaja 2002: 111; see de Witte 2002 and Nzongola-Ntalaja 2002: 107–12). Eduardo Mondlane was assassinated by parcel bomb by the Portuguese secret police PIDE in Dar-es-Salaam on 3 February 1969. Minter refers to a report in *Private Eye*, 9 May 1969 detailing cooperation between West German intelligence officers and PIDE, which included cooperation in the campaign against Frelimo culminating in the assassination of Mondlane (Minter 1972: 136). Amílcar Cabral was assassinated by Portuguese agents in Conakry on 20 January 1973. Samora Machel died in a plane crash on 19 October 1986. He was returning from a summit in Zambia when the aircraft, heading towards Maputo, crashed into the side of a hill at Mbuzini in South Africa. It is believed on the basis of considerable evidence that the crash was caused deliberately by South African military forces but the circumstances have never been formally explained.

2 The contradictory nature of the struggles for decolonisation, rooted in the class structures of society mediated by ideologies of ethnicity, race, nationalism and by the uneven spatial configurations of social conditions, underlines precisely the need for careful substantive analysis rather than careless generalisation. Such real contradictions and complexities prevent any unmediated move from philosophical analysis of oppression, struggle and

transformatory praxis to substantive pronouncements, such as sometimes appear in Bhaskar's elaboration of dialectical critical realism.

3 See Universidade Eduardo Mondlane 1988b chapter 6, Mondlane 1976 chapter 5, Isaacman and Isaacman 1976, 1983, Munslow 1983 part II, Birmingham 1992 chapter 2, Minter 1972 chapter 3.

4 These included the Batepá Massacre in São Tomé in February 1953 when 1,032 plantation workers were killed by Portuguese troops; the Pijiguiti massacre in Guinea Bissau on 3 August 1959, when 50 dockworkers were killed; the massacre of more than 600 unarmed demonstrators in Mueda, Cabo Delgado in Mozambique on 16 June 1960; and the killing of hundreds of Angolans in a counter-attack against a campaign against cotton cultivation in 1961 (Torp *et al.* 1989: 135–6, Minter 1972: 56, Mondlane 1976: 125–6).

5 See Mondlane 1976, de Brito 1991, Munslow 1980, Munslow 1983, Birmingham 1992, Hall and Young 1997 and Davidson 1975.

6 These groups were the National Democratic Union of Mozambique (UDENAMO), formed in 1960 in Southern Rhodesia; the Mozambique African National Union (MANU), formed in 1961 in Kenya; and the National Union for Mozambican Independence (UNAMI), formed in Malawi in 1961. Eduardo Mondlane was mainly responsible for bringing them together, with support from Julius Nyerere (Fauvet 1984, Mondlane 1976: 127–30).

7 In the 1960s most of the uranium required for nuclear power came from the Congo; 99 per cent of US imports of cobalt came from Africa; around half of the world's industrial diamonds were produced in Congo; the US imported virtually all its manganese, required for high-grade steel, one third of which came from Gabon and 10 per cent from South Africa; and Africa's copper was considered by the US State Department 'a vital element in our peacetime economy' (Department of State 1964: 3, cited in Duignan and Gann 1984: 288). The United States relied on South Africa for 65 per cent of vanadium imports, 44 per cent of antimony, 35 per cent of platinum, over 30 per cent of chromite and ferro-chrome, and 27 per cent of gold (see Duignan and Gann 1984: 300 and Ogunbadejo 1985). By the end of the 1970s 'southern Africa had assumed an important role as a supplier of urgently needed metals for the American economy' (Duignan and Gann 1984: 311). A Report prepared for the congressional subcommittee on mining and minerals confirmed America's dependence on South African minerals (Council on International Economic Policy 1974 cited in Lockwood 1976: 14).

8 See Minter 1972: 74–81, Costa Pinto 2001: 16–19, Mahoney 1983: 188–91, Emerson 1967: 70–6, Noer 1985 and Samuels and Haykin 1979.

9 See Munslow 1983 chapter 11, Depelchin 1983: 79–83, Meyns 1981, Hall and Young 1997: 11–19, Frelimo 1977.

10 See Martin and Johnson 1986, Minter 1986a, Davies *et al.* 1988 and Hanlon 1989.

11 Robert Gersony, a consultant to the US Bureau for Refugee Programs, carried out research into the causes of the high numbers of refugees fleeing from Mozambique in the late 1980s. His report summarised findings from nearly 200 interviews conducted in 42 locations in Mozambique, Malawi, Zimbabwe, South Africa and Tanzania with refugees who had fled from locations throughout Mozambique, from northern, central and southern provinces. He documented reports of extreme levels of systematic violence and brutality perpetrated by MNR forces against the Mozambican population especially in rural areas, revealing the deliberate strategy of societal destruction and terrorisation. Gersony summarised his findings:

> the level of violence reported to be conducted by RENAMO against the civilian population of rural Mozambique is extraordinarily high. Roughly 170 refugees, each representing one family, who arrived in 1987/1988, collectively reported about 600 murders by RENAMO of unarmed civilians, in the absence of resistance or defense. [. . . and] many hundreds of cases of systematic forced portering,

beatings, rape, looting, burning of villages, abductions and mutilations. These patterns of systematic abuse represent many hundreds, if not thousands, of individual instances reported by this small sample. Conservative projections based on this data would yield extremely high levels of abuse. That the accounts are so strikingly similar by refugees who have fled from northern, central and southern Mozambique suggests that the violence is systematic and coordinated and not a series of spontaneous, isolated incidents by undisciplined combatants. [. . .] the relationship between RENAMO and the civilian population, according to the refugee accounts, revolves almost exclusively around a harsh extraction of labor and food. [. . .] There are virtually no reports of attempts to win the loyalty – or even the neutrality – of the villagers. The refugees report virtually no effort by RENAMO to explain to the civilians the purpose of the insurgency, its proposed program or its aspirations. If there is a significant sector of the population which is sympathetic to this organization, it was not reflected in the refugee accounts.

(Gersony 1988)

7 Neo-colonialism and the reproduction of poverty: contemporary dialectics of accumulation and dispossession

1 These are contained in the United Nations Millennium Declaration, adopted by the General Assembly in September 2000. The Declaration specifically resolves, by the year 2015, to halve the proportion of the world's people whose income is less than one dollar a day and the proportion of people who suffer from hunger; to halve the proportion of people who are unable to reach or to afford safe drinking water; to ensure that children everywhere, boys and girls alike, will be able to complete a full course of primary schooling and that girls and boys will have equal access to all levels of education; to have reduced maternal mortality by three quarters, and under-five child mortality by two-thirds, of their current rates; to have halted, and begun to reverse, the spread of HIV/AIDS, the scourge of malaria and other major diseases that afflict humanity; to provide special assistance to children orphaned by HIV/AIDS; and by 2020, to have achieved a significant improvement in the lives of at least 100 million slum dwellers as proposed in the 'Cities Without Slums' initiative. See United Nations General Assembly, United Nations Millennium Declaration, Resolution A/RES/55/2, http://www.un.org/millennium/declaration/ares552e.pdf

2 This contradiction was identified in 1960 by Robert Triffin. See O'Brien and Williams 2004: 226–8, Helleiner 2005: 158–60, Eichengreen 1996 and Triffin 1961.

3 At IMF meetings during 1964 the European representatives emphasised the need for the United States to take 'corrective internal measures' to reduce its payments deficit. However the major cause of America's deficit was not internal monetary imbalance but America's strategic military spending, specifically the war in Vietnam (Hudson 2003: 296–9).

4 However US monetary policy effectively forced the revaluation of European currencies as well as the Japanese Yen, and in December 1971 the US compelled further revaluation (Hudson 2003: 334–47, Gowan 1999: 20–1).

5 It is beyond the scope of this account to examine the nature and causes of stagnation of the advanced industrialised economies of the United States and Europe during the twentieth century. For differing explanations see Mandel 1978, Amin *et al.* 1982 and Brenner 2002. The growth in speculative capital described below and the concentration of capital through mergers and acquisitions since the 1980s are not symptoms of nor have they enabled the revitalisation of the productive base of capitalism in America and Europe. Furthermore, much of the economic growth achieved in the United States and the United Kingdom during the 1980s was based on expansion of the military-industrial complex – the militarisation of the economy (Davis 1985). Meanwhile, as

argued below, the effects of the crisis have been imposed elsewhere. Through enforced restructuring

> the most powerful partners seek to transfer the maximum possible burden of the crisis to the weakest partners – the peripheries of the South and now the East – in order to play down its consequences at home and to avoid its becoming dramatic, even if such a tactic does not help to find a solution to the crisis.
>
> (Amin 1993: 4–5)

6 The question of the extent to which deliberate intention has informed the global restructuring since the 1970s, in particular in the Third World enforced by the IFIs, is not easy to answer. Several analyses suggest that what was initially a response to crisis evolved into deliberate strategy. Analyses such as those of Gowan, Hudson and Ould-Mey identify a more deliberate strategy of global domination pursued since the mid-1970s by the United States (Gowan 1999, Hudson 2003) along with the other major industrialised powers of the G7 (Ould-Mey 1996, especially 29–53): 'Adjustment did not come out of unintentional developments of the world economy and did not develop from the pressure of domestic interest groups in developing countries. It was a relatively well-planned policy by the Group of Seven, whose regular summit meetings since 1975 "reflect a heightened recognition of the need for close cooperation as a result of the growing integration of the world economy and the globalization of financial markets" ' (Ould-Mey 1996: 29, citing US Department of State, *Dispatch*, 2(37), 16 September 1991: 694).

7 '[T]he United States is scarcely a debtor nation in the same sense as Brazil or Mexico. Wall Street money-centre banks and the US Treasury remain sufficiently hegemonic to enforce interest-tribute from the Third World and an unwonted "Marshall Plan in reverse" from Europe and Japan' (Davis 1985: 49). Hudson (2003) provides an extended analysis of this new monetary basis of America's global dominance.

8 This was either an unintended consequence of OPEC's decision following the 1973 Arab–Israeli war or, as Gowan and others have argued, the strategic result that America had sought to achieve (Gowan 1999: 21, Kubursi and Mansur 1994: 321–2, Terzian 1985). Kubursi and Mansur (1994) document America's strategic attempts to influence a rise in the price of oil in the early 1970s, but point out that nevertheless 'it was not American urging that triggered the 1973–74 oil price hike. It came unexpectedly. Egyptian president Anwar Sadat's decision to start the fourth Arab–Israeli war on the morning of October 6, 1973, caught everyone, including the Arab oil producers of OPEC, by surprise. As it unfolded, however, the oil shock did not come as a surprise to the Nixon administration; all the desired effects were in place, while OPEC would be publicly held responsible for the negative consequences in the court of American public opinion' (1994: 323). Furthermore Hudson (2003: 352) identifies the global rise in inflation after 1971 as 'a major reason prompting [the OPEC economies] . . . to quadruple oil prices'.

9 However Gowan records that 'The US banks themselves were initially far from happy about recycling the petrodollars to countries in the South. The US government had to lean on them to do so and had to provide incentives for such lending' (1999: 22).

10 High inflation is harmful to money capital because it erodes the value of royalties, and this was a major reason behind the policy decision to increase interest rates (Gowan 1999: 39, Duménil and Lévy 2004: 69).

11 The world market prices of primary commodities fell 15 per cent in 1981 and 12 per cent in 1982. Between 1980 and 1987 the price of non-oil commodities relative to manufactured goods fell by 45 per cent. See Chu and Morrison 1984, Maizels 1992.

12 For data and analysis of Africa's structure, composition and terms of trade see UNCTAD 2003.

13 The International Labour Organisation has listed the countries which have suffered economic/financial crisis between 1990 and 2003: Albania, Algeria, Angola, Argentina, Armenia, Azerbaijan, Bahamas, Barbados, Belarus, Benin, Bolivia, Bosnia

and Herzegovina, Brazil, Bulgaria, Burkina Faso, Cameroon, Chad, Central African Republic, Congo, Chile, China, Colombia, Costa Rica, Côte d'Ivoire, Croatia, Czech Republic, Democratic Republic of Congo, Dominican Republic, Ecuador, Egypt, Estonia, El Salvador, Ethiopia, Finland, Georgia, Guatemala, Guyana, Haiti, Hong Kong (China), Honduras, Hungary, Indonesia, Japan, Islamic Republic of Iran, Jamaica, Kazakhstan, Republic of Korea, Kyrgyzstan, Lao People's Democratic Republic, Latvia, Lebanon, Lithuania, the former Yugoslav Republic of Macedonia, Madagascar, Mali, Malawi, Malaysia, Mauritania, Mexico, Republic of Moldova, Mozambique, Nicaragua, Niger, Nigeria, Norway, Pakistan, Peru, Philippines, Poland, Romania, Russian Federation, Rwanda, Senegal, Serbia and Montenegro, Singapore, Slovakia, Slovenia, Sri Lanka, Sudan, Suriname, Sweden, Taiwan (China), Tajikistan, Thailand, Togo, Turkey, Turkmenistan, Ukraine, Uruguay, Venezuela, Zambia, Zimbabwe (International Labour Organisation 2004: 40).

14 The Fund created the Structural Adjustment Facility in 1986, followed by the Enhanced Structural Adjustment Facility in 1987 (Williams 1994: 63). Essentially the same basic relations of imposed financial discipline and deepening, widening policy reforms through the mechanism of conditionality have continued under the current Poverty Reduction and Growth Facility.

15 It is important to recognise the dynamic and changing nature of the IMF as an international organisation. Its role and influence has changed over the years since its establishment, according to changing conditions in the international political economy and the changing relative power of the United States, Europe and the countries of the Third World acting as a group in international politics. As Williams has carefully demonstrated, the Fund has at times responded to the various demands of Third World countries (1994 chapter 4). However it remains a capitalist financial institution with a fundamental commitment to principles of free trade, espousing a neo-liberal ideology, and remains structurally dominated by the Western industrialised powers.

16 It is the case that the Western industrialised powers' own policies are often directly opposed to central tenets of the structural adjustment imposed on the Third World, as UNCTAD report in measured tones: 'many industrialized countries have persistently pursued protectionist domestic agricultural policies, which prioritize income stabilization and protection of their farming populations at the cost of some $1 billion a day. Conversely, in Africa, where agriculture employs approximately 70 to 80 per cent of the workforce, a great majority of whom live on less than $1 per day per person, similar concerns have fallen on deaf ears. Not only has the international community not been inclined to go far enough in addressing the issue of income or commodity price stabilization, but poor countries have been encouraged to liberalize their agricultural sectors though structural adjustment programmes in the past two decades' (UNCTAD 2003: 29–30).

17 These were the Structural Adjustment Facility (SAF), 1987–89; the first Enhanced Structural Adjustment Facility (ESAF), 1990–95; the second ESAF, 1996–99; the Poverty Reduction and Growth Facility (PRGF), 1999–2003; and the latest PRGF, 2004–07.

18 It must be emphasised that neo-liberal reform has also increased inequality and created impoverishment and insecurity for many in the West. High levels of consumption in the West are also enabled by increasing personal debt, which has risen significantly over the past two decades especially in the United States and United Kingdom. This problem is gradually spreading to other Western economies, see for example Marques *et al.* 2000. In the United Kingdom total consumer credit in 2004 was two and a half times greater than in 1993, rising from just under £60 billion in 1987 to around £170 billion in 2004. In 2002, 22 per cent (around one in four) of families with three children and 31 per cent (nearly one in three) of families with four or more children were in arrears (debts that people cannot pay) (Summerfield and Gill 2005: 91–2).

19 The SDR (Special Drawing Right) is an international reserve asset which was created by the IMF in 1969. Its value is based on a basket of key international currencies, and

it serves as the unit of account of the IMF and some other international organizations (IMF 2005b).

20 Castel-Branco *et al.* report that in 1995 'the United States government, through its Embassy, threatened to reduce food aid if the government was not prepared to concede monopoly rights for exploitation of the gas reserves in Pande (Inhambane Province) to the US company, Enron' (2001: 7). There are various projects to develop key transport corridors, such as those from Maputo inland to South Africa, from Beira inland to Zimbabwe and Malawi and from Nacala inland to Malawi, through attracting foreign investment, thus reinforcing the regionally uneven pattern of development established in Southern Africa under colonial capitalism. For critical analysis of the Maputo Development Corridor see Söderbaum and Taylor 2001 and 2003.

21 A large rectangular cotton cloth, printed with different designs, worn by women.

22 One *conto* is a thousand *meticais*.

Conclusion

1 Again, it is always necessary to qualify this discussion with acknowledgement of inequality and poverty in Western capitalist societies. Nevertheless the general level of and possibilities for need satisfaction are starkly different, as indicated in some of the facts presented in the introduction.

Bibliography

Abrahamsson, H. and Nilsson, A. (1995) *Mozambique: The Troubled Transition. From Socialist Construction to Free Market Capitalism*, London and New Jersey: Zed Books.

Abt Associates Inc. (1998) *A Preliminary Assessment of the Enabling Environment for Cashew in Mozambique*, Maryland.

Abu-Lughod, J. L. (1989) *Before European Hegemony: The World System A.D. 1250–1350*, New York: Oxford University Press.

Addison, A. and Macdonald, I. (1995) *Rural Livelihoods and Poverty in Mozambique*, Maputo: Poverty Alleviation Unit, Ministry of Planning and Finance.

Adekunle, J. O. (2000) 'East African States' in Falola, T. (ed.) *Africa (Vol. 1): African History Before 1885*, Durham, NC: Carolina Academic Press.

Adesina, J. O. (1994) *Labour in the Explanation of an African Crisis*, Dakar: CODESRIA.

African Development Bank (2002) *Africa Development Report 2002: Rural Development for Poverty Reduction in Africa*, Oxford: Oxford University Press.

Agência de Informação de Moçambique (1978) *Dossier. 4th Session of the Central Committee of Frelimo*. 7–16 August, Maputo.

Ahmad, A. (1983) 'Imperialism and Progress' in Chilcote, R. H. and Johnson, D. L. (eds) *Theories of Development: Mode of Production or Dependency?* London: Sage Publications.

Ahmad, A. (1985) 'Class, Nation, and State: Intermediate Classes in Peripheral Societies' in Johnson, D. L. (ed.) *Middle Classes in Dependent Countries*, Beverly Hills, CA, London and New Delhi: Sage Publications.

Ahmad, A. (1992) *In Theory: Classes, Nations, Literatures*, London: Verso.

Ahmad, A. (1997) 'Postcolonial Theory and the "Post-" Condition', *Socialist Register 1997*, 353–81.

Ahmad, A. (ed.) (2001) *On the National and Colonial Questions: Selected Writings*, New Delhi: LeftWord.

Ahmad, A. (2004) *Iraq, Afghanistan and the Imperialism of Our Time*, New Delhi: LeftWord Books.

Ahmad, E. (1980) 'Post-Colonial Systems of Power', *Arab Studies Quarterly*, 2 (4): 350–63.

Ahmad, E. (1983) 'The Neo-Fascist State: Notes on the Pathology of Power in the Third World' in Friedman, J. S. and Vidal, G. (eds) *First Harvest: The Institute for Policy Studies, 1963–83*, New York: Grove Press (first published in *Arab Studies Quarterly*, 3 (2), 1981).

Ake, C. (1973) 'Explaining Political Instability in New States', *Journal of Modern African Studies*, 11 (3): 347–59.

Almond, G. A. (ed.) (1974) *Comparative Politics Today: A World View*, Boston, MA: Little, Brown.

Almond, G. A. and Coleman, J. S. (1960) *The Politics of Developing Areas*, Princeton, NJ: Princeton University Press.

Almond, G. A. and Powell, G. B. (1966) *Comparative Politics: A Developmental Approach*, Boston, MA: Little, Brown.

Alpers, E. A. (1969) 'Trade, State, and Society among the Yao in the Nineteenth Century', *Journal of African History*, 10 (3): 405–20.

Alpers, E. A. (1975) *Ivory & Slaves in East Central Africa: Changing Patterns of International Trade in the Later Nineteenth Century*, London: Heinemann.

Amadiume, I. (1997) *Re-inventing Africa: Matriarchy, Religion, and Culture*, London: Zed Books.

Amin, S. (1972) 'Underdevelopment and Dependence in Black Africa – Origins and Contemporary Forms', *Journal of Modern African Studies*, 10 (4): 503–24.

Amin, S. (1976) *Unequal Development: An Essay on the Social Formations of Peripheral Capitalism*, New York: Monthly Review Press.

Amin, S. (1993) 'Replacing the International Monetary System?', *Monthly Review*, 45 (5): 1–12.

Amin, S. (1994) *Re-Reading the Postwar Period: An Intellectual Itinerary*, New York: Monthly Review Press.

Amin, S. (2003) *Obsolescent Capitalism: Contemporary Politics and Global Disorder*, London: Zed Books.

Amin, S., Arrighi, G., Frank, A. G. and Wallerstein, I. (1982) *Dynamics of Global Crisis*, London and Basingstoke: Macmillan.

Anderson, P. (1983) *In the Tracks of Historical Materialism*, London: Verso.

Anghie, A. (1999) 'Finding the Peripheries: Sovereignty and Colonialism in Nineteenth-Century International Law', *Harvard International Law Journal*, 40 (1): 1–80.

Anghie, A. (2005) *Imperialism, Sovereignty and the Making of International Law*, Cambridge: Cambridge University Press.

Angotti, T. (1981) 'The Political Implications of Dependency Theory', *Latin American Perspectives*, 8 (3/4): 124–37.

Anstey, R. (1976) 'The British Slave Trade 1751–1807: A Comment', *Journal of African History*, 17 (4): 606–7.

Apter, D. E. (1958) 'A Comparative Method for the Study of Politics', *American Journal of Sociology*, 64, 221–37.

Apter, D. E. (1965) *The Politics of Modernization*, Chicago, IL: University of Chicago Press.

Apter, D. E. (1968) *Some Conceptual Approaches to the Study of Modernization*, Englewood Cliffs, NJ: Prentice-Hall.

Apter, D. E. (1973) *Political Change*, London: Frank Cass.

Apthorpe, R. and Gasper, D. (eds) (1996) *Arguing Development Policy: Frames and Discourses*, London: Frank Cass.

Arce, A., Villarreal, M. and de Vries, P. (1994) 'The Social Construction of Rural Development: Discourses, Practices and Power' in Booth, D. (ed.) *Rethinking Social Development: Theory, Rresearch and Practice*, Harlow: Longman.

Archer, M. (1990) 'Human Agency and Social Structure: A Critique of Giddens' in Clark, J., Modgil, C. and Modgil, S. (eds) *Anthony Giddens: Consensus and Controversy*, London: The Falmer Press.

Archer, M. (1995) *Realist Social Theory: The Morphogenetic Approach*, Cambridge and New York: Cambridge University Press.

Archer, M., Bhaskar, R., Collier, A., Lawson, T. and Norrie, A. (eds) (1998) *Critical Realism: Essential Readings*, London: Routledge.

Arthur, C. J. (2002) 'The Spectral Ontology of Value' in Brown, A., Fleetwood, S. and Roberts, J. M. (eds) *Critical Realism and Marxism*, London: Routledge.

Askin, S. (1990) 'Mission to Renamo: The Militarization of the Religious Right', *Issue: A Journal of Opinion*, 18 (2): 29–38.

Augelli, E. and Murphy, C. N. (1988) *America's Quest for Supremacy and the Third World: A Gramscian Analysis*, London: Pinter Publishers.

Augelli, E. and Murphy, C. N. (1997) 'Consciousness, Myth and Collective Action: Gramsci, Sorel and the Ethical State' in Gill, S. and Mittelman, J. H. (eds) *Innovation and Transformation in International Studies*, Cambridge: Cambridge University Press.

Austin, K. (1994) *Invisible Crimes: US Private Intervention in the War in Mozambique*, Washington, DC: Africa Policy Information Center.

Avineri, S. (1969) *Karl Marx on Colonialism and Modernization*, New York: Doubleday.

Ayers, A. J. (2004) *The Constitution of African Democracy Through the Global Political Economy*, DPhil Thesis, University of Sussex.

Ayers, A. J. (2006) 'Beyond the Imperial Narrative: African Political Historiography Revisited' in Gruffydd Jones, B. (ed.) *Decolonising International Relations*, Lanham, MD: Rowman and Littlefield.

Balogun, F. O. (1995) *Adjusted Lives: Stories of Structural Adjustments*, Trenton, NJ: Africa World Press.

Baran, P. A. (1968) *The Political Economy of Growth*, New York: Modern Reader.

Barongo, J. R. (1978) 'Understanding African Politics: The Political Economy Approach', *African Review: Journal of African Politics, Development and International Affairs*, 8 (3/4): 63–76.

Barry, B. (1979) 'The Subordination of Power and the Mercantile Economy: The Kingdom of Waalo, 1600–1831' in Cruise O'Brien, R. (ed.) *The Political Economy of Underdevelopment: Dependence in Senegal*, London: Sage.

Barry, B. (1998) *Senegambia and the Atlantic Slave Trade*, Cambridge: Cambridge University Press.

Barry, B. (1965) *Political Argument*, London: Routledge and Kegan Paul.

Bartolovich, C. and Lazarus, N. (eds) (2002) *Marxism, Modernity and Postcolonial Studies*, Cambridge: Cambridge University Press.

Basu, A. and Srinivasan, K. (2002) *Foreign Direct Investment in Africa – Some Case Studies*, International Monetary Fund, Working Paper 02/61, Washington, DC.

Baxi, U. (1998) 'Voices of Suffering and the Future of Human Rights', *Transnational Law and Contemporary Problems*, 8, 125–70.

Beachey, R. W. (1976a) *A Collection of Documents on The Slave Trade of Eastern Africa*, London: Rex Collings.

Beachey, R. W. (1976b) *The Slave Trade of Eastern Africa*, London: Rex Collings.

Bedjaoui, M. (1979) *Towards a New International Economic Order*, New York: Holmes and Meier Publishers.

Belshaw, D. (2002) 'Strategising Poverty Reduction in sub-Saharan Africa: The Role of Small-Scale Agriculture (presidential address)', *Journal of Agricultural Economics*, 53 (2): 161–93.

Benn, H. (2004) 'A Shared Challenge: Promoting Development and Human Security in Weak States', Speech at Center for Global Development, Washington DC, 23 June 2004.

Benn, S. I. and Peters, R. S. (1959) *Social Principles and the Democratic State*, London: Allen and Unwin.

Bernstein, H. (1979) 'Sociology of Underdevelopment vs. Sociology of Development?' in Lehmann, D. (ed.) *Development Theory: Four Critical Studies*, London: Frank Cass.

Berry, S. (1993) *No Condition is Permanent: The Social Dynamics of Agrarian Change in sub-Saharan Africa*, Madison, WI: University of Wisconsin Press.

Bhaba, H. K. (1994) *The Location of Culture*, London: Routledge.

Bhaskar, R. (1980) 'Scientific Explanation and Human Emancipation', *Radical Philosophy*, 26: 16–28.

Bhaskar, R. (1986) *Scientific Realism and Human Emancipation*, London: Verso.

Bhaskar, R. (1989) *Reclaiming Reality: A Critical Introduction to Contemporary Philosophy*, London: Verso.

Bhaskar, R. (1991) *Philosophy and the Idea of Freedom*, Oxford: Basil Blackwell.

Bhaskar, R. (1993) *Dialectic: The Pulse of Freedom*, London: Verso.

Bhaskar, R. (1994) *Plato Etc. The Problems of Philosophy and Their Resolution*, London: Verso.

Bhaskar, R. (1997) *A Realist Theory of Science*, 3rd edn, London: Verso (first published 1975).

Bhaskar, R. (1998) *The Possibility of Naturalism: A Philosophical Critique of the Contemporary Human Sciences*, 3rd edn, London: Routledge (first published 1979).

Bhaskar, R. (2003) *From Science to Emancipation: Alienation and the Actuality of Enlightenment*, London: Sage.

Bhaskar, R. and Collier, A. (1998) 'Explanatory Critiques' in Archer, M., Bhaskar, R., Collier, A., Lawson, T. and Norrie, A. (eds) *Critical Realism: Essential Readings*, London: Routledge.

Bhila, H. H. K. (1992) 'Southern Zambezia' in Ogot, B. A. (ed.) *General History of Africa (Volume V): Africa from the Sixteenth to the Eighteenth Century*, Paris, Oxford and Berkeley, CA: UNESCO, James Currey and University of California Press.

Bieler, A. and Morton, A. D. (2004) 'A Critical Theory Route to Hegemony, World Order and Historical Change: Neo-Gramscian Perspectives in International Relations', *Capital and Class*, 82: 85–113.

Biersteker, T. J. (1978) *Distortion or Development? Contending Perspectives on the Multinational Company*, Cambridge, MA: MIT Press.

Biersteker, T. J. (1990) 'Reducing the Role of the State in the Economy: A Conceptual Exploration of IMF and World Bank Prescriptions', *International Studies Quarterly*, 34 (4): 477–92.

Biersteker, T. J. (1993) 'Evolving Perspectives on IPE: 20th Century Contexts and Discontinuities', *International Political Science Review*, 14 (1): 7–33.

Birmingham, D. (1992) *Frontline Nationalism in Angola and Mozambique*, New Jersey, London and Trenton, NJ: James Currey and Africa World Press.

Birmingham, D. (1993) *A Concise History of Portugal*, Cambridge: Cambridge University Press.

Black, C. E. (1966) *The Dynamics of Modernization: A Study in Comparative History*, New York: Harper Torchbooks.

Blackburn, R. (1997) *The Making of New World Slavery: From the Baroque to the Modern, 1492–1800*, London and New York: Verso.

Blair, T. (2005) 'I believe this is Africa's best chance for a generation', *The Guardian*, 12 March: 22.

Blaut, J. M. (1993) *The Colonizer's Model of the World: Geographical Diffusionism and Eurocentric History*, London: The Guildford Press.

Blaut, J. M. (2000a) *Eight Eurocentric Historians*, London: The Guildford Press.

Blaut, J. M. (2000b) 'Marxism and Eurocentric Diffusionism' in Chilcote, R. H. (ed.) *The Political Economy of Imperialism: Critical Appraisals*, Lanham, MD: Rowman and Littlefield.

Booth, D. (1985) 'Marxism and Development Sociology: Interpreting The Impasse', *World Development*, 13 (7): 761–87.

Booth, D. (1994a) 'Rethinking Social Development: An Overview' in Booth, D. (ed.) *Rethinking Social Development: Theory, Research and Practice*, Harlow: Longman.

Booth, D. (ed.) (1994b) *Rethinking Social Development: Theory, Research and Practice*, Harlow: Longman.

Booth, K. and Smith, S. (eds) (1995) *International Relations Theory Today*, Cambridge: Polity Press.

Borstelmann, T. (1993) *Apartheid's Reluctant Uncle: The United States and Southern Africa in the Early Cold War*, New York: Oxford University Press.

Borstelmann, T. (2001) *The Cold War and the Color Line: American Race Relations in the Global Arena*, Cambridge, MA and London: Harvard University Press.

Botchwey, K. (1977) 'Marxism and the Analysis of the African Reality', *Africa Development*, 2 (1): 9–15.

Bourdieu, P. (1977) *Outline of a Theory of Practice*, Cambridge: Cambridge University Press.

Bourdieu, P. (1990) *The Logic of Practice*, Cambridge: Polity Press.

Bowman, L. W. (1971) 'South Africa's Southern Strategy and its Implications for the United States', *International Affairs*, 47 (1): 19–30.

Boxer, C. R. (1961) *Four Centuries of Portuguese Expansion, 1415–1825: A Succinct Survey*, Johannesburg: Witwatersrand University Press.

Boxer, C. R. (1969) *The Portuguese Seaborne Empire 1415–1825*, London: Hutchinson.

Brennan, T. (1997) *At Home in the World: Cosmopolitanism Now*, Cambridge, MA: Harvard University Press.

Brennan, T. (2003) 'The Subtlety of Caesar', *Interventions*, 5 (2): 200–6.

Brenner, R. (1977) 'The Origins of Capitalist Development: a Critique of Neo-Smithian Marxism', *New Left Review*, 104: 25–92.

Brenner, R. (2002) *The Boom and the Bubble: the US in the World Economy*, London: Verso.

Brewer, A. (1990) *Marxist Theories of Imperialism: a Critical Survey*, 2nd edn, London and New York: Routlegde.

Brockway, T. P. (1968) *Basic Documents in United States Foreign Policy*, Princeton, NJ: Van Nostrand.

Brooker, C. (2004) 'Screen Burn', *The Guide*, Saturday, 2 October–Friday, 8 October: 52.

Brown, A. (2002) 'Developing Realistic Philosophy: From Critical Realism to Materialist Dialectics' in Brown, A., Fleetwood, S. and Roberts, J. M. (eds) *Critical Realism and Marxism*, London: Routledge.

Brown, C. (2004) 'Not different enough?' *International Studies Review*, 6: 327–9.

Bull, H. and Watson, A. (eds) (1984) *The Expansion of International Society*, Oxford: Clarendon Press.

Burnham, P. (1991) 'Neo-Gramscian Hegemony and the International Order', *Capital and Class*, 45: 73–92.

Butterfield, H. and Wight, M. (eds) (1966) *Diplomatic Investigations*, London: Allen and Unwin.

Buttigieg, J. A. (1992) 'Introduction' in Buttigieg, J. A. (ed.) *Antonio Gramsci, Prison Notebooks. Volume I*, Oxford and New York: Columbia University Press.

Cabral, A. (1969) *Revolution in Guinea: An African People's Struggle. Selected texts by Amílcar Cabral*, London: Stage 1.

Cabral, A. (1973) *Return to the Source: Selected Speeches of Amílcar Cabral*, (ed.) Africa Information Service, New York and London: Monthly Review Press.

Callinicos, A. (2002) 'Imperialism', *Millennium: Journal of International Studies*, 31 (2): 319–26.

Cammack, D. (1987) 'The "Human Face" of Destabilization: The War in Mozambique', *Review of African Political Economy*, 14 (40): 65–75.

Campbell, H. (1988) 'The Teaching and Research of Political Economy in Africa with Specific Reference to East Africa', *African Review: Journal of African Politics, Development and International Affairs*, 15 (1): 89–106.

Capela, J. (1977) *O Imposto de Palhota e a Introdução do Modo de Produção Capitalista nas Colónias*, Porto: Afrontamento.

Capela, J. (1978) *Escravatura: Conceitos; A empresa de Saque*, Porto, Afrontamento: (2.a edição, revista).

Cardoso, F. H. and Faletto, E. (1979) *Dependency and Development in Latin America*, Berkeley, CA: University of California Press.

Carney, D. (ed.) (1998) *Sustainable Rural Livelihoods: What Contribution Can We Make?* London: Department for International Development.

Carr, E. H. (1939) *The Twenty Year's Crisis*, New York: Harper and Row.

Castel-Branco, C., Cramer, C. and Hailu, D. (2001) *Privatization and Economic Strategy in Mozambique*, Discussion Paper no. 2001/64, World Institute for Development Economics Research, United Nations University. Online. Available HTTP: <http://www.wider.unu.edu/publications/dps/dp2001–64.pdf> (accessed 24 April 2004).

Castro, A. (1972a) *Estudos de História sócio-económica de Portugal*, Lisbon: Editorial Inova.

Centro de Estudos Africanos (1981) 'Interview: Forced Labour by Those who Lived Through It', *Mozambican Studies*, 2: 26–35.

Centro de Estudos Africanos (1982) 'Strategies of Social Research in Mozambique', *Review of African Political Economy*, 25: 29–39.

Centro de Estudos Africanos (1987) *Não Vamos Esquecer!* Centro de Estudos Africanos, Maputo.

Chambers, R. (1983) *Rural Development: Putting the Last First*, London: Longman.

Chambers, R., Pacey, A. and Thrupp, L.-A. (1989) *Farmer First: Farmer Innovation and Agricultural Research*, London: Intermediate Technology Publications.

Chan, S. (ed.) (1990) *Exporting Apartheid: Foreign Policies in Southern Africa 1978–1988*, New York: St Martin's Press.

Chan, S. and Venâncio, M. (1998) *War and Peace in Mozambique*, Basingstoke: Macmillan Press.

Chefo, C. (2003) *Cultura da pobreza: Um estudo da lixeira do Hulene na cidade de Maputo*, unpublished thesis (Tese de licenciatura), Universidade Eduardo Mondlane.

Chilcote, R. H. (1974) 'Dependency: A Critical Synthesis of the Literature', *Latin American Perspectives*, 1 (1): 4–29.

Chilcote, R. H. (1991) *Amílcar Cabral's Revolutionary Theory and Practice*, Boulder, CO: Lynne Rienner.

Chilundo, A. G. (2001) *Os Camponeses e os Caminhos de Ferro e Estradas em Nampula (1900–1961)*, Maputo: Promédia.

Chimni, B. S. (1987) *International Commodity Agreements: A Legal Study*, London: Croom Helm.

Chimni, B. S. (1993) *International Law and World Order: A Critique of Contemporary Approaches*, New Delhi: Sage.

Chimni, B. S. (2003) 'Third World Approaches to International Law: A Manifesto' in Anghie, A., Chimni, B. S., Mickelson, K. and Okafor, O. (eds) *The Third World and International Order: Law, Politics and Globalization*, Leiden/Boston, MA: Martin Nijhoff Publishers.

Chu, K.-Y. and Morrison, T. K. (1984) 'The 1981–1982 Recession and Non-Oil Primary Commodity Prices', *IMF Staff Papers*, 31 (1): 93–140.

Ciment, J. (1997) *Angola and Mozambique: Postcolonial Wars in Southern Africa*, New York: Facts on File.

Clarke, S. (1987) 'Capitalist Crisis and the Rise of Monetarism', *Socialist Register*, 1987: 393–427.

Cleaver, K. M. and Donovan, W. G. (1995) *Agriculture, Poverty, and Policy Reform in Sub-Saharan Africa. World Bank Discussion Paper*, World Bank, Washington, DC.

Coker, C. (1985) *NATO, the Warsaw Pact and Africa*, Basingstoke: MacMillan.

Colaço, J. C. (2001) 'Lixeiros da cidade de Maputo', *Estudos Moçambicanos*, 18: 25–74.

Collier, A. (1979) 'Materialism and Explanation in the Human Sciences' in Ruben, D.-H. and Mepham, J. (eds) *Issues in Marxist Philosophy (Vol. 2). Materialism*, Brighton: Harvester Press.

Collier, A. (1981) 'Scientific Socialism and the Question of Socialist Values' in Mepham, J. and Ruben, D.-H. (eds.) *Issues in Marxist Philosophy (Vol. 4). Social and Political Philosophy*, Brighton: Harvester Press.

Collier, A. (1988) 'Retrieving Structural Marxism', *Economy and Society*, 17 (4): 543–52.

Collier, A. (1989) *Scientific Realism and Socialist Thought*, London: Harvester Wheatsheaf.

Collier, A. (1990) *Socialist Reasoning: An Inquiry into the Political Philosophy of Scientific Socialism*, London: Pluto Press.

Collier, A. (1994) *Critical Realism: An Introduction to the Philosophy of Roy Bhaskar*, London: Verso.

Collier, A. (1995) 'The Power of Negative Thinking', *Radical Philosophy*, 69: 36–9.

Collier, A. (1997) 'Unhewn Demonstrations', *Radical Philosophy*, 81: 22–26.

Collier, A. (1998) 'Language, Practice and Realism' in Parker, I. (ed.) *Social Constructionism, Discourse and Realism*, London: Sage Publications.

Collier, A. (2001a) *Christianity and Marxism: A Philosophical Contribution to Their Reconciliation*, London: Routledge.

Collier, A. (2001b) 'Real and Nominal Absences' in López, J. and Potter, G. (eds) *After Postmodernism: An Introduction to Critical Realism*, London: Sage.

Collier, A. (2002) 'Dialectic in Marxism and Critical Realism' in Brown, A., Fleetwood, S. and Roberts, J. M. (eds) *Critical Realism and Marxism*, London: Routledge.

Collier, A. (2003a) 'Critical Realism and the Heritage of the Enlightenment' in Collier, A. *In Defence of Objectivity: On Realism, Existentialism and Politics*, London: Routledge.

Collier, A. (2003b) *In Defence of Objectivity: On Realism, Existentialism and Politics*, London: Routledge.

Corbridge, S. (1990) 'Post-Marxism and Development Studies: Beyond the Impasse', *World Development*, 18 (5): 623–39.

Corbridge, S. (1994) 'Post-Marxism and Post-Colonialism: The Needs and Rights of Distant Strangers' in Booth, D. (ed.) *Rethinking Social Development: Theory, Research and Practice*, Harlow: Longman.

Costa, E. (1901) 'Estudo Sobre a Administração Civil das nossas Possessões Africanas, apresentado ao Congresso Colonial – 1901', *Boletim da Sociedade de Geografia*, 19 (7–12): 624–5.

Costa Pinto, A. (2001) *O Fim do Império Português: A Cena Internacional, a Guerra Colonial, e a Descolonização, 1961–1975*, Lisbon: Livros Horizonte.

Council on International Economic Policy (1974) *Special Report: Critical Imported Materials*, Washington DC.

Couto, M. (2002) 'Pobres dos nossos ricos', *Savana*, 13 December.

Covane, L. A. (2001) *O Trabalho Migratório e a Agricultura no Sul de Moçambique (1920–1992)*, Maputo: Promédia.

Cox, R. W. (1981) 'Social Forces, States and World Orders: Beyond International Relations Theory', *Millennium: Journal of International Studies*, 10 (2): 126–55.

Cox, R. W. (1987) *Production, Power and World Order: Social Forces in the Making of History*, New York: Columbia University Press.

Cox, R. W. (1990) 'Towards a Counterhegemonic Conceptualisation of World Order', Notes prepared for the *Governance-without-Government* Workshop, Ojai, CA, February 1990, Mimeo.

Cox, R. W. (2001) 'The Way Ahead: Toward a New Ontology of World Order' in Wyn Jones, R. (ed.) *Critical Theory and World Politics*, Boulder, CO: Lynne Rienner.

Cramer, C. (2001) 'Privatisation and Adjustment in Mozambique: a "Hospital Pass"?' *Journal of Southern African Studies*, 27 (1): 79–103.

Cramer, C. and Pontara, N. (1998) 'Rural Poverty Alleviation in Mozambique: What's Missing from the Debate?', *Journal of Modern African Studies*, 36 (1): 101–38.

Cramer, C. and Pontara, N. (1999) 'A Reply to Pitcher', *Journal of Modern African Studies*, 37 (4): 711–22.

Creaven, S. (2000) *Marxism and Realism: A Materialistic Application of Realism in the Social Sciences*, London: Routledge.

Crocker, C. A. (1980) 'South Africa: Strategy for Change', *Foreign Affairs*, 59 (2): 323–51.

Crocker, C. A. (1992) *High Noon in Southern Africa: Making Peace in a Rough Neighbourhood*, New York and London: W W Norton.

Crollen, L. (1973) *Portugal, The U.S. and NATO*, Leuven: Leuven University Press.

Cueva, A. (1976) 'A Summary of Problems and Perspectives of Dependency Theory', *Latin American Perspectives*, 3 (4): 12–16.

Curtin, P. D. (1969) *The Atlantic Slave Trade: A Census*, Madison: University of Wisconsin Press.

Curtin, P. D. (1976) 'Measuring the Atlantic Slave Trade Once Again: A Comment', *Journal of African History*, 17 (4): 595–605.

da Costa, A. N. (1982) *Penetração e impacto do capital mercantil português em Moçambique nos séculos XVI e XVII: O caso de Muenemutapa*, Maputo: Cadernos Tempo.

da Costa, I. N. (1987) *Contribuição para o estudo do colonial-fascismo em Moçambique*, Maputo, Universidade Eduardo Mondlane: Arquivo Histórico de Moçambique.

da Silva Cunha, J. M. (1960) *Questões Ultramarinas e Internacionais, 10 volume*, Lisbon: Edições Ática.

Davidson, B. (1970) 'Arms and the Portuguese', *Africa Report*, May: 10–11.

Davidson, B. (1975) 'The Politics of Armed Struggle: National Liberation in the African Colonies of Portugal' in Davidson, B. (ed.) *Southern Africa: The New Politics of Revolution*, Harmondsworth: Penguin.

Davies, R. and O'Meara, D. (1984) 'The State of Analysis of the Southern African Region: Issues Raised by South African Strategy', *Review of African Political Economy*, 29: 64–76.

Davies, R. and O'Meara, D. (1985) 'Total Strategy in Southern Africa: An Analysis of South African Regional Policy since 1978', *Journal of Southern African Studies*, 11 (2): 83–209.

Davies, R., O'Meara, D. and Dlamini, S. (1988) *The Struggle for South Africa*, Vol. 1, London: Zed Books.

Davis, J. (1970) 'Allies in Empire: US Economic Involvement', *Africa Today*, 17 (4): 1–18.

Davis, M. (1985) 'Reaganomics' Magical Mystery Tour', *New Left Review*, 149: 45–65.

Davis, M. (1987) 'From Fordism to Reaganism: The Crisis of American Hegemony in the 1980s' in Bush, R., Johnson, G. G. and Coates, D. (eds) *The World Order: Socialist Perspectives*, Cambridge: Polity Press.

de Almeida, E. F. (1957) *Governo do Distrito de Moçambique: Relatório*, Lisbon: Agência Geral do Ultramar.

de Brito, L. (1991) *Le Frelimo et la Construction de l'Etat National au Mozambique*, PhD thesis, Université de Paris VIII.

de Witte, L. (2002) *The Assassination of Lumumba*, London: Verso.

Dearden, R. (1972) ' "Needs" in education' in Hirst, P. and Peters, R. (eds) *Development of Reason*, London: Routledge and Kegan Paul.

Deleuze, G. and Guattari, F. (1984) *Anti-Oedipus: Capitalism and Schizophrenia*, London: Athlone.

Department for International Development (1999) *Sustainable Livelihoods and Poverty Elimination* (*Background Briefing*), London.

Department of State (1964) *The United States and Africa*, Washington DC.

Depelchin, J. (1981) 'The Transformations of the Petty-Bourgeoisie and the State in Post-colonial Zaire', *Review of African Political Economy*, 22: 20–41.

Depelchin, J. (1983) 'African Anthropology and History in the Light of the History of FRELIMO', *Contemporary Marxism*, 7: 69–88.

Depelchin, J. (1992) 'The History of States and the States of History: Ways of Denying the History of the Oppressed' in Depelchin, J. *From the Congo Free State to Zaire (1885–1974): Towards a Demystification of Economic and Political History*, Dakar: CODESRIA.

Devisse, J. and Labib, S. (1984) 'Africa in Inter-Continental Relations' in Niane, D. T. (ed.) *Africa from the Twelfth to the Sixteenth Century*, London, Berkeley, CA and Paris: Heinemann, University of California Press, UNESCO.

Diamond, L., Linz, J. J. and Lipset, S. M. (eds) (1990) *Politics in Developing Countries: Comparing Experiences with Democracy*, Boulder, CO: Lynne Rienner.

Diamond, R. A. and Fouquet, D. (1970) 'Portugal and the United States: Atlantic Islands and European Strategy as Pawns in African wars', *Africa Report*, 15 (5): 15–17.

Dirlik, A. (1994) 'The Postcolonial Aura: Third World Criticism in the Age of Global Capitalism', *Critical Inquiry*, 20: 328–56.

DNPP (1984) *Pela Paz: Acordo Nkomati*, Maputo: Direcção Nacional de Propaganda e Publicidade.

dos Santos, A. L. (1959) *Relatório do Governo do Distrito de Moçambique*, Lisbon: Agência Geral do Ultramar.

Doyal, L. (1993) 'Thinking about Human Need', *New Left Review*, 201: 113–28.

Doyal, L. and Gough, I. (1991) *A Theory of Human Need*, London: Macmillan.

Drinkwater, M. J. (1992) 'Visible Actors and Visible Researchers: Critical Hermeneutics in an Actor-Oriented Perspective', *Sociologia Ruralis*, 32 (4): 367–88.

Du Bois, W. E. B. (1896) *The Suppression of the African Slave Trade to the United States of America, 1638–1870*, Cambridge, MA: Harvard University Press.

Du Bois, W. E. B. (1935) *Black Reconstruction in America: An Essay Toward a History of the Part which Black Folk Played in the Attempt to Reconstruct Democracy in America, 1860–1880*, New York: Meridian Books (1964).

Du Bois, W. E. B. (1946) *The World and Africa: An Inquiry into the Part which Africa has Played in World History*, New York: International Publishers (1996).

Duayer, M. and Medeiros, J. L. (2005) 'Lukács' Critical Ontology and Critical Realism,' *Journal of Critical Realism*, 4 (2): 395–425.

Duignan, P. and Gann, L. H. (1984) *The United States and Africa: A History*, Cambridge and New York: Cambridge University Press and Hoover Institution.

Duménil, G. and Lévy, D. (2004) *Capital Resurgent: Roots of the Neoliberal Revolution*, Cambridge, MA: Harvard University Press.

Duménil, G. and Lévy, D. (2005) 'The Neo-Liberal (Counter-)Revolution' in Saad-Filho, A. and Johnston, D. (eds) *Neoliberalism: A Critical Reader*, London: Pluto.

Dunne, T., Cox, M. and Booth, K. (1999) *The Eighty Years' Crisis: International Relations 1919–1999*, Cambridge: Cambridge University Press.

Dyer, H. C. and Mangasarian, L. (eds) (1989) *The Study of International Relations: The State of the Art*, Basingstoke: Macmillan.

Eckstein, H. and Apter, D. E. (eds) (1963) *Comparative Politics: A Reader*, New York: The Free Press.

Edwards, M. (1989) 'The Irrelevance of Development Studies', *Third World Quarterly*, 11 (1): 116–35.

Egerö, B. (1990) *Mozambique: A Dream Undone. The Political Economy of Democracy, 1975–1984*, Uppsala: Nordiska Afrikainstitutet.

Eichengreen, B. J. (ed.) (1985) *The Gold Standard in Theory and History*, New York: Methuen.

Eichengreen, B. J. (1996) *Globalizing Capital: A History of the International Monetary System*, Princeton, NJ: Princeton University Press.

Eisenstadt, S. N. (1965) *Essays on Comparative Institutions*, New York: John Wiley and Sons.

Eisenstadt, S. N. (1966) *Modernization: Protest and Change*, Englewood Cliffs, NJ: Prentice-Hall.

Eisenstadt, S. N. (ed.) (1968) *Comparative Perspectives on Social Change*, Boston, MA: Little, Brown and Co.

Eisenstadt, S. N. (1973) *Tradition, Change and Modernity*, New York: John Wiley.

Eisenstadt, S. N. and Rokkan, S. (eds) (1973) *Building States and Nations*, Beverly Hills, CA: Sage Publications.

El-Khawas, M. A. (1972) 'Mozambique and the United Nations', *Issue*, Winter 1972: 30–5.

El-Khawas, M. A. (1974) 'Foreign Economic Involvement in Angola and Mozambique', *African Review: Journal of African Politics, Development and International Affairs*, 4 (2): 300–14.

El-Khawas, M. A. (1975) 'American Involvement in Angola and Mozambique' in El-Khawas, M. A. and Kornegay F. A., Jr (eds) *American–Southern African Relations: Bibliographic Essays*, Westport, CT and London: African Bibliographic Center, Greenwood Press.

El-Khawas, M. A. and Cohen, B. (1976) *The Kissinger Study of Southern Africa: National Security Study Memorandum 39 (Secret)*, Westport, CT: Lawrence Hill & Co.

Ellis, F. and Freeman, H. A. (2004) 'Rural Livelihoods and Poverty Reduction Strategies in Four African Countries', *Journal of Development Studies*, 40 (4): 1–30.

Emerson, R. (1967) *Africa and United States Policy*, Englewood Cliffs, NJ: Prentice-Hall.

Emmanuel, A. (1972) *Unequal Exchange: A Study of the Imperialism of Trade* (trans. Brian Pearce), New York: Monthly Review Press.

Enes, A. (1946) *Moçambique – Relatório Apresentado Ao Governo (3.a edição)*, Lisbon.

Engels, F. (1859) 'Review of Karl Marx, *A Contribution to the Critique of Political Economy*' in *Karl Marx and Frederick Engels, Selected Works (Volume One)*, Moscow: Progress Publishers.

Escobar, A. (1984–85) 'Discourse and Power in Development: Michel Foucault and the Relevance of his Work for the Third World', *Alternatives*, X: 377–400.

Escobar, A. (1995) *Encountering Development: The Making and Unmaking of the Third World*, Princeton, NJ: Princeton University press.

Esteva, G. and Prakash, M. S. (1998) *Grassroots Post-Modernism: Remaking the Soil of Cultures*, London: Zed Books.

European Parliament (2001) *Report on the Mission of a Delegation of the Committee on Development and Cooperation to Mozambique, 14–18 September 2001*, European Parliament Committee on Development and Cooperation, Brussels.

Evans, P. (1979) *Dependent Development: The Alliance of Multinational, State, and Local Capital in Brazil*, Princeton, NJ: Princeton University Press.

Fagan, G. H. (1999) 'Cultural Politics and (post) Development Paradigm(s)' in Munck, R. and O'Hearn, D. (eds) *Critical Development Theory: Contributions to a New Paradigm*, London: Zed Books.

Falola, T. (ed.) (2000) *Africa (Vol. 1): African History Before 1885*, Durham, NC: Carolina Academic Press.

Fals Borda, O. and Rahman, A. (ed.) (1991) *Action and Knowledge: Breaking the Monopoly with Participatory Action-Research*, New York: Apex Press.

Fanon, F. (1967a) 'The Pitfalls of National Consciousness' in Fanon, F. *The Wretched of the Earth*, Harmondsworth: Penguin.

Fanon, F. (1967b) 'Racism and Culture' in Fanon, F. *Toward the African Revolution: Political Essays*, New York: Monthly Review Press.

Fanon, F. (1967c) *Toward the African Revolution: Political Essays*, New York: Monthly Review Press.

Fanon, F. (1967d) *The Wretched of the Earth*, Harmondsworth: Penguin.

Fauvet, P. (1984) 'Roots of Counter-Revolution: The Mozambique National Resistance', *Review of African Political Economy*, 29: 108–21.

Ferguson, J. (1990) *The Anti-Politics Machine: 'Development', Depoliticization, and Bureaucratic Power in Lesotho*, Cambridge: Cambridge University Press.

Fernández, R. and Ocampo, J. F. (1974) 'The Latin American Revolution: A Theory of Imperialism, not Dependence', *Latin American Perspectives*, 1: 4–29.

Fieldhouse, D. K. (1982) *The Colonial Empires: A Comparative Survey from the Eighteenth Century*, 2nd edn, London: Macmillan.

Fine, B. (2004) 'Addressing the Critical and the Real in Critical Realism' in Lewis, P. A. (ed.) *Transforming Economics: Perspectives on the Critical Realist Project*, London and New York: Routledge.

First, R., Steele, J. and Gurney, C. (1973) *The South African Connection: Western Investment in Apartheid*, Harmondsworth: Penguin Books.

Fitzgerald, R. (1977a) 'Abraham Maslow's Hierachy of Needs: An Exposition and Evaluation' in Fitzgerald, R. (ed.) *Human Needs and Politics*, Pergamon.

Fitzgerald, R. (1977b) 'The Ambiguity and Rhetoric of "need" ' in Fitzgerald, R. (ed.) *Human Needs and Politics*, Pergamon.

Fleetwood, S. (2001) 'What kind of *Theory* is Marx's Labour *Theory* of Value?' *Capital and Class*, 73: 41–77.

Flew, A. (1977) 'Wants or Needs, Choices or Demand' in Fitzgerald, R. (ed.) *Human Needs and Politics*, Pergamon.

Foucault, M. (1970) *The Order of Things*, London: Tavistock.

Frank, A. G. (1967) *Capitalism and Underdevelopment in Latin America*, New York: Monthly Review Press.

Frank, A. G. (1972) *Lumpen-bourgeoisie, Lumpen-Development: Dependence, Class and Politics in Latin America*, New York and London: Monthly Review Press.

Frank, A. G. (1978) *Dependent Accumulation and Underdevelopment*, Basingstoke: Macmillan.

Frankfurt, H. (1984) 'Necessity and Desire', *Philosophy and Phenomenological Research*, 45: 1–13.

Fraser, I. (1998) *Hegel and Marx: The Concept of Need*, Edinburgh: Edinburgh University Press.

FRELIMO (1977) *Central Committee Report to the Third Congress*, Mozambique, Angola and Guiné Information Centre, London.

Gamer, R. E. (1976) *The Developing Nations: A Comparative Perspective*, Boston, MA: Allyn and Bacon.

Gardner, K. and Lewis, D. (1996) *Anthropology, Development and the Post-Modern Challenge*, London: Pluto Press.

Geldof, B. (2005) 'Africa has become a living wound. Now we have the chance to heal it', *The Independent*, 11 March.

George, J. (1988) 'The Study Of International Relations And The Positivist/Empiricist Theory of Knowledge: Implications for The Australian Discipline' in Higgott, R. (ed.) *New Directions in International Relations*, Canberra: Australian National University.

George, J. and Campbell, D. (1990) 'Patterns Of Dissent And The Celebration of Difference: Critical Social Theory and International Relations', *International Studies Quarterly*, 34 (3): 269–93.

Geras, N. (1999) 'The View from Everywhere', *Review of International Studies*, 25: 157–63.

Gersony, R. (1988) *Summary of Mozambican Refugee Accounts of Principally Conflict-Related Experience in Mozambique: Report submitted to Ambassador Moore and Dr Chester A. Crocker*, Bureau for Refugee Programs, US Department of State. Online. Available HTTP: <http://www.usaid.gov/regions/afr/conflictweb/reports/gersony/gersony_mozambique.pdf> (accessed 5 May 2005).

Gibbins, C. (ed.) (2005) *Family Spending. A Report on the 2003–04 Expenditure and Food Survey*, Basingstoke: Palgrave Macmillan, Office for National Statistics.

Giblin, J. (1986) 'Famine and Social Change during the Transition to Colonial Rule in North Eastern Tanzania, 1880–1896', *African Economic History*, 15: 85–105.

Giddens, A. (1981) *A Contemporary Critique of Historical Materialism*, London: Macmillan.

Giddens, A. (1984) *The Constitution of Society: Outline of the Theory of Structuration*, Cambridge: Polity Press.

Gifford, P. and Roger Louis, W. (1987) 'Introduction' in Gifford, P. and Roger Louis, W. (eds) *Decolonization and African Independence: The Transfers of Power 1960–1980*, New Haven, CT: Yale University Press.

Gill, S. (1991a) *American Hegemony and the Trilateral Commission*, Cambridge: Cambridge University Press.

Gill, S. (1991b) 'Historical Materialism, Gramsci, and International Political Economy' in Murphy, C. N. and Tooze, R. (eds) *The New International Political Economy*, Boulder, CO: Lynne Rienner.

Gill, S. (1993a) 'Epistemology, Ontology, and the "Italian school" ' in Gill, S. (ed.) *Gramsci, Historical Materialism and International Relations*, Cambridge: Cambridge University Press.

Gill, S. (1993b) 'Gramsci and Global Politics: Towards a post-Hegemonic Research Agenda' in Gill, S. (ed.) *Gramsci, Historical Materialism and International Relations*, Cambridge: Cambridge University Press.

Gill, S. (ed.) (1993c) *Gramsci, Historical Materialism and International Relations*, Cambridge: Cambridge University Press.

Gill, S. (1995) 'Globalisation, Market Civilisation, and Disciplinary Neoliberalism', *Millennium: Journal of International Studies*, 24 (3): 399–423.

Gill, S. (1997) 'Transformation and Innovation in the Study of World Order' in Gill, S. and Mittelman, J. H. (eds) *Innovation and Transformation in International Studies*, Cambridge: Cambridge University Press.

Gill, S. (2003) *Power and Resistance in the New World Order*, Basingstoke: Palgrave Macmillan.

Gill, S. and Law, D. (1989) 'Global Hegemony and the Structural Power of Capital', *International Studies Quarterly*, 33: 475–99.

Gill, S. and Law, D. (1993) 'Global Hegemony and the Structural Power of Capital' in Gill, S. (ed.) *Gramsci, Historical Materialism and International Relations*, Cambridge: Cambridge University Press

Godinho, V. M. (1971) *Estrutura da Antiga Sociedade Portuguesa*, Lisbon: Editora Arcádia.

Gomes, A. (1984) 'Southern Africa 1984: Nkomati Accord (Briefing)', *Review of African Political Economy*, 29: 144–50.

Government of Mozambique (1995a) *The Poverty Reduction Strategy for Mozambique*, Maputo: Poverty Alleviation Unit, Ministry of Planning and Finance.

Government of Mozambique (1995b) *Rural Livelihoods and Poverty in Mozambique*, Maputo: Poverty Alleviation Unit, Ministry of Planning and Finance.

Government of Mozambique (2001) *Action Plan for the Reduction of Absolute Poverty (2001–2005)*, Maputo.

Government of Mozambique (2004) *Republic of Mozambique – Letter of Intent, Memorandum of Economic and Financial Policies, and Technical Memorandum of Understanding*, Maputo.

Governo de Moçambique (1995) *Estratégia para a Redução da Pobreza em Moçambique*, Maputo: Unidade de Alívio da Pobreza, Ministério do Plano e Finanças.

Gowan, P. (1999) *The Global Gamble: Washington's Faustian Bid for World Dominance*, London: Verso.

Gran, P. (1996) *Beyond Eurocentrism: A New View of Modern World History*, New York: Syracuse University Press.

Grillo, R. D. (1997) 'Discourses of Development: the View from Anthropology' in Grillo, R. D. and Stirrat, R. L. (eds) *Discourses of Development: Anthropological Perspectives*, Oxford: Berg.

Grillo, R. D. and Stirrat, R. L. (eds) (1997) *Discourses of Development: Anthropological Perspectives*, Oxford: Berg.

Grovogui, S. N. (1996) *Sovereigns, Quasi Sovereigns, and Africans: Race and Self-Determination in International Law*, Minneapolis, MN: University of Minnesota Press.

Grumley, J. (1999) 'A Utopian Dialectic of Needs? Heller's Theory of Radical Needs', *Thesis Eleven*, 59: 53–72.

Guelke, A. (1980) 'Southern Africa and the Super-Powers', *International Affairs*, 56 (4): 648–64.

Gunn, R. (1989) 'Marxism and Philosophy: a Critique of Critical Realism', *Capital and Class*, 37: 86–116.

Hall, M. and Young, T. (1997) *Confronting Leviathan: Mozambique since Independence*, London: Hurst and Company.

Halliday, F. (1986) *The Making of the Second Cold War*, London: Verso.

Halperin, S. (2004) *War and Social Change in Modern Europe: The Great Transformation Revisited*, Cambridge: Cambridge University Press.

Halpern, M. (1963) *The Politics of Social Change in the Middle East and North Africa*, Princeton, NJ: Rand.

Handel, M. (1981) *Weak States in the International System*, London: Frank Cass.

Hanlon, J. (1989) *SADCC in the 1990s: Development in the Frontline,* London: Economic Intelligence Unit.

Hanlon, J. (2002) 'Bank Corruption Becomes Site of Struggle in Mozambique', *Review of African Political Economy*, 91: 53–72.

Hardt, M. and Negri, A. (2000) *Empire*, Cambridge, MA: Harvard University Press.

Harrison, D. (1988) *The Sociology of Modernization and Development*, London: Routledge.

Harvey, D. (1999) *The Limits to Capital*, London: Verso.

Harvey, D. (2004) 'The "New" Imperialism: Accumulation by Dispossession', *Socialist Register 2004*, 63–87.

Hearn, J. (1998) 'The NGO-isation of Kenyan society: USAID and the Restructuring of Health Care', *Review of African Political Economy*, 25 (75): 89–100.

Helleiner, E. (1994a) 'From Bretton Woods to Global Finance: A World Turned Upside Down' in Stubbs, R. and Underhill, G. R. D. (eds) *Political Economy and the Changing Global Order*, Basingstoke: Macmillan.

Helleiner, E. (1994b) *States and the Re-emergence of Global Finance: From Bretton Woods to the 1990s*, Ithaca, NY: Cornell University Press.

Helleiner, E. (2005) 'The Evolution of the International Monetary and Financial System' in Ravenhill, J. (ed.) *Global Political Economy*, Oxford: Oxford University Press.

Heller, A. (1980) 'Can "True" and "False" needs be posited?" in Lederer, K. (ed.) *Human Needs*, Cambridge, MA: Oelgeschlager, Gunn and Hain.

Heller, A. (1983) *Dictatorship over Needs*, Oxford: Blackwell.

Henkel, H. and Stirrat, R. (2001) 'Participation as Spiritual Duty; Empowerment as Secular Subjection' in Cooke, B. and Kothari, U. (eds) *Participation: The New Tyranny?* London: Zed Press.

Hilton, A. (1985) *The Kingdom of Kongo*, Oxford: Clarendon.

Hinsley, F. H. (1963) *Power and the Pursuit of Peace: Theory and Practice in the History of Relations between States*, Cambridge: Cambridge University Press.

Hobart, M. (ed.) (1993a) *An Anthropological Critique of Development: The Growth of Ignorance*, London: Routledge.

Hobart, M. (1993b) 'Introduction: The Growth of Ignorance?' in Hobart, M. (ed.) *An Anthropological Critique of Development: The Growth of Ignorance*, London: Routledge.

Hobden, S. and Wyn Jones, R. (2001) 'Marxist Theories of International Relations' in Baylis, J. and Smith, S. (eds) *The Globalization of World Politics: An Introduction to International Relations*, 2nd edn, Oxford: Oxford University Press.

Hobsbawm, E. (1995) *The Age of Extremes: The Short Twentieth Century 1914–1991*, London: Abacus.

Hobsbawm, E. (1997) *The Age of Capital 1848–1875*, London: Abacus.

Hoffman, S. (1975) 'Regulating the New International System' in Kilson, M. (ed.) *New States in the Modern World*, Cambridge, MA: Harvard University Press.

Hollis, M. and Smith, S. (1990) *Explaining and Understanding International Relations*, Oxford: Clarendon Press.

Hopkins, A. G. (1975) 'On Importing Gunder Frank into Africa', *African Economic History Review*, 2: 13–21.

Hudson, M. (2003) *Super Imperialism: The Origin and Fundamentals of U.S. World Dominance*, 2nd edn, London: Pluto Press.

Huntington, S. P. (1965) 'Political Development and Political Decay', *World Politics*, 17 (3): 386–430.

Huntington, S. P. (1968) *Political Order in Changing Societies*, New Haven, CT: Yale University Press.

Hyam, R. (ed.) (1992a) *The Labour Government and the End of Empire 1945–1951. Part I: High Policy and Administration*, London: HMSO.

Hyam, R. (ed.) (1992b) *The Labour Government and the End of Empire 1945–1951. Part III: Strategy, Politics and Constitutional Change*, London: HMSO.

IMF (2000) *Policies for Faster Growth and Poverty Reduction in Sub-Saharan Africa and the Role of the IMF: An IMF Issues Brief*, International Monetary Fund, Washington, DC.

IMF (2001) *Mozambique: Joint Staff Assessment of the Poverty Reduction Strategy Paper*, International Monetary Fund and International Development Association, Washington, DC.

IMF (2004) *Republic of Mozambique: Ex Post Assessment of Mozambique's Performance Under Fund-Supported Programs*, International Monetary Fund, IMF Country Report No. 04/53, Washington, DC.

IMF (2005a) *International Financial Statistics*, ESDS International, University of Manchester. Online. Available HTTP: <http://www.esds.ac.uk> (accessed 29 March 2005).

IMF (2005b) *Special Drawing Rights (SDRs) Factsheet*, International Monetary Fund. Online. Available HTTP: <http://www.imf.org/external/np/exr/facts/sdr.htm> (accessed 12 June 2005).

Inikori, J. E. (1976a) 'Measuring the Atlantic Slave Trade: A Rejoinder', *Journal of African History*, 17 (4): 607–27.

Inikori, J. E. (1976b) 'Measuring the Atlantic Slave Trade: An Assessment of Curtin and Anstey', *Journal of African History*, 17 (2): 197–223.

Inikori, J. E. (1979) 'The Slave Trade and the Atlantic Economies 1451–1870' in UNESCO (ed.) *The African Slave Trade from the Fifteenth to the Nineteenth Century*, Paris: United Nations Educational, Scientific and Cultural Organization.

Inikori, J. E. (2000) 'Africa and the Trans-Atlantic Slave Trade' in Falola, T. (ed.) *Africa, vol. 1: African History before 1885*, Carolina: Carolina Academic Press.

Inikori, J. E. (2002) *Africans and the Industrial Revolution in England: A Study in International Trade and Economic Development*, Cambridge: Cambridge University Press.

International Fund for Agricultural Development (2001) *Rural Poverty Report 2001: The Challenge of Ending Rural Poverty*, Oxford: Oxford University Press.

International Labour Organisation (2004) *Economic Security for a Better World*, International Labour Office, Geneva.

IRIN News (2002) *Focus on Mozambique: Poverty and Maternal Mortality*, Online. Available HTTP: <<http://malawihere.com/viewnews.asp?id=744&recnum=1331&catid=>> (accessed 24 April 2004).

Isaacman, A. (1995) *Cotton is the Mother of Poverty: Peasants, Work, and Rural Struggle in Colonial Mozambique, 1938–1961*, Portsmouth, NH: Heinemann.

Isaacman, A. and Chilundo, A. G. (1995) 'Peasants at Work: Forced Cotton Cultivation in Northern Mozambique 1938–1961' in Isaacman, A. and Roberts, R. (eds) *Cotton, Colonialism and Social History in Sub-Saharan Africa*, Portsmouth, NH: Heinemann.

Isaacman, A. and Isaacman, B. (1976) *The Tradition of Resistance in Mozambique*, London: Heinemann.

Isaacman, A. and Isaacman, B. (1983) *Mozambique: From Colonisation to Revolution, 1900–1982*, Boulder, CO: Westview Press.

Isaacman, A., Pililão, A., Macamo, E., Homem, M. J., Stephen, M. and Adam, Y. (1979) 'A Resistência popular à cultura forçada de algodão em Moçambique, 1930–1961', Universidade de Eduardo Mondlane, Brigada de História do Curso de Letras, Actividades de Julho 1979, Maputo, Mimeo.

Ishemo, S. L. (1989) 'Forced Labour, Mussoco, Famine and Migration' in Zegeye, A. and Ishemo, S. L. (eds) *Forced Labour and Migration: Patterns of Movement within Africa*, London, Munich and New York: Hans Zell.

Ishemo, S. L. (1995) *The Lower Zambezi Basin in Mozambique: A Study in Economy and Society, 1850–1920*, Aldershot: Avebury.

Jackson, R. H. (1990) *Quasi-States: Sovereignty, International Relations, and the Third World*, Cambridge: Cambridge University Press.

Jackson, R. H. and Rosberg, C. G. (1982) 'Why Africa's Weak States Persist: The Empirical and the Juridical in Statehood', *World Politics*, 35 (1): 1–24.

James, C. L. R. (1938) *The Black Jacobins: Toussaint L'Ouverture and the San Domingo Revolution*, New York: Dial Press.

Jani, P. (2002) 'Karl Marx, Eurocentrism, and the 1857 Revolt in British India' in Bartolovich, C. and Lazarus, N. (eds) *Marxism, Modernity and Postcolonial Studies*, Cambridge: Cambridge University Press.

Jenkins, R. (1987) *Transnational Corporations and Uneven Development: The Internationalisation of Capital and the Third World*, London: Methuen.

Jewsiewicki, B. and Létourneau, J. (eds) (1985) *Mode of Production: The Challenge of Africa*, Ste-Foy, Quebec: Editions Safi Press.

Johnson, C. (1981) 'Dependency Theory and the Processes of Capitalism and Socialism', *Latin American Perspectives*, 8 (3/4): 55–81.

Johnson, D. L. (1981) 'Economism and Determinism in Dependency Theory', *Latin American Perspectives*, 8 (3/4): 108–117.

Johnson, D. L. (1985) 'Class Roots of Dictatorship in South America: Local Bourgeoisies and Transnational Capital' in Johnson, D. L. (ed.) *Middle Classes in Dependent Countries*, Beverly Hills, CA, London and New Delhi: Sage Publications.

Johnson, D. S. (1991) 'Constructing the Periphery in Modern Global Politics' in Murphy, C. N. and Tooze, R. (eds) *The New International Political Economy*, Boulder, CO: Lynne Rienner.

Joseph, J. (1998) 'In Defence of Critical Realism', *Capital and Class*, 65: 73–106.

Joseph, J. (2000) 'A Realist Theory of Hegemony', *Journal for the Theory of Social Behaviour*, 30 (2): 179–202.

Joseph, J. (2001) 'Critical Realism: Essential Readings (review)', *Historical Materialism: Research in Critical Marxist Theory*, (8): 507–17.

Joseph, J. (2002) 'Five Ways in which Critical Realism Can Help Marxism' in Brown, A., Fleetwood, S. and Roberts, J. M. (eds) *Critical Realism and Marxism*, London: Routledge.

Kalleberb, A. L. (1966) 'The Logic of Comparison: A Methodological Note on the Study of Political Systems', *World Politics*, 19 (1): 69–82.

Kamat, S. (2004) 'The Privatization of Public Interest: Theorizing NGO Discourse in a Neoliberal Era', *Review of International Political Economy*, 11 (1): 155–76.

Kaplan, R. (1996) *The Ends of the Earth: A Journey at the Dawn of the 21st century*, New York: Random House.

Kasaba, R. (1992) '"By Compass and Sword!" The Meanings of 1492', *Middle East Report*, Septermber–October 1992: 6–10.

Kaufman, R. R., Chernotsky, H. I. and Geller, D. S. (1975) 'A Preliminary Test of the Theory of Dependency', *Comparative Politics*, 7 (3): 303–30.

Kedourie, E. (1984) 'A New International Disorder' in Bull, H. and Watson, A. (eds) *The Expansion of International Society*, Oxford: Clarendon Press.

Kiernan, V. G. (1974) 'The Marxist Theory of Imperialism and Its Historical Formation' in *Marxism and Imperialism: Studies*, London: Edward Arnold.

Kilson, M. (1966) *Political Change in a West African State: A Study of the Modernization Process in Sierra Leone*, Cambridge: Harvard University Press.

Kilson, M. (1975a) 'Cleavage Management in African Politics: The Ghana case' in Kilson, M. (ed.) *New States in the Modern World*, Cambridge, MA: Harvard University Press.

Kilson, M. (ed.) (1975b) *New States in the Modern World*, Cambridge, MA: Harvard University Press.

Kilson, M. (1975c) 'Preface' in Kilson, M. (ed.) *New States in the Modern World*, Cambridge, MA: Harvard University Press.

Kirk-Greene, A. H. M. (ed.) (1979) *The Transfer of Power: The Colonial Administrator in the Age of Decolonisation*, Oxford: Inter-Faculty Committee for African Studies, University of Oxford.

Kolko, G. (1988) *Confronting the Third World: United States Foreign Policy 1945–1980*, New York: Pantheon Books.

Koskenniemi, M. (2000) *International Law and Imperialism*, Hull: University of Hull, Studies in Law.

Krasner, S. D. (1985) *Structural Conflict*, Berkeley, CA: University of California Press.

Krasner, S. D. (1996) 'The Accomplishments of International Political Economy' in Smith, S., Booth, K. and Zalewski, M. (eds) *International Theory: Positivism and Beyond*, Cambridge: Cambridge University Press.

Kubursi, A. A. and Mansur, S. (1994) 'The Political Economy of Middle Eastern Oil' in Stubbs, R. and Underhill, G. R. D. (eds) *Political Economy and the Changing Global Order*, Basingstoke: Macmillan.

Kuper, L. and Smith, M. G. (ed.) (1969) *Pluralism in Africa*, Berkeley, CA: The University of California Press.

Laclau, E. (1971) 'Feudalism and Capitalism in Latin America', *New Left Review*, 67: 19–38.

Lall, S. (1975) 'Is "Dependence" A Useful Concept in Analysing Underdevelopment?' *World Development*, 3 (11–12): 799–810.

Larrain, J. (1989) *Theories of Development: Capitalism, Colonialism and Dependency*, Cambridge: Polity Press.

Larsen, N. (2000) 'DetermiNation: Postcolonialism, Poststructuralism, and the Problem of Ideology' in Afzal-Khan, F. and Seshadri-Crooks, K. (eds) *The Pre-Occupation of Postcolonial Studies*, Durham, NC: Duke University Press.

Lasswell, H. D. (1965) 'The Policy Sciences of Development', *World Politics*, 17 (2): 286–309.

Lawson, T. (1997) *Economics and Reality*, London: Routledge.

Leggasick, M. (1977) 'The Concept of Pluralism: A Critique' in Gutkind, P. C. W. and Waterman, P. (eds) *African Social Studies: A Radical Reader*, London: Heinemann.

Lemarchand, R. (1972) 'Political Clientelism and Ethnicity in Tropical Africa: Competing Solidarities in Nation-Building', *American Political Science Review*, 66 (1): 68–90.

Lenin, V. I. (1917) *Imperialism, the Highest Stage of Capitalism. A Popular Outline*, Peking: Foreign Languages Press (1975).

Lerner, D. (1958) *The Passing of Traditional Society*, Glencoe: The Free Press.

Leys, R. and Tostensen, A. (1982) 'Regional Co-operation in Southern Africa: The Southern African Development Co-ordination Conference', *Review of African Political Economy*, 23: 52–71.

Linklater, A. (1990) *Beyond Realism and Marxism: Critical Theory and International Relations*, Basingstoke: Macmillan.

Linklater, A. (1998) *The Transformation of Political Community: Ethical Foundations of the post-Westphalian Era*, Cambridge: Polity Press.

Linklater, A. (2001) 'The Changing Contours of Critical International Relations Theory' in Wyn Jones, R. (ed.) *Critical Theory and World Politics*, Boulder, CO: Lynne Rienner.

Lockwood, E. (1976) 'Preface' in El-Khawas, M. A. and Cohen, B. (eds) *The Kissinger Study of Southern Africa: National Security Study Memorandum 39 (Secret)*, Westport, CT: Lawrence Hill & Co.

Long, N. (ed.) (1989) *Encounters at the Interface: A Perspective on Social Discontinuities in Rural Development*, Wageningen: University of Wageningen Press.

Long, N. (1992) 'From Paradigm Lost to Paradigm Regained? The Case for An Actor-Oriented Sociology of Development' in Long, N. and Long, A. (eds) *Battlefields of Knowledge: The Interlocking of Theory and Practice in Social Research and Development*, London: Routledge.

Long, N. and van der Ploeg, J. D. (1994) 'Heterogeneity, Actor and Structure: Towards a Reconstitution of the Concept of Structure' in Booth, D. (ed.) *Rethinking Social Development: Theory, Research and Practice*, Harlow: Longman.

Luxemburg, R. (1913) *The Accumulation of Capital*, London: Routledge and Kegan Paul (1963).

Lyon, P. (1973) 'New States and International Order' in James, A. (ed.) *The Bases of Inter-national Order: Essays in Honour of C. A. W. Manning*, Oxford: Oxford University Press.

Lyotard, J. F. (1984) *The Postmodern Condition: A Report on Knowledge* (trans. Geoff Bennington and Brian Massumi), Manchester : Manchester University Press.

McGowan, P. J. (1976) 'Economic Dependency and Economic Performance in Black Africa', *Journal of Modern African Studies*, 14 (1): 25–40.

McGowan, P. J. and Smith, D. L. (1978) 'Economic Dependency in Black Africa: An Analysis of Competing Theories', *International Organization*, 32: 179–235.

Machel, S. (1973) 'Solidarity is Mutual Aid' in de Bragança, A. and Wallerstein, I. (eds) *The African Liberation Reader: Documents of the National Liberation Movements, Volume 3: The Strategy of Liberation*, London: Zed Press.

Machel, S. (1982) 'White Mozambicans. A Message by the President of FRELIMO, on the day of the Mozambican Revolution, 25 August 1971' in de Bragança, A. and Wallerstein, I. (eds) *The African Liberation Reader: Documents of the National Liberation Movements. Volume 2: The National Liberation Movements*, London: Zed Press.

McInnes, N. (1977) 'The Politics of Needs and Who Needs Politics' in Fitzgerald, R. (ed.) *Human Needs and Politics*, Rushcutters Bay: Pergamon Press.

McKay, V. (ed.) (1966) *African Diplomacy: Studies in the Determinants of Foreign Policy*, New York: Praeger.

MacLean, J. (1981) 'Marxist Epistemology, Explanations of "Change" and the Study of International Relations' in Buzan, B. and Jones, B. (eds) *Change and the Study of International Relations: The Evaded Dimension*, London: Frances Pinter.

McLennan, G. (1981) *Marxism and the Methodologies of History*, London: Verso.

Mafeje, A. (1981) 'On the Articulation of Modes of Production (review article)', *Journal of Southern African Studies*, 8 (1): 123–38.

Magdoff, H. (1978) *Imperialism, from the Colonial Age to the Present: Essays*, New York: Monthly Review Press.

Magill, K. (1994) 'Against Critical Realism', *Capital and Class*, 54: 113–36.

Mahoney, R. D. (1983) *JFK: Ordeal in Africa*, New York: Oxford University Press.

Maizels, A. (1992) *Commodities in Crisis: The Commodity Crisis of the 1980s and the Political Economy of International Commodity Policies*, Oxford: Clarendon Press.

Mamdani, M. (1976) *Politics and Class Formation in Uganda*, London: Heinemann.

Mamdani, M. (1982) 'Karamoja: Colonial Roots of Famine in North-East Uganda', *Review of African Political Economy*, 25: 66–73.

Mamdani, M. (1983) *Imperialism and Fascism in Uganda*, London: Heinemann.

Mamdani, M. (1986) 'The Colonial Roots of the Famine in Karamoja: A Rejoinder', *Review of African Political Economy*, 36: 85–92.

Mamdani, M. (1990) 'The Social Basis of Constitutionalism in Africa', *Journal of Modern African Studies*, 28 (3): 359–374.

Mamdani, M. (1994) 'A Critical Analysis of the IMF programme in Uganda' in Himmelstrand, U., Kinyanjui, K. and Mburugu, E. (eds) *African Perspectives on Development: Controversies, Dilemmas and Openings*, Nairobi: East African Educational Publishers.

Mamdani, M. (1995) 'A Critique of the State and Civil Society Paradigm in Africanist Studies' in Mamdani, M. and Wamba-dia-Wamba, E. (eds) *African Studies in Social Movements and Democracy*, Dakar: CODESRIA.

Mamdani, M. (1996a) *Citizen and Subject: Contemporary Africa and the Legacy of Late Colonialism*, Princeton, NJ: Princeton University Press.

Mamdani, M. (1996b) 'Introduction' in *Citizen and Subject: Contemporary Africa and the Legacy of Late Colonialism*, Princeton, NJ: Princeton University Press.

Mamdani, M. (2004) *Good Muslim, Bad Muslim: America, the Cold War, and the Roots of Terror*, New York: Pantheon Books.

Mandel, E. (1978) *Late Capitalism*, London: Verso.

Manicas, P. T. (1987) *A History and Philosophy of the Social Sciences*, Oxford: Blackwell.

Manji, F. and O'Coill, C. (2002) 'The Missionary Position: NGOs and Development in Africa', *International Affairs*, 78 (3): 567–83.

Mar, E. J. E. (1975) *Exploração Portuguesa em Moçambique 1500–1973*, Kastrup: African Studies Editorial.

Marques, M. M. L., Neves, V., Frade, C., Lobo, F., Pinto, P. and Cruz, C. (2000) *O Endividamento Dos Consumidores*, Coimbra: Almedina.

Marsden, R. (1999) *The Nature of Capital: Marx after Foucault*, London and New York: Routledge.

Martin, D. and Johnson, P. (1986) 'Mozambique: To Nkomati and Beyond' in Johnson, P. and Martin, D. (eds) *Destructive Engagement: Southern Africa at War*, Harare: Zimbabwe Publishing House.

Martins, H. (2001) 'Samora na luta armada (1965–1968)' in Sopa, A. (ed.) *Samora, Homen do Povo*, Maputo: Maguezo.

Marx, K. (1844) *Economic and Philosophical Manuscripts of 1844*, Moscow: Progress Publishers (1977).

Marx, K. (1847) *The Poverty of Philosophy*, New York: Prometheus Books (1995).

Marx, K. (1852) 'The Eighteenth Brumaire of Louis Bonaparte' in *Karl Marx and Frederick Engels, Selected Works in three volumes (Volume One)*, Moscow: Progress Publishers (1969).

Marx, K. (1853) 'The Future Results of the British Rule in India' in *On Colonialism*, Moscow: Foreign Languages Publishing House.

Marx, K. (1857) 'Introduction to a Critique of Political Economy' in Arthur, C. (ed.) *Karl Marx and Frederick Engels. The German Ideology. Part One*, London: Lawrence and Wishart (1974).

Marx, K. (1858) *Grundrisse*, London: Penguin (1993).

Marx, K. (1859) *A Contribution to the Critique of Political Economy*, Moscow: Progress Publishers (1970).

Marx, K. (1861) 'Letter to Lassalle, 16 January' in *Karl Marx and Friedrich Engels, Selected Correspondence*, Moscow: Progress Publishers (1975).

Marx, K. (1863) *Theories of Surplus Value (Vol. 3)*, Moscow: Progress Publishers (1971).

Marx, K. (1867) *Capital (Vol. 1)*, London: Penguin (1990).

Marx, K. (1878) 'Letter to the editorial board of *Otechestvennye Zapiski*' in Shanin, T. (ed.) *Late Marx and the Russian Road: Marx and 'the Peripheries of Capitalism'*, London: Routledge and Kegan Paul (1983).

Marx, K. (1885) *Capital (Vol. 2)*, London: Penguin (1992).

Marx, K. (1894) *Capital (Vol. 3)*, London: Penguin (1991).

Marx, K. and Engels, F. (1845–46a) *The German Ideology*, New York: Prometheus Books (1998).

Marx, K. and Engels, F. (1845–46b) 'The German Ideology' in *Karl Marx and Friedrich Engels, Collected Works (Vol. 5)*, London, Moscow and New York.

Marx, K. and Engels, F. (1848) *Manifesto of the Communist Party*, Peking: Foreign Languages Press (1975).

Mbuende, K. (1986) *Namibia, the Broken Shield: Anatomy of Imperialism and Revolution*, Lund: Liber.

Mehmet, O. (1999) *Westernizing the Third World: The Eurocentricity of Economic Development Theories*, 2nd edn, London and New York: Routledge.

Mepham, J. and Ruben, D.-H. (eds) (1979) *Issues in Marxist Philosophy (Vol. 3). Epistemology, Science and Ideology*, Brighton: Harvester Press.

Meyns, P. (1981) 'Liberation Ideology and National Development Strategy in Mozambique', *Review of African Political Economy*, 22: 42–64.

Ministry of Agriculture and Fisheries (1992) *The Determinants of Household Income and Consumption in Rural Nampula Province: Implications for Food Security and Agricultural Policy Reform*, Maputo.

Ministry of Planning and Finance (MPF), Eduardo Mondlane University and International Food Policy Research Institute (1998) *Understanding Poverty and Well-Being in Mozambique: The First National Assessment 1996–97*, Maputo.

Ministry of Planning and Finance (MPF), International Food Policy Research Institute and Purdue University (2004) *Poverty and Well-being in Mozambique: The Second National Assessment*, Maputo.

Minter, W. (1972) *Portuguese Africa and the West*, New York and London: Monthly Review Press.

Minter, W. (1986a) 'Destructive Engagement: The United States and South Africa in the Reagan Era' in Johnson, P. and Martin, D. (eds) *Destructive Engagement: Southern Africa at War*, Harare: Zimbabwe Publishing House.

Minter, W. (1986b) *King Solomon's Mines Revisited: Western Interests and the Burdened History of Southern Africa*, New York: Basic Books.

Minter, W. (1994) *Apartheid's Contras: An Inquiry into the Roots of War in Angola and Mozambique*, London: Zed Books.

Misturelli, F. and Heffernan, C. (2001) 'Perceptions of Poverty among Poor Livestock Keepers in Kenya: A Discourse Analysis Approach', *Journal of International Development*, 13 (7): 863–75.

Mitchell, J. C. (1960) *Tribalism and the Plural Society*, London:

Mohri, K. (1979) 'Marx and "Underdevelopment"', *Monthly Review*, 31 (4): 32–42.

Mondlane, E. (1976) *Lutar por Moçambique*, Lisbon: Livraria Sá da Costa Editora.

Monteiro, Ó. (2001) 'Samora e o Mundo' in Sopa, A. (ed.) *Samora, Homen do Povo*, Maputo: Maguezo.

Moore, D. B. and Schmitz, G. G. (eds) (1994) *Debating Development Discourse: Institutional and Popular Perspectives*, Basingstoke: Macmillan.

Morera, E. (1990) *Gramsci's Historicism*, London: Routledge.

Morgenthau, H. J. (1948) *Politics Among Nations: The Struggle for Power and Peace*, New York: Knopf.

Morrison, D. G. and Stevenson, H. M. (1972) 'Cultural Pluralism, Modernization and Conflict: An Empirical Analysis of Sources of Political Instability in African Nations', *Canadian Journal of Political Science*, 5: 82–103.

Mortimer, R. A. (1984) *The Third World Coalition in International Politics*, 2nd edn, Boulder, CO and London: Westview Press.

Morton, A. D. (2003) 'Social Forces in the Struggle over Hegemony: Neo-Gramscian Perspectives in International Political Economy', *Rethinking Marxism*, 15 (2): 153–79.

Mosse, M. (2001) 'Os Últimos Dias de Samora' in Sopa, A. (ed.) *Samora, Homen do Povo*, Maputo: Maguezo.

Mouzelis, N. (1988) 'Sociology of Development: Reflections on the Present Crisis', *Sociology*, 22 (1): 23–44.

Mugomba, A. T. (1976) 'NATO, the Southern Oceans and Southern Africa', *African Review: Journal of African Politics, Development and International Affairs*, 6: 15–33.

Muldoon, J. (1994) *The Americas in the Spanish World Order: The Justification for Conquest in the Seventeenth Century*, Philadelphia, PA: University of Pennsylvania Press.

Munck, R. (1981) 'Imperialism and Dependency: Recent Debates and Old Dead-Ends', *Latin American Perspectives*, 8 (3/4): 162–79.

Munck, R. (1999) 'Deconstructing Development Discourse: Of Impasses, Alternatives and Politics' in Munck, R. and O'Hearn, D. (eds) *Critical Development Theory: Contributions to a New Paradigm*, London: Zed Books.

Munck, R. (2000) 'Dependency and Imperialism in Latin America: New Horizons' in Chilcote, R. H. (ed.) *The Political Economy of Imperialism: Critical Appraisals*, Lanham, MD: Rowman and Littlefield.

Munslow, B. (1978) 'The Liberation Struggle in Mozambique and the Origins of Post-Independence Political and Economic Policy' in Allen, C. (ed.) *Mozambique: Seminar Proceedings*, Edinburgh: Edinburgh University, Centre of African Studies.

Munslow, B. (1980) *Frelimo and the Mozambican Revolution*, PhD thesis, University of Manchester.

Munslow, B. (1983) *Mozambique: The Revolution and its Origins*, London: Longman.

Munslow, B. (ed.) (1985) *Samora Machel: An African Revolutionary. Selected Speeches and Writings*, London: Zed Books.

Murphy, C. N. (2001) 'Critical Theory and the Democratic Impulse' in Wyn Jones, R. (eds) *Critical Theory and World Politics*, Boulder, CO: Lynne Rienner.

Murphy, C. N. and Tooze, R. (1991a) 'Getting Beyond the "common sense" of the IPE Orthodoxy' in Murphy, C. N. and Tooze, R. (eds) *The New International Political Economy*, Boulder, CO: Lynne Rienner.

Murphy, C. N. and Tooze, R. (1991b) 'Introduction' in Murphy, C. N. and Tooze, R. (eds) *The New International Political Economy*, Boulder, CO: Lynne Rienner.

Narayan, D., Patel, R., Schafft, K., Rademacher, A. and Koch-Schulte, S. (2000a) *Voices of the Poor: Can Anyone Hear Us?* New York: Oxford University Press, published for the World Bank.

Narayan, D. and Petesch, P. (2002) *Voices of the Poor: From Many Lands*, New York: Oxford University Press, published for the World Bank.

Narayan, D., Chambers, R., Kaul Shah, M. and Petesch, P. (2000b) *Voices of the Poor: Crying Out for Change*, New York: Oxford University Press, published for the World Bank.

Nederveen Pieterse, J. (2000) 'Trends in Development Theory' in Palan, R. (ed.) *Global Political Economy: Contemporary Theories*, London: Routledge.

Neil-Tomlinson, B. (1977) 'The Nyassa Chartered Company 1892–1928', *Journal of African History*, 18 (1): 109–128.

Neil-Tomlinson, B. (1978) 'The Growth of a Colonial Economy and the Development of African Labour: Manica and Sofala and the Mozambique Chartered Company, 1892–1942' in Allen, C. (ed.) *Mozambique: Seminar Proceedings*, Edinburgh: Edinburgh University, Centre of African Studies.

Nessa, N. and Gallagher, J. (2004) 'Diet, Nutrition, Dental Health and Exercise' in *The Health of Children and Young People*, Office for National Statistics, London.

Neufeld, M. (1995) *The Restructuring of International Relations Theory*, Cambridge: Cambridge University Press.

Neufeld, M. (2001) 'What's Critical about Critical International Relations Theory?' in Wyn Jones, R. (ed.) *Critical Theory and World Politics*, Boulder, CO: Lynne Rienner.

Newitt, M. (1973) *Portuguese Settlement on the Zambesi: Exploration, Land Tenure and Colonial Rule in East Africa*, London: Longman.

Newitt, M. (1995) *A History of Mozambique*, London: Hurst and Company.

Nhabinde, S. A. (1999) *Destabilização e Guerra Económica no Sistema Ferro-Portuário de Moçambique, 1980–1997*, Maputo: Livraria Universitária, Universidade Eduardo Mondlane.

Niane, D. T. (ed.) (1984a) *Africa from the Twelfth to the Sixteenth Century*, London, Berkeley, CA and Paris: Heinemann, University of California Press, UNESCO.

Niane, D. T. (1984b) 'Relationships and Exchanges among Different regions' in Niane, D. T. (ed.) *Africa from the Twelfth to the Sixteenth Century*, London, Berkeley, CA and Paris: Heinemann, University of California Press, UNESCO.

Nimtz, A. (2002) 'The Eurocentric Marx and Engels and Other Related Myths' in Bartolovich, C. and Lazarus, N. (eds) *Marxism, Modernity and Postcolonial Studies*, Cambridge: Cambridge University Press.

Nkrumah, K. (1962) *Towards Colonial Freedom: Africa in the Struggle Against World Imperialism*, London: Heinemann.

Nkrumah, K. (1963) *Africa Must Unite*, London: Panaf Books.

Nkrumah, K. (1965) *Neo-colonialism: the Last Stage of Imperialism*, London: Nelson.

Noer, T. J. (1985) *Black Liberation: The United States and White Rule in Africa, 1948–1968*, Columbia: University of Missouri Press.

Nowell, C. E. (1982) *The Rose-Coloured Map: Portugal's Attempt to Build an African Empire from the Atlantic to the Indian Ocean*, Lisbon: Junta de Investigações Cientificas do Ultramar.

Nzongola-Ntalaja, G. (1987) *Revolution and Counter-Revolution in Africa: Essays in Contemporary Politics*, London: Zed Books.

Nzongola-Ntalaja, G. (2002) *The Congo from Leopold to Kabila: A People's History*, London: Zed Books.

Nzula, A. T., Potekhin, I. I. and Zusmanovich, A. Z. (1979) *Forced Labour in Colonial Africa*, London: Zed Press.

O'Brien, R. (1995) 'International Political Economy and International Relations: Apprentice or Teacher?' in Macmillan, J. and Linklater, A. (eds) *Boundaries in Question: New Directions in International Relations*, London: Pinter Publishers.

O'Brien, R. and Williams, M. (2004) *Global Political Economy: Evolution and Dynamics*, Basingstoke: Palgrave Macmillan.

O'Connell, J. (1967) 'The Inevitability of Instability', *Journal of Modern African Studies*, 5: 181–91.

Oculi, O. (1987) *Food and the African Revolution*, Zaria, Nigeria: Ahmadu Bello University Bookshop.

Ogunbadejo, O. (1985) *The International Politics of Africa's Strategic Minerals*, London: Frances Pinter.

Okeke, C. N. (2001) 'The Debt Burden: An African Perspective', *International Lawyer*, 35: 1489–505.

Ollman, B. (1993) *Dialectical Investigations*, London: Routledge.

Ollman, B. (2003) *The Dance of the Dialectic*, Urbana, IL and Chicago, IL: University of Illinois Press.

Onimode, B. (1982) *Imperialism and Underdevelopment in Nigeria: The Dialectics of Mass Poverty*, London: Zed Press.

Onimode, B. (1989) 'Introduction' in Onimode, B. (ed.) *The IMF, the World Bank, and the African Debt: The Economic Impact*, London: Institute for African Alternatives, Zed Books.

Ortiz, R. D. (1992) 'Aboriginal People and Imperialism in the Western Hemisphere', *Monthly Review*, 44 (4): 1–11.

Ould-Mey, M. (1996) *Global Restructuring and Peripheral States: The Carrot and the Stick in Mauritania*, Lanham, MD: Rowman and Littlefield.

Ould-Mey, M. (2003) 'Currency Devaluation and Resource Transfer from the South to the North', *Annals of the Association of American Geographers*, 93 (2): 463–84.

Owen, W. F. (1833) *Narrative of Voyages to Explore the Shores of Africa, Arabia and Madagascar*, London.

Oyebade, A. (2000) 'Euro-African Relations to 1885' in Falola, T. (ed.) *Africa, vol. 1: African History before 1885*, Carolina: Carolina Academic Press.

Pagden, A. (1995) *Lords of All the World: Ideologies of Empire in Spain, Britain and France c.1500–c.1800*, New Haven, CT: Yale University Press.

Palan, R. (2000) 'The Constructivist Underpinnings of the New International Political Economy' in Palan, R. (ed.) *Global Political Economy: Contemporary Theories*, London: Routledge.

Palma, G. (1978) 'Dependency: A Formal Theory of Underdevelopment or a Methodology for the Analysis of Concrete Situations of Underdevelopment?', *World Development*, 6: 881–924.

Parboni, R. (1986) 'The Dollar Weapon: From Nixon to Reagan', *New Left Review*, I/158: 5–18.

Parfitt, T. (2002) *The End of Development? Modernity, Postmodernity and Development*, London: Pluto Press.

Parker, S. (2005) 'Bush Vows to Help Africa on Trade, Aid', *Voice of America*, 8 June. Online. Available HTTP: <http://www.voanews.com/english/2005-06-08-voa66.cfm> (accessed 15 June 2005).

Parsons, T. (1960) *Structure and Process in Modern Societies*, Glencoe, IL: The Free Press.

Pasha, M. K. (1996) 'Globalisation and Poverty in South Asia', *Millennium: Journal of International Studies*, 25 (3): 635–56.

Patomäki, H. (2002) *After International Relations: Critical Realism and the (Re)construction of World Politics*, London: Routledge.

Pauly, L. W. (1993) 'From Monetary Manager to Crisis Manager: Systemic Change and the International Monetary Fund' in Morgan, R., Lorentzen, J., Leander, A. and Guzzini, S. (eds) *New Diplomacy in the Post-Cold War World: Essays for Susan Strange*, London: Macmillan.

Pauly, L. W. (1994) 'Promoting a Global Economy: The Normative Role of the International Monetary Fund' in Stubbs, R. and Underhill, G. R. D. (eds) *Political Economy and the Changing Global Order*, Basingstoke: Macmillan.

Pauly, L. W. (2000) 'Capital Mobility and the New Global Order' in Stubbs, R. and Underhill, G. R. D. (eds) *Political Economy and the Changing Global Order*, 2nd edn, Ontario: Oxford University Press.

Penvenne, J. (1995) *African Workers and Colonial Racism. Mozambican Strategies and Struggles in Lourenço Marques, 1877–1962*, Portsmouth NH: Heinemann.

Pereira-Leite, J. H. (1989) *La Formation de l'economie coloniale au Mozambique: Pacte colonial et industrialisation*, PhD Thesis, Ecole de Haute Etudes Sciences Social.

Petras, J. (1981) 'Dependency and World System Theory: A Critique and New Directions', *Latin American Perspectives*, 8 (3/4): 148–55.

Petras, J. and Veltmeyer, H. (2001) 'NGOs in the Service of Imperialism' in Petras, J. and Veltmeyer, H. *Globalization Unmasked: Imperialism in the 21st Century*, Halifax and London: Fernwood Publishing and Zed Books.

Phiri, K. M., Kalinga, O. J. M. and Bhila, H. H. K. (1992) 'The Northern Zambezia-Lake Malawi Region' in Ogot, B. A. (ed.) *General History of Africa (Volume V): Africa from the Sixteenth to the Eighteenth Century*, Paris, Oxford and Berkeley, CA: UNESCO, James Currey and University of California Press.

Pimentel, J. S. (1904) *No Distrito de Moçambique – Memórias, Estudos e Considerações*, Lourenço Marques.

Pinto, F. L. de V. and Carreira, A. (1979) 'Portuguese Participation in the Slave Trade: Opposing Forces, Trends of Opinion within Portuguese Society, Effects on Portugal's Socio-economic Development' in UNESCO (ed.) *The African Slave Trade from the Fifteenth to the Nineteenth Century*, Paris: United Nations Educational, Scientific and Cultural Orginaization.

Pitcher, M. A. (1999) 'What's Missing from "What's missing"? A reply to C. Cramer and N. Pontara, "Rural Poverty Alleviation in Mozambique: What's Missing from the Debate?"' *Journal of Modern African Studies*, 37 (4): 697–709.

Pletsch, C. E. (1981) 'The Three Worlds, or the Division of Social Scientific Labor, *c.*1950–1975', *Comparative Studies in Society and History*, 23: 565–90.

Porpora, D. V. (1989) 'Four Concepts of Social Structure', *Journal for the Theory of Social Behaviour*, 19 (2): 195–211.

Porpora, D. V. (1993) 'Cultural Rules and Material Relations', *Sociological Theory*, 11 (2): 212–29.

Post, K. W. J. (1963) *The Nigerian Federal Elections of 1959: Politics and Administration in a Developing Political System*, London: Oxford University Press.

Pratten, S. (1993) 'Structure, Agency and Marx's Analysis of the Labour Process', *Review of Political Economy*, 5 (4): 403–26.

Pye, L. W. (1966) *Aspects of Political Development*, Boston, MA: Little, Brown.

Pye, L. W. and Verba, S. (eds) (1965) *Political Culture and Political Development*, Princeton, NJ: Princeton University Press.

Radice, H. (ed.) (1975) *International Firms and Modern Imperialism: Selected Readings*, Harmondsworth: Penguin Books.

Rahnema, M. (1991) 'Global Poverty: A Pauperizing Myth', *Interculture*, 24 (2): 4–51.

Rahnema, M. (1997) 'Towards Post-development: Searching for Signposts, a New Language and New Paradigms' in Rahnema, M. and Bawtree, V. (eds) *The Post-Development Reader*, London: Zed Books.

Ramsay, M. (1992) *Human Needs and the Market*, Aldershot: Avebury.

Ramsay, M. (1997) *What's Wrong with Liberalism? A Radical Critique of Liberal Political Philosophy*, London: Leicester University Press.

Ray, D. (1973) 'The Dependency Model and Latin America: Three Basic Fallacies', *Journal of Interamerican Affairs and World Studies*, 15 (1): 4–20.

Reid, E. (1977) *Time of Fear and Hope: The Making of the North Atlantic Treaty, 1947–1949*, Toronto: McClelland and Stewart.

Rengger, N. and Hoffman, M. (1992) 'Modernity, Postmodernism and International Relations' in Doherty, J., Graham, E. and Malek, M. (eds) *Postmodernism and the Social Sciences*, New York: St Martin's Press.

Rengger, N. J. (1999) *International Relations, Political Theory and the Problem of Order: Beyond International Relations Theory?* London and New York: Routledge.

Renton, D. (ed.) (2001) *Marx on Globalisation*, London: Lawrence and Wishart.

Rickards, L., Fox, K., Roberts, C., Fletcher, L. and Goddard, E. (2004) 'Housing and Consumer Durables' in *Living in Britain: Results from the 2002 General Household Survey*, London: Office for National Statistics.

Rivkin, A. (ed.) (1968) *Nations By Design: Institution Building in Africa*, Garden City, NY: Anchor Books.

Roberts, J. M. (1999) 'Marxism and Critical Realism: The Same, Similar, or Just Plain Different?', *Capital and Class*, 68: 21–49.

Roberts, J. M. (2001) 'Critical Realism and the Dialectic', *British Journal of Sociology*, 52 (4): 667–85.

Roberts, J. M. (2002) 'Abstracting Emancipation: Two Dialectics on the Trail of Freedom' in Brown, A., Fleetwood, S. and Roberts, J. M. (eds) *Critical Realism and Marxism*, London: Routledge.

Robinson, C. J. (2001) *An Anthropology of Marxism*, Aldershot: Ashgate.

Rodney, W. (1972) *How Europe Underdeveloped Africa*, London and Dar es Salaam: Bogle-L'Ouverture and Tanzanian Publishing House.

Rotberg, R. I. (ed.) (2003) *When States Fail: Causes and Consequences*, Princeton, NJ: Princeton University Press.

Rothstein, R. L. (1977) *The Weak in the World of the Strong: The Developing Countries in the International System*, New York: Columbia University Press.

Rothstein, R. L. (1979) *Global Bargaining: UNCTAD and the Quest for a New International Economic Order*, Princeton, NJ: Princeton University Press.

Roxborough, I. (1979) *Theories of Underdevelopment*, Basingstoke: Macmillan Education.

Ruggie, J. G. (1982) 'International Regimes, Transactions and Change: Embedded Liberalism in the Postwar Economic Order', *International Organization*, 36 (2): 379–415.

Rupert, M. (1995) *Producing Hegemony*, Cambridge: Cambridge University Press.

Rupert, M. (1997) 'Globalisation and Contested Common Sense in the United States' in Gill, S. and Mittelman, J. H. (eds) *Innovation and Transformation in International Studies*, Cambridge: Cambridge University Press.

Rupert, M. (2000) *Ideologies of Globalization: Contending Visions of a New World Order*, London: Routledge.

Rupert, M. (2003) 'Globalising Common Sense: a Marxian-Gramscian (Re-)vision of the Politics of Governance/Resistance', *Review of International Studies*, 29: 181–98.

Rustow, D. A. (1967) *A World of Nations: Problems of Political Modernization*, Washington, DC: Brookings Institute.

Sá da Bandeira, V. de (1873) *O Trabalho Rural Africano e a Administração Colonial*, Lisbon.

Sachs, W. (ed.) (1992) *The Development Dictionary: A Guide to Knowledge as Power*, London: Zed Books.

Said, E. (1994) *Culture and Imperialism*, London: Vintage.

Samuels, M. A. and Haykin, S. M. (1979) 'The Anderson Plan: An American Attempt to Seduce Portugal Out of Africa', *Orbis: A Journal of World Affairs*, 23 (3): 649–69.

San Juan, E. J. (1998) *Beyond Postcolonial Theory*, New York: St Martin's Press.

Sardar, Z. (1999) 'Development and the Locations of Eurocentrism' in Munck, R. and O'Hearn, D. (eds) *Critical Development Theory: Contributions to a New Paradigm*, London: Zed Books.

Saurin, J. (1996) 'Globalisation, Poverty, and the Promises of Modernity', *Millennium: Journal of International Studies*, 25 (3): 657–80.

Sayer, D. (1983) *Marx's Method: Ideology, Science and Critique in 'Capital'*, 2nd edn, Brighton: Harvester Press.

Sayer, D. and Corrigan, P. (1983) 'Late Marx: Continuity, Contradiction and Learning' in Shanin, T. (ed.) *Late Marx and the Russian Road: Marx and 'the Peripheries of Capitalism'*, London: Routledge and Kegan Paul.

Schuurman, F. (ed.) (1993) *Beyond the Impasse: New Directions in Development Theory*, London: Zed Books.

Scoones, I. and Thompson, J. (eds) (1994) *Beyond Farmer First: Rural People's Knowledge, Agricultural Research and Extension Practice*, London: Intermediate Technology Publications.

Scott, J. C. (1990) *Domination and the Arts of Resistance: Hidden Transcripts*, New Haven, CT and London: Yale University Press.

Seers, D. (1979) 'The Congruence of Marxism and Other Neoclassical Doctrines' in Hill, K. Q. (ed.) *Toward a New Strategy for Development*, New York: Pergamon Press.

Seidman, A. and Seidman, N. (1977) *U.S. Multinationals in Southern Africa*, Dar Es Salam: Tanzania Publishing House.

Serra, C. (1980) 'Colonial Capitalism in Zambezia 1855–1930', *Mozambican Studies*, 1: 33–52.

Serra, C. (1986a) *Como a Penetração Estrangeira Transformou o Modo de Produção dos Camponeses Moçambicanos – o exemplo da Zambézia (∓ 1200–1964); Volume 1: os Moçambicanos antes da penetração estrangeira*, Maputo: Universidade Eduardo Mondlane/Imprensa Nacional de Moçambique.

Serra, C. (1986b) *Como a Penetração Estrangeira Transformou o Modo de Produção dos Camponeses Moçambicanos – o exemplo da Zambézia (∓ 1200–1964); Volume 2: dos mercadores estrangeiros à ocupação militar-imperialista*, Maputo: Universidade Eduardo Mondlane/Imprensa Nacional de Moçambique.

Serra, C. (1997a) *Combates Pela Mentalidade Sociólogica*, Maputo: Livraria Universitária.

Serra, C. (1997b) *Novos Combates Pela Mentalidade Sociólogica*, Maputo: Livraria Universitária.

Serra, C. (2001) 'Tudo o que é sólido se esfuma', *Estudos Moçambicanos*, 18: 5–23.

Serra, C. (2003) *Em Cima de Uma Lâmina – Um Estudo Sobre Precaridade Social em Três Cidades de Moçambique*, Maputo: Livraria Universitária.

Shaikh, A. (1979) 'Foreign Trade and the Law of Value: Part I', *Science and Society*, 43 (3): 281–302.

Shaikh, A. (1980) 'Foreign Trade and the Law of Value: Part II', *Science and Society*, 44 (1): 27–57.

Shaikh, A. (1981) 'The Laws of International Exchange' in Nell, E. J. (ed.) *Growth, Profits and Property: Essays in the Revival of Political Economy*, Cambridge: Cambridge University Press.

Sharpe, P. (2003) *The Philosophical Significance of Roy Bhaskar's Dialectical Critical Realism*, Self-Published.

Sherclif, J. (1958) 'Portugal's Strategic Territories', *Foreign Affairs*, 31 (2): 321–25.

Shivji, I. G. (1976) *Class Struggles in Tanzania*, London and Dar es Salaam: Heinemann and Tanzania Publishing House.

Shivji, I. G. (1986) *Law, State and the Working Class in Tanzania c.1920–1964*, London: James Currey.

Silva Cunha, J. M. de (1955) *O Trabalho Indigena: Estudo de Direito Colonial*, Lisbon.

Simler, K. R., Mukherjee, S., Dava, G. L. and Datt, G. (2004) *Rebuilding After War: Micro-Level Determinants of Poverty Reduction in Mozambique*, Washington, DC: International Food Policy Research Institute.

Singer, M. R. (1972) *Weak States in a World of Powers: The Dynamics of International Relationships*, New York: The Free Press.

Singham, A. W. (ed.) (1977) *The Non-Aligned Movement in World Politics*, Westport, CT: Lawrence Hill and Company.

Singham, A. W. and Hune, S. (1986) *Non-Alignment in an Age of Alignments*, Westport, CT: Lawrence Hill and Company.

Sklair, L. (1988) 'Transcending the Impasse: Metatheory, Theory and Empirical Research in the Sociology of Development and Underdevelopment', *World Development*, 16 (6): 697–709.

Smith, S. (1987) 'Paradigm Dominance in International Relations: The Development of International Relations as a Social Science', *Millennium: Journal of International Studies*, 16 (2): 189–206.

Smith, S. (1996) 'Positivism and Beyond' in Smith, S., Booth, K. and Zalewski, M. (eds) *International Theory: Positivism and Beyond*, Cambridge: Cambridge University Press.

Smith, S., Booth, K. and Zalewski, M. (eds) (1996) *International Theory: Positivism and Beyond*, Cambridge: Cambridge University Press.

Smith, T. (1979) 'The Underdevelopment of Development Literature: The Case of Dependency', *World Politics*, 31 (2): 247–88.

Söderbaum, F. and Taylor, I. (2001) 'Transmission Belt for Transnational Capital or Facilitator for Development? Problematising the Role of the State in the Maputo Development Corridor', *Journal of Modern African Studies*, 39 (4): 675–95.

Söderbaum, F. and Taylor, I. (eds) (2003) *Regionalism and Uneven Development in Southern Africa: The Case of the Maputo Development Corridor*, Aldershot: Ashgate.

Soper, K. (1981) *On Human Needs: Open and Closed Theories in a Marxist Perspective*, Brighton: Harvester.

Soper, K. (1993) 'A Theory of Human Needs (review article)', *New Left Review*, 197: 113–28.

Southall, A. W. (ed.) (1961) *Social Change in Modern Africa*, London: Oxford University Press, International African Institute.

Springborg, P. (1981) *The Problem of Human Needs and the Critique of Civilisation*, London: Allen and Unwin.

Stannard, D. E. (1992) *American Holocaust: Columbus and the Conquest of the New World*, Oxford: Oxford University Press.

Stockholm International Peace Research Institute (SIPRI) (1975a) *Arms Trade Registers: The Arms Trade with the Third World*, Cambridge MA: MIT Press.

Stockholm International Peace Research Institute (SIPRI) (1975b) *The Arms Trade with the Third World*, Harmondsworth: Penguin.

Subrahmanyam, S. (1997) 'Connected Histories: Notes towards a Reconfiguration of Eurasia', *Modern Asian Studies*, 31 (3): 735–62.

Subrahmanyam, S. (2005) *Explorations in Connected History (two volumes)*, Oxford: Oxford University Press.

Sued-Badillo, J. (1992) 'Christopher Columbus and the Enslavement of Amerindians in the Caribbean', *Monthly Review*, 44 (3): 71–102.

Summerfield, C. and Gill, B. (eds) (2005) *Social Trends*, Basingstoke: Palgrave Macmillan, Office for National Statistics.

Suret-Canale, J. (1971) *French Colonialism in Tropical Africa, 1900–1945*, London: Hurst.

Sutton, J. E. G. (1972) *Early Trade in Eastern Africa*, Dar es Salaam: East African Publishing House.

Sylvester, R. and Sparrow, A. (2005) 'Vast Majority Think African Aid is Wasted, Poll Shows' *Telegraph*, 4 June 2005.

Taylor, J. G. (1979) *From Modernization to Modes of Production: A Critique of the Sociologies of Development and Underdevelopment*, Basingstoke: Macmillan Press.

Taylor, P. (1959) 'Need Statements', *Analysis*, 19 (5): 106–11.

Terzian, P. (1985) *OPEC: The Inside Story*, London: Zed Books.

Teschke, B. (2003) *The Myth of 1648: Class, Geopolitics and the Making of Modern International Relations*, London: Verso.

Thomas, C. Y. (1974) *Dependence and Transformation: The Economics of the Transition to Socialism*, New York: Monthly Review Press.

Thomas, C. Y. (1984) *The Rise of the Authoritarian State in Peripheral Societies*, New York: Monthly Review Press.

Thomson, G. (1987) *Needs*, London: Routledge and Kegan Paul.

Timpanaro, S. (1980) *On Materialism*, London: Verso.

Tooze, R. (1988) 'The Unwritten Preface: International Political Economy and Epistemology', *Millennium: Journal of International Studies*, 17 (2): 285–93.

Tooze, R. (1990) 'Understanding the Global Political Economy: Applying Gramsci', *Millennium: Journal of International Studies*, 19 (2): 273–80.

Tooze, R. and Murphy, C. N. (1996) 'The Epistemology of Poverty and the Poverty of Epistemology: Mystery, Blindness, and Invisibility', *Millennium: Journal of International Studies*, 25 (3): 681–707.

Topik, S. (1998) 'Dependency Revisited: Saving the Baby from the Bathwater', *Latin American Perspectives*, 25 (6): 95–9.

Torp, J. E., Denny, L. M. and Ray, D. I. (1989) *Mozambique, São Tomé and Príncipe: Politics, Economics and Society*, London and New York: Pinter.

Triffin, R. (1961) *Gold and the Dollar Crisis: The Future of Convertibility*, New Haven, CT: Yale University Press.

Trovillot, M.-R. (1995) *Silencing the Past: Power and the Production of History*, Boston, MA: Beacon Press.

Tucker, V. (1999) 'The Myth of Development: Critique of a Eurocentric Discourse' in Munck, R. and O'Hearn, D. (eds) *Critical Development Theory: Contributions to a New Paradigm*, London: Zed Books.

Turshen, M. (1984) *The Political Ecology of Disease in Tanzania*, New Brunswick, NJ: Rutgers University Press.

Udokang, O. (1975) 'Portuguese African Policy: A Critical Re-appraisal', *African Review: Journal of African Politics, Development and International Affairs*, 6: 289–312.

UNCTAD (2002) *The Least Developed Countries Report 2002*, United Nations Conference on Trade and Development, Geneva and New York.

UNCTAD (2003) *Economic Development in Africa: Trade Performance and Commodity Dependence*, United Nations Conference on Trade and Development, Geneva and New York.

UNCTAD (2004) *Economic Development in Africa: Debt Sustainability, Oasis or Mirage?* United Nations Conference on Trade and Development, Geneva and New York.

Underhill, G. R. D. (2000) 'Global Issues in Historical Perspective' in Stubbs, R. and Underhill, G. R. D. (eds) *Political Economy and the Changing Global Order*, 2nd edn, Ontario: Oxford University Press.

UNDP (1998) *Mozambique. Peace and Economic Growth: Opportunities for Human Development*, United Nations Development Programme, National Human Development Report, Maputo.

UNDP (2004) *Human Development Report*, New York: United Nations Development Programme.

United Nations (1960) *1514 (XV) Declaration on the Granting of Independence to Colonial Countries and Peoples*, UN General Assembly, Fifteenth Session. Online. Available HTTP: <http://www.un.org/Depts/dpi/decolonization/declaration.htm> (accessed 8 December 2004).

United Nations (1970) *A Principle in Torment: II. The United Nations and Portuguese Administered Territories*, New York.

United Nations (1973) *Report of Sub-Committee I, Special Committee on the Situation with Regard to the Implementation of the Declaration on the Granting of Independence to Colonial Countries and Peoples, A/AC.109/L.893*, New York, 31 July.

Universidade Eduardo Mondlane (ed.) (1983) *História de Moçambique Volume 2: Aggressão Imperialista (1886–1930)*, Maputo: Cadernos Tempo e Departamento de História, Universidade Eduardo Mondlane.

Universidade Eduardo Mondlane (ed.) (1988a) *História de Moçambique Volume 1: Primeiras sociedades sedentárias e impacto dos mercadores (200/300–1886)*, 2nd edn, Maputo: Cadernos Tempo e Departamento de História, Universidade Eduardo Mondlane.

Universidade Eduardo Mondlane (ed.) (1988b) *História de Moçambique Volume 3: Moçambique no auge do colonialismo, 1930–1961*, Maputo: Cadernos Tempo e Departamento de História, Universidade Eduardo Mondlane.

US Government (1964) *Status Report on NSAM No. 295 of April 24, 1964 – South Africa*, 30 July 1964.

Vail, L. and White, L. (1980) *Capitalism and Colonialism in Mozambique*, Minneapolis, MN: University of Minnesota Press.

van den Berghe, P. L. (1971) 'Ethnicity: The African Experience', *International Social Science Journal*, 23 (4): 507–18.

van der Pijl, K. (1998) *Transnational Classes and International Relations*, London: Routledge.

Vandergeest, P. and Buttel, F. H. (1988) 'Marx, Weber and Development Sociology: Beyond the Impasse', *World Development*, 16 (6): 683–95.

Vasquez, J. A. (1995) 'The Post-positivist Debate: Reconstructing Scientific Enquiry and International Relations after Enlightenment's fall' in Booth, K. and Smith, S. (eds) *International Relations Theory Today*, Cambridge: Polity Press.

Villamil, J. J. (ed.) (1979) *Transnational Capitalism and National Development: New Perspectives on Dependence*, Harvester: Hassocks.

Vines, A. (1991) *Renamo: Terrorism in Mozambique*, London: James Currey.

Wade, R. (2002) 'US Hegemony and the World Bank: The Fight over People and Ideas', *Review of International Political Economy*, 9 (2): 201–29.

Walker, R. J. B. (1993) *Inside/Outside: International Relations as Political Theory*, Cambridge: Cambridge University Press.

Wallbank, T. W. (1964) *Documents On Modern Africa*, Princeton, NJ: Van Nostrand.

Walsh, C. E. (2004) 'October 6, 1979', *Federal Reserve Bank of San Francisco Economic Letter*, (35).

Warren, B. (1980) *Imperialism: Pioneer of Capitalism*, London: Verso.

Watson, A. (1992) *The Evolution of International Society: A Comparative Historical Analysis*, London and New York: Routledge.

Weber, H. (2002) 'The Imposition of a Global Development Architecture: The Example of Microcredit', *Review of International Studies*, 28 (3): 237–55.

Weber, H. (2004) 'The New Economy and Social Risk: Banking on the Poor?' *Review of International Political Economy*, 11 (2): 356–86.

Weeks, J. (1981) 'The Differences between Materialist Theory and Dependency Theory and Why They Matter', *Latin American Perspectives*, 8 (3/4): 118–23.

White, A. (1975) *Modal Thinking*, Oxford: Blackwell.

White, H. (1999) 'Why is Africa Poor?' Lecture given at the University of Sussex as part of the Sussex Development Lecture series, Autumn 1999.

Wield, D. (1983) 'Mozambique: Late Colonialism and Early Problems of Transition' in White, G., Murray, R. and White, C. (eds) *Revolutionary Socialist Development in the Third World*, Brighton: Wheatsheaf Books.

Williams, E. (1987) *Capitalism and Slavery*, London: André Deutsch (first published Chapel Hill, NC: University of North Carolina Press, 1944).

Williams, M. (1987) 'Africa and the International Economic System: Dependency or Self-reliance?' in Wright, S. and Brownfoot, J. N. (eds) *Africa in World Politics: Changing Perspectives*, Basingstoke: Macmillan.

Williams, M. (1991) *Third World Cooperation: The Group of 77 in UNCTAD*, London: Pinter.

Williams, M. (1994) *International Economic Organisations and the Third World*, London: Harvester Wheatsheaf.

Williams, M. (1996) 'International Political Economy and Global Environmental Change' in Vogler, J. and Imber, M. F. (eds) *The Environment and International Relations*, London: Routledge.

Williams, P. and Chrisman, L. (eds) (1993) *Colonial Discourse and Post-Colonial Theory*, London: Harvester Wheatsheaf.

Williams, W. E. (1936) *Africa and the Rise of Capitalism*, Masters Thesis, Howard University.

Wohlgemuth, P. (1963) *The Portuguese Territories and the United Nations*, New York: Carnegie Endowment for International Peace.

Wolf, E. R. (1997) *Europe and the People Without History*, Berkeley, CA: University of California Press.

Wolfensohn, J. D. (2004) *Speech at Annual Meeting of the Governors of the World Bank and International Monetary Fund (news report)*, Online. Available HTTP: <http://web.worldbank.org/WBSITE/EXTERNAL/TOPICS/EXTPOVERTY/0,contentMDK:20264454~pagePK:148956~piPK:216618~theSitePK:336992,00.html> (accessed 12 October 2004).

Wolpe, H. (ed.) (1980) *The Articulation of Modes of Production*, London: Routledge and Kegan Paul.

Wood, E. M. (1995) *Democracy Against Capitalism: Renewing Historical Materialism*, Cambridge: Cambridge University Press.

Wood, E. M. (1999) *The Origins of Capitalism*, New York: Monthly Review Press.

Wood, E. M. (2001) 'Eurocentric Anti-Eurocentrism' *Against the Current*, May/June. Online. Available HTTP: <http://www.solidarity-us.org/indexATC.html> (accessed 14 November 2004).

World Bank (1990) *World Development Report: Poverty*, Washington, DC: Oxford University Press.

World Bank (1993) *Mozambique Vision Document*, Maputo.

World Bank (1996a) *Agricultural Sector Memorandum Volume 1: Executive Summary*, Washington, DC.

World Bank (1996b) *From Plan to Market: World Development Report 1996*, Oxford: Oxford University Press.

World Bank (1999) *Methodology Guide: Consultations with the poor*, Washington, DC: Poverty Group, PREM.

World Bank (2001) *World Development Report: Attacking Poverty*, Washington, DC: Oxford University Press.

World Bank (2003) *Mozambique: Country Assistance Strategy*, Washington, DC: World Bank. Online available HTTP: <http://www-wds.worldbank.org/servlet/WDSContentServer/WDSP/1B/2004/07/09/00001209_20040709092054/Rendered/PDF/267470corr.pdf> (accessed 24 January 2006).

World Bank (2005) *Global Development Finance*, ESDS International, University of Manchester. Online available HTTP: <http://www.esds.ac.uk> (accessed 29 March 2005).

World Vision-Mozambique (1998) *World Vision Cashew Policy Vision Document*, Maputo.

Wright, G. (1989) 'US Foreign Policy and Destabilisation in Southern Africa', *Review of African Political Economy*, (45/46): 159–68.

Wright, R. (2000) *Stolen Continents: Conquest and Resistance in the Americas*, London: Phoenix Press.

Wyn Jones, R. (2001) 'Introduction: Locating Critical International Relations Theory' in Wyn Jones, R. (ed.) *Critical Theory and World Politics*, Boulder, CO: Lynne Rienner.

Young, R. (1990) *White Mythologies: Writing History and the West*, London: Routledge.

Zack-Williams, A. B. (1983) 'Merchant Capital and Underdevelopment: The Process Whereby Sierra Leone Social Formation Became Dominated by Merchant Capital 1896–1961', *African Review: Journal of African Politics, Development and International Affairs*, 10 (1): 54–73.

Zartman, W. I. (1966) *International Relations in the New Africa*, Englewood Cliffs, NJ: Prentice-Hall.

Zartman, W. I. (1967) 'Africa as A Subordinate State System in International Relations', *International Organization*, 21 (3): 545–64.

Zeleza, P. T. (1983) 'African History: The Rise and Decline of Academic Tourism', *Ufahamu*, 13 (1): 9–42.

Zeleza, P. T. (1997) *Manufacturing African Studies and Crises*, Dakar: CODESRIA.

Zeleza, P. T. (2003) 'The Production of Historical Knowledge for Schools' in Falola, T. (ed.) *Ghana in Africa and the World: Essays in Honour of Adu Boahen*, Trenton, NJ: Africa World Press.

Zolberg, A. R. (1966) *Creating Political Order: The Party-States of West Africa*, Chicago, IL: Rand-McNally.

Zolberg, A. R. (1968) 'The Structure of Political Conflict in the New States of Tropical Africa', *American Political Science Review*, 62 (1): 70–87.

Index